Rick Steves.

Italy

D0917522

for Food
Lovers

Rick Steves & Fred Plotkin

Contents

PART I

The Basics

Introduction

This is a guide to Italian food. But it's also a book about the Italian people—their ingenuity, their traditions, and their evangelical zeal for quality. It's about the *sensuality* of Italy, expressed through its food, wine, and culinary philosophy. It will lead you to the Italy that you can see, taste, smell, touch, and hear, where flavors, fragrances, scenery, art, music, and people are all sources of pleasure—known in Italy as *piacere*.

Garibaldi with a Fork

Before we dig in, first let's meet Giuseppe Garibaldi—a name you'll see wherever you go in Italy. There may be a street named Via Garibaldi, a Piazza Garibaldi, a Bar Garibaldi, or any number of civic institutions named for the

man who is often thought of as the George Washington of Italy.

Giuseppe Garibaldi (1807-1882) was the military leader of the Risorgimento, a decades-long movement that culminated in the creation of a modern Italian nation in 1870. The Risorgimento brought together, for the first time, the Italian Peninsula's many city-states, kingdoms, duchies, papal territories, and lands under foreign domination. The nation created by Garibaldi and the Risorgimento stretches from the Alps (with apple strudel and *Deutsch*-speaking natives), to former outposts of the Venetian Republic and the Austro-Hungarian Empire, to the fog-draped valleys and fertile farmlands of central Italy, to city-states that peaked in the Middle Ages or Renaissance, to the ancient ruins of Rome, to the wild sprawl of Naples at the base of a temperamental volcano, to the sunbaked and Greek-inflected

south, to two giant islands that each have their own unique culture and history. It's staggering to imagine the ambition—the sheer gall—of Garibaldi and his peers, who wove these disparate parts of the peninsula into a single country.

One of the joys of traveling through Italy is observing how this internal diversity has remained strong, more than 150 years after Garibaldi. Through Mussolini, world wars, membership in the European Union, economic crisis, a global pandemic, and much more, Italy is still Italy. Except it's also many Italys—regions, provinces, cities, neighborhoods—each with its own personality.

Italians use the word *campanilismo* to describe their super-local approach to cultural identity. It means the sense of community, pride, and devotion shared by those within earshot of a town's *campanile,* or bell tower. A *campanilista* will tell you that the pasta typical of his town is the best in Italy, and certainly better than the (essentially identical) one from the next town over. Within the region of Emilia-Romagna, the cities of Parma and Reggio Emilia—separated

by less than 20 miles—cultivate a centuries-old enmity about who has the better cheeses, hams, and *salame.* And if you meet a woman from the Sicilian city of Siracusa, she likely won't identify herself as *italiana,* but as *siciliana*—if not *siracusana.*

As you explore Italy, it's all too easy to become a mindless sightseer, lured in by interchangeable, tourist-friendly restaurants with a giant English menu out front listing the same dishes you can order in Little Italy back home. Instead, try traveling as a food lover—as Garibaldi with a fork: tuning into the subtle

regional differences as you move from place to place, making a point to sample the very best of what each region or town has to offer, while at the same time celebrating what makes Italy, Italy.

About This Book

Rick Steves Italy for Food Lovers is a handbook for those wanting to experience Italy not only through its great sights, but also through its cuisine. The core of this book is a reincarnation of *Italy for the Gourmet Traveler* by Fred Plotkin—a town-by-town, restaurant-by-restaurant guide to Italian cuisine (first published in 1996, with updated editions through 2014). For many years, Rick admired Fred's masterpiece, which was *the* undisputed, definitive guide to Italian food culture. And over time, as Rick and Fred became friends, we hatched an idea: What if we revived that book, updated it, and adapted it for today's traveler? And so, *Rick Steves Italy for Food Lovers* was born.

Over the decades that Fred has spent living and traveling in Italy, he has come to think of himself as a Garibaldi with a fork. He has slept and eaten in most of the towns Garibaldi visited—and many he didn't, taking notes on everything he ate and drank. Along the way, Fred delighted locals with his interest in and affection for their foods, customs, and history. In this book, he'll share much of this acquired *campanilismo* with you—along with the encouragement to go and discover these places for yourself.

Meanwhile, Rick prides himself as being the "everyperson" traveler— a typical American who enjoys travel and good food, but who lacks Fred's deep expertise. As his life's work, Rick seeks to embolden all travelers to wade into the joys of Europe— making his favorite continent accessible and meaningful to first-timers and veteran travelers alike. Rick might not know the difference, exactly, between a Barolo and a Barbaresco, but he knows what he likes.

Together, we've worked hard to ensure that this new guide is up-to-the-moment relevant to the needs of today's traveler, while also taking advantage of Fred's knowledge of the timeless joys of Italian cuisine. With many combined decades of Italian travel (and eating) under our collective belts, our goal is to help travelers not only appreciate Italian food, but also to understand it deeply—to think about food the way that Italians do. We want to introduce you to the flavors that Italians grew up with and cherish.

For simplicity, in the chapters that follow, we'll shed our respective egos and become "I." But you'll notice that each of our personalities sneaks in here and there—and at times we'll call out some personal observations and memories. And at the end of the book, we've each curated a list of our 50 favorite eateries from all across Italy.

This isn't a guidebook of sightseeing strategies, itinerary tips, and listings for hotels, museums, or even restaurants. For that, you'll want to pick up a proper guidebook. (Might we suggest the Rick Steves guidebook series—either our all-Italy books, or city and regional guides on Venice, Rome, Florence and Tuscany, the Cinque Terre, and Sicily?) Rather, this book is designed to complement other travel information with a focus on food. It's designed to be something you can take along to Italy and flip through while you're waiting for your flight, sitting on the train, or relaxing over dinner. Or simply enjoy reading it at home, as an armchair gourmand.

This book is organized into four parts.

The first part covers the basics: how to find a good restaurant, how Italian meals differ from ones back home, and how to take advantage of Italy's fine grocery stores and markets to assemble a picnic, pick up some souvenirs, or cook for yourself.

The second part dives into the food, describing what you'll find on the plate, course by course—from tasty *antipasti* to toothsome pastas to hearty steaks to delicious gelato— plus Italy's coffee culture and remarkable wine scene.

Then comes the heart of the book: a region-by-region rundown covering the entirety of Italy's "boot," from knee to toe. Italy has 20 regions, and for each one, we've included an overview of the landscape, history, and food culture; descriptions of towns and cities of interest to the traveler (from either a culinary or a sightseeing point of view); extensive descriptions of food and wine specialties; and a digestible little list of local tastes you should be sure not to miss while in that region.

ITALY'S REGIONS

The final part of the book covers our 100 favorite restaurants across Italy—Rick's 50 Favorites and Fred's 50 Favorites—and includes a comprehensive Italian Food Glossary that you can use to decode local menus or whet your appetite for what to look for on the road.

Here's a user's guide for this book: Before your trip, read through the chapters on Italian food, the regions you're visiting, and the "100 Favorites" at the end—taking note of items that might enhance your trip. Then use those sections on the road to travel with a new culinary savvy. And, for the sake of packing light, please consider tearing out only the sections you need for your trip.

This book is designed for anybody curious about Italian food, from utter novices to seasoned gourmands. Depending on your personal experience level, some sections may feel too elementary (especially the early chapters) or too advanced (the region-by-region chapters). With a little browsing, you'll find the guidance that meets you wherever you are on the learning curve. And given the beautiful complexity of Italian food culture, even sophisticated travelers who've been to Italy year after year might pick up some tips and insights that have eluded them… even when reading the more "basic" sections.

Regardless of your level of expertise coming in, we're going all-in on Italian customs. We use Italian terms liberally, just as Italians do (the plural of *enoteca* isn't "enotecas"—it's *enoteche*). If you're not very familiar with the language, this might feel overwhelming…not unlike the many Italians you'll meet who will keep chatting away at you, in their language, even as you protest that you only speak English. Just go with it: Let your trip be a crash course in

Italian ways. By diving in feet-first, you'll be surprised how much you pick up along the way. After experiencing Italy as a food lover—after traveling as Garibaldi with a fork—for the rest of your life, every whiff or bite of a beloved dish will rekindle a memory, transporting you instantly back to that amazing meal you had on a floodlit piazza. A sensory flashback—what better souvenir exists?

Why Is Italian Food So Great?

Italian cuisine is the world's most international food. Pizza, pasta, and Parmigiano-Reggiano can be found around the globe. Yet nowhere does Italian cooking equal what you can find in its native country. That's because the quality and freshness of the ingredients can seldom be equaled abroad. And the unique mindset of Italian chefs can't be fully exported: an accumulated intelligence, tradition, appreciation of flavor, and understanding of texture. Savoring Italian cuisine, *in Italy,* is sightseeing for your palate.

Italian food was once completely geared to seasonal availability of foods. Although modern food storage techniques and importation have made many ingredients available year-round, Italians still tend to eat certain foods only when they're fresh from local farmers. Even urbanites possess a surprisingly sophisticated knowledge of agricultural cycles. In some towns, the arrival of seasonal foods is celebrated with a festival, called a *sagra,* that has ancient roots both in pagan culture (thanking the land and the deities for the food) and in Catholicism. Considering Italy's determination to eat fresh and with the seasons, here are a few key words to look for: *fatto in casa* (homemade), *per oggi*

(for today), *stagione* (season), and *nostrano* (our).

Similarly, many dishes (especially desserts) originated as a special treat for Carnival (Mardi Gras), Easter, or Christmas. Often these items became so beloved that they're now available year-round.

One delightful outgrowth of this faithfulness to tradition is that flavors are that much bolder. Almost every dish in Italy has local roots and is best eaten in its place of origin. While spaghetti with fresh tomato sauce can be found throughout Italy, nowhere is it more delicious than in its native Campania. Tomatoes that grow in the local volcanic soil have an irreplaceable flavor, and the people of that same land have an innate knowledge of how to use them.

Many of those classic dishes are also distinguished by their simplicity, which is often rooted in hardship. Especially in the South, simple dishes originated as *cucina povera*—the "cuisine of the poor." Centuries of poverty forced Italian chefs to become creative and to harness the very best that each ingredient had to offer. The best and most famous

Italian dishes don't use high-end ingredients: noodles with a basic sauce of tomato and garlic; eggplant dusted with breadcrumbs and scant cheese, then baked; dried salted cod *(baccalà)* that's been rehydrated and mixed with flavorful vegetables. These are foods designed to stretch limited resources. It speaks to the ingenuity and soulfulness of Italian culinary tradition that they're also utterly delicious.

Another beautiful aspect of Italian cuisine is *abbinamento:* the proper matching of flavors and textures, along with pairings of

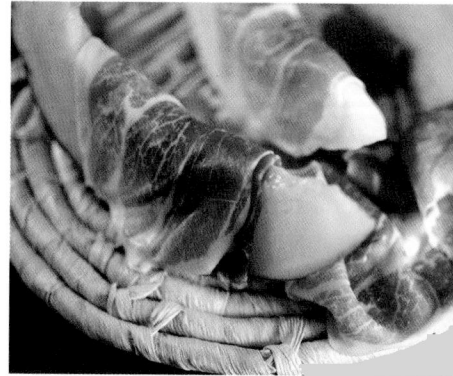

Holiday and Festival Foods

Many of Italy's traditional dishes originated as seasonal specialties—either because that's when a food would make its annual appearance, or because the dish was associated with a holiday or a festival. Especially in the traditionally poor South, holidays like Easter or Christmas may have been the only time all year that locals would splurge on hearty meats or sweets.

In February, Carnival (Carnevale) culminates in *Martedì Grasso* ("Fat Tuesday")—a flurry of indulgence that precedes the onset of Lent. Venice's Carnival, with its elaborate masquerade traditions, is the most famous, but many other towns and cities have similar celebrations. Most foods related to Carnival are sweets, many of which—including Sicily's *cannoli*—have become available year-round.

Lent (La Quaresima) is the 40 days that lead up to Easter. Because it coincides with the final weeks of winter, Lent is a lean time. Traditionally, during Lent Italians would abstain from eating meat on Fridays, which Christians believe is the day Jesus died. (The word "carnival" comes from a phrase that roughly means to "put away meat"). This partly explains the affinity even landlocked Italians have for fish (such as *baccalà*, salt-preserved cod), especially on Fridays. Some specialties, such as the meatless Ligurian layered salad called *cappon magro*, originated as a Lenten dish.

Easter (Pasqua) sees the return of meat, the end of lean winter months, and the appearance of more springtime produce. Typically, Easter is celebrated with a feast of slow-roasted lamb (or another animal, such as goat or suckling pig). As in the US, hard-boiled eggs are often consumed at Eastertime. Many areas have elaborate, everything-but-the-kitchen-sink baked Easter dishes—such as Trentino's *smacafam* ("hunger-killer") or Liguria's *torta pasqualina,* with 33 layers (one for each year of Jesus' life). And certain cakes (such as Campania's citrusy *pastiera*) are special for Easter, as well. Celebrations spill over from Easter Sunday into Monday, which is called La Pasquetta ("Little Easter"); if the weather permits, this is the day for a picnic.

The Christmas (Natale) season sees the arrival both of winter and a whole new array of seasonal foods. In the North, Christmas markets are

Left: Italians celebrate many special occasions with little colorful candied almonds called *confetti;*
Right: Chocolate eggs for Pasqua (Easter)

Babbo Natale (Italy's Santa) makes an appearance at many Christmas markets.

lubricated by mulled wine and other wintry, hot drinks. Milan's patron saint feast day (San Ambrogio, December 7) coincides with the early days of the Christmas season, providing double the reason to celebrate—including with *panettone,* the yeast cake that originated at the holidays and is now eaten anytime. Trentino-Alto Adige enjoys *Zelten,* a Germanic Christmas fruitcake, while Verona indulges with golden *pandoro* cake, and Naples enjoys marzipan cakes called *pasta reale.* In the South, look for sweet, deep-fried dough balls (such as Naples' *struffoli* and Puglia's *pettole*). Christmas Eve (vigilia di Natale) meals often include seafood—especially eel—and the Christmas Day feast features meat. And for New Year's (Capodanno), Italians eat lentils—which resemble small coins—for good fortune in the coming year.

Each Italian town also has its own patron saint, whose feast day *(giorno di festa)* is celebrated in boisterous fashion, and sometimes with special foods. For example, the feast of St. Joseph (San Giuseppe), on March 19, is Italy's answer to Father's Day. It's celebrated in Rome and the South by eating special cream puffs called *bignè di San Giuseppe* (or, in Naples, deep-fried balls of dough called *zeppole*).

Finally are the seasonal festivities called *sagra,* which coincide with the annual arrival of a favorite local ingredient. Think of these as "harvest festivals" that occur anytime a new fruit or vegetable ripens. These are celebrated with a special verve in the South, perhaps thanks to a heritage of poverty that has bred a mindset of abundance.

Timing a visit to Italy to coincide with a holiday can drape your trip with festive tinsel—and provide a chance to indulge in special holiday foods.

foods and wines. Italians sometimes describe this as "a good marriage." For example, a fresh slice of *melone* (cantaloupe) or a thin slice of salty prosciutto are each delicious on their own. But paired together, they're a revelation. Italians also know which flavors *don't* go together. Never ask for Parmigiano to go with your *spaghetti alle vongole* (with clams); to an Italian, cheese and seafood or fish seldom mix.

We might think of "Italian food," but the country's cuisine is far from monolithic. If you're eating well (in other words, at places catering to locals rather than tourists), what's on the plate will differ entirely based on where you are and when you're there. An Italian once told me that,

by looking at a menu from a good restaurant, a smart eater could tell which region (or even town) it came from, and the time of year. That's why a major feature of this book are chapters covering each of Italy's 20 regions, focusing on what you'll find in that place (and often, *only* in that place).

The intense regionality of Italian ingredients is reflected in a legal designation called DOP *(Denominazione d'Origine Protetta)*—a European Union-administered "Protected Designation of Origin," meaning that to earn a certain name, the product must come from a specific, controlled, and protected location. "San Marzano" tomatoes or "Parmigiano-Reggiano" cheese or "Prosecco" sparkling wine are each produced exclusively in a legally defined zone. (There's a similar classification for wines, called DOC and DOCG, which is explained in the Italian Wine chapter.) This book doesn't make note of DOP products—which are too numerous to mention—but you'll likely see that terminology throughout your travels in Italy.

Yes, supermarkets, McDonald's, and processed foods have made inroads in Italy. But most Italians still have a deep and persistent reverence for the land. This is reflected in the Slow Food movement, founded in the Piedmont region in the 1980s. Slow Food strives to defend the irreplaceable virtues and traditions of cooking, eating, agriculture, and social interaction at the table. Think of it as a preservation society, not for buildings or public spaces, but for food. You'll see the red snail of Slow Food in the front window of many restaurants, promising a slow-down-and-savor-the-flavors approach.

A related trend is "zero kilometer" cooking, in which every ingredient for a meal is grown within a

kilometer of where it's eaten. This approach makes even "traditional" Italy feel fresh and vital.

But Italian dining isn't just about the food: It's convivial and pleasurable—captured by the expression *A tavola non si invecchia* ("At the table one does not age"). Italians don't adopt formal "restaurant manners," but remain relaxed; having dinner together is a fun, social experience, even at high-end places. Each *mise-en-table* is its own little drama, comedy, farce, or tragedy. It's an opportunity to observe, for instance, four generations of a family carry on with each other. Kids feel comfortable expressing themselves, elderly relatives are closely watched and doted upon, and everyone goofs around, with an occasional outburst of disagreement.

This may sound clichéd, but it's true: One of Italy's great virtues is the way its people relish human contact. When you shop in a food store, pay a bill at a bar, or sit next to someone on a bus, there is a moment of contact that is made sweet by the tendency of most Italians to want that moment to be a nice one. You don't need to

Italians hand down culinary traditions from one generation to the next. On a special day each summer, this village's older kids teach the younger ones how to make good ravioli.

share a common language for these encounters to be meaningful. A smile, a *buongiorno* (good morning), a *grazie* (thank you)—these are all you need. Italians are grateful when you attempt to communicate in their language, even just a bit. To facilitate these connections, spend a little time studying the Italian Survival Phrases in the back of this book. You'll be rewarded for your effort.

Rick Steves' Travel Philosophy

Travel is intensified living—maximum thrills per minute and one of the last great sources of legal adventure. Travel is freedom. It's recess, and we need it.

Affording travel is a matter of priorities. (Make do with the old car.) You can eat and sleep—simply, safely, and enjoyably—anywhere in Europe for $100 a day plus transportation costs. In many ways, spending more money only builds a thicker wall between you and what you traveled so far to see. Europe is a cultural carnival—its best acts are free, and the best seats are the cheap ones.

Experiencing the real Europe requires catching it by surprise, going casual..."through the Back Door." A tight budget forces you to travel close to the ground, among the people. Never sacrifice sleep, nutrition, safety, or cleanliness to save money. Simply enjoy the local-style alternatives to expensive hotels and restaurants.

Connecting with people carbonates your experience. Extroverts have more fun. If your trip is low on magic moments, kick yourself and make things happen. If you don't enjoy a place, maybe you don't know enough about it. Seek the truth. Recognize tourist traps. Give a culture the benefit of your open mind. See things as different, but not better or worse. Any culture has plenty to share. When an opportunity presents itself, make it a habit to say "yes."

Of course, travel, like the world, is a series of hills and valleys. Be fanatically positive and militantly optimistic. If something's not to your liking, change your liking.

Our Earth is home to almost eight billion equally precious people. It's humbling to travel and find that other people don't have the "American Dream"—they have their own dreams. Europeans like us, but with all due respect, they wouldn't trade passports. Can travel be a political act? Yes. Travelers learn that the world is basically a good place filled with joy and love, and that caring for our environment and finding international solutions can be a win-win rather than a win-lose.

Thoughtful travel engages us with the world. It reminds us what is important and teaches new ways to measure quality of life. I believe that if Americans were required to travel before they could vote, the US would be safer, stronger, and happier. That's why rather than saying, "Have a safe trip," I say, "Keep on travelin'."

Globetrotting destroys ethnocentricity and helps us understand and appreciate other cultures. Rather than fear the diversity on this planet, celebrate it. Among your most prized souvenirs will be the strands of different cultures you choose to knit into your own character. The world is a cultural yarn shop, and good travelers are weaving the ultimate tapestry. Join in!

Italy for the Pleasure Activist
by Fred Plotkin

I define myself as a pleasure activist, a concept not everyone understands or embraces. Pleasure activism goes well beyond simple hedonism. Nor is it about shopping, consuming, or acquisition.

Nearly all of us have been given the gift of five senses: sight, hearing, smell, taste, and touch. But most people scarcely use their senses—and miss out on a great deal of pleasure. They see but do not observe. They hear but do not listen. They smell and taste but do not savor. They touch but do not feel.

I believe that the best way to use our senses is to not constantly analyze what is being perceived. Rather, what we take in becomes part of our bank of information, knowledge, and experience. We put all thoughts out of our head and open our senses more fully and actively—to discover the pleasures and complexities that await us.

Pleasure activism is also the recognition of the value of experiences. One bite of chocolate or one sip of wine is immensely rewarding. The second bite or sip can tell us more, if we let it. Otherwise, it's merely a repetition of the first experience.

Similarly, if we meet a new person and open all of our senses to him or her, we have a much stronger experience of why that person is so compelling.

It would be too pat to say that the fullest use of our senses is the secret to happiness. But any behavior that can contribute to our becoming more fully human and insightful is to be prized. That, to me, is pleasure activism. And Italy—with its splendid food culture, visual art, music, spectacular natural beauty, and extraordinary people—is a *paradiso* for the pleasure activist.

Dining Out

The Italians are masters of the art of fine living. That means eating long and well. Lengthy, multicourse meals and endless hours sitting in outdoor cafés are the norm. Americans eat on their way to an evening event and complain if the check is slow in coming. For Italians, the meal is an end in itself, and only rude servers rush you. This chapter covers tips on how to find good eateries and advice for dining out like an Italian.

Finding a Place to Eat

When restaurant-hunting, choose a spot filled with locals, not the place with the big neon signs boasting, "We speak English and accept credit cards." Restaurants parked on famous squares generally serve bad food at high prices to tourists. These are easy to spot: The big, flashy multilingual

menu posted outside is identical to other restaurants all over town. Another sure sign is the *menù turistico,* a set meal of the most mundane dishes—spaghetti with tomato sauce, breaded veal cutlet, green salad, and fruit salad. These can be comfortingly familiar and low-stress. But if you choose one of these, you'll usually get crank-'em-out food and service ranging from indifferent to surly.

Challenge yourself to find something more distinctive and memorable. Venturing even a block or two off the main drag leads to higher-quality food and more attentive service at a better price. Locals eat better at lower-rent, family-run places. My very favorite type of Italian eatery is a classic "mom-and-pop" where Dad is very busy in the kitchen while Mom charms visitors in the dining room (or vice versa). Children, grandparents, aunts, and uncles all help out in one way or another.

One sure sign of a great eatery is a short, handwritten menu in Italian only. It's short because they're going to cook up only what they can sell for the day. It's handwritten because it's shaped by whatever's fresh in the market that morning. And it's in Italian—and *only* Italian—because they're targeting local, return customers rather than tourists. If I see one of these menus pinned to the door, I know I'm in for a great meal.

The best places are hardly a secret. If your sights are set on a particular eatery, to avoid disappointment, confirm opening hours and ideally make a reservation *(una prenotazione)*. (You can do this by phone or, sometimes, on the restaurant's website; if you encounter a language barrier, your hotel can help.)

Most eateries are closed *(chiuso)* for a day or a day and a half each week, often Sunday *(domenica)* and/or Monday *(lunedì)*; this is listed on the door with the words *chiuso per turno* or *chiusura settimanale. Chiuso per ferie* means they're closed for vacation (common in big cities in July and August, and off-season in resort areas).

Most restaurant kitchens close between their lunch and dinner service. Good restaurants don't reopen for dinner before 7 p.m., and some not until 8. If you arrive at reopening time, most restaurants will be empty. Small restaurants with a full slate of reservations for 8:30 or 9 can sometimes accommodate walk-in diners willing to eat a quick, early meal. And some very popular places offer two seatings, so you can choose early or late.

What time you arrive can really

When restaurant-hunting, I look for places with a short, handwritten menu in Italian only.

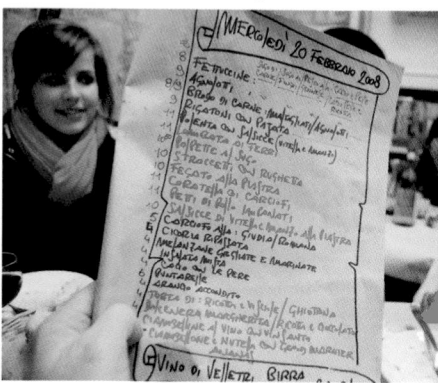

shape your experience. If you go early, it may seem sedate and touristy; if you go later, it's higher-energy, packed with locals, and potentially overwhelming for a tourist who doesn't speak the language. There's no right or wrong—just your preference. Here's a tip: If you scope out a place at 7 p.m. and it looks like a tourist trap, try coming back at 9. You may find it has transformed into a local favorite.

Italy bans smoking in indoor pub-lic places. While people still smoke on outdoor *terrazze,* you'll rarely smell it inside.

At the Restaurant

When entering a restaurant with-out reservations, talk to the host or catch a server's eye and signal to be sure it's OK to sit at a table that isn't marked "reserved" *(riservato).* You may be asked to wait, or you may be turned away.

THE MENU
Once seated, you'll be handed a menu (or be directed to a QR code to access the menu online with your smartphone). Note that in Italian, the word *menù* can refer to the printed menu (also called la *lista*), or it can refer to a fixed-price meal. The menu

is organized in sections, based on the courses traditionally served at a complete meal: *antipasto* (appetizer), *primo* (first course, typically pasta or soup), *secondo* (main dish, meat or fish) plus *contorni* (side dishes), and *dolce* (dessert) or fruit.

Many eateries also post a handwritten list of the day's specials, usually based on what the chef found fresh at the market. These are often noted with the word *oggi* (today)—sometimes followed by *lo chef consiglia* (the chef recommends) or *consigliamo* (we recommend).

It can be worth paying a little more for an inventive fixed-price meal that shows off the chef's cre-ativity. These come in various forms: Remember that a *menù turistico* is a made-for-tourists plate of Italian food clichés for one fixed price. But locals have their own, typically more interesting version of this, usually called a *prezzo fisso* or sometimes *menù del giorno* (menu of the day). If you choose wisely, these fixed-price meals can be a good-value way to sample some variety. For a smaller appetite, some restaurants serve a *piatto unico,* with smaller portions of each course on one plate (for instance, a meat, starch, and vegetable).

Other key menu terms: *incluso* or *compreso* means "included"; *escluso* or *non compreso* means the opposite. For example, for a fixed-price meal, beverages may not be included (*bevande escluse* or *bevande non comprese*).

One thing that's often included is the service charge—you'll see the phrase *servizio compreso.* For more on tipping and cover-charge cus-toms, see the sidebar on page 25.

Some restaurants have only a chalkboard menu, and a few don't have a printed menu at all; the server or proprietor simply recites the day's

Ristorante Ricardo • IL MENÙ
Via Buon Appetito 35, Roma

Menù del giorno
(primo, secondo, dolci)................€30

Some restaurants offer a fixed-price, three-course meal of the day.

Menù degustazione
(antipasto, 2 primi, secondo, contorno, dolce, bevande comprese)...€50

The tasting menu is literally the full meal deal—multiple courses (often with choices) for one fixed price.

ANTIPASTI
Bruschetta..............................€4
Carciofi alla romana.....................€6
Prosciutto di Parma.....................€8
Affettati misti.........................€12

Starter—usually cold cuts (salumi), cheeses, and other small dishes.

PRIMI
Pappardelle al ragù...................€8
Tortellini in brodo.........................€9
Risotto alla milanese..................€10
Minestrone.................................€6

"First course" is pasta, soup, risotto, or polenta.

SECONDI
Ossobuco...................................€12
Brodetto....................................€14
Bistecca alla fiorentina............€3/etto
Pesce spada alla ghiotta..........€2/etto

"Second course" is heartier—usually meat or fish.

Steak or seafood may be priced by the *etto* (100 grams, about ¼ pound).

CONTORNI
Insalata mista..............................€5
Radicchio......................................€3
Patate arroste.............................€4
Cannellini.....................................€4

Contorni (vegetable side dishes) may come with the *secondo*, or be ordered separately. Salads (insalate) are served with or after the *secondo*.

DOLCI
Sottobosco.....................................€5
Tiramisù della casa.......................€4
Vin Santo e biscotti........................€8

Dessert—save room or find a nearby gelateria and go for a moonlit stroll.

Specialties of the house (della casa) are usually worth trying.

Drinks, also called *bevande*.

BIBITE
Vino della casa...¼ L.– €5, ½ L.– €7, L.– €10
Acqua minerale.................½ L.– €5, Litro – €5

Mineral water comes bottled—still (non gassata) or carbonated (gassata).

House wine (usually good and affordable) is served by the carafe (¼, ½, or 1 full liter). Finer wines by the bottle (bottiglia) are found on the wine list (lista dei vini).

pane e coperto – €2,50 • servizio compreso

Many restaurants add a per person cover charge to your bill.

Service here is included (compreso). Tip modestly, simply by rounding up your bill.

Note: A full meal is simply too much food for most diners. A good rule of thumb is for each person to order any two courses. So a couple can share, for example, one antipasto, two pastas, and a dessert. **Buon appetito!**

offerings, based on the cook's mood and the morning market. This is a good sign, though it can be confusing for a tourist (who, unlike regulars, doesn't know the price range up front—it's fine to ask).

On menus at high-end restaurants, premium items (such as fish, seafood, steak, and anything truffle-forward) don't list a price, but rather the Italian version of "market price": s.q. (*secondo quantità,* according to the amount) or *p.v.* (*prezzo da vedere,* price to be determined). And some dishes might indicate the price *per etto* (100 grams, or 3.5 ounces— about a quarter-pound) or, occasionally, by the kilogram (1,000 grams, or 2.2 pounds). Before ordering these, it's fine to ask, *Quanto costerebbe, più o meno?* ("How much would it cost, more or less?") For these high-end items, you might be shown a fish or a steak for your approval.

Especially for steak, restaurants may require a minimum order of four or five *etti* (which diners can share). And some special dishes come in larger quantities meant to be shared by two people. The shorthand way of showing this on a menu is "X2"

(for two), but the price listed could indicate the cost per person.

THE SERVICE

In Italy, being a server is a valued vocation, done with dignity, professionalism, and pride; Italians treat waitstaff with respect, rather than as servants. To echo this sentiment— and to get in your server's good graces—refer to them as *Signore* or *Signora:* "Sir" or "Ma'am."

Here are a few things you may hear from your server: First, they'll ask what you'd like to drink *(Da bere?).* When ready to take your order, they'll ask *Prego?* and maybe *E dopo?* ("And then?") to see what else you might want; just reply *È tutto* ("That's all"). They'll bring your food with a *Buon appetito!*—wishing you a good meal.

When you want the bill, mime-scribble on your raised palm or request it: *Il conto, per favore.* Or the server might notice when you're done—Italians signal this by placing their utensils on the plate with the handles pointing to the right. The server might confirm by asking *Finito?* Then you'll likely be asked if you'd like dessert *(Qualcosa*

Coperto (Cover Charge), *Servizio* (Service Charge), and Tipping

Avoid surprises by familiarizing yourself with two common Italian restaurant charges: *coperto* (cover charge) and *servizio* (service charge). You won't encounter them in every restaurant, but both charges, if assessed, by law must be listed on the menu.

The **coperto** is a minor fee (typically €1.50-3/person) covering the cost of the bread and the clean tablecloth. (It's sometimes called *pane e coperto*—"bread and cover.") It's not negotiable, even if you don't eat the bread. And it's not a tip. Think of it as a fee paid to the owner that entitles you to use the table for as long as you like.

The **servizio** is a 10- to 15-percent "service charge" that goes to the server. It's similar to the mandatory gratuity that American restaurants often add for groups of six or more. These days, most Italian restaurants don't charge this separately; rather, they include service in their prices—you'll see *servizio compreso*. (At places that do levy a separate *servizio* charge, you don't need to leave an additional tip.)

Italian servers are well-paid and are not as reliant on additional **tips** as servers are back home. Even so, if you're pleased with the service, it's polite to add a small tip *(una mancia)*. This is much smaller than the standard 20 percent in the US. A common tip at a simple restaurant or pizzeria is €1 per person (or simply round up the bill); at a finer restaurant, leave a few euros per person. While you could leave coins on the table, it's more discreet and classy to simply round up the bill when paying. (For instance, if the bill is €46 or €47, hand the server €50 and tell them to keep the change.) If paying with a credit card, be prepared to tip separately with cash or coins; most credit card receipts don't have a tip line.

If you're bothered by either the *servizio* or the *coperto,* keep in mind that there's no added tax (it's included in the listed prices) and additional tipping is minimal—so actually, you wind up paying closer to the listed price in Italy than you do back home.

di dolce?) and coffee *(Un caffè?),* and, finally, if you want anything else *(Altro?).*

If you're satisfied, you can say *Buono!* (good), *Delizioso!* (delicious), or even *Complimenti!* (compliments). Servers are genuinely pleased to know you've enjoyed the food.

Remember: Good service isn't rushed. Americans sometimes find it stressful to have to ask for the check and may be surprised (and annoyed) at how long it takes to arrive. You may have to ask more than once. For Italians, dining out is an end in itself; they savor the experience of lingering at the table after a meal, as food digests and conversation percolates. If you find yourself impatient after dinner, experiment with taking on this

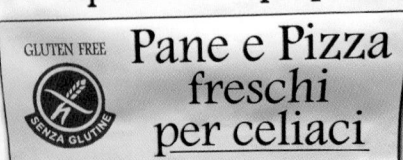

Left: While it's not common in all of Italy, you may find some restaurants with gluten-free options *(per celiaci)*; **Right:** Credit cards are widely accepted at Italian restaurants.

Italian mindset. Or, if you just can't wait to get on with your evening, be politely assertive: Request the check when you receive the last item you order, be ready to pay when it arrives…and don't be surprised if it still takes a while.

Simpler places don't have table service; instead, you'll order at a counter. At traditional bars, you'll first order and pay at the cashier, then take the receipt to the counter to be served your food. And you might pay more if you sit than if you stand up. For more on this, see "Bars" on page 40.

THE BILL

Most Italian restaurants are honest in their pricing, but it's always smart to carefully review the bill; if anything seems odd, ask. In Italy, the fear of *brutta figura* (casting an "ugly fig-ure") will usually shame someone into rectifying the problem. But be polite (if firm) about it to avoid becoming the *brutta figura* yourself.

Credit cards are widely accepted, but there are a few holdouts; if in doubt, call or check online in advance to know whether you need to hit an ATM first.

After you pay, you are legally required to be given a printed receipt *(scontrino),* and you are legally required to take it with you as you leave the business.

Special Concerns

This section offers advice for trav-elers with food allergies or dietary restrictions, and for those who are traveling with kids.

FOOD ALLERGIES AND DIETARY RESTRICTIONS

Broadly speaking, Italy doesn't cater to special diets as well as the US. For instance, non-dairy milks are uncom-mon at cafés. You're more likely to find a higher awareness—and more options (such as strictly vegetarian or vegan offerings)—in bigger cities. Still, things can be hit-or-miss; at one restaurant, the server will "get it" instantly and help you navigate the menu, while at the next, you might get confused stares.

Vegetarians can dine very well on

Key Phrases for Dietary Restrictions

Sono vegetariano/a.   →   I am a vegetarian.
(*-o* for male, *-a* for female).

Non mangio nè _____ *, nè* _____ .   →   I do not eat _____ or _____ .

_____ *e* _____ *OK.*   →   _____ and _____ are OK.

Fill in the blanks with these terms:

Carne: Meat.   *Formaggio:* Cheese.
Pesce: Fish.   *Latte:* Milk.
Frutti di mare: Seafood.   *Frumento:* Wheat.
Pollo: Chicken.   *Soia:* Soy.
Uova: Egg.   *Glutine:* Gluten.

For example: Translation:
Sono vegetariano.   →   I am a vegetarian.
Non mangio nè carne, nè pollo.   →   I don't eat meat or chicken.
Pesce e formaggio OK.   →   Fish and cheese are OK.

If you need more specific terms, look them up before your trip (Google Translate is helpful; I also include several terms and phrases in my *Rick Steves Italian Phrase Book & Dictionary*). Jot them down or print them out, and keep them handy.

many pasta dishes, pizza, vegetable-based *antipasti* and *contorni,* and salads. But be careful—some Italians think "vegetarian" means "no red meat" or "not much meat." If you are a vegan or strict vegetarian, you'll have to make things very clear (see the sidebar).

The *contorni* (side dishes) section of the menu is a good place to look for interesting plant-based dishes. In fact, when having a traditional multicourse meal, vegetarians can skip the *secondo* and order several *contorni* instead.

Travelers with celiac disease, gluten sensitivity, or food allergies will find that Italians—again, especially in bigger cities—are becoming more aware of how to cater to their needs. That said, even if you come armed with translations, locals won't always be familiar with terms such as "gluten." To avoid misunderstandings, explicitly name what you cannot eat. Keep the translation straightforward: "I am allergic to barley, wheat, and rye. I cannot eat bread, pasta, couscous, or other foods containing barley, wheat, or rye."

Some travelers carry a laminated card listing their allergies in Italian, which they simply hand to servers in restaurants to avoid confusion. (For example, you can download free translated "chef cards" at www.foodallergy.org/resources/food-allergy-chef-cards.) It's also helpful

especially when traveling; or people who have a gluten sensitivity—rather than an allergy—but still "cheat" from time to time. If you're in that category, there's no better time to flex than when you're in Italy. Those who've done so report that the purity of Italian ingredients (locally sourced, fresh and seasonal, less processed) makes them easier to stomach than what they get back home.

TRAVELING WITH CHILDREN

Taking your kids to Italy can be a wonderful opportunity to introduce them to a new world of flavors. But if your child is a picky eater, they'll face a very steep learning curve.

Start the day with a good, substantial breakfast and plan for snack breaks. Buying bread, cheese, fruit, and drinks in the morning means you can picnic anytime, anywhere. Italian grocery stores are an adventure for kids, so bring them along to help shop—and to pick out some local treats to try.

Kid-friendly foods found everywhere include fresh bread *(pane)* and pasta (plain is *pasta in bianco,* and pasta with butter is *pasta al burro;* grated cheese will be served on the side). Pizza is another favorite. Kids like simple toppings, such as *Margherita* (tomato, basil, and mozzarella) and *diavola* ("spicy," often the Italian version of American pepperoni). (If you ask for *peperoni,* you'll get sweet peppers.) Peanut butter is virtually unknown in Italy; instead, try a sandwich with cocoa-hazelnut Nutella spread *(un panino con la Nutella).* If your kids find certain condiments make anything palatable (I'm looking at you, ketchup), pack a small bottle to help make unfamiliar foods more appealing.

Popular drinks for families on the road are *frullati* (smoothies), *frappé* (shakes), *aranciata* (orange soda),

to know that the European Union has a classification system for food allergens, which are denoted by numbers that often appear on menus (for example, gluten is #1 and peanuts are #5). Familiarize yourself with these numbers (just search for "EU food allergens") as another way to safeguard against eating the wrong things.

There are many resources for specific dietary needs. Food bloggers review restaurants based on their vegan offerings, offer tips on health-food stores that sell gluten-free products, and so on. Do a little homework and scout options before your trip.

That said, the reality is that traveling with dietary restrictions will limit your ability to fully experience Italian cuisine. I have some friends who self-identify as "flexitarians": They do their best to be vegetarian at home, but occasionally do eat meat,

limonata (lemonade), *spremuta d'arancia* (fresh-squeezed orange juice), and *cioccolata calda* (thick hot chocolate).

Eat dinner early (at about 7 p.m.); restaurants are less kid-friendly after 9. You'll see Italian families dining at sit-down restaurants. But their kids are accustomed to being out for a long evening—and yours might not be. Bring something to occupy them while lingering, or look for a place where younger kids can move around without bothering others or where you can take food out to eat at a scenic park or piazza: self-service places (such as a *rosticceria*), *pizza rustica* shops, bars (children are welcome), or fast-food restaurants. Restaurants with outdoor seating allow parents to have a relaxed and scenic meal while keeping an eye on well-behaved youngsters exploring nearby. In general, don't expect highchairs to be available; in a pinch, use your stroller.

Eating Well on a Budget

Experiencing Italian food and wine can feel like an indulgence, but it doesn't have to be expensive. While it's possible to blow through a lot of money eating in Italy, by choosing restaurants and dishes carefully, you can have an even better experience for less money... and come home with a few euros in your pocket for the next trip.

The top tip is to avoid touristy, obvious restaurants on the main drag or piazza—the ones with big neon signs and multilingual menus. These cater to tourists and specialize in extracting the most money possible from their guests. Instead, go looking for a place focused on cultivating a loyal, local return clientele—with good food and welcoming service at reasonable prices. These can often be found just a few blocks, or even just steps, from the obvious tourist traps. A short, hand-written menu that's only in Italian is an excellent sign of quality. The listings in the "100 Favorites" chapter, and in the Rick Steves guidebooks, are a start, but travelers are wise to master the art of finding these places on their own.

If splurging, do so in smaller towns. A basic big-city *trattoria* might cost as much as a high-end *ristorante* in smaller towns and villages. To stretch your euros, consider picnicking and grabbing cheap takeout in urban centers, then going all-out for a memorable meal in the countryside.

If your accommodations charge extra for breakfast, skip it and instead have an espresso or cappuccino with a pastry standing at the counter in a local bar. This is very affordable, and far more Italian than a hotel breakfast buffet.

In general, when getting drinks or food at a bar, notice the tiered pricing system: You'll pay less to stand at the counter than if you sit at a table. If you're just looking for a jolt of caffeine, slam down your *caffè* at the bar, alongside the budget-conscious locals. (In fact, the Italian government regulates how much even the fanciest grand café can charge for a stand-up shot of espresso.)

If you're seeking a quick, simple, affordable meal, don't overlook Italy's many casual take-out alternatives to a pricey restaurant. *Pizza rustica* shops, *paninoteche,* and cafeteria-style *tavola calda* bars or *rosticcerie* are all described on page 36 of the Types of Eateries chapter.

Picnicking—the traveler's equivalent of raiding the refrigerator for a basic, cheap meal—is another great way to stretch your budget while exploring local flavors; it's even better if you assemble it at a thriving market. The Food Shopping chapter includes plenty of picnic tips.

If you've had a big lunch, consider taking part in the *"apericena"* custom that's increasingly common in the North. This is a pun combining *aperitivo* (aperitif, a late-afternoon/pre-dinner drink) and *cena* (dinner). An *aperitivo* might be pricey, but it typically comes with free snacks—a bowl of chips or nuts. And at some bars, it includes an impressive smorgasbord of little finger foods. If you're in need of only a small dinner, you can discreetly turn your cocktail into a light meal. For more on this, see page 58.

At restaurants offering a complete, multicourse meal, don't feel obligated to order one of each course (*antipasto, primo, secondo,* dessert). That's too much food for most diners, and your bill can add up. The general rule of thumb is that each diner can order any two courses. So two people, for example, can share an *antipasto,* two *primi,* and a dessert.

In general, sharing not only cuts costs but also lets you sample more flavors—stretching your budget per taste. Also look for places offering *bis*—two half-portions of pasta on one plate, rather than having to order two full portions.

Italian restaurant desserts can be hit-or-miss. Instead of ordering a fancy dessert costing several euros, politely decline and go for an after-dinner walk in search of a cone of cheap, delicious gelato. Or get a bottle of dessert wine (such as Vin Santo) and some dry *biscotti,* and enjoy that light dessert back at your hotel.

Don't have tunnel vision for the famous wines. Table wines are much more affordable and often exceptional. At a meal, there's no expectation that you order a high-end bottle, and in fact, the *vino da tavola* pairs perfectly with your meal, since it was produced in the same area.

Also, some famous areas have a more affordable alternative grown nearby. In Tuscany, Brunello di Montalcino comes with a huge price tag, but Rosso di Montalcino (grown nearby, using similar methods and grapes) costs half as much.

Types of Eateries

Italy has a wide array of restaurants, from hole-in-the-wall takeaway shops to midrange *trattorie* to white-tablecloth, Michelin-starred splurges. You can have a memorable meal in any of these; above all, a "good eatery" has nothing to do with the price tag—it's simply one where you feel that the food has been cooked *for you,* and where eating it is a joy.

Let's begin at the high end and work our way down.

Take-Your-Time, Sit-Down Meals

RISTORANTI AND TRATTORIE

A ***ristorante*** (literally, "place to be restored") is the cream of the crop; they range from moderate to very expensive (especially in cities). The menu reflects the talents of the chef and/or local specialties. In big cities, these can also offer an opportunity to sample specialties from other towns or regions (for example, a Ligurian restaurant in Rome). Italian *ristoranti* tend to be less ambitious than a French temple of gastronomy, where elegant waiters serve elaborately conceived dishes in very formal settings. Rather, *ristoranti* have decor that's pleasant but (with a few swanky exceptions) not over-the-top. Service is gracious and attentive, but never stiff.

I find that in small towns, seeking

A *trattoria* is a casual, welcoming restaurant.

out a serious *ristorante* is the best way to find a more interesting menu of quality dishes, while still at a cost that's moderate when compared to big cities.

A **trattoria** is a notch below a *ristorante* in price, but the food is often just as good, if not better. (The main difference is that a *ristorante* is more formal and often features top-end options, such as truffles or lobster.) Most *trattorie* are family-run, casual, welcoming, and offer home-cooked meals at moderate prices. The clientele is a mix of savvy visitors and neighborhood regulars who know the owners and enjoy the special reception they receive going somewhere that feels like family.

Roman *trattorie* (once you get outside the touristy center) are in a class by themselves. The food is earthy, white wine flows gently, the walls are artfully decorated with paintings, and you'll feel like you're in a family's dining room, with friends and neighbors dropping in all night. Don't be shy about striking up a conversation with the next table.

They might pour you some wine, or perhaps invite you for a coffee or gelato after dinner.

OSTERIE AND ENOTECHE
The **osteria** (occasionally called **locanda**) originated as a place to drink wine accompanied by food. This being Italy, the food is usually very good: maybe a soup or a simple pasta dish, followed by roasted meat or poultry, or slices of quality cold cuts *(salumi)* and cheese. An *osteria* often has long, shared tables—a great opportunity to connect with Italians. The *osteria* has become, in some cases, more like a full restaurant, while often sticking close to their simple, wine-focused origins. (Note: A few pricey restaurants bill themselves as an *osteria* in an effort to be casually chic.)

A more urban version of the *osteria* is the **enoteca** (plural *enoteche*). This term—roughly translated as "wine library"—has various meanings. Usually it's a wine bar where light food is served—ideal if you've gotten one meal ahead of your needs and are

looking simply for a glass of wine and *spuntini* (light snacks). Surrounded by the office crowd, you can get a salad, a plate of *salumi* and cheeses, or a simple seasonal dish, along with a glass of good wine (see blackboards for the day's selection and price per glass). Any food that's offered will pair beautifully with the wine.

An *enoteca* might also be a shop that sells bottles of wine. A third type of *enoteca* is operated by a consortium of wine producers to showcase their particular product. (For more on *enoteche,* see page 116 in the Italian Wine chapter.)

AGRITURISMI **AND HOTEL DINING**

Another place for good food at modest prices is at a farm, specifically a "tourist farm" or **agriturismo** (called **maso** in the Italian Alps). While *agriturismi* are often thought of as accommodations, many also have restaurants, some of which are open to nonguests. Some *agriturismi* have gone high-end, with fine restaurants on site. The selection is typically limited, but the food can't be fresher.

If you're staying at a resort in the Alps or at the coast, especially in a rural setting, your **hotel's restaurant** might be the only place to eat nearby. When you book your stay, you'll be asked whether you want *mezza pensione* (breakfast plus another meal—usually dinner) or *pensione completa* (breakfast, lunch, and dinner). Prices for a full pension usually are not much more than those for a half-pension. While this can be a good value and a convenience, don't commit to this if you'll want to explore and have a wider variety of meals off-property. Occasionally a hotel might require at least half-pension in peak season.

Pizza Types and Toppings

The classic choice is *pizza Margherita.* Originating in Naples—the birthplace of pizza—it's topped only with crushed fresh tomatoes (ideally San Marzano), mozzarella cheese, basil leaf, and perhaps a drizzle of olive oil. This option is hard to beat, and it's patriotic: Its toppings represent the colors of the Italian flag (red, white, and green), and it's named for Margherita of Savoy, the first queen of a united Italy after the Risorgimento.

Here are a few other pizza types and toppings:

Acciughe: Anchovies.

Bianca: White pizza, with no tomatoes.

Capricciosa: This is the "surprise me" option, with toppings at the whim of the *pizzaiolo* (pizza maker). In practice it's usually the same items from a *quattro stagioni* (ham, mushrooms, artichokes, and olives), but all mixed up rather than separated in quarters.

Carciofi: Artichokes.

Cipolla: Onions.

Diavola: Spicy hot.

Frutti di mare: Seafood.

Funghi: Mushrooms.

Ortolana or *vegetariana:* "Greengrocer-style," with vegetables.

Marinara: Tomatoes, garlic, oregano (no cheese).

Melanzane: Eggplant.

Prosciutto: Ham.

Quattro stagioni: "Four seasons," with tomato, mozzarella, and usually one-quarter each of ham, mushrooms, artichokes, and olives. There's also *quattro formaggi,* four different cheeses.

Salsiccia: Sausage.

Siciliana: Capers, olives, and often anchovies.

Tonno: Tuna.

Viennese: "Vienna-style," with German sausage, tomato, and mozzarella.

Note that if you ask for "pepperoni" on your pizza, you'll get *peperoni* (green or red peppers); instead, try requesting *salsiccia piccante,* or *salame piccante* (the closest thing to American pepperoni).

There are other variations, too. A *pizza ripiena* ("stuffed") is thicker, with "toppings" stuffed between an upper and lower crust. A *calzone* is a folded pizza turnover with various fillings. And a *farinata* (sometimes called *cecina* or *torta di ceci*) is a savory crêpe made from chickpeas.

Fast and Casual

For more affordable meals in a hurry, Italy offers several options. In general, to get food to take away, say *da portare via.*

PIZZA PLACES

Italians head to a **pizzeria** at dinner-time to order a one-person pie. In Naples, where pizza was born and still is better than anywhere else, pizzas are traditionally baked in a wood-burning oven *(forno a legna).* In recent years, many pizzerias have transformed into near-*trattorie*, adding small menus of pasta and other standard dishes. In general, these items are lower both in price and quality; the best advice is to go to a

pizzeria for pizza and a *trattoria* for other food.

Some shops sell **pizza rustica** (also called *pizza al taglio* or *pizza al trancio*)—thick pizza baked in a large rectangular pan and sold by weight. This, rather than floppy New York-style slices, is the standard option for Italians on the go. If you simply ask for a piece, you may wind up with a gigantic slab and be charged top euro. Instead, clearly indicate how much you want: *un etto*—100 grams—is a hot and cheap snack; *due etti*—200 grams—makes a light meal. Or show the size with your hands: *tanto così* ("this much"). They may ask if you want it *riscaldata*—heated up. The correct answer is *sì.*

DELIS, CAFETERIAS, AND BUFFETS

Don't confuse a pizzeria with a **pizzicheria**—this somewhat archaic term describes a small grocery store, often with a deli case. That is similar to a **salumeria**, a shop specializing in *salumi* (cold cuts). These can be good places to stock up for a picnic, and sometimes they might make you a sandwich to order. But be careful when selecting meats and cheeses—high-end ingredients can add up to a very expensive bill.

The Italian version of a cafeteria or a full-service corner deli—where you can order food at a counter to be dished up—is a *rosticceria* or a *tavola calda*. The **rosticceria** ("roasting place"), more common in central and southern Italy, dates from a time when not everyone had the facilities to roast their own food at home. It remains a great place to buy a roast chicken or something more exotic, such as duck, goose, or rabbit; they also sell accompanying sides such as roasted potatoes and sautéed greens (spinach or escarole). A **tavola calda** ("hot table")

Above: A deli can make you a tasty sandwich *presto*—just point to what you want. But be careful! Top-end items can add up to a big bill; **Below:** A cafeteria feeds locals (and savvy visitors) affordably.

is an inexpensive, point-and-shoot, buffet-style restaurant (sometimes called a *caffetteria*). Here you can purchase prepared foods such as baked pasta, *risotto,* baked or roasted meats, and vegetables that can be casually eaten standing up, at a table, or taken out. (In the North, you might see a *tavola fredda*—"cold table"—which is more like a snack bar.) Unfortunately, these are fading away as fast-food chains make inroads in Italy, which is a shame—Italy's traditional takeaway shops are easy, generally tasty, and a great value.

Another vanishing institution is the **mensa.** More like a classic caf-eteria, it's connected to a university or a place of work. Railway workers have a *mensa* near most major train stations, and large factories have *mense* as well. A *mensa* is almost always subsidized, so prices for nour-ishing, though unastonishing, meals are amazingly cheap. Usually you need a *tessera* (identification card or monthly pass) to dine at a *mensa,*

but there are occasional exceptions, especially at universities.

SANDWICH SHOPS AND QUICK BITES
In big cities, especially Milan, you can grab a decent lunch at a **panino-teca** (sandwich shop). These are a byproduct of the shrinking lunch break; gone are the days of two- or three-hour lunches, and office drones (especially the workaholic *milanesi*) now grab a quick bite between meetings. At a *paninoteca,*

the sandwiches are often premade, filled with good-quality meats, fish, and vegetables—just point to what you want. A *panifico* (bakery) may also have sandwiches. For more on sandwiches, see the sidebar.

In Liguria and on the coast, a *friggitoria* (fry shop) sells deep-fried fish and sea creatures, eaten standing up or as you walk down the street. Locals might take their fried goodies home, where they supplement them with veggies and other dishes.

For heavy snacks in the early evening, look for a bar that has free happy hour munchies for the after-work crowd. For more on this *aperitivo* custom, see page 58.

When on a road trip, drivers enjoy grabbing a bite at Italy's many **Autogrill** eateries—a rest stop (often spanning a highway, or with facilities on both sides of the *autostrada*) that has a variety of hot and cold foods, sometimes of surprisingly good quality.

International food is relatively rare in Italy. And many purists (including one of this book's co-authors) might question why anyone in their right mind would eat anything but Italian food in one of the world's great culinary destinations. But for those seeking a change of pace, most towns have an Asian eatery or two, and big cities like Rome and Milan have various options featuring non-Italian cuisine (Thai, Mexican, Indian, and so on). Poke and sushi are also becoming popular, especially in the North. Keep in mind that to Italians, "exotic" cuisine doesn't necessarily come from a foreign country; to the people of Milan, going to a Sicilian, Venetian, or Calabrian restaurant feels almost international.

One ubiquitous feature is the

Sandwiches

The generic word for "sandwich" is *panino* (plural *panini*), often served on a small baguette. In central Italy, *porchetta* stands serve tasty rolls stuffed with slices of roast suckling pig. Here are some other variations:

Focaccia: On puffy, chewy Ligurian bread.

Piadina: On the flatbread of Emilia-Romagna; not unlike a "wrap," but folded over rather than wrapped.

Rosetta: On a round roll with a hard crust and an airy center, especially common in central Italy but available everywhere.

Schiacciata: A thin, "squashed" bread sprinkled with sea salt and olive oil (similar to a focaccia), often used to make sandwiches—especially in Tuscany.

Semel: On a big, puffy roll (common in the Alps and Florence).

Toast: Thin, basic sandwich—usually ham and cheese—on crustless white bread, heated up upon ordering; very typical in bars.

Tramezzini: Triangular sandwiches made on crustless white bread, with a thin strip of mayo, and filled with some combination of tuna, prosciutto, mozzarella, tomatoes, asparagus, and sliced hard-boiled eggs. These are also typical in bars, especially in Venice.

stand or hole-in-the-wall shop selling **döner kebab.** Originating in Turkey, a *döner kebab* consists of slow-roasted, ultra-thin-sliced chicken, veal, or lamb stuffed into pita bread *(panino)* or a wrap *(piadina),* along with tomatoes, onions, lettuce, tangy yogurt sauce, and (optional) hot chili sauce. A vegetarian alternative is falafel (a fried garbanzo-bean patty) served with the same works. Shops with more traffic tend to be better bets, with fresher meat and toppings; it's also a good sign if they serve the yogurt drink *ayran,* indicating that they cater to local émigrés. While hardly high cuisine, and arguably not "Italian" whatsoever, *döner kebab* has become a staple for Italians seeking a quick, cheap, filling, flavorful bite on the run.

Food tours offer smartly curated tastes of local specialties with tidbits of information…filling you in while filling you up.

Food Tours and Cooking Classes

For a more hands-on, interactive approach to Italian food, consider a food tour or a cooking class. These can be vivid, memorable, and an excellent value for those really wanting to understand Italian cuisine.

Typical **food tours** last about three or four hours, come with a mile or so of walking, and include four to eight stops. The best ones move at a brisk pace and max out at eight or ten people—small enough to squeeze into small shops and boutique restaurants. A good food guide fluidly intersperses history, tradition, and local food culture while giving you a glimpse into daily life in a characteristic neighborhood. The style of the tour varies: Some are

mobile feasts, where you stand and share a plate of little bites, while others feature a progression of sit-down dining experiences. In any case, you'll often eat (at least) enough food to approximate a hearty sit-down meal, which you should take into consideration when weighing the expense. It's smart to do food tours early in your trip, giving you more time to put your guide's tips into practice.

The best casual **cooking classes** are taught by trained chefs with actual restaurant backgrounds (rather than hobbyists or unemployed locals embarking on a second career); take place in a real kitchen environment (rather than a stuffy classroom or "show" kitchen); have a spirit of fun and interaction; involve small groups (allowing more personal interaction with the instructor); and—perhaps most important—are hands-on rather than demonstration-based. You'll typically spend a couple of hours cooking, and then sit down to a hard-earned (if not always flawlessly executed) meal. Some classes also include a shopping trip to the market. They'll send you on your way with the recipes you prepared.

Bars

And finally, we come to Italy's ubiquitous bars. An Italian bar isn't so much a tavern as an inexpensive café. These neighborhood hangouts serve coffee, mini pizzas *(pizzette),* basic sandwiches (*toasts* and *tramezzini*—see the "Sandwiches" sidebar, earlier), and drinks from the cooler. This is where locals go for a

breakfast of cappuccino and a fresh brioche or *cornetto* (croissant). And then, throughout the day, bars are the place to drop in for a coffee or another drink. Many bars are small—if you can't find a table, you'll need to stand or find a ledge to perch on outside.

Visiting a bar comes with a particular procedure: Upon entering, look around to decide what you want, then go to the cashier *(la cassa)* to order and pay. Often, a list with two sets of prices is posted near the cashier: *al banco* (standing at the bar) or *al tavolo* (seated). Unless you really plan to settle in and watch the world go by, have your drink at the bar.

Upon paying, you're handed a receipt *(scontrino)*. Take that to the bartender (whose clean fingers handle no dirty euros) and tell them what you want. It's customary to set a few euro cents on the bar as you place your order.

Throughout Italy, you can get coffee standing at the counter of any establishment, no matter how fancy, and pay the same low, government-regulated price (generally about a euro). All bars have a WC *(toilette, bagno)* in the back, available to customers…and the discreet public.

In addition to coffee (see page 92), bars sell tea, tisanes (herbal infusions), milk, beer, *cioccolata calda* (thick hot chocolate), mineral water, and bottled juices (apple, apricot, peach, and pear) or freshly squeezed *spremuta* (orange, grapefruit, or lemon juice). Wine is affordable and available by the glass. Stronger drinks include grappa, as well as imported Scotch, gin, and whiskey; Italians seldom have the strong stuff, and those bottles often languish on shelves for months.

Whether you buy liquor or soft drinks (Coca-Cola is *una Coca*), you will probably not see ice *(ghiaccio)* unless you ask for it; Italians believe ice dilutes the flavor of drinks.

A **bar-pasticceria** doubles as a pastry shop. Some bars also sell ice cream, but I prefer to have my gelato in a *gelateria*.

A **café** or **caffè** is usually a bar with tables and wait service, for which you will pay a higher price. These are often fancy and very beautiful, and you can linger at your table for as long as you wish. (The line separating bars and cafés is slushy; for example, some places that call themselves bars also have table service.)

Food Shopping

Eating meals in restaurants is one thing. But shopping for your own ingredients—in hole-in-the-wall shops or open-air markets—is an experience all its own. It's fun to pick up a few things for a picnic, to cook at "home" (if your accommodations have a kitchen), or to bring back as a souvenir. This chapter covers the types of shops where you might stock up, some advice for navigating street markets, and tips for assembling a memorable Italian picnic.

Food Shops

Towns big and small boast a variety of specialty food shops, where the owners carefully select or produce their wares and sell them with great pride. Here are some of the types of stores you'll find in Italy:

Alimentari: All-purpose corner grocery store selling bread, milk,

cheese, cold cuts, dry goods, and perhaps some fruit and vegetables.

Caseificio: Cheese producer.

Confetteria: Confectionary shop, with candies and *confetti* (special almond candies for special occasions—see page 282).

Drogheria: Dry-goods store selling a wide selection of coffees, teas, cookies, cereals, flours, spices, candies, seeds, detergents, soaps, etc. These often feature some interesting local specialties.

Enoteca: This can simply be a wine shop selling bottles, or it can also be a wine bar with light food.

Erboristeria: This distinctly Italian institution sells herb-based products such as teas, soaps, liqueurs, and herb oils for cooking or medicinal purposes, as well as fresh and dried herbs. Many *erboristerie* will concoct special combinations to treat specific medical conditions.

Frutta e verdura: Fruit-and-vegetable seller.

Gastronomia: This high-end food shop often sells elegant, prepared foods at a fraction of the price you'd pay in a restaurant. *Gastronomie* are popular with busy professionals who don't have time to cook but want to eat well at home.

Gelateria: Ice-cream parlor.

Latteria: Dairy shop, selling fresh milk, cheeses, and butter.

Macelleria: Butcher shop, which often also sells *salumi* (cold cuts). You might notice that many butchers sell canned food for dogs and cats—a holdover from the time when people bought scraps to feed their pets.

Panetteria (or **panificio**): Bread baker that sometimes sells plain cakes and cookies *(biscotti)* as well. In general, the standard bread of a town (such as *pane toscano* in Florence) is sold at a fixed low price to keep it affordable; specialty breads can be pricier.

Pasticceria: Pastry shop for cakes and cookies; some also have a coffee bar.

Pastificio: Pasta shop, usually featuring fresh pasta *(pasta fresca)*.

Pescheria: Fish seller. (A **mercato ittico** is a fish market.)

Pizza al taglio: Shop selling squares of *pizza rustica* by the slice; while handy, this falls far short of a fresh, oven-baked pizza from a pizzeria.

Pizzicheria (or **pizzicagnolo**): Similar to an *alimentari*.

Polleria: Poultry store for chicken, turkey, pheasant, duck, quail, goose, and sometimes rabbit.

Salumeria (or **salsamenteria**): Similar to a delicatessen, this is the place to buy *salumi* (cold cuts), and usually some cheeses, too. Some will make a sandwich for you.

Salumificio: Producer of *salame* and sausages.

Tabaccaio (or **tabaccheria**): Italy's ubiquitous tobacconists (marked by a blue-and-white sign with a big "T") are neighborhood minimarts. Yes, they sell cigarettes, but these government-regulated shops also have postage stamps, postcards, stationery, and light snacks like candy bars. These are also handy places to pay for street parking, purchase city bus and subway tickets, and try your luck in the government lotto.

Torrefazione: Coffee roaster where you can buy freshly roasted coffee beans. Italians rarely pre-grind beans—they only grind when they're ready to use them.

Vini e oli: Old-fashioned store that sells wine and olive oil.

And, of course, Italy has its share of **supermercati.** While not as gigantic as American big-box stores, an Italian *supermercato* is a well-stocked, convenient, if less characteristic one-stop shop. If you're new to Italy, exploring its aisles can be an adventure in seeing how Italians shop, live, and eat. In addition to produce, dairy, meats, and dry goods, many have a deli case and pizza counter. Dominant chains include Esselunga, Conad, Carrefour, and Co-Op.

It can also be fun to browse a **kitchenware shop** (which can go by various names, including *ferramenta*—hardware store). In most of Italy, much of the artisanal work you see has its roots in the kitchen: gleaming copper pots, sturdy wooden spoons to stir polenta, or wonderful ceramics, china, and glassware. All of these were born of necessity, but they've evolved into objects of beauty. Italian handicrafts or housewares make fine souvenirs and gifts, and they'll let you re-create some of your favorite recipes back home. Look for items marked *Made in Italy* to avoid cheap imports.

Eating with the Seasons

Italian chefs love to serve fresh produce and seafood at its tastiest. Each region in Italy has its seasonal specialties, which you'll see displayed in open-air markets. Here are a few examples of what's fresh when:

April-May: Calamari (Venice), romanesco broccoli (similar to cauliflower), fava beans (Rome), green beans, artichokes.

April-May and Sept-Oct: Black truffles.

April-June: Asparagus, zucchini flowers, zucchini.

May-June: Mussels, cantaloupe, loquats, strawberries.

May-Aug: Eggplant, clams.

July-Sept: Figs, cherries, peaches, apricots, plums.

Oct-Nov: Mushrooms, white truffles, persimmons, chestnuts.

Nov-Feb: *Radicchio* (Venice), cardoon (wild artichoke), *puntarelle* (chicory shoots; Rome).

Il Mercato (The Market)

Italy's street markets are a delight to explore. Nothing compares to the festive animation of sellers hawking their wares as they flirt with and cajole potential shoppers. This is where people meet to exchange gossip about children, parents, spouses, friends, and lovers. Markets are where Italians cement their sense of community. And, of course, the star of the show is what's being sold: Newly picked fruits and vegetables, local nuts and seeds, fresh young cheeses, just-caught fish, fragrant herbs, simple wine, pure oil, and fresh breads are all best near the place they are born.

Markets are busiest in the mornings; some stalls begin to close down after lunchtime. Keep in mind that some of the most authentic and affordable eateries in any city are tucked in the market zone: hole-in-the-wall local faves, unpretentious food counters, and takeaway stalls designed to feed hungry local shoppers.

In most markets, food sellers buy from farms and suppliers, and their quality depends on their contacts. But some larger markets might have a section labeled *coltivatori diretti,* with stalls run by the people who raise the crops. Here you'll get less of the hard sell; these producers let their produce speak for itself. And it does: fresh basil, rosemary, and lavender that were picked this morning. Tiny zucchini flowers for stuffing with cheese and herbs. Figs from someone's tree. Or whatever else a farmer might bring in. Everything is at the peak of freshness. It may not always be cosmetically perfect, but the flavor and fragrance are.

Edible Souvenirs

Taking a few carefully selected culinary items home is tempting: a tiny bottle of precious-as-gold *aceto balsamico tradizionale* from Modena, a shrink-wrapped hunk of *pecorino* or Parmigiano-Reggiano cheese, some top-quality extra virgin olive oil, a bottle of *limoncello* or Brunello di Montalcino, and so on.

First, think carefully about what you'll actually be able to get home. Consider airport security measures. Anything liquid (from a jar of honey to a bottle of grappa) is best transported in your checked luggage, packed very carefully to avoid breaks and leaks. Don't try to bring alcohol, other liquids, or liquid-packed foods in your carry-on bag unless you've purchased it at a duty-free shop at the airport. You'll increase your odds of getting it onto a connecting flight if it's packaged in a "STEB"—a secure, tamper-evident bag. But stay away from liquids in opaque, ceramic, or metallic containers, which usually cannot be successfully screened (STEB or no STEB).

Also consider what you're allowed to bring in through US Customs. Many processed and packaged foods are allowed, including cheeses, dried herbs, jams, baked goods, candy, chocolate, oil, vinegar, condiments, and honey. Fresh fruits and vegetables and most meats are not allowed, with exceptions for some canned items. Always declare any food items in your luggage. Those cute food-sniffing dogs in the customs line make it not worth the risk to try to sneak in that leftover prosciutto, even if it's wrapped in your underwear.

As for alcohol, you can bring in one liter duty-free per person; that's basically one bottle of Chianti Classico or one bottle of *limoncello*. Any additional alcohol will be subject to duty. For details on allowable goods, customs rules, and duty rates, visit http://help.cbp.gov.

Items sent home are subject to the same duty rates, shipping costs are high (especially for alcohol, which must be packed carefully), and the Italian postal service can be notoriously unreliable—all of which makes shipping edible souvenirs home less enticing than it sounds. There are some wine and food shops that cater to visitors by offering convenient (if pricey) shipping options. Others might work with an importer in the United States, who can ship your purchases domestically (which is much simpler). Still, the best advice may be to pack home a few carefully selected favorites, try to find a good Italian food or wine importer in your community to stock up between trips...and then have even more reason to go back to Italy.

Market Measurements

The unit of measure can differ from item to item. If a price is listed without a unit, then it's usually per kilo, but confirm just in case by asking *Il prezzo per kilo?* Here are some of the ways you'll see prices listed:

Al kg or **al kilo:** By the kilogram (2.2 pounds).

Per ½ kg or **per 500 gr:** By the half-kilogram or *mezzo-kilo* (just over a pound).

Per etto or **per 100 gr:** By the 100-gram unit (about 3.5 ounces). This is, after the kilo, the most common unit. When shopping for a picnic, it's easy to remember that each *etto* is approximately a quarter-pound.

Pezzo or **l'uno:** By the piece.

Manciata or **mazzo:** By the bunch.

Fetta: By the slice.

Be prepared to see food in a more natural state than you'll ever see at the supermarket back home. Root vegetables can be clumped with dirt. Dead animals hang from hooks with their fur and feathers still on. Butchers will, if asked, clean and trim meat, poultry, and game.

At most markets, bargaining for food is discouraged. Prices are set and posted. If you don't like them, go to another stand. For those on a tight budget, prices may drop just before closing time. Expect to pay cash, and keep an eye out for pickpockets.

It's fun to observe the artistry with which many food sellers arrange and display their products—an example of aesthetics expressed in everyday life. Vendors are happy to sell small quantities of produce, but it's customary to let the merchant choose for you. Say *per oggi* (for today) and they'll grab you something ready to eat.

Many cities—such as Bologna, Genoa, Florence, Padua, and Rome—have old indoor market halls where citizens enjoy gathering. Other places—such as Asti, Bolzano, Trento, Modena, and Palermo—have outdoor markets on piazzas and streets. In each case, the local market offers clues into how locals eat. For instance, you'll quickly notice that some cities or regions are more meat-forward, while others abound with fruits and vegetables.

If you're staying in the same place for several days, you'll discover how easy it is to get to know some of the market vendors. Before long, they'll slip that extra piece of fruit into your bag in gratitude for your

The *mercato* can be a fine place to meet locals...
and to stock up on local picnic fixings.

patronage. Take advantage of the vendor's kindness and expertise: They love to educate you about the proper handling and use of ingredients.

In small towns and villages, the market scene is a one-day-a-week traveling food fest on wheels (some merchants make their rounds in a regional cycle). In this case, do what you can to make this lively scene.

In many cities, a clothing-and-housewares market comes to town once a week, adding an animated bustle to the streets. This is a good place to pick up gloves, sweaters, umbrellas, coffee makers, and all the wonderful little gadgets that are so useful in Italian kitchens.

Picnic Tips

Enjoy a few picnics while you're in Italy. You'll eat better while spending half as much as those who eat exclusively in restaurants. In my book, there's no better travel experience than a picnic sourced from local markets and grocers, eaten outdoors with a lively piazza, peaceful park, or rejuvenated harborfront as a backdrop. (While picnicking

feels perfectly Italian, be discreet, and respect any signs that forbid picnics.) Be warned: The challenging thing about picnicking may be trying to get in a bite between all the people wishing you a happy *buon appetito!*

A picnic can even be an adventure in high cuisine. Be daring. Try the fresh *ricotta,* pesto, olives, and any regional specialties the locals are excited about. And it's good for your budget: At home, we save time and money by raiding the refrigerator to assemble a pick-up dinner. In Italy, the equivalent is the corner deli, bakery, produce market, or *alimentari.*

For the most colorful experience, gather your ingredients in the morning at a produce market. Supplement that with a visit to an *alimentari* or *salumeria* to pick up cold cuts, cheeses, and other picnic supplies. Almost every grocery store has a deli case featuring prepared items like stuffed peppers, *lasagne,* olives, or chicken, all usually sold by weight; if you want it reheated, remember the word *riscaldare.* And remember that *rosticcerie* sell inexpensive food to go—you'll find options such as *lasagne,* rotisserie chicken, and

This happy gang is living simply and well on the cheap: enjoying a picnic in Assisi, St. Francis' hometown.

sides including roasted potatoes and spinach.

Some grocery stores, *salumerie,* and any *paninoteca* (sandwich shop) can make a sandwich to order. Just point to what you want, and they'll stuff it into a *panino.*

Remember that many foods are priced by the *etto* (100 grams, very roughly a quarter-pound). A typical picnic for two might be fresh rolls, *un etto* of cheese, and *un etto* of meat. For two people, I might get *un etto* of prosciutto and *due panini* (two rolls). Add two tomatoes, three carrots, two apples, yogurt, and a liter box of juice. Total: about €10.

If ordering *antipasti* (such as grilled or marinated veggies) at a deli counter, you can ask for *una porzione* in a takeaway container *(contenitore).* Use gestures to show exactly how much you want. To set a price limit of 5 or 10 euros on what you order, say *"Da [cinque/dieci] euro, per favore."* The word *basta* (enough) works as a question or as a statement.

If you'll be picnicking a lot, buy a good knife with a can opener and corkscrew in Italy. Resealable plastic baggies (large and small) are great for containing messy food and packing up leftovers. Bring a reusable cup as well as a spoon and fork for eating takeout soups and salads. And a large cloth napkin can make a handy little picnic tablecloth.

PART II

Italian Food 101

Italian Meals & Courses

È l'ora di mangiare—it's time to eat! But Italians eat their meals at slightly different times—and in a different way—than you might be used to back home.

In general, Italians eat meals a bit later than we do. At 7 or 8 in the morning, they have a light breakfast. Lunch comes sometime between 1 and 3 p.m., and dinner not until about 8. To bridge the gap, people drop into a bar in the late afternoon for an *aperitivo* (aperitif) with snacks.

Lunch and dinner tend to be earlier in the North, and move progressively later as you travel south—so your lunch in the alpine town of Bolzano might be served at noon, while in Palermo, Sicily, it may not come until 2:30. While you can try to find a meal at other times, you'll have fewer options (i.e., fast food and restaurants catering to tourists). Adopt the Italian schedule for a more authentic experience.

This chapter explores each of these meals and outlines the traditional course-by-course flow of a traditional lunch or dinner. And the next several chapters delve into more detail on each course, roughly in the order you'll encounter them as you make your way through a big meal.

Breakfast (*Prima Colazione*)

Italian breakfasts, like Italian bath towels, are small: The classic version, eaten at a neighborhood bar, is simply a cappuccino, a pastry or a roll with butter and marmalade, and perhaps fruit juice. (The red orange juice—*spremuta d'arancia rossa*—is made from Sicilian blood oranges.) Midrange and high-end hotels tend to have more options, possibly including yogurt, cereal, cold cuts and sliced cheese, and hard-boiled eggs (scrambled or fried eggs are less common). Small budget hotels may leave a basic breakfast in your room (coffee and a stale, individually packaged croissant and/or roll).

Even if your hotel includes breakfast, consider skipping it and heading for a real Italian breakfast at a nearby bar or *pasticceria* (pastry shop). Once there, for a truly local experience, stand at the counter for a coffee and

pastry. While the *cornetto* (croissant) is most common, you'll find a range of *pasticcini* (pastries, sometimes called *dolci*—sweets). Look for *otto* (an 8-shaped pastry, often filled with custard, jam, or chocolate), *sfoglia* (filo-dough crust that's fruit-filled, like a turnover), or *bombolone* or *ciambella* (a doughnut filled with custard or chocolate)—or ask about local specialties. For example, some Sicilians have a breakfast of sweet, icy *granita* stuffed into a brioche.

Lunch *(Pranzo)* and Dinner *(Cena)*

Travelers notice that sometimes, lunch is considered the main meal of the day, while at other times, people seem to favor a big dinner. And in either case, both meals tend to be eaten later than back home. To understand these peculiarities, it helps to appreciate Italy's history.

Traditionally, lunch was considered the main meal. Farmers would rise at dawn to milk cows, collect eggs, and then work in the fields all morning to build up an appetite. Lunch was substantial—filling the

farmer up and, with wine, making him drowsy. An afternoon nap would follow. In the relative cool of the late afternoon, he'd return to his labors, do the evening milking, and work until there was no more light. The urban equivalent of this was a sub-stantial meal, either at home or at a *trattoria* or *mensa,* followed by a nap or a stroll before returning to work. In general, lunch in the North would begin as early as 12:00 or 12:30, and the return to work would happen sometime between 2 and 3 p.m. In central and southern Italy, the closing

time might be later, and the return to work might not happen until 4 or 5.

Because lunch was such a big meal, dinner was a lighter affair. It might include soup followed by vegetables and *salumi* or cheese. Alternatively, people would have a pizza. People sometimes wonder why Italians seem so fit, while consuming foods that we're told are fattening. I suspect it's because they go to bed with stomachs that are not stuffed, and therefore don't store calories as they sleep.

Historically, poor people filled up on a single grain-based course; in central and southern Italy, it was pasta, while northerners ate rice or polenta. These would be flavored with vegetables, inexpensive fish, or bits of meat and gravy. (To this day, certain rustic dishes are romanticized as holdovers from *cucina povera*— "cuisine of the poor.")

Italians who were more *benestanti* (well-off) had a meal consisting of a *primo* (soup, pasta, or rice), a *secondo* (a protein, such as meat or fish), a *contorno* (a salad or vegetable side dish), and then a *dolce* (dessert, generally fruit). This became the standard meal format across Italy as affluence arrived in the postwar era. And, of course, a meal always ends with an espresso to leave a pleasant flavor in the mouth.

What to Try, Where

When in Rome, eat as the Romans do. Here's a quick "hit list" of favorite items to seek out in some of Italy's major destinations. In the regional chapters, you'll find much more about each dish, plus a longer list of foods and wines to be sure to try while you're there.

WHEN IN...	BE SURE TO TRY...
Piedmont	White truffles, creamy cheeses (like Fontina and Gorgonzola), and top-quality wines (including Barolo and Barbaresco).
Milan	Nurse an *aperitivo* (pre-dinner drink—Aperol or Campari *spritz*, perhaps) with elegant finger foods, followed by saffron-flavored *risotto alla milanese* or *ossobuco* (veal shank in lemony sauce).
Dolomites	Big, hearty *canederli* dumplings, apple strudel, and Gewürztraminer wine.
Venice	*Cicchetti* (bar snacks), Prosecco cocktails like the Bellini, and weird sea creatures pulled from the lagoon.
Cinque Terre (Riviera)	Pillowy focaccia bread, pesto on *trofie* pasta, anchovies (come on—give them a try), and *biscotti* dunked in the sweet dessert wine Sciacchetrà.
Emilia-Romagna	Prosciutto di Parma, *mortadella* (the original "bologna"), Parmigiano-Reggiano cheese, top-quality *aceto balsamico tradizionale,* and fresh-made filled pastas.

A larger meal might start with an *antipasto* (appetizer) before the *primo,* and could insert some *formaggio* (cheese) before the dessert. (Of course, there are regional variations: *Antipasti* are more common in Piedmont and Puglia, while the cheese course is typical in Lombardy and Sardinia.)

Recent generations have seen some changes to these traditions. Workdays have lengthened and the lunch period has shrunk, particularly in many northern cities. Quicker meals are consumed at or near the office rather than at home. The faster lunch means that the evening meal has taken on greater importance for

Florence and Tuscany	World-class red wines such as Brunello di Montalcino, Vino Nobile di Montepulciano, Chianti Classico, or a "Super Tuscan"; rustic pasta (such as *pappardelle* or *pici*) with a hearty sauce such as *antara* (duck) or a *ragù* of wild boar *(cinghiale);* and *bistecca alla fiorentina* (top-quality, rare-grilled T-bone).
Rome and Lazio	Rich, flavorful pasta dishes like *spaghetti alla carbonara, cacio e pepe, amatriciana,* and *arrabbiata,* plus deep-fried goodies including *supplì* (little fried balls of rice and mozzarella).
Naples and Amalfi Coast (Campania)	Real Neapolitan pizza, fresh mozzarella (preferably *di bufala*—from water buffalo milk), flavorful tomatoes, *sfogliatelle* (crunchy, fried, filled pastries), and the lemon-infused liqueur *limoncello.*
Sicily	Tasty-but-challenging street foods (from the deep-fried rice balls *arancine* to *pani ca' meusa,* spleen sandwich); incomparable *agrumi* (citrus fruits); plus *granita* (sweet slushy ice), *cannoli,* and other sugar-bomb desserts.
Sardinia	Top-quality *pecorino* (sheep's cheese), the crispy shepherd's bread *pane carasau,* and slow-roasted suckling pig.
The South	Rustic pastas; spicy *salumi* (such as *capocollo, soppressata, 'nduja, lucanica*); soft, milky cheeses (provolone, *burrata, caciocavallo, scamorza*); and spicy foods liberally seasoned with *peperoncino rosso* (hot red pepper).
The North	Polenta; rice (often in the form of *risotto*); buttery, creamy cheeses (mascarpone, Asiago, Gorgonzola); and *bollito misto* (a mix of boiled meats and interesting sauces).

both socializing and nutrition. (On Sundays and most religious holidays, however, lunch remains the major meal.)

With greater affluence, Italians now eat more elaborate meals when they dine out. On special occasions or at business meals, a dinner may include six or more courses, each accompanied by a wine pairing.

International health and fitness standards have also influenced Italians, some of whom now reject the standard four-course meal in favor of something lighter. This might mean eating only a dish of pasta and a piece of fruit at lunch, then soup, salad, a piece of cheese, and fruit at dinner.

These changes have put a financial pinch on Italian restaurateurs—especially because the idea of

Top: An *antipasti* platter can be a light meal in itself; **Bottom:** For many visitors, the *primo* (often pasta) is the most interesting part of the meal.

"turning over" a table is not common here. (Once you're seated, the restaurant doesn't count on seating other diners there for the rest of the evening.) That's why prices for dining have tended to pull either to the inexpensive or expensive extreme as restaurateurs seek their niche. The inexpensive places are either pasta-and-pizza joints with adequate food, or those with imaginative cooks who have looked back to the tradition of peasant cooking and reintroduced tasty dishes that use affordable ingredients. On the opposite end, fancy restaurants charge more for elaborate dishes, making dining out an *event* rather than just a meal.

All of this muddies the water for travelers who want to eat according to "local" customs. Here's my advice: Begin by following the customary Italian model: light breakfast; maybe a midmorning snack, if you need it; and a standard (big) lunch at around 1 p.m., followed by a stroll and/or nap. Then, in the early evening, dive into the *passeggiata* and *aperitivo* scene (see sidebar), followed by a light dinner—maybe just a pizza—at 8 p.m. (or even later in the South).

Courses

A complete Italian meal—either lunch or dinner—consists of multiple courses, explained in more detail in the following chapters.

ANTIPASTI (APPETIZERS)

The appetizer course commonly includes *salumi* (cold cuts and cured meats), local cheeses *(formaggi),* and often vegetables—typically marinated or grilled. Note that while some cheeses are eaten as *antipasti,* others are served before or instead of the dessert course.

PRIMI (FIRST COURSES)

Many of the foods for which Italian cuisine is so famous come in the category of the *primo piatto* ("first dish"): pasta, *risotto,* polenta, and soup. At dinnertime, it's often customary to have soup rather than a grain-based *primo.* (In some parts of the North, menus might call the first course *minestra* instead.)

SECONDI (MAIN COURSES), *CONTORNI* (SIDE DISHES), AND *INSALATE* (SALADS)

A "second dish" *(secondo piatto),* equivalent to our main course, is more substantial: meat *(carne),* poultry *(pollame),* fish *(pesce),* or seafood *(frutti di mare).* After those delicious *antipasti* and *primi,* it's rare for the American diner to have room left for a *secondo.* (And my Italian friends freely admit the *secondo* is the least interesting part of their cuisine.) Pace yourself: To get a complete meal, consider sharing one *primo* and one *secondo.*

A vegetable side dish *(contorno)* may come with the *secondo,* but more often must be ordered separately. Typical *contorni* are *insalata mista* (mixed salad), spinach, roasted potatoes, or grilled veggies. The *contorno* can be an interesting, if overlooked, part of the menu.

Sometimes—especially with salads—the *contorno* is eaten after the *secondo,* rather than alongside it. The idea is that you want the flavors of the salad to stand out rather than compete with the taste of the meat or fish.

DOLCI (DESSERTS)

For many, no meal is complete without a sweet *(dolce).* On most menus, you'll find typical Italian desserts such as *tiramisù* and *panna cotta* as well as local favorites. Servers are accustomed to diners splitting

Top: *Primi* can include pasta, rice, soup, or polenta; **Bottom:** The *secondo* (main course), usually meat or fish, may be served with *contorni* (side dishes), such as potatoes.

a single dessert—just ask for extra forks. Fruit *(frutta)* is often eaten as a dessert. A shot of espresso *(un caffè)* is typically served after dessert. And yet another, perfectly reasonable option is to skip dessert at the restaurant and wander around licking a cone of gelato instead.

A FEW MORE TIPS

When settling in to dine, many travelers find that a complete, multicourse meal amounts to simply too much food (and the euros can add up in a hurry). It's a relief to know that each diner is not expected or required to

Passeggiata and *Aperitivo*

While it's not technically a part of the dining custom, no trip to Italy is complete without cultivating an appreciation for the **passeggiata:** that pre-dinner stroll in which the entire community is out, aimlessly ambling along the main streets and piazzas. *Fare la passeggiata* is an opportunity to see and be seen. People run into friends, relatives, and business associates, and invite them for a coffee, a gelato, or an *aperitivo* (see below). Every city has a designated area where people stroll like this—usually a wide, traffic-free street or a broad piazza. No matter where you go, figure out where the *passeggiata* takes place...and join in.

The *passeggiata* pairs perfectly with an **aperitivo:** a pre-dinner drink enjoyed around 6 or 7 p.m. The drink itself may not be cheap (around €8-12), but it usually includes some snacks. Traditionally this was simply crackers, chips, or nuts. But increasingly, bars (especially in the North) are touting their free happy-hour buffets—sometimes nicknamed *"apericena"* (*cena* means dinner). These places lay out an enticing array of meats, cheeses, grilled vegetables, and other *antipasti*-type dishes, and you're welcome to nibble while you nurse your drink.

The *apericena* is intended as an appetizer course before heading out for dinner—you're invited to have a couple of hearty snacks with each drink you pay for. For light eaters who've had a too-big lunch, this could wind up being enough to skip dinner. Drop by a few bars around this time to scope out their buffets before choosing. Or opt for a place with a big view and simpler snacks—either way, you'll get your money's worth.

For a list of typical *aperitivo* cocktails, see page 98 in the *Bevande* chapter.

Two Italian customs to sample: Enjoy an *aperitivo* with new friends on a twilit piazza (left); and join the locals in the evening *passeggiata* (right).

order something for each course. In fact, to avoid overeating (and to stretch your budget), sharing dishes is a smart strategy. A good rule of thumb is for each person to order any two courses. For example, a couple can order and share one *antipasto,* one *primo,* one *secondo,* and one dessert; or two *antipasti* and two *primi;* or whatever combination appeals.

Small groups can mix *antipasti* and *primi* family-style (skipping *secondi*). If you do this right, you can eat well in better places for less than the per-person cost of a *menù turistico* in a cheap place.

Speaking of variety, some restaurants have a self-service *antipasti* buffet; at others, the server can assemble a plate at your direction. You'll pay by the size of the plate (large or small, like a salad bar). This can be a great way to eat fast, cheap, and healthy while sampling many local specialties.

Antipasti (Appetizers)

The word *antipasti* only begins to suggest the endless selection of tasty foods that are meant to take the edge off your appetite and make your mouth water as you begin your meal. While the *antipasto* (literally, "before the meal") is not obligatory, it has become increasingly popular as Italy has become more affluent. (Many dishes that formed the center of an Italian meal in poorer times are now served in small portions to start the meal off.)

What you'll find in the *antipasti* course reflects the region you're visiting: In many places (including Piedmont and Puglia), *antipasti* are vegetable-based. In coastal areas (Liguria, Campania, Puglia, Sicily, and parts of Veneto), you'll find seafood. Regions that specialize in prosciutto and *salumi* (Emilia-Romagna, Friuli-Venezia Giulia, Tuscany, and Umbria, among others) will typically present a platter of *affettati misti*, a combination of the best local cold cuts. For a wider variety, look for *antipasto misto* (*salumi,* cheeses, and vegetables). Or you may see the word *tagliere*—"cutting board"—a selection of *salumi* and cheeses on a wooden board.

This chapter covers some of the items you'll most likely see in the *antipasto* course: *salumi* (cold cuts), cheeses, vegetables, other *antipasti,* and bread. I've also included a primer on olive oil, which can show up, in one form or another, in just about any and every Italian dish.

Salumi (Cold Cuts)

Salumi (meats preserved in salt, from the Latin word for "salted")—sometimes called *affettati* ("sliced")—are an Italian staple. While most American cold cuts are cooked, in Italy they're far more commonly "raw"—that is, cured by salting, air-drying, or smoking.

Salumi come in various forms. One of these, confusingly, is **salame** (plural *salami*)—a tightly packed casing with various meats (usually pork) and spices that is dried and then sliced. This was a food of the poor: While the better parts of a pig became prosciutto and were sold at a high price, *salame* used the less desirable parts. To try the local variation, ask for *salame locale*. In Tuscany, *salame* often contains fennel seeds (and is called *finocchiona*), while in the South, it's frequently spiked with dried *peperoncino rosso* (chili pepper). In Piedmont

it can be flavored with wine. Our "Genoa salami" is called *salame di Sant'Olcese* in its homeland.

The term **"prosciutto"** comes from the phrase "dry over time." But it refers to ham—usually from the hind leg of the pig—which comes in two broad varieties.

Prosciutto cotto is boiled ham, sliced thin. *Spalla cotta* is boiled pork shoulder, a less expensive cut.

Prosciutto crudo is exquisite air-cured ham—what Americans think of when we imagine prosciutto, and one of the iconic foods of Mediterranean Europe. It's typically sliced paper-thin (except in Tuscany) and can be predominantly sweet *(dolce)* or salty *(salato)*. Prosciutto is eaten straight or paired with *melone* (cantaloupe) or *fichi* (fresh figs). Most people say the best comes from Parma, although a vocal minority prefers the *prosciutto* from San Daniele in Friuli-Venezia Giulia. Other good variations come from Carpegna in the Marche and from the Valle d'Aosta, where it's cured with herbs.

Culatello, made in Emilia-Romagna exclusively from the right

hind leg of the pig, is among the most prized *salumi* (see page 209).

Pork products are used in a staggering variety of other ways. **Mortadella** is a large, pink, smooth pork sausage from Bologna. It often contains cubes of fat and even pistachios. (While similar to the product that Americans call bologna, *mortadella* is sublime, and bologna is baloney.) In the Dolomites, **speck** is smoked bacon, often served in slices. **Pancetta,** popular in central and southern Italy, is unsmoked bacon that's typically cooked with eggs or tomatoes to dress pasta; this is sometimes used interchangeably with **guanciale,** tender pork cheek. **Lonzino** is delectable cured pork loin. And **lardo** is pork lard (fatback), made fragrant with herbs and spices, sliced very thin, and melt-on-the-tongue delicious. Popular in Piedmont, Valle d'Aosta, and Tuscany, *lardo* has less cholesterol than butter and fewer calories than olive oil; the best is **lardo di Colonnata,** from the Carrara marble quarries in Tuscany.

You'll find even more varieties of *salumi* in the South. **Soppressata** is a simple dry *salame* that has some kick, and **'nduja** is a super-spicy, smoky, soft, spreadable pork sausage with a texture like a bright-red pâté. **Capocollo** (sometimes called *capicola* or, in the North, *coppa*) is peppery pork shoulder; this is also found in central Italy (Tuscany, Umbria, and Lazio).

There are also various versions of raw beef. **Bresaola** is air-cured (in other words, beef prepared similarly to prosciutto; *della Valtellina,* from Lombardy's Alps, is low-fat and top quality). Salt-cured beef from Trentino is **carne salada.** And **carpaccio** is thinly sliced raw beef served

with olive oil, lemon juice, greens, and shaved Parmigiano-Reggiano.

Smoked breast of goose *(petto d'oca affumicato)* or duck *(petto di anatra affumicato)* is popular in Lombardy and other parts of the North.

Formaggi (Cheeses)

There is a saying in Lombardy: *Il magnar non vale un'acca se alla fine non sa di vacca.* Loosely translated: "A meal isn't worth a damn if it doesn't end with the taste of the cow."

There are rivers of cow's milk in Lombardy, and much of the nation's best cheese is produced there. But every Italian region makes cheese from the milk of cows, sheep, and goats.

Italian cheeses come in various forms: *a pasta molle* (with a soft consistency, like *ricotta* or mozzarella), *a pasta semidura* (semi-hard, like Fontina or provolone), and *a pasta dura* or *grana* (hard, crumbly, and granular, like Parmigiano-Reggiano). Many cheeses taste very different depending on how long they're aged—from *fresco* ("fresh," soft and mild) to *stagionato* ("aged," hard and sharp).

Here are a few of the big-name Italian cheeses that you'll find throughout Italy, even outside their place of origin:

Parmigiano-Reggiano, from Emilia-Romagna and Lombardy, is the king of cheeses—a pungent, crumbly, aged cow cheese, ideal either for eating on its own or grating over pasta.

Grana can be used as a generic term for grating cheeses, but most often it refers to **grana padano** ("*grana* of the Po"), a fine, nutty, hard cheese that's often used as a less expensive alternative to Parmigiano-Reggiano.

Pecorino is sheep's-milk cheese

(*pecora* means "ewe"). Fresh *pecorino* is buttery and delicious; the area around Pienza, in Tuscany (where it's made by Sardinian transplants), is a great place to sample it. The versions produced in Sardinia and Lazio are hard, grating cheeses; the Lazio version is called **pecorino romano.** It's sharper than Parmigiano-Reggiano and better suited for the spicier pasta sauces of central and southern Italy.

Ricotta is made of curds—a byproduct of the cheesemaking process—that are cooked a second time (*ricotta* means "re-cooked"). The result is a wonderful, soft, creamy cheese that is eaten cool by itself or with flavorings such as fruit, sugar, or even freshly ground coffee. It's delicate and very nice at breakfast on bread. *Ricotta* is also used in cheesecakes and in fillings for pasta or for dessert *cannoli*. **Ricotta salata** is a firmer, salty version—not unlike feta—that can be grated over pasta.

Mozzarella, which originated in Campania, is a soft, milky, fresh cheese stored in water. The very best is **mozzarella di bufala,** from the milk of water buffalo. Many mozzarellas

Top to bottom: A classic Italian cheese shop; various types of *pecorino*; mozzarella and *ricotta*

are made with a combination of buffalo's milk (giving it a special tanginess) and cow's milk; one that's made entirely from cow's milk is often called **fior di latte.**

The South (where cheese can be called **cacio**) has several variations of mozzarella-like, soft, milky cheese. **Burrata** is a ball of mozzarella wrapped around a buttery, almost liquid center. **Scamorza** is a firmer mozzarella. **Provolone**—now common throughout Italy and around the world—also originated in the South. And **caciocavallo**—the misnamed "horse cheese"—is a cow's-milk cheese that's pear-shaped so it can be lashed at the top and hung to dry, like a saddlebag.

Gorgonzola is a pungent, blue-veined cheese from Piedmont and Lombardy. It can be either *dolce* (sweet and creamy) or *piccante* (sharp).

Fontina (from the Valle d'Aosta) and **Montasio** (from Friuli-Venezia Giulia) are excellent semi-hard, nutty, Gruyère-style mountain cheeses.

Mascarpone is a buttery sweet cheese from Emilia-Romagna and Lombardy that's often used in making desserts such as *tiramisù*.

And **Asiago,** most associated with Veneto, is a hard cow cheese that comes either *mezzano* (young, firm, and creamy) or *stravecchio* (aged, pungent, and granular).

Verdure (Vegetables)

Veggies often show up in the *antipasti* course. These are often **sott'oli** (oil-cured vegetables such as olives, mushrooms, artichokes, and tomatoes) or **sott'aceti** (vegetables pickled in vinegar, such as carrots, celery, peppers, and onions; a mix of pickled vegetables is called *giardiniera*). *Cipollotti* are miniature onions marinated in oil.

Vegetables can also be grilled *(alla griglia),* baked *(al forno),* or stuffed *(ripieni). Pinzimonio* are raw vegetables dipped in olive oil; this is served as an *antipasto* in some parts of the country, while in others they serve it to cleanse the palate toward the end of a meal. And in Piedmont, raw vegetables are dipped in hot olive oil with anchovies and garlic—a dish called *bagna cauda.*

Especially in Rome, you'll see artichokes *(carciofi)*—either "Roman-style" *(alla romana),* simmered with garlic and mint; or "Jewish-style" *(alla giudìa),* flattened and deep-fried.

In the South, *peperoncini* (peppers) are used liberally—especially *peperoncino rosso,* spicy red pepper.

The small, intensely hot *diavolillo* (or *diavolicchio*) can be minced and mixed in oil, or dried and ground into a powder; in either form, it's added to a recipe for an extra kick.

Pane (Bread)

Bread is placed on the table to nibble on while you wait for your first course. Italians do not butter their bread, and they don't typically dip it in olive oil. (The idea of starting every meal by dunking bread into a bowl of olive oil with *balsamico* and dried herbs is an invention of Italian restaurants in the US. Many touristy restaurants in Italy have imported this "custom.")

There are some wonderful bread-based *antipasti*. The most famous is also the simplest: **bruschetta** (broo-SKAY-tah). This begins with a rustic hunk of bread, which is toasted, rubbed with raw garlic, drizzled with good olive oil, and sprinkled with sea salt. Some versions add other toppings, most commonly chopped fresh tomatoes. You'll never quite be able to replicate the joy of a good Italian *bruschetta* back home. That's because the bread, the oil, and the other ingredients all come from the same land and pair perfectly. Another bread-based *antipasto* is *crostini*— more delicate little toasts topped with liver pâtés or other meat or veggie pastes.

Bread varies radically throughout Italy. In the Alps, there are many rye breads *(pane di segale)*. In Piedmont are *grissini* (breadsticks). Liguria has thick, pillowy focaccia. Emilia-Romagna has bone-dry breads that go well with that region's rich foods. Tuscany has salt-free bread, often

Left: *Crostini* are little bread rounds with various toppings; **Right:** Italy's deep-fried tasties are worth sampling.

drizzled with fresh olive oil. Lazio, Abruzzo, and Puglia have large loaves of delicious *pane casareccio* ("home-style" bread). Sardinia makes distinct breads, including the crisp, unleavened, simple shepherd's bread *pane carasau*. And so on.

Because pasta and bread are both starches, Italians consider them redundant. If you order only a pasta dish, bread may not come with it; you can request it, but you may be charged extra. If you're ordering a complete meal at a traditional or formal place, the server may bring you a basket of bread with the *antipasto*, then remove it for the *primo*, and finally bring it back again for the *secondo*.

The best possible use for bread? Tear off a little chunk and use it to sweep up the delicious drippings of sauce that remain in your bowl after finishing a pasta dish. Called *fare la scarpetta*—"doing the little shoe"—this was once seen as inelegant, but now everyone does it.

More *Antipasti*

Other popular *antipasti* include *involtini* (stuffed rolls of meat or vegetables) and *sarde in saor* (sweet-and-sour-marinated sardines).

Deep-fried items are also popular: *crocchette* (croquettes), *fiori di zucca* (lightly fried squash blossoms, filled with mozzarella and anchovies), *filetti di baccalà* (batter-fried salted cod), and—in the South—*arancine* or *suppli* (two different types of deep-fried rice balls). *Fritti* is an assortment of little fried munchies, often croquettes, mozzarella, or olives stuffed with meat *(olive all'ascolana)*.

In coastal areas, *insalata di mare* is seafood that has been cooked, removed from its shell, chilled, and tossed with lemon juice, olive oil, and perhaps some parsley. Unless well made, this dish can be rubbery. Certain shellfish, such as clams and mussels, can be filled with breadcrumbs and other flavors and then baked *(al forno)*.

Olio d'Oliva (Olive Oil)

If you're used to generic, store-bought olive oil back home, sampling some vivid-green, spicy, astringent, fresh-pressed extra-virgin olive oil in Italy is a revelation.

Extra-virgin olive oil (*olio d'oliva extra vergine*) is the best quality, from the first pressing of the olives after the autumn harvest. The best and freshest olive oil is used for dressing salads and an all-purpose condiment, drizzled over virtually any food: You may be offered *un filo d'olio*—"a thread of oil"—on top of *pasta e fagioli* soup, boiled fish, or pasta. *Aglio e olio,* a plate of spaghetti tossed with olive oil and garlic, is a classic dish of *la cucina povera* ("cuisine of the poor") that is recently in vogue.

As the oil ages and loses its specialness, chefs use it for cooking. This is also the primary use of lower-quality oils, which are produced by heating olives and pressing them multiple times to extract more oil. In fact, olive oil is the primary cooking fat in most of Italy.

Most aficionados believe that Tuscany (specifically the area around Siena and Lucca) produces Italy's best olive oil, though a knowledgeable minority believe that the best olive oil comes from Liguria, Lake Garda, or Umbria. Puglia produces the most—about one-third of Italy's total production.

Many olive oil producers open their doors to curious travelers. For a proper tasting, you'll pour a small amount of oil into a tiny cup, examining its rich green-and-yellow hue for color and clarity. Hold the cup in your hands to gently warm up the oil, encouraging the natural esters to release its fragrance. Then put a bit of the oil on the tip and the sides of your tongue and let its taste permeate your mouth. Is it smooth, peppery, tart, harsh, or some other sensation? When tasting it in isolation, you may be surprised by how pure olive oil tickles your throat, even to the point of discomfort; this is a sign of quality and freshness, and will fade as the oil ages. Find an oil that has attributes that you enjoy, then take or ship some home. Store it in a dark, dry place and use it within a year.

Olive oil is best when fresh; unlike the fine wines grown in the very same fields, it ages poorly. Better producers list a date on the bottle; dusty bottles in a shop are a bad sign and should be avoided. And don't be misled by opaque bottles painted with idyllic scenes of rolling hills and cypress trees; these often disguise and distract from the oil's poor quality. If shopping back home, note that most mass-market oils sold stateside are actually a mix of older and varying-quality oils, sometimes from multiple countries.

Primi (First Courses)

The first course *(primo piatto)* is where you'll find many of the quintessential Italian foods—especially pasta, but also *risotto,* polenta, and soup. For many travelers, the *primo* is the best part of the meal, and can easily be a meal in itself.

Pasta

Pasta is the most famous *primo* of all, and arguably the world's favorite food. Noodles of one type or another exist in cuisines of many nations, and Italian noodles have made their way to every corner of the planet. And yet, anyone who's been to Italy will tell you that pasta simply tastes better here.

There are hundreds of varieties of Italian pasta, each one specifically used to highlight a certain sauce, meat, or regional ingredient. Pasta is divided into two broad categories:

Pastasciutta is dry-stored pasta, which is boiled until *al dente* (chewy, "to the tooth") and tossed with a sauce.

Pasta fresca is fresh pasta that is cut into noodles and served with sauce; or it's cut in sheets *(sfoglie),* filled with different ingredients, folded, cooked, and then served with butter, cream, broth, or sauce.

DRY PASTA *(PASTASCIUTTA)*

Pastasciutta (or *pasta secca*) is made of wheat flour and water in an almost infinite variety of shapes. Don't make the mistake of thinking that dry pasta is inferior to fresh. If prepared well, it can be just as satisfying as

Italian pasta can be sold fresh (*pasta fresca,* left) or dry (*pastasciutta,* right).

something handmade. And it's useful, since it can be stored in a pantry, then quickly transformed into a delicious dish. When Italians gather to make an impromptu meal, they might call it a *spaghettata*—a big dish of spaghetti thrown together with whatever's in the pantry.

There are two general types of dry pasta: *pasta lunga* (long pasta) and *pasta corta* (short pasta).

Pasta lunga, also called strand pasta, are noodles long enough to twist around a fork. The most famous are spaghetti, which are native to Naples. But the noodles can be round, such as *capellini* (thin "little hairs"), *vermicelli* ("little worms"), and *bucatini* (long and hollow—*bucato* means "with a hole"); or they can be flat and ribbon-shaped, such as *linguine* (narrow "little tongues"), *fettuccine* (wider "small ribbons"), *tagliatelle* (even wider), and *pappardelle* (very wide, best with meat sauces). If a pasta is a bit thicker, -*one* is added to the end; if it's a bit thinner, -*ine,* -*ette,* or -*elle* is added. For example, *spaghettini* are skinnier than spaghetti, while *spaghettoni* are thicker.

Pasta lunga are used with smooth vegetable sauces as well as sauces of seafood or vegetables that have small bits that can be gathered in the strands.

Pasta corta ("short pasta") are smaller, designed to be scooped or speared with a fork. They go well with creamy sauces and chunkier meat sauces. The most common are dried tubular pastas called *maccheroni;* these come in endless forms, such as *penne* ("quills") and *maccheroncini* (tiny macaroni). Tubular pastas come either *lisce* (smooth) or *rigate* (grooved—so sauce clings better).

Many short pastas are named for their shapes. *Rigatoni* ("ridged") are exactly that: large, ridged tubes. Others include *conchiglie* ("shells"), *farfalle* ("butterflies"—a.k.a. bowtie pasta), *orecchiette* ("little ears," from Puglia), or *cavatappi* ("corkscrews"). These names can be a delight in themselves. *Ziti*—"grooms"—are traditionally served at weddings. *Marziani* are pasta spirals that resemble "Martian" antennae. (These are also called *radiatori,* since they also resemble an old-fashioned radiator.) And then

ITALIAN PASTA TYPES

DRY-STORED PASTA *(PASTASCIUTTA)*

LONG PASTA *(PASTA LUNGA)*

Spaghetti		Linguine	
Capellini		Fettuccine	
Vermicelli		Tagliatelle	
Bucatini		Pappardelle	

SHORT PASTA *(PASTA CORTA)*

Penne	*(lisce =* smooth)	Orecchiette	
Penne rigate	*(rigate =* ridged)	Cavatappi	
Maccheroncini		Ziti	
Rigatoni		Marziani/Radiatori	
Conchiglie		Strozzapreti	
Farfalle		Stringozzi	

FRESH PASTA *(PASTA FRESCA)*

FLAT PASTA *(SFOGLIA)*

Cannelloni		Tagliatelle	
Manicotti		Taglierini	
Lasagne		Tagliolini	

FILLED PASTA *(PASTA RIPIENA)*

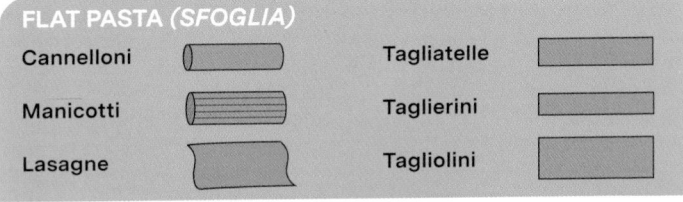

Ravioli   Agnolotti   Tortellini

OTHER PASTAS

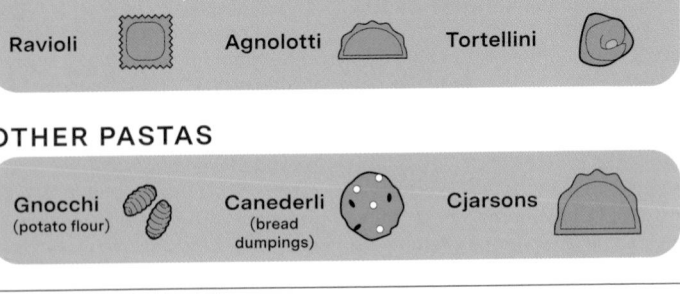

Gnocchi (potato flour)   Canederli (bread dumplings)   Cjarsons

there's *strozzapreti*—literally "priest-choker"; and *stringozzi*—named for the long leather cord that was used to strangle papal tax collectors in the Middle Ages.

FRESH PASTA *(PASTA FRESCA)*

Pasta fresca is made with flour, eggs, and sometimes a little water, hand-kneaded to just the right consistency. Then it's rolled out and cut into strips, which are run through a roller machine (either electric or hand-turned) to create long, flat sheets of fresh pasta called **sfoglia.** The *sfoglia* can be used in three ways:

The sheets can be cut into squares and rectangles, which are rolled or layered with various fillings, then baked. These include *cannelloni, manicotti,* and, of course, *lasagne.*

Or the sheets can be cut into narrower noodles such as *tagliatelle, taglierini,* and *tagliolini (tagliare* means "to cut"). In Rome, noodles similar to *tagliatelle* are called *fettuccine;* very broad noodles in Tuscany are called *pappardelle.* (Note that these can also be dried, but are better when fresh.)

Or the sheets can be cut into little squares, circles, and triangles that are filled with meat, cheese, herbs, or vegetables, and then folded—creating **filled pastas** *(pasta ripiena).* The most famous of these are ravioli and *tortellini,* but they come in a wide variety (for example, *agnolotti* or *mezzelune* are filled pasta shaped like a "priest's hat" or "half-moon"). Cheese-filled pastas are often dressed with a tomato or meat sauce, while meat-filled pastas might be served in broth, *alla panna* (in cream), or with butter and either sage, mushrooms, or truffles.

Fresh pasta is produced almost everywhere, but it's most common in the North and at its best in Emilia-Romagna. For example, in Liguria,

Top: Many types of fresh pasta use the same dough, cut in different widths; **Bottom:** Gnocchi are a pillowy pasta variation.

fresh pasta is often filled with herbs. Along the shores of the Adriatic, it's frequently filled with fish. In Lombardy, much of the filled pasta contains meat, while the towns of Mantua and Cremona make *tortelli di zucca*—containing pumpkin, ground macaroons *(amaretti),* and minced *mostarda* (fruit that has been pickled with mustard seed).

OTHER PASTAS

Some pastas do not quite fit into the above categories. For example, **gnocchi**—among the oldest pastas known—are puffy little clouds of dough made either with riced

Pasta Sauces and Preparations

Each pasta is designed to go with a particular sauce, topping, or other preparation. Here are some that you'll often see throughout Italy; for many of these, you'll find more details in the chapter covering the region where it originates. On menus, these words are usually preceded by *in* or *alla* ("in the style of").

Aglio e olio: Garlic and olive oil.

Alfredo: Sweet butter and heaps of Parmigiano-Reggiano cheese.

Amatriciana: Guanciale (pork cheek), tomatoes, *pecorino romano* cheese, and chili peppers, usually served with *bucatini* (from Amatrice in Lazio).

Arrabbiata: "Angry"—spicy tomato sauce with chili peppers; it's often served with penne and is popular in Lazio and elsewhere in the South.

Bolognese: "Bologna-style" meat and tomato sauce.

Boscaiola: "Woodsman-style," with mushrooms, herbs, and often sausage or ham.

Brodo: Broth (typical for filled pastas, especially in Emilia-Romagna).

Burro e salvia: Butter and sage.

Cacio e pepe: Pecorino romano cheese and fresh-ground pepper.

Ciociara: Sauce of tomatoes, mozzarella, *pecorino romano,* and oregano.

Carbonara: A Roman style of preparing spaghetti with raw eggs, *guanciale* (pork cheek), *pecorino romano* cheese, and fresh-ground pepper.

Carrettiera: Spicy and garlicky, with olive oil and little tomatoes.

Diavola: "Devil-style," spicy hot.

Forno, al: Oven-baked.

Frutti di mare: Seafood.

Genovese: Also called pesto: basil ground with pine nuts, Parmigiano-Reggiano cheese, garlic, and olive oil.

Gricia: Cured *guanciale* (pork cheek) and *pecorino romano* cheese.

Marinara: Usually tomato, often with garlic and onions, but can also be a seafood sauce ("sailor's style").

Mollicata: Simple sauce of tomato, onion, red wine, breadcrumbs, and sometimes anchovy.

Norma: Tomato, eggplant, basil, and *ricotta salata* (Sicily).

Pajata (or *pagliata):* Calf intestines (Rome).

Pescatora: Seafood ("fisherman style").

Pesto: See *"Genovese,"* above.

Pomodoro: Tomato.

Puttanesca: "Prostitute-style," tomato sauce with anchovies and/or tuna, black olives, capers, and garlic; found throughout the country but typical of the area from Rome to Naples. Because it's quick to make, it's thought this was a dish a prostitute could whip up for a speedy meal between clients.

Ragù: Meat sauce.*

Scoglio: Mussels, clams, and tomatoes.

Sorrentina: "Sorrento-style," with tomatoes, basil, and mozzarella (usually over gnocchi).

Sugo di lepre: Rich sauce made of wild hare.

Tartufi: Truffles (also called *tartufata).*

Vongole: Clams.

*The original *ragù* is a special sauce made in Bologna with beef, pork, chicken livers, tomatoes, milk, and other flavors. These days there are many regional variations of *ragù* (especially within Emilia-Romagna and Tuscany), which are generally heavy on pork and/or beef. However, in the South—where meat was hard to come by—a *ragù* might have a very small amount of meat (sometimes even removed after cooking) used to flavor a tomato- and vegetable-focused sauce. For example, *ragù di piccione* is a sauce made with squab (young pigeon).

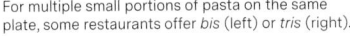

For multiple small portions of pasta on the same plate, some restaurants offer *bis* (left) or *tris* (right).

potatoes and flour, or entirely with flour. (They're sometimes described as "dumplings"—but that's misleading, because dumplings are generally heavy, and proper gnocchi are pillow-light.) Small gnocchi are *gnocchetti.*

Gnocchi di semola (or **gnocchi alla romana**) is something different: disks made with semolina that are baked with cheese and butter. These—like all types of gnocchi—are much loved in Rome; in fact, as you'll notice on menus, many Romans eat gnocchi every Thursday.

In the mountainous areas of Trentino, Alto Adige, and northern Veneto, **canederli** are large, dense dumplings made of bread and flavorings such as cheese, herbs, *speck* (bacon), prosciutto, or liver. *Canederli* are often served in soup or topped with melted butter and cheese. Many restaurants in this region serve a sampler with three or four different types of *canederli* on one plate.

Pizzoccheri are buckwheat noodles typical of the Valtellina in Lombardy. They may be fresh or dried, and after being cooked, they're combined with cheeses, garlic, and cabbage or spinach.

Passatelli, native to Romagna and common in much of central Italy, are made of cheese, egg, breadcrumbs, flour, nutmeg, and lemon. The dough is either formed into little dumplings or pushed through a press to form cylindrical lengths. *Passatelli* are cooked and served in broth.

PASTA PROTOCOL

In Italy, pasta is served in relatively small portions, unless it's intended as the only course in a meal. Much less sauce is put on pasta than you might expect: When the noodles are tossed, they should be coated in sauce, with just a little left at the bottom of the plate. And most pastas are topped with a small amount of freshly grated cheese.

While pasta is technically considered a "first course," many diners—and not just tourists—often make it the main feature of a meal. Remember, even when ordering from a multicourse menu, it's perfectly fine for two diners to, say, split an *antipasto,* two pastas, and a dessert.

Some restaurants might let you order two half-portions, either served in succession or on the same plate (in which case it's called *bis*). In rare

circumstances, they may even serve you three small portions *(tris).* If you just can't decide, try asking if this is possible.

Riso (Rice)

In northern Italy, rice was historically a more common staple than wheat. To this day, it's used for both *risotto* and soups throughout Veneto, Lombardy, and Piedmont (where the city of Vercelli hosts Europe's largest rice market).

The classic Italian rice dish, **risotto,** is as widely known as it is misunderstood. Outside of Italy, this term is often used to describe mushy rice with a muddle of various ingredients. But a properly executed Italian *risotto* is delicate and time-consuming: Rice is lightly toasted in butter, then cooked with broth that's added a little at a time, over a long period (typically 20 to 25 minutes); as the broth is absorbed, the rice is stirred continuously. The starch from the rice mixes with the liquid, giving it a creamy texture. Once the rice is cooked, grated cheese is stirred

in. The final result is firm rice in a creamy sauce that you can eat with a fork.

Risotto comes in many regional and local variations. The most famous is *risotto alla milanese,* Milan-style with saffron. Other preparations call for wine rather than broth; this can be a robust red such as Barolo or Amarone, or something as delicate as Champagne or spumante. Wherever you travel in northern Italy, you'll find *risotti* made with an astonishing range of ingredients: fish, seafood, meat, poultry, vegetables, herbs, and sometimes even fruit.

If the *risotto* takes a long time to reach your table…that's a very good sign. Scratch-made *risotto* sometimes requires at least two diners to make it worth the effort. There are simpler variations, too; these days, many restaurants parboil rice, then finish it with ingredients once an order is placed.

In Milan, when there are leftovers, they make delicious *risotto al salto,* little cakes of *risotto* that are fried in butter until they are crunchy.

There are other uses for rice

in Italy. *Paniscia* (or *panissa*), from eastern Piedmont, is drier than *risotto* and contains rice, sausage, beans, and other flavors. *Insalata di riso* is made during the summer with cold cooked rice and chopped fresh vegetables, prosciutto, chunks of cheese, and sometimes oil-marinated vegetables. *Bomba di riso, sartù di riso,* and *timballo di riso* are baked rice casseroles that use either poultry or meat plus vegetables.

And then there's *arancine:* balls of rice, often stuffed with cheese and ground meat, that are deep-fried and sometimes served with tomato sauce; these are most common in Sicily and the South. Rome has the similar *supplì,* which are smaller, and the ingredients are mixed up rather than stuffed.

Italians also use rice to make dessert: *Torta di riso* is a rice cake that often contains *ricotta* cheese. And *riso* gelato tastes like rice and is usually embedded with grains of cooked rice.

Polenta

Polenta is another popular, traditional starch alternative in the North (especially the central and eastern parts). It's such a standard dish in Veneto that the rest of Italy has nicknamed people from this region "polenta eaters."

For centuries, this boiled cereal was the staff of life—a substitute for bread—and it became the ideal counterpart to just about anything: a little gravy, a bit of fish, a small game bird, melted cheese, or sugar and cinnamon as a dessert. Families would make a large pot of polenta on Monday, which the children would eat for the remainder of the week. Each day a piece would be cut off to cook with other available ingredients such as cheese, vegetables, or perhaps a stew. Only on Sunday were meals more elaborate. This was the way the poor ate for centuries; things only changed with the affluence that arrived after World War II.

Until the exploration of the Americas, polenta was made with millet, chickpeas, or buckwheat. But with the arrival of maize from the New World in the early 16th century, cornmeal became the preferred ingredient. Making polenta is a laborious process: Fill a large copper pot with cornmeal and water, then stir the mixture continuously as it thickens over about 45 minutes.

Polenta comes in many forms, from soft and mushy (left) to solid bricks carved out of a block and grilled (right).

Eventually it becomes soft and creamy. When stirring, the cook is careful not to scrape the sides or bottom of the pot, which results in a hard crust that can be salted and served as an appetizer. (These days, instant polentas are popular, as are tubes of premade polenta.) Polenta can be served as a soft porridge or cooled and cut into firm slabs to reheat later.

You may find polenta in small pieces as part of an *antipasto;* in larger amounts with cheese, mushrooms, or sauce as a *primo;* or in a piece or a creamy dollop as a side dish to slow-cooked meat or fish. (It's the standard accompaniment to salt cod, *baccalà;* and to Venetian calf liver and onions, *fegato alla veneziana.*)

Polenta can vary in how toothsome it is; generally speaking, it tends to be firmer as you move farther east. Lombards prefer it creamy and infused with cheese, while in Veneto, they cook it and cut it into rectangular bricks that can be served at room temperature or sometimes grilled.

Minestra (Soup)

Minestra means "soup," so *minestrone* is "big soup"—a rich soup with vegetables, beans, and either rice, pasta, or barley. Another famous Italian soup, which comes in many regional variations, is *pasta e fagioli,* pasta-and-bean soup.

Brodo is a broth, usually of chicken or capon (a rooster). It might be served with noodles as a soup, or used as a cooking liquid for pasta (especially in Emilia-Romagna).

Crema and *passato* are terms that suggest a velvety soup, usually vegetable-based (often with dairy cream added), rather than one full of chunky ingredients. And near the sea, you might find *impepata di cozze,* soup with mussels in the shell. *Zuppa* implies thick and substantial, like a stew—for example, *zuppa di trippa* (tripe soup). But be careful: Some dishes called *zuppa* appear elsewhere in the meal. *Zuppa di pesce* is a fish stew that sometimes appears as a *primo* but is hearty enough to be a main course or a whole meal. And *zuppa ingelese* is a rum-soaked *(inzuppato)* sponge cake dessert that is loosely translated as "trifle" (see page 91).

As with everything else in Italy, soups come in wonderful local variations. For example, Tuscany has *ribollita* ("reboiled"), a twice-cooked soup with beans, cabbage, and bread. In Rome, there's *stracciatella alla romana,* an egg-drop soup made with chicken broth. And Campania has *minestra maritata*—a "married soup" of meat and vegetables.

Secondi (Main Courses), *Contorni* (Side Dishes) & *Insalate* (Salads)

For many travelers, an *antipasto* and a *primo* are enough to have us crying *basta!* But try to save room, on occasion, for a *secondo piatto*—the Italian main course, where you'll find most of the meat, poultry, and seafood.

Accompanying (or, occasionally, following) the *secondo,* you'll also have *contorni* (side dishes) or an *insalata* (salad)—which, outside of the *antipasto,* is where you'll get most of your veggies in an Italian meal.

Secondi (Main Courses)

CARNE (MEAT) AND *POLLAME* (POULTRY)

Beef *(manzo),* pork *(maiale),* lamb *(agnello),* veal *(vitello),* and poultry *(pollame)* can be prepared a wide variety of ways: braised or stewed *(brasato, stufato,* or *in umido),* grilled *(alla griglia* or *ai ferri),* fried *(fritto),* sautéed *(saltato* or *in padella),* baked *(al forno),* or roasted or broiled *(arrosto).*

For a sampler plate of roasted meats (usually veal, pork, and lamb), look for *arrosto misto.* **Bollito misto** is eaten in the colder months in the North (especially Veneto, Emilia-Romagna, Lombardy, and Piedmont). This might include pork, poultry, sausages, oxtail, tongue, and veal, all boiled and served with a variety of sauces. In a restaurant, a cart is rolled to your table for you to select the meats you prefer. Sauces include *salsa verde* (an herb-and-caper

sauce) and *pearà* (a bone-marrow sauce from Verona). The classic *bollito misto* is also served with *mostarda,* fruit that has been pickled with mustard seed.

Steaks are typically served on the rare end of the American spectrum (especially *bistecca alla fiorentina,* the classic Tuscan T-bone). Remember that steaks and other premium items may be priced by the *etto* (100 grams); if on a budget, ask for an estimated total price before ordering.

For reasons of economy and health, meats such as veal or beef are pounded flat, or sliced very thin to make *scaloppine. Cotoletta alla milanese* is the classic breaded veal chop—similar to a Wiener Schnitzel. Sometimes thin pieces of meat (or fish) are rolled and filled, creating *involtini. Straccetti* ("rags") are strips of meat sautéed and served with arugula and cherry tomatoes or mushrooms; *tagliata* is thin slices of grilled tenderloin, typically topped with arugula.

Ossobuco is a veal shank, commonly braised in broth with carrots, onions, and tomatoes. *Saltimbocca*

alla romana is thinly sliced veal that "leaps into your mouth" (as its name implies); it's layered with prosciutto and sage, then pan-cooked.

Pork, usually prepared as *salumi* (cold cuts), is most often served as an appetizer (see page 60). But a few main courses do feature pork, typically either stewed or roasted. Tender, seasoned, roasted pork *(porchetta)* comes in various forms, and can be eaten as a *secondo* or simply stuffed in a bun as a sandwich. Sardinia has the similar *porceddu*—a slow-roasted suckling pig.

Arista describes an excellent cut of meat—either pork or veal—roasted lovingly with olive oil, rosemary, garlic, pepper, and salt. *Abbacchio* is spring lamb (a sheepish or bashful person might be called *abbacchiato*).

Italians are also big consumers of **poultry** and other birds such as chicken *(pollo),* rooster *(gallo),* capon *(cappone),* duck *(anatra),* turkey *(tacchino),* goose *(oca),* squab *(piccione),* pheasant *(fagiano),* guinea fowl *(faraona),* partridge *(pernice),* and quail *(quaglia).* Many dishes call for the boneless breast *(petto)* of these birds, often prepared as veal cutlets might be. *Pollo alla cacciatora* is "hunter-style" chicken with red wine, rosemary, garlic, tomato, and often mushrooms.

"HARDSHIP MEATS" AND *CACCIAGIONE* (GAME)

Italian chefs have always been creative and economical, employing every possible protein source—especially during times of hardship (of which Italian history has had many). When a pig was slaughtered (usually once a year, in late fall or winter), every imaginable part was used. For example, in Modena the trotter (foot) would be stuffed with minced meat and boiled—creating the dish called *zampone,* which is eaten at New Year's with lentils for luck.

For cattle, the choicer cuts are sold at high prices in small quantities. Then the less popular parts are slow-cooked with wine and vegetables. The Romans call this the **quinto quarto** ("fifth quarter")— what's left after the animal has been drawn, quartered, and butchered: brains *(cervello),* tongue *(lingua),* heart *(cuore),* lungs *(polmoni),* kidneys *(rognone),* digestive tract (*trippa* or *lampredotto*), pancreas (a.k.a. sweetbreads, *animelle*), liver *(fegato),* and other assorted organs *(frattaglie),* along with the head, feet, and tail.

While these ingredients were traditionally used by poor people for home cooking, the "nose-to-tail" trend has brought them into vogue in many of today's trendy restaurants. Give the *quinto quarto* a try—when prepared well, these dishes can be delicious, nutritious, and affordable (though very high in cholesterol). For example, *coda alla vaccinara* is oxtail braised with garlic, wine, tomato, and celery. *Trippa* (tripe) can come either *alla fiorentina,* Florence-style, sautéed with vegetables in a

tomato sauce, sometimes baked with Parmigiano-Reggiano; or *alla romana,* Rome-style, braised with onions, carrots, and mint.

Italians have many variations on headcheese—unwanted cuts of meat (often organs) preserved in meat gelatin. Look for the word *testa* (head), such as *testa in cassetta* or *coppa di testa.* Also be careful with *soppressata:* In the South, this word means a spicy salami, but in Tuscany, it could be headcheese.

In the search for protein, Italian chefs turned to a variety of **game** *(cacciagione):* rabbit *(coniglio),* hare *(lepre),* wild boar *(cinghiale),* kid *(capretto),* horse *(cavallo),* pony *(puledro),* frogs *(rane),* snails *(lumache),* and deer *(cervo).*

Some of these ingredients sound unappetizing, even shocking. It's helpful to keep the historical context of poverty in mind. There's an old proverb: *Quando un contadino mangia un pollo, o è ammalato l'uno o è ammalato l'altro.* ("When a peasant eats a chicken, either one or the other is sick.") In other words, because chickens provide eggs, a peasant would never eat one—unless the chicken stops laying eggs, or eating the chicken would help heal a sick person. This was the brutal everyday economy that faced the typical Italian through much of history.

Although today most Italians can afford more expensive ingredients, some still choose to eat these "comfort foods" that taste good and help them feel connected to tradition. For instance, scanning menus in Veneto, you might see pasta with horsemeat sauce, or a dish including *pastissada de caval* (such as a salad with strips of horsemeat or a horsemeat stew).

The decision as to whether a particular animal is suitable to eat is always personal and often emotionally charged. Some people regard

Fish is sometimes served whole, by weight. (More than one portion shown.)

animals such as horses as a natural part of the food chain, while others would never consider eating them. Should the practice of eating horse meat be abandoned because affluence means it's no longer necessary?

By describing these dishes—both here and in the regional chapters—I'm not condoning or encouraging you to eat them. I simply wish to provide a comprehensive survey of the Italian culinary scene, and respect each reader's choice regarding whether to partake or to protest.

PESCE (FISH) AND FRUTTI DI MARE (SEAFOOD)

Italians eat a much broader range of fish and seafood than do most Americans. These include everything from tiny fish that are cooked whole, all the way up to enormous ugly fish with delicious flesh. In the North, river trout *(trota)* and lake fish are consumed; in the South, magnificent swordfish *(pesce spada)* and tuna *(tonno)* are staples. Anything you get is likely fresh. In fact, when fish or

seafood is bought frozen *(surgelato)* by a restaurateur, it must by law be indicated on a menu.

Like steak, high-end fish dishes may be priced by the *etto* (100 grams). Unless the menu indicates a fillet *(filetto),* fish is usually served whole with the head and tail. However, you can ask your server to select a small fish and fillet it for you. One elegant preparation is *al cartoccio*—in parchment. As with meat, in coastal areas you might see a mix of fish and/or seafood on a skewer with vegetables *(spiedino).*

Stoccafisso and **baccalà**—dried cod and dried salted cod—have been imported from Norway for 500 years. This inexpensive ingredient was a staple for the poor, who developed many dishes using it. When handled correctly, the dried fish is soaked and rinsed enough to rid it of most salt, then fried or slow-cooked. In Lazio, *baccalà dorato* is deep-fried. In Veneto's Vicenza, *baccalà alla vicentina* is cooked with milk and onions and served with polenta. And on the Tuscan coast, *baccalà alla*

livornese is cooked with tomato and herbs. Although the Catholic Church long ago lifted the rule of no meat on Fridays, that's still the day you'll most likely see cod on menus in most of Italy.

Fresh **anchovies** *(alici),* preserved anchovies *(acciughe),* and sardines *(sarde)* are economical fish that appear in many forms, especially in the South and in Liguria. If you've only had preserved anchovies, and assume you don't like them, you must try them here in Italy. When served fresh and prepared creatively, anchovies can be a revelation.

In coastal areas, fried fish is affordable and popular—especially at a ***friggitoria*** (fry shop—roughly, the Italian equivalent of an English "chippie"). A *fritto misto* is an assortment of deep-fried calamari, prawns, and various small fish.

In Emilia-Romagna and Lombardy, sturgeon *(storione)* is popular. Centuries ago, the Jews of Romagna were the only people who ate sturgeon eggs...until everyone else found out how good caviar can be.

In Sicily, Sardinia, and coastal areas, ***bottarga*** is the dried pressed roe of tuna or mullet—sometimes called "poor man's caviar." It's usually served in shaved curls over pasta, although it also appears as an *antipasto* spritzed with generous amounts of lemon.

Shellfish *(crostacei)* is eaten all over coastal Italy and is also found in the interior: lobster *(aragosta)* from Sardinia, prawns *(scampi* and *gamberoni),* smaller shrimp *(gamberi* and *gamberetti),* mussels *(cozze* and *muscoli),* clams *(vongole* and *arselle),* octopus *(polpo* or *polipo),* squid *(calamari),* and more. Cuttlefish (similar to squid) is commonly eaten; *seppie al nero* is served in its own ink, often over spaghetti or with polenta.

Eel *(anguilla)* is consumed in much of Italy, often stewed in tomato sauce *(in umido).*

Another good option is **fish or seafood stew,** which has different names throughout the country; some include *zuppa di pesce, brodetto, cacciucco,* and *cassola.* (You may be familiar with cioppino, an Italian-American dish based on these.)

Contorni (Side Dishes)

The *contorni* are where you'll likely find most of the vegetables during a typical Italian meal. *Contorni* lend themselves to family-style sharing. Because they tend to be lighter and healthier, I err on the side of over-ordering these to round out the meal and sample interesting flavors.

One of the joys of dining in Italy is its amazing range of vegetables, almost all of superb quality. Some vegetables are eaten raw, while others are cooked and then served either hot or cold. Some are drizzled with a little olive oil, and others (such as chilled cooked spinach) taste great with a spritz of fresh lemon juice. Remember: Seasonality is important. Many Italians dote on *primizie,* the first vegetables of the season, because of their delicacy and flavor.

Each region has vegetable specialties: tomatoes in Campania, eggplants in Sicily and Calabria, artichokes and peas in Lazio, fava beans and chicory in Puglia, sweet peppers in Piedmont, *radicchio* and asparagus in Veneto, beans in Tuscany, and so on. In each region, and in the Food Glossary at the end of the book, you'll find more comprehensive coverage of which veggies to look for in the area you're visiting.

One especially common feature in the *contorni* is **potatoes** *(patate).* These can be roasted (*arrosto,* usually served with salt and rosemary), oven-baked *(al forno),* fried *(fritte),* or boiled *(bollite).* Mashed potatoes, called *purè,* go well with boiled meats.

Another commonly seen side dish is *peperonata,* made of cooked sweet peppers; it marries well with many roasted or boiled meats.

Insalate (Salads)

In an Italian meal, the salad often comes either with, or sometimes after, the main course—rather than early in the meal, as it might be back home. Italians think deeply about digestion, and believe greens provide a much-needed cushion for the richness of the *secondo.* If you order only a pasta and a salad, the server may bring them in that order, which is the opposite of what you might expect; astute severs ask if you want it *insieme* ("together").

Tartufi (Truffles)

A truffle *(tartufo)* is a tuber—technically a subterranean fungus—with an unmistakable, earthy, pungent flavor and a high price tag.

A truffle grows entirely underground, usually at a depth of around three to ten inches, in damp earth near the roots of certain trees—especially oak, poplar, and willow. Truffles can't be "planted" per se, but areas hospitable to truffle growth can be seeded with spores to encourage them to appear. Since no part of the plant grows aboveground, they're difficult to find—a job typically done by trained dogs (or, historically, pigs). Once found, the truffle is gently dug up (before the dog can eat it) using a special little shovel called a *vanghino*. An unearthed truffle is far from pretty—it looks like a tough, dirty pinecone.

There are two major types: Black truffles, or *tartufo nero,* are more widespread and have a rough, spiny surface. White truffles—which Italians call *tartufo bianco*—have a deeper, more pungent flavor and a smooth, rounded, whitish surface; these are also quite rare and command the highest prices. The Marzuolo (or *bianchetto*) truffle, also white, is somewhat less prized but still tasty.

Each type of truffle has two growing seasons, summer and winter. If visiting a truffle-growing region, find out if your visit coincides with a period when truffles are unearthed (most common in the late fall or winter; October and November are big truffle months). Because truffles don't keep their kick for long (just a few days) and don't travel well, enjoying some during truffle season in Italy is a highlight.

In Italian cooking, truffles are used sparingly for flavor. Delicate white truffles might be shaved or grated over pasta or scrambled eggs. Black truffles, which are tougher and have peppery notes, can be added to certain recipes (such as *risotto*) and might also be shaved over dishes. But *attenzione,* eh? A common tourist-baiting trick is to prepare a dish with truffle-infused oil and charge fresh-truffle prices. To ensure you're getting your money's worth, they should grate the truffle before your eyes.

Major truffle-growing areas include Piedmont (especially near Alba—famous for its white truffles), Umbria (the town of Norcia is known for its black truffles), and Molise (which fairly recently discovered rich deposits of white truffles). You'll also find some in Tuscany, Romagna, Marche, and Abruzzo.

Insalata verde (or simply *insalata*) is all greens. **Insalata mista** contains greens, tomatoes, and perhaps onions, carrots, cucumbers, or other vegetables.

The word *insalata* comes from *sale* (salt). Originally lettuces were highly salted when they were dressed, in part because Italians (especially Romans) have a fondness for salt. There is an old expression: *Insalata, ben salata / poco aceto, molto oliata / mille volte rivoltata.* ("Greens, well-salted / little vinegar, well-oiled / tossed one thousand times.") Italians follow these instructions for a properly dressed salad: Sprinkle the greens with a healthy amount of salt and a touch of vinegar. Then pour enough oil on top to cover the leaves and toss the greens repeatedly to combine the ingredients. Everything is measured by the eye and by touch. (Note the difference from the American approach of pouring premixed dressing over the entire salad.)

If you want your salad (or anything else) without salt, say *senza sale;* if you want just a little salt, say *con poco sale.*

On your table, you may find an *oliera*—a little tray or caddy with a bottle of vinegar and a bottle of oil, plus salt and pepper shakers, allowing you to dress your own salad to taste. Unfortunately, in some areas (especially where not much oil or vinegar is produced), the quality of these condiments is middling.

There are also some special salads. **Insalata caprese**—from the isle

Top: *Insalata mista;* **Bottom:** *Insalata caprese*

of Capri in Campania, but available in much of the country—is sliced tomato topped with fresh mozzarella, basil leaves, and olive oil. *Insalata russa* ("Russian salad") is a vegetable salad with mayonnaise. And *misticanza,* originating in Rome, is a mixed green salad of arugula, chicory-like *puntarelle,* and anchovy.

Dolci (Desserts)

o finish a meal, Italians often favor either fruit or gelato—which are the main focus of this chapter. I've also described some classic desserts for those with even more of a sweet tooth.

Frutta (Fruit)

Italians track the passage of time with the annual arrival of fruits and vegetables. When something comes into season—such as cherries in June or grapes in September—it's eaten with great delight, because it's at the peak of its flavor. In fact, an Italian superstition calls for making a wish the first time you eat a fruit of a season.

While there are countless examples, ***melone***—cantaloupe—embodies Italy's abundance of top-quality fruit. Having a wedge of fresh, juicy *melone* in Italy is, for many

Americans, like tasting it for the very first time. And if you've never tried wrapping a chunk of cantaloupe in a slice of prosciutto, that's a "must-do" experience that you owe your taste buds while in Italy. The pairing is explosively flavorful.

At fancier places, when you order *frutta* for dessert, you may get a bowl of fruit pretty enough to inspire Caravaggio—with a bowl of cold water to wash it yourself. Far more commonly, restaurants prepare a daily, seasonal fruit salad called

Left: Fresh fruit—such as *melone*—can be the perfect dessert; **Right:** ...or it can be baked into a *crostata*.

macedonia. To keep the apples and pears from discoloring, fresh lemon juice is squeezed onto the fruit. This might mean that, by late in the day, the *macedonia* is mushy and sour—so you might want to see it before ordering.

Another popular dessert is **sottobosco.** This delicacy is a fruit salad of small wild berries such as strawberries, raspberries, blackberries, blueberries, and currants, topped with a bit of lemon juice and, if you want, some sugar. These berries are also called *frutti di bosco* ("fruits of the forest") and might be served over ice cream or with *crespelle* (crêpes).

One classic Italian dessert is the **crostata**—a fruit or jam tart, usually open-faced but occasionally with a lattice top. Most common are apple *(mela)*, pear *(pera)*, cherry (*ciliegia* or *amarena*), apricot *(albicocca)*, peach *(pesca)*, plum *(prugna)*, and fig *(fico)*. Smaller, individual-sized tarts are called *crostatine.*

Italy is proud of its **citrus fruits.** For example, oranges *(arance)* appear first in the winter in the warmer climates (such as Sicily). Note that in Italy, especially in the South, what's described as an "orange" might be a blood orange *(arance rosse)*, which has blood-red flesh and a different, more intense flavor, with hints of raspberry. These may be called *tarocco* or *sanguinelle.*

Lemons, too, are prized—especially on Campania's Amalfi Coast, south of Naples. Some gigantic, bumpy "lemons" you'll see here are actually citrons, called *cedri,* and are more for show—they're pulpier than they are juicy, and make a good marmalade. The juicy *sfusato sorrentino,* grown only in Sorrento, is shaped like an American football, while the *sfusato amalfitano,* with knobby points on both ends, is less juicy but equally aromatic. These two kinds of luscious lemons are used in sweets such as gelato, *sorbetto, granita, limoncello,* and *delizia al limone* (a dome of fluffy cake filled and slathered with a thick whipped lemon cream).

For any citrus fruit, look for a *spremuta*—fresh-squeezed juice. (For more on juices, see page 97 in the *Bevande* chapter.)

Gelato

Italian gelato is generally considered the best ice cream in the world. It's different from other ice creams because it's lower in fat and has much more intense flavor. And good gelato is made with just a few quality ingredients: whole milk (no cream), sugar, sometimes fresh eggs, and genuine flavorings.

While many restaurants make their own gelato—which can be good—I prefer to head for a **gelateria.** The best *gelaterie* make their own. Look for the words *artigianale, nostra produzione,* or *produzione propria,* indicating that the gelato is made on the premises. Gelato that's stored in covered metal tins (rather than white plastic) is more likely to be homemade. Seasonal flavors are also a good sign.

Another tip: Look for mellow hues and avoid colors that don't appear in nature. No self-respecting *gelataio* would use artificial flavors or colors. For example, strawberry *(fragola)* is made with real berries that are pureed—unlike American-style ice cream that uses frozen berries suspended in chilled cream. Travelers' palates sometimes recoil when faced with the intensity and purity of real, natural flavors.

There are two broad categories of gelato: fruit-flavored (strawberry, cherry, banana, and so on) and cream (which includes flavors such as chocolate, coffee, hazelnut, pistachio, and vanilla).

When you buy a cup (*coppa* or *coppetta*) or a cone *(cono),* you'll typically specify two or three flavors. Most *gelaterie* clearly display prices and sizes. But in the textbook *gelateria* scam, the tourist simply names flavors and the clerk selects a fancy, expensive chocolate-coated waffle cone, piles it high with huge scoops, and cheerfully charges the tourist €10. To avoid rip-offs, point to the price or say what you want—for instance, a €3 cup: *Una coppetta da tre euro.*

A key to gelato appreciation is sampling liberally and choosing flavors that go well together. Ask for a taste: *Un assaggio, per favore?* You can also ask what flavors go well together: *Quali gusti stanno bene insieme?* Generally speaking, fruit flavors and cream flavors each go well with others in the same category. But there are some delightful exceptions: While coffee and strawberry might be strange, chocolate with banana, coconut, or pear is delicious.

Gelaterie often have other offerings as well. **Sorbetto** is sorbet

Gelato Flavors

After Eight: Chocolate and mint.

Bacio: Chocolate hazelnut, named for Italy's popular "kiss" candies.

Caffè: Coffee.

Cassata: With dried fruits.

Ciliegia: Cherry.

Cioccolato: Chocolate.

Cocco: Coconut.

Crema: Plain (similar to vanilla).

Crème caramel: Caramel custard (flan).

Croccantino: "Crunchy," with toasted nut bits.

Fior di latte: Creamy milk.

Fragola: Strawberry.

Frutti di bosco: Mixed berries.

Gianduia (or *gianduja*): Chocolate-hazelnut.

Lampone: Raspberry.

Macedonia: Mixed fruits.

Malaga: Similar to rum raisin.

Menta: Mint.

Nocciola: Hazelnut.

Noce: Walnut.

Riso: With bits of rice mixed in.

Stracciatella: Vanilla with chocolate shreds (the closest you'll get to chocolate chip).

Tartufo: Super chocolate.

Torrone: Nougat.

Zabaione: Named for the egg yolk-and-Marsala wine dessert; the flavor is reminiscent of eggnog.

Zuppa inglese: "English trifle"—sponge cake, custard, chocolate, and cream.

Other flavors are easy to decode: *banana, vaniglia, pistacchio,* **Nutella,** and so on. Remember, a cup is *coppa* or *coppetta,* and a cone is *cono.* Most places top it with whipped cream *(con panna).*

(made with fruit, but no milk or eggs). Especially in Sicily, **granita** (plural *granite*) is a sweet, slushy, icy, refreshing treat. Far from the "Italian ice" you might see stateside, a real *granita* is a liquid (usually coffee, almond, or sugared lemon juice) that has been frozen and then allowed to partially melt. It's light on the tongue, strong in flavor, and great on a hot day. Rome has the similar (but coarser) **grattachecca**—shaved ice flavored with syrup.

A **cremolata** is a gelato-*granita* float. **Frullato** is a drink made of pureed fruit with some milk and ice added—sort of a lighter version of a milkshake. And for a jolt of caffeine with your treat, **caffè affogato** is a scoop of *fior di latte* or vanilla gelato "drowned" in a shot of hot espresso, often accompanied by a little cookie.

Other Desserts

While Italians once enjoyed cakes and pastries mainly for an afternoon tea or coffee break, they've increasingly become part of multicourse meals. What you'll find on menus varies regionally: Apple strudel is ubiquitous in mountainous regions that have more Germanic influence, while Friuli-Venezia Giulia and Veneto have delicious cakes with nuts and spices.

Most northern and central regions have creamy desserts such as the classic **tiramisù**—literally "pick-me-up," this is made with espresso-soaked ladyfingers, cocoa powder, mascarpone, and sometimes sweet Marsala wine. Others in this category include *crème caramel* (caramel custard, a.k.a. flan), *bonèt* (a chocolate, coffee, or nut pudding made in Piedmont), and *budino di mandorla* or *di cioccolato* (almond or chocolate pudding).

Semifreddo ("half cold") is a mix of ice cream and whipped cream, typically chilled in blocks and served in slices with a sauce. **Panna cotta** ("cooked cream") is a custard-like dessert, served with berries or other toppings.

Southern Italy, especially Sicily, makes sumptuous desserts with liqueurs, nut creams and pastes, and lots of *ricotta* cheese (such as the *ricotta* that fills the deep-fried pastry tube in **cannoli**). *Cassata* is a Sicilian cake made of sponge cake, *ricotta* cheese, chocolate, marzipan, candied fruit, and other goodies.

Other desserts to look for: *Tartufo* is a dark-chocolate gelato ball with a cherry inside (originally from Calabria, but now everywhere);

Above: *Tiramisù;* **Below:** *Panna cotta*

torta di mele is an apple cake; *prof-iterole* is a cream-filled pastry with warm chocolate sauce; *zabaione* (or *zabaglione*) is a custard of egg yolks, sugar, and sweet wine; *zeppole* are deep-fried doughnuts filled with custard; and *zuppa inglese* ("English soup") is the Italian answer to trifle: rum-soaked cake layered with custard, whipped cream, and chocolate. In fancy restaurants, you might be served tiny pastries called *mignon* or *piccola pasticceria.*

Italy also enjoys an abundance of excellent **dessert wines,** which are usually accompanied by dry cookies called *biscotti* or *amaretti.* In Tuscany, sweet Vin Santo is served with crunchy almond cookies called *cantuccini.* In Liguria's Cinque Terre, it's the Sciacchetrà dessert wine. If it's a wine of high quality, the "proper" thing is to alternate nibbles of cookies with sips of wine. But it's hard to resist the urge to channel your inner kid and simply dunk the cookies into the wine. (Why else would the cookies be shaped long and skinny?) I find a nice glass of dessert wine with cookies is a light, delicious, and memorable way to cap a meal; often I'm very happy to have chosen that rather than a big, sweet, gloppy dessert.

A glass of dessert wine, a few dunkable cookies, and a floodlit lane make for a wonderful way to complete an Italian meal.

Bevande (Drinks)

While wine *(vino)* is a topic—and a chapter—all its own, here we'll cover other types of drinks, including coffee, mineral water, soft drinks, beer, liquor, and grappa.

Italian Coffee Culture

Italians are among Europe's most avid coffee drinkers. And while "Italian" coffee culture appears to have migrated across the Atlantic—in the form of Starbucks and its clones—it's lost a great deal in translation. One of the joys of traveling in Italy is becoming fluent in the local coffee scene.

Italians organize their lives around coffee. There's the breakfast coffee, the social coffees throughout the day, the one that follows lunch, and perhaps one after supper. Are Italians overcaffeinated? Keep in mind they consume smaller amounts—usually a shot at a time—rather than slugging back giant American-style "ventis" or a big cup of drip coffee (which contains more caffeine than an espresso shot). By the end of the day, the typical Italian has probably ingested no more caffeine than the typical American. And, almost certainly, they've enjoyed it a great deal more.

When an Italian offers you a coffee *(ti offro un caffè)*, it's a gesture of graciousness and friendship. You get into a brief quarrel over who pays, and then you politely lose and say *grazie*. This doesn't come with strings attached; it's simply another one of those Italian moments of human contact lived to the fullest.

Remember, when ordering coffee in a bar, you'll pay first at the register, then take the receipt to the barista to make your drink. The price depends on whether you drink it sitting or standing up. Most Italians consume their coffee standing shoulder-to-shoulder at the bar. (For details, see "Bars" on page 40.)

Italian coffee begins with espresso, to which milk and/or foam are added in various amounts. As the

day goes on, the amount of added milk decreases. Italians believe that having too much milk after lunch is bad for digestion. Even so, many baristas are willing—perhaps with a raised eyebrow—to serve milky drinks to tourists in the afternoon.

The basic building block of Italian coffee culture is **un caffè**—a shot of espresso, typically served in a small ceramic demitasse cup (2-3 fluid ounces), filled about halfway. It should be freshly brewed with very hot water and beans that have just been ground. Usually, a well-made espresso will have a *crema,* a slight

orange-brown foam on top. Many Italians reflexively add sugar to their *caffè.* Coffee consumed without sugar is called *amaro* (bitter), which is a misnomer since the best coffee is naturally slightly sweet.

If you want a more intense coffee, you use less water; this is called a **caffè ristretto** or **caffè corto.** Conversely, if you want it less intense, ask for a **caffè lungo,** made with more water. A **caffè americano** is espresso diluted with quite a bit of hot water, coming close to an American-style drip coffee (which is uncommon in Italy). A **caffè corretto,** an espresso "corrected" by adding a shot of grappa or brandy, is not for the fainthearted.

Adding milk or foam to an espresso brings about a wide array of coffee drinks. A **caffè macchiato** is an espresso "stained" with a little milk, served in a small cup. This is for people who'd rather not stomach straight espresso, while still keeping milk consumption to a minimum (making it socially acceptable even later in the day). Don't confuse this with its opposite, the **latte macchiato**—a tall glass with layers

ITALIAN COFFEE DRINKS

UN CAFFÈ
(ESPRESSO)

CAFFÈ
MACCHIATO

CAFFÈ RISTRETTO
(Less water than
a regular *caffè*)

CAFFÈ LUNGO
(More water than
a regular *caffè*)

CAFFÈ
AFFOGATO

Gelato

CAFFÈ
CORRETTO

Grappa

CAFFÈ
AMERICANO

CAPPUCCINO

CAFFÈ LATTE

MAROCCHINO

Layers
of Cocoa
Powder

LATTE MACCHIATO

LEGEND

Espresso
Milk
Milk Foam
Water

of hot milk and foam, "stained" with a splash of espresso.

A **cappuccino** is an espresso in a large cup with foamed milk on top. It's named for the hooded Capuchin monks, with their brown robes.

A **caffè latte** is espresso, sometimes "lengthened" with hot water, to which heated milk is added (what the French call *cafe au lait*). Unlike a cappuccino, the coffee and milk in a *caffè latte* are blended. The flavor combination of coffee and milk is about fifty-fifty. (Don't order a *"latte,"* which simply means "milk"—in Italy, it's a *caffè latte*.)

A **marocchino** ("Moroccan") consists of layers of espresso, cocoa powder, and foamed milk, with a dusting of cocoa powder on top. It's usually served in a glass so you can see the layers. The similar **mocaccino** is larger and uses hot chocolate instead of cocoa.

Chilled coffee drinks ("cold brew" and the like) have not been as widely embraced in Italy as stateside. Still, they do have **caffè freddo,** a glass of chilled espresso; or, during summer in warm southern climates, the refreshing **caffè latte freddo,** which is cold coffee (often sugared) to which cold milk is added. You may even see a **cappuccino freddo;** while the slushy Frappuccino is an American invention, this is the next closest thing. A **shakerato** is espresso, ice, and sugar shaken up until frothy. For something even more decadent, **caffè affogato** is a scoop of gelato "drowned" in a shot of hot espresso. And especially in Sicily, a refreshing alternative is a coffee **granita** (sweet slushy ice; if you ask for *con panna,* they'll top it with whipped cream, creating a sort of frozen *caffè latte*).

If you don't want caffeine, add the word **decaffeinato** to your order (for example, *un cappuccino decaffeinato*). A decaffeinated espresso is called a **caffè Hag**—for a popular name brand—sometimes served in an orange cup. Another decaf option is **caffè d'orzo,** which is brewed with toasted barley (but no actual coffee) that supposedly approximates the flavor of coffee. This is an acquired taste that some people come to enjoy.

At home, most Italians brew their coffee in the ubiquitous stovetop **Moka** pot. Invented in 1933 by Alfonso Bialetti, this iconic, all-metal little pot is a percolator. If you stay in an Italian home, try it out: Fill the bottom of the pot with water (to just below the little steam-vent hole); fill the middle "basket" with coffee; then insert the basket into the lower pot, screw it onto the upper pot, and place it on the burner. As the water boils, it's pushed up through the grounds and coffee appears in the upper chamber. Listen for the bubbling sound—indicating that the last of the lower liquid has reached the upper chamber. Once that begins to quiet, remove it from the heat. The resulting coffee is concentrated—a bit closer to espresso than to drip coffee (for an American-style brew, you may need to dilute it with hot water).

And, of course, many Italians have their own at-home espresso machines, too; some of these use Nespresso-like capsules.

Left: "*Cappuccino* with a Capuchin";
Right: Moka pot

Italy has many public fountains designed to get an easy, refreshing drink on the go. Just avoid any marked *acqua non potabile.*

Acqua (Water) and Soft Drinks

Travelers are sometimes frustrated that Italian restaurant servers "push" bottled water instead of tap water. It's not because they're trying to upsell you. It's because Italians are highly selective about water; they simply can't understand why you wouldn't want good water to accompany your good food.

Today, **tap water** *(acqua del rubinetto)* is perfectly safe to drink everywhere in Italy. In some

areas—including parts of the Alps, the province of Parma, Norcia in Umbria, and Lazio—it's excellent. (There are a few exceptions: At some decorative fountains, in the little bathrooms on board trains, and in some restrooms, you may see the words *acqua non potabile*—meaning that this water is not drinkable).

But historically, tap water was not always potable—especially in the South. So, Italians developed an affinity for **mineral water** *(acqua minerale),* typically bottled from protected sources. In short, minerals are essential to proper body functioning, and Italians believe *acqua minerale* is a good way to get them. Browse the bottled water aisle of an Italian grocery store and you'll find as many varieties of H_2O as we have types of Coke and Pepsi. Each label is loaded with technical data about mineral composition, and sometimes a small essay by a university professor about the healthful properties of the water.

Usually at a meal, you'll order *vino e acqua;* fortunately, both of these— table wine and bottled water—are generally inexpensive. Bottled water is served by the half-liter *(mezzo litro)* or liter *(un litro)*. Ask for **con gas** for bubbles, or **naturale** if you prefer still water *(gassata* also means carbonated; *senza gas* or *non gassata* are uncarbonated).

Some brands, such as Ferrarelle, are naturally sparkling and are called *frizzante.* Things can get very specific; *acqua leggermente effervescente* (lightly carbonated water) is a good choice for diners who want a little fizziness without big bubbles. As you travel through Italy, go on a little quest for your favorite water.

When you're on the go, half-liter bottles of mineral water are available everywhere for about €1—or even less in supermarkets. I either refill my water bottle with tap water, or invest in a big, cheap bottle of mineral water at the grocery store for refills.

All of that said, you can try requesting tap water at restaurants. But now you know why you might get some funny looks. (And even if you do get tap water, it will never be served with ice cubes.)

Juice **(succo)** comes in little bottles, while **spremuta** means freshly squeezed juice—commonly served in bars and worth the extra euros. Most common is orange juice *(arancia);* from February through April, it's sometimes made from Sicilian blood oranges *(arance rosse)*. You'll also see lemon *(limone)* and grapefruit *(pompelmo)*.

In grocery stores, you can get a liter of O.J. for the price of a Coke or coffee. Look for *100% succo* or *senza zucchero* (without sugar)—or be surprised by something diluted and sugary sweet. I like to buy juice in cheap liter boxes, drink some in my hotel room, and then store the rest in an empty water bottle for my next stop.

Tè freddo (iced tea) is usually from a can—sweetened and flavored with lemon or peach. Lemonade is **limonata.** Try looking for some interesting soft drinks. For instance, **chinotto** tastes vaguely like a bitter, less sweet Dr. Pepper.

Birra (Beer) and Hard Drinks

BEER

Italy is thought of as wine country. And traditionally, Italian beers have been unexciting: the big brands are mass-produced, Budweiser-type lagers Peroni and Moretti. Beer was long considered a drink of poor people, or something you'd have with pizza for a cheap buzz. (Italians never drink beer with meat.)

But now the global trend for

Above: The Aperol *spritz* is a popular Italian *aperitivo*. You'll see these bright-orange drinks everywhere; **Below:** At most places, an *aperitivo* comes with light snacks.

craft beer *(birra artigianale)* has taken hold in Italy. Even in smaller cities, you may see microbreweries pouring their own brews. (*Birrificio* means "brewery"; a *birreria* is a beer bar/pub that typically serves food.) What's on tap is often inspired by the same trends you'll find stateside—IPAs, ambers, stouts, saisons, sours, seasonal beers, and so on—though naturally, Italian brewers get creative with local ingredients and novel approaches.

Beer on tap is *alla spina.* Get it *piccola* (33 cl, 11 oz), *media* (50 cl, about a pint), or *grande* (a liter). A *lattina* is a can and a *bottiglia* is a bottle.

COCKTAILS: *APERITIVI* AND *DIGESTIVI*

Italians appreciate both *aperitivi* (palate-stimulating, pre-dinner cocktails) and *digestivi* (after-dinner drinks designed to aid digestion). These are the liquid bookends of an Italian meal.

The **aperitivo** custom pairs well with the evening *passeggiata* and often comes with hearty snacks (see page 58). The most popular cocktail-hour drink may be the **spritz:** Prosecco (or white wine) and soda livened up with either **Campari** (carmine-red bitters with a secret blend of herbs and orange peel) or **Aperol** (sweeter, softer, bright-orange bitters with herbal, citrusy under-tones). Another version of the *spritz* is the **Hugo** (Prosecco, elderberry syrup, and soda served with mint leaves). Originally from northeastern Italy, the *spritz* is now found everywhere.

Vermouths (both red and white) from **Carpano, Cinzano, Martini,** or

Riccadonna can be served straight, on the rocks, with a splash of soda, or as part of drinks like **Punt e Mes** (sweet red vermouth and red wine). Venice has a trio of drinks named after local artists: **Bellini** (Prosecco and white peach juice), **Tiziano** (Prosecco and grape juice), and **Tintoretto** (Prosecco and pomegranate juice). Other choices include the Yankee-sounding but very Italian **Americano** (vermouth with bitters, brandy, and lemon peel), **Garibaldi** (also known as Campari-Orange, a mixture of Campari and orange juice), and **Cynar** (bitters flavored with artichoke—this is enjoyed both as an *aperitivo* and a *digestivo*).

For a traditional, stronger cocktail, bartenders can make all of the classics. Or try something local; for instance, a **Negroni** is a potent mix of equal parts Campari, vermouth, and gin.

Digestivi are designed to aid the digestive process; many Italians would not think of finishing a meal without one. Choices fall into three categories: a bittersweet, syrupy herbal drink called *amaro;* something sweeter, like *limoncello;* and grappa.

Amaro recipes are closely held secrets, but most are a grape brandy infused with ingredients that include herbs, flowers, citrus peel, and spices (with an alcohol content of 20 to 40 percent). Many restaurants have their own *amaro* recipe. Although *amaro* means "bitter," the flavor varies greatly, from light and sweet (such as the Nonino brand, from Friuli) to medium (Averna, from Sicily) to quite bitter (Fernet Branca, a nasal-passage-clearing brand from Milan).

Other popular commercial brands found all over Italy include Ramazzoti (from Milan), Montenegro (from Bologna, with a distinctive bottle), Strega (from Campania), and Amaro Lucano (from Basilicata). Alpine *amari,* which use mountain herbs, include Braulio (from Valtellina in Lombardy), with piney, menthol notes; and Centerbe (from Abruzzo), characterized by its greenish color and a throat-burning sensation.

If your tastes run sweeter, try any of these flavored liqueurs: *amaretto* (almond; the most famous is from Saronno, north of Milan), Frangelico (hazelnut), *limoncello* (lemon; the best is from the South—see page 273),

nocino (walnut, from Emilia-Romagna), and *sambuca* (anise, often served with coffee beans). Other very sweet options include the fortified wines Marsala (from Sicily) and Vin Santo ("holy wine" that's ideal for dunking dry cookies).

And if you want something even stronger…try a grappa or *acquavite*.

FIREWATER (GRAPPA AND *ACQUAVITE*)

Ranging from 35 to 70 percent alcohol, the twin Italian firewaters grappa and *acquavite* are an acquired taste.

Grappa, a byproduct of the winemaking process, originated as a beverage of the poor. Wine would be given to the lord of the land, and the peasants would distill the leftover grape skins to make a coarse, powerful brandy *(grappa del contadino)*. It was meant to keep them warm through the winter and, with its sugar content, to provide energy; along with polenta, this was one of the staples of poor northern Italians (especially in Veneto, Friuli, and Trentino) all the way through the postwar era. The middle and upper

classes would never have considered drinking rustic, backward grappa.

In recent generations, this perception has shifted; with affluence, grappa has gone from a source of nutrition to something to sip at the end of a meal. And over time, it evolved in sophistication: Instead of using any old grape skins, higher-end producers (such as the Nonino family in Friuli) began using skins from leading wine producers. The theory was that the skins from better wine grapes would make better grappa. The Noninos also pioneered the use of *monovitigno* grappas: using the skins from just

one kind of grape to make the flavor more distinct. These days, every winemaker in Italy wants to make a few extra euros with their leftover grape skins. *Stravecchio* is an aged, mellower variation on grappa.

Acquavite ("water of life") is similar to grappa: a distillation of fruit such as apples, raspberries, cherries, pears, plums, and apricots. It's most common in the North (where fruit abounds) and can be expensive.

Italians take grappa (or *acquavite*) tasting very seriously. The beverage usually comes in slender decorative bottles and is served in a small glass, held by the stem. Swirl the liquid gently, give it a smell, then take a tiny sip onto your tongue, raise it to your palate, and let it evaporate. Yes, it burns a little, but allow the fragrance and flavor to permeate your mouth, throat, and nasal passages. Let this sip slowly disappear, then pause a bit and sense the *ritorno*—the flavor that returns to your mouth a few moments later. For a good grappa, this will be the best flavor; for a bad one, it will be the worst. Then take another little sip and repeat.

If you enjoy it, buy a bottle to take home and store in a dark, cool place: A good bottle should last for years, though there'll be a slight rounding of flavor.

Finer restaurants often have a cart packed with various grappa bottles that you'll hear rumbling and tinkling toward your table at the end of the meal. The server is more than happy to help you make a selection.

Italian Wine

Galileo wrote, "Wine is light held together by water." Wine *(vino)* is a huge part of the Italian culinary world—as much a way of life as it is a beverage. Ideal conditions here for grapes (warm Mediterranean climate, well-draining soil, and an abundance of hillsides), plus centuries of know-how, have made the Italian Peninsula a paradise for grape growers, winemakers, and wine drinkers.

Italian Wine 101

Travelers often remark on how inexpensive and good Italian wine can be: In restaurants, a house wine *(vino della casa)* is usually cheaper than soft drinks or even bottled water. That's because wine is a sacred staple, consumed alongside every lunch and dinner, whether at home or dining out. (Italy is routinely among the world's top 10 countries in per capita wine consumption.)

Many Italians make their own wine or obtain it from a friend or relative (a cheap, local, everyday wine might be called *vino del contadino*—"farmer's wine"—or even *vino dello zio,* "uncle's wine"). Or, lacking a family or farm connection, Italians stock up on table wine at a local winery, some with a "filling station" efficiency for selling in bulk.

In most years, Italian winemakers produce more wine than any other country—more than four million liters annually. Production is mainly red *(rosso)* and white *(bianco)* wines. Rosé *(rosato)* is less traditional—though as it's become trendy stateside and elsewhere, more Italian vintners are experimenting with it. A sparkling wine is *frizzante* or *spumante;* Prosecco is a bubbly white wine from northeastern Italy (Veneto and Friuli). (These days, as with French "champagne," some

Many Italians buy table wine affordably in bulk… and pump their own.

Americans use the term "prosecco" generically—and improperly—to describe any Italian sparkling white; for more on the *real* Prosecco, see page 190.)

Within each type of wine you'll find a wide variation in quality and price. But even the most basic table wine *(vino da tavola)* or house wine can be deliciously drinkable. (Though on occasion, it can also be pretty rough.)

If you want to move up the quality ladder, go beyond the *vino da tavola.* Like Italian food, wines are highly localized—it can be hard to find many wines outside of their place of origin. Italians are extremely loyal to their local *vino,* and a major feature of this book's regional chapters is a rundown of the wines from each place. Naturally, each wine pairs perfectly with the food that grows in the same area. For example, in Tuscany, nothing complements an aged local *pecorino* cheese quite like a nice Chianti.

Italian wines are sometimes named for the grape (such as "cabernet sauvignon" or "chardonnay"). In other cases, they're named for

the zone (like Chianti); others are a specific type (such as Brunello di Montalcino, Barolo, or Sciacchetrà). Higher-quality wines are legally protected with the denomination DOC (pronounced "doke") or—even better—DOCG (pronounced "D-O-chee-gee"). For more on these, see the "Deciphering Wine Labels" side-bar, later in this chapter.

The most famous DOCG wines have a small production and other restrictions, which can make them quite expensive. If you're on a tight budget, try looking for a

History of Italian Wine

Faded frescoes in Etruscan tombs give us reason to believe that wine was already being made—and consumed—in Italy 4,000 years ago. And when the ancient Greeks colonized Italy, they called it Enotria, Land of the Grape. The Greeks were the first to undertake widespread wine production on the Italian Peninsula, even creating a system of *enodotti:* pipelines that transported wine to the ports for shipping back to Athens.

As the Romans gained control of the Italian Peninsula, their lasting contribution was the unification of the cultivation of vines, wheat, and olives: the great trinity of Mediterranean agriculture. Wine had already become entwined with pagan rituals. Bacchus was an important god in the Roman pantheon, and a successful harvest was celebrated with a raucous bacchanalian festival. As Christianity spread across Italy, wine also became heavily used in religious sacraments. In this way, wine has always been part of the delicate balance between the sacred and the profane that typifies Italian history.

After the fall of Rome, as barbarians ravaged the land, it was priests, nuns, and monks—who had become expert winemakers—who rescued old vines, replanting them within church walls to preserve them through those dark centuries. Well into the Middle Ages and beyond, wine was mainly for local consumption. Landed peasants produced wine for their lord, keeping some lower-quality wine for themselves. Those fortunate enough to own land made just enough wine for their own family's use, with perhaps a bit left over to trade or barter. It wasn't until the late 17th century that certain wines, like Chianti, began to be officially named and codified.

By the 19th century, the rise of wine journalism in England drew more attention to the craft. French wines were lavished with laudatory coverage, while Italian wines were ignored or considered lower tier. Unfortunately, this thinking persisted until recent times—consumers and even many Italian winemakers, until not that long ago, believed that Chianti was inferior to Bordeaux, or that the wines of Piedmont couldn't stand up to those from Burgundy. It didn't help that, through the 20th century, most Italian wines shipped abroad were overproduced, inexpensive reds

designed to provide an affordable taste of the Old Country to newly arrived immigrants in North America. Some winemakers, suffering an inferiority complex, even uprooted traditional grape varieties and replaced them with trendy chardonnay and cabernet sauvignon grapes.

Things shifted in 1963 with the introduction of the DOC designation *(Denominazione di Origine Controllata)*. This legislated that certain wines could only be so named if they adhered to strict controls on the type, quantity, and location of the grapes grown. For example, to be called "Chianti," a wine must come from that specific area (between Florence and Siena) and be made of at least 70 percent sangiovese grapes. This succeeded in bringing a consistency of quality and a sense of pride to Italian wines; later it was augmented with an additional category—DOCG *(Denominazione di Origine Controllata e Garantita)*—to identify wines of unmistakably high quality. And in the 1990s, a new designation arrived—IGT *(Indicazione Geografica Tipica)*—that allowed for international-style wines that use non-native grapes and modern methods.

Technological advances further bolstered the quality of Italian wines. Today well over 300 types are graced with the coveted DOC designation, more than 75 are DOCG, and more than 130 are IGT—you'll notice these proudly stamped on labels. And these days, Italy exports more wine than any nation on earth. Most important to local winemakers, Italian wines are renowned for their quality; aficionados worldwide recognize that Italian wine is right up there with anything that France or California has to offer.

ITALIAN WINE REGIONS

50 Kilometers
50 Miles

Trieste

Major Italian Wines

1. Barolo (Piedmont)
2. Barbaresco (Piedmont)
3. Moscato (Piedmont)
4. Gewürztraminer (Trentino)
5. Amarone (Veneto)
6. Prosecco (Veneto)
7. Ribolla Gialla & Pignolo (Friuli-Venezia Giulia)
8. Sciacchetrà (Liguria)
9. Chianti Classico (Tuscany)
10. Super Tuscans (Tuscany)
11. Brunello di Montalcino (Tuscany)
12. Vino Nobile di Montepulciano (Tuscany)
13. Orvieto Classico (Umbria)
14. Verdicchio (Marche)
15. Frascati (Lazio)
16. Aglianico del Vulture (Basilicata)
17. Salice Salentino (Puglia)
18. Cirò (Calabria)
19. Etna (Sicily)
20. Marsala (Sicily)

BIANCO DEI COLLI MACERATESI

Adriatic Sea

MONTEPULCIANO D'ABRUZZO
Pescara
TREBBIANO D'ABRUZZO
ABRUZZO
Sulmona   Larino
MOLISE
BIFERNO
PENTRO
Campobasso
CAMPANIA   PUGLIA
Bari   Martina Franca
ALEATICO DI PUGLIA   PATRIGLIONE
FIANO
Naples
AGLIANICO DEL VULTURE 16   GIOIA DEL COLLE   Brindisi
Sorrento   Amalfi   Potenza   Matera   Taranto   SALICE SALENTINO 17
Furore   COLLI LUCANI
BASILICATA   PRIMITIVO DI MANDURIA
Maretea   Gulf of Taranto
CALABRIA
CIRÒ 18   CIRÒ
MELISSA   Crotone   Ionian Sea
Catanzaro

Tropea

Note: Italy is covered in vineyards. Not all wine regions are shown.

Messina   GRECO DI BIANCO
Palermo   Randazzo   Reggio Calabria
Cefalù   ETNA 19   Taormina
SICILY   Enna   Catania
Agrigento
Siracusa
Noto
Ragusa   CERASUOLO DI VITTORIA

LEGEND

Wine Region
Wine Road
Italy's Major Wines

more affordable alternative grown nearby. For example, in Tuscany, the world-famous Brunello di Montalcino can break the bank, but Rosso di Montalcino—made in the same zone with similar grapes, in a similar way, but aged for a shorter period of time—costs half as much. This tip helps locals navigate high prices among wines that have become popular with tourists, inflating the market.

Since around the 1970s, some winemakers have been looking beyond traditional Italian grapes and methods to create exciting new blends. A classic example are the famous "Super Tuscans," which blend native sangiovese grapes with imported cabernet sauvignon varieties from France, and are produced according to modern, international methods.

In addition to enjoying wines in restaurants, if you're serious about sampling wine, make a point to do a tasting *(degustazione)* at a wine shop (*enoteca*—see page 33) or a vineyard. This chapter is designed to equip you with what you need to know to navigate the world of Italian wine.

WINEMAKING

With its varied landscape and its tradition of artisanal perfectionism, Italy is ideally suited to the art and science of winemaking. After all, wine is an expression of a terrain, of climate, of the grape, and of the person who makes it.

While the Italians don't have a specific word for it, they share an understanding of the French concept of *terroir:* Grapes are heavily influenced by the very specific terrain, soil type, altitude, climate, and exposure to sun of the land where they grow. Even on the same plot of land, a grape will produce different wine if grown on one side or the other of a hill. Wine labels boast about the grapes that came from the "sunny side" of the vineyard (*bricco* in Piedmont, *ronco* in Friuli, and *poggio* in Tuscany).

Of course, conditions change from year to year, which also affects the properties of the wine. Large industrial winemakers strive for consistency, taking variations in climate and grape quality into account in trying to vinify a wine to resemble the production from previous years. Consumers who buy industrial wine look for uniformity,

not variation. Smaller producers have more variety in their product from year to year. To aficionados, those changes are a feature, not a bug: The unique taste of a given year's wine reflects not only the story of the wine, but also the lives of the people who made it.

Winemaking technology has advanced in recent years, with machines that can help pick grapes and turn them into wine. But the vintner must still make critical decisions that shape the final product: when to pick the grapes, how long they should be fermented (and at what temperature), whether wine should be stored in stainless steel tanks or wooden barrels (or both), and for how long, and so on.

Debate rages among winemakers about whether traditional ways, or new ones, produce the best results. For most of Italy's history, almost all wine was made in wooden vats and transferred to wooden barrels to ferment, then age. With the affluence and technological advances of the postwar era, some winemakers began to use stainless-steel tanks. Each approach has its advantages: Stainless steel is more sanitary and the temperature is easier to regulate, giving the winemaker more precise control over the fermentation process. But wood mellows wines that naturally have a high acid content, and can add certain notes of distinctive flavor. (In fact, many of the protected DOC and DOCG wines must spend a specified time in wood, which imparts that special character. And some are required to further age in the bottle before being sold.) Many winemakers use a combination, starting in steel and then transferring to wood to develop a deeper flavor and fragrance.

Complicating matters was the arrival (in the 1980s) of the *barrique*—expensive, small barrels made of French or Slavonian oak, used for aging certain wines (a trend that began with California chardonnays). While some appreciate the oaky notes, others (including one of this book's co-authors) find that you wind up tasting the tree more than the grape.

These "new" methods have a way of entering Italy through the North, then gradually disseminating through the country. Winemakers who honed their craft in Piedmont or Veneto might migrate south, to humbler places like Sicily or Puglia—combining local grapes with cutting-edge techniques to create exciting new wines.

This speaks to the delicate balance of new and old in Italian winemaking. While the landscape can sustain both innovation and tradition, I'm particularly moved by the way that a fine, traditional Italian wine represents decades of hard work, tradition, and love from the same family. It's a powerful experience to be served a glass of wine by the family that has been making it for generations. Imagine: Standing in a dimly lit cellar, the head of household pours you a glass of wine, placing her hand just so on the bottle's label to frame the family name…as her aging grandfather, sitting in the corner, proudly looks on.

Visiting a winery allows you to better understand the winemaking process, get to know the people, and taste a variety of wines—sometimes using the very same grapes—by the same producer, providing you with a vivid lesson on how the specifics of production can have a huge impact on the final result. Tasting wine is a subjective pastime, and one of the joys of traveling in Italy is the journey to becoming an aficionado. For more, see the "Wine Tourism" section, later.

Deciphering Wine Labels

An Italian wine label can teach you plenty and help you make a good selection. For starters, the label typically lists the harvest year, the alcohol percentage, perhaps the name of the vintner(s), and sometimes the grapes that were used. You'll also see some indication of where the wine was produced—either a town name, a region name, or initials indicating the location (for example, VR for Verona or MC for Macerata).

In general, Italian wines fall into four official categories:

Vino da Tavola (VdT): Table wine, made from local grapes that can be grown anywhere in Italy; this is typically inexpensive but can still be delicious. Many restaurants, even modest ones, take pride in their house wine *(vino della casa),* bottling their own or partnering with a local winery. Nowadays, a *vino da tavola* can also be a high-end, niche wine, especially in Tuscany—the price will tell you.

Denominazione di Origine Controllata (DOC, pronounced "doke"): This meets national standards for high-quality wine. Made from grapes grown in a defined area, it's usually quite afford-able and good.

Denominazione di Origine Controllata e Garantita (DOCG, pronounced "D-O-chee-gee"): The highest grade, this meets national standards for the highest-quality wine (made with grapes from a defined area whose quality is "controlled and guaran-teed"). In general, these wines are from

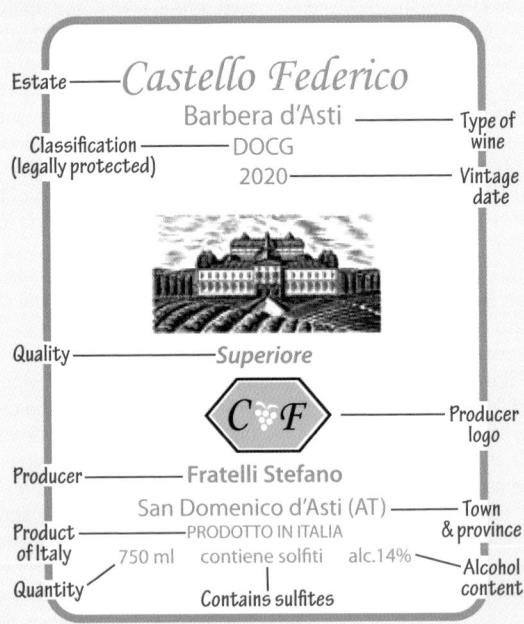

Estate —— *Castello Federico*

Barbera d'Asti —— Type of wine

Classification —— DOCG
(legally protected)

2020 —— Vintage date

Quality —— *Superiore*

Producer logo

Producer —— Fratelli Stefano

San Domenico d'Asti (AT) —— Town & province

Product of Italy —— PRODOTTO IN ITALIA

750 ml   contiene solfiti   alc.14% —— Alcohol content

Quantity

Contains sulfites

lower-yield vineyards, are aged longer, and undergo a taste test by a panel of experts. They can be identified by the pink or green label on the neck...and the high price tag.

Indicazione Geografica Tipica (IGT): This broad group of wines doesn't meet the standard for DOC or DOCG status—usually because they've used non-traditional grapes or methods—but they've been designated as "typical" of a particular area. (While it's a matter of taste, some IGT wines can rival, or even surpass, wines in the DOC or DOCG designation.)

Finally, you may also see these terms on wine labels:

Riserva: DOCG or DOC wine matured for an even longer period than is required by law.

Classico: From a defined, select area within a zone.

Superiore: Higher quality (usually) and often higher alcohol content.

Annata: Year of harvest.

Vendemmia: Harvest.

Tenuta: Property.

Fattoria: Farm, rural wine estate.

Castello: Castle on or near the property.

Azienda agricola: Wine estate that grows its own grapes and bottles their wine.

Azienda vinicola: Company that buys grapes from other growers.

Cantine: Cellars.

Imbottigliato all'origine: Bottled by the producer.

Contiene solfiti: Contains sulfites (a warning for those who are allergic).

Ordering and Tasting Wine

IN RESTAURANTS

Most restaurants have two broad categories of wine: house wine and bottled wine.

At most meals, Italians simply order the **house wine** (vino della casa), which is considered vino sfuso—"loose," meaning that the wine is served in a carafe. Choose a glass (about 5 oz, un bicchiere), a quarter-liter (8.5 oz, un quarto), half-liter (17 oz, un mezzo litro), or a full liter (34 oz, un litro). For a good, light, affordable, straightforward wine at a meal, order una caraffa di vino della casa (a carafe of the house wine).

For a **finer wine,** ask to see the lista dei vini or carta dei vini (wine list). Some places might have a few bottles of high-quality wine open to serve by the glass. But more often, you'll buy the entire bottle (bottiglia).

To order a single glass of red or white wine, say, "Un bicchiere di vino rosso/bianco." Your server will likely default to the house wine but may offer you something from an open bottle.

AT A WINE TASTING

If you're already comfortable tasting wines, skip ahead to the next section. But if you're relatively new to wine tastings, here are some tips for evaluating what you're served.

A proud Italian vintner once told me, "You taste the wine three times: First with your eyes, then with your nose, and finally with your mouth." Follow these steps to get this full experience.

Once the wine is poured into the glass, hold it up to the light and **view the color.** Any type of wine should be clear and not cloudy. The palette of a red wine can range from inky purple to ruby red; it's common for an older red to appear brick-red along the edges of the glass. White wines can be yellowish, greenish, or clear, but beware of one that's *too* yellow—this can indicate that it is oxidized, meaning it has been exposed to air due to a bad cork or being kept too long. Speaking of the cork, examine it to be sure it's intact and not deteriorating. Smell it. If a wine is "corked," it has a distinctive, unpleasant aroma.

Next, **aerate the wine.** Swirl the liquid gently and observe how it clings and streaks down the inside of the glass. These streaks of glycerin, called "legs," are more pronounced in full-bodied wines. The legs can also be an indication of higher alcohol content. Swirling aids in the aeration of the wine, which releases more of

the bouquet. Stick your nose in the glass and **inhale deeply.**

Now look your partner in the eye, say *salute,* and **take a small sip.** Let the liquid cover your tongue and completely fill the bottom of your mouth. (Develop the technique of inhaling slightly through your mouth while it's partly filled with wine, which propels the aromas up into the nasal cavity.) Ponder which taste notes you can detect, either with your nose or with your palate. Quality wines are said to have good "mouthfeel," meaning they possess a nice texture and viscosity along with a pleasing flavor.

Now it's time to **swallow, then savor the aftertaste.** The flavor of some wines (especially whites and rosés) disappears immediately—a "short finish." In contrast, the best wines (particularly reds) have a lingering, long finish: They fade away slowly, leaving you eager for the next sip. During the finish, you may notice different notes than you first smelled or tasted.

Remember that many Italian wines—particularly the bigger, robust reds, such as Barolo—are tannic, which makes them ideally suited for having with food…but, frankly, not particularly palatable on their own. I once visited a winemaker in the Tuscan hills who was very proud of his Brunello di Montalcino. Sipping a glass, I asked him if this was a good wine to relax with out on the terrace at the end of a long day. He winced a bit and said, "Um, no. We have another wine for that"—something lighter, more refreshing. *This* wine, he explained, was for eating with grilled meat and other hearty dishes. And sure enough, when tasting the wine with a chunk of the local steak, *bistecca alla fiorentina,* the flavor of both changed dramatically for the better.

When buying bottles of wine, consider not just what you like, but how you'll drink it: on its own, with a meal, at a picnic? And never be afraid to ask follow-up questions of the server or shop clerk. Italians love the opportunity to share their knowledge and enthusiasm for wine.

Wine-Tasting Terms

When tasting wine, it helps to know a few Italian terms. If you're not familiar with Italian grapes and wines, it can be challenging for an outsider to know what to expect. The clerk at a wine shop or wine tasting wants to help you find something that suits your tastes and your palate. Read through these phrases and think about what constitutes, for you, an appealing wine. Then use them to guide your exploration and find a new favorite.

ENGLISH	ITALIAN	PRONOUNCED
wine	*vino*	VEE-noh
red	*rosso*	ROH-soh
white	*bianco*	bee-AHN-koh
rosé	*rosato*	roh-ZAH-toh
sparkling	*spumante/frizzante*	spoo-mahn-tay/ freed-ZAHN-tay
I'd like to sample a typical local wine.	*Vorrei provare un vino locale tipico.*	voh-REH-ee proh-VAH-ray oon vee-noh loh-KAH-lay TEE-pee-koh
What do you suggest?	*Cosa suggerisce?*	KOH-zah soo-jeh-REE-sheh
I like ___. (fill in type of wine)	*Mi piace il ___.*	mee pee-AH-chay eel
I like something that is ___ and ___.	*Preferisco qualcosa di ___ e ___.*	preh-feh-REE-skoh kwahl-KOH-zah dee ___ ay ___
sweet	*dolce*	DOHL-chay
semi-sweet ("friendly")	*amabile/abboccato*	ah-MAH-bee-lay/ ah-boh-KAH-toh
semi-dry	*semi-secco*	seh-mee-SEH-koh
(very) dry	*(molto) secco*	(mohl-toh) SEH-koh
light/heavy	*leggero/gustoso*	LEH-jeh-roh/ goo-STOH-zoh
full-bodied	*corposo/pieno*	kor-POH-zoh/ pee-EH-noh

ENGLISH	ITALIAN	PRONOUNCED
young	*giovane*	JOH-vah-nay
old	*vecchio*	VAY-kee-oh
mature	*maturo*	mah-TOO-roh
fruity	*fruttato*	froo-TAH-toh
earthy	*terroso*	teh-ROH-zoh
tannic	*tannico*	TAH-nee-koh
elegant	*elegante*	eh-leh-GAHN-tay
smooth	*morbido*	MOR-bee-doh
sharp	*spigoloso*	spee-goh-LOH-zoh
easy to drink	*facile da bere*	FAH-chee-lay dah beh-ray
complex	*complicato*	kohm-plee-KAH-toh
balanced	*armonico*	ahr-MOH-nee-koh
long finish	*persistente*	pehr-sees-TEHN-tay
fresh, crisp, acidic	*fresco*	FRAY-skoh
flavor	*sapore*	sah-POH-ray
harvest	*vendemmia*	vehn-DAYM-ee-ah
grapes	*uva*	OO-vah
vines	*viti*	VEE-tee

An *enoteca* (wine shop) allows you to sample several local wines before choosing a bottle to buy.

Wine Tourism

Italy affords many opportunities to delve into the wine scene, beyond simply ordering a glass or bottle at dinner.

One of the best ways to explore local wine is to visit an **enoteca** (described on page 33). Sometimes this is simply a wine bar, offering glasses of regional wines paired with light local dishes. Other times it's a wine shop with no food at all. And on occasion—especially when called an *enoteca regionale* or *enoteca pubblica*—it can be an outgrowth of a consortium (*consorzio*) of local wine producers. In addition to being a fine place to sample wine, *enoteche* are also hubs of information for the local wine scene and a good place to seek advice on which vineyards you can visit.

The advantage of an *enoteca* is the chance to enjoy small tastes of the area's very best and most expensive wines. In the past, bottles of fine wine—once opened—had to be finished in short order. But newer technology inserts a needle through the cork to extract small amounts of wine without opening up the entire

bottle. This innovation—which you'll see in use at wine shops around Italy—means that you can treat yourself to a $10 taste of a top-end wine, rather than paying $100 for the entire bottle.

Another good option is to visit a **vineyard** (*vigneto*) to tour the vines and production facility. (While most often the wine is produced on site, in a few cases—such as with Vino Nobile di Montepulciano—the grapes are harvested and taken to another location to make and age the wine.)

Many American travelers are accustomed to the belly-up-to-the-bar, Napa Valley-style tasting room, where you can simply drop in when they're open, perhaps pay a nominal fee to taste a few wines, buy a bottle or two, then head to the next place. These exist in Italy, but they are mainly large or trendy producers, which limits your options.

By contrast, most Italian wineries require a reservation. It's a simple process: Do some homework, establish which wineries you're interested in, and reach out in advance—by phone or email—to set up a time to visit. (Your hotelier might be able to help with this.) These organized visits require a time commitment, as they typically include both an hour-long tour and a deliberate, guided tasting of several wines—often, for a bit more money, paired with local foods, or even an entire meal. But it's also a more personal, in-depth, and memorable experience.

If you're paying for a wine tasting (*degustazione*), you aren't obligated to buy. But if a winery is doing a small tasting just for you, they're hoping you'll buy a bottle or two.

If your goal is to settle into a vineyard-strewn countryside, consider the option of staying at an **agriturismo**—a working farm that also provides services (accommodations, restaurants, etc.) and activities for travelers. Many *agriturismi* produce their own wine and would be eager to show you a (typically less formal) production facility. And they are often located near other wineries, enabling you to efficiently connect several.

Another option is driving the **wine roads** *(strade del vino)* that crisscross major winegrowing areas. These are tourist routes that are well-marked with directional signs and are designed to help you scenically weave together wineries. One nice feature of the wine roads is that they're more likely to include a variety of tasting options, including ones that don't require a reservation. If you're interested in a certain wine area, do some research to see if it has a wine road. (One of Italy's best, most scenic wine roads is in Trentino-Alto Adige, described on page 170.) Keep in mind that Italy has strict blood-alcohol limits for drivers; this is not a place to get caught driving under the influence. (Some wineries offer a "to go" taste for the designated driver to enjoy later.)

You'll be tempted to buy a few bottles (or cases) of your favorites. But be mindful of the hassle and expense of getting these home. In your checked luggage, you're legally allowed just one liter (effectively one bottle) of wine duty-free; after that, you'll pay duty to bring it to the United States. (In my experience, different airports vary as to how carefully they check the number of bottles you're bringing home.)

Depending on where you live, it

may be possible to ship wine to your home. But the shipping and duty costs can be significant, even if the wine itself is well-priced. And rules for importing wine vary by state, so you'll need to do some homework.

As more and more Italian wines are being exported, you may find it's much easier—and, potentially, less expensive—to seek out your favorites once you've returned home. Some wineries work with specific importers in the US, which may be able to ship you some wines domestically. If you find a wine you enjoy in Italy, snap a photo of the label, then swing by your neighborhood wine merchant back home to see if they can order you some bottles (or something similar).

Many smaller winemakers simply don't export—they produce only for local consumption. For this reason, the best plan of all may be to buy a few bottles along the way and savor them as you go—giving you one more reason to return to Italy for the next round.

PART III

Italy, Region by Region

Italy's Regions

Italian food is highly regional. What's on offer in one place can be entirely different from what you'll find 100, 50, or even 10 miles away. While the preceding chapters were designed to give you a 30,000-foot view of Italian food and drink, this section of the book dives deep into each of Italy's many regional cuisines. In other words, it's time to travel as Garibaldi with a fork.

Italy has 20 regions. I've covered each one individually and organized them geographically: the North; Central Italy; the South; and the Islands. (For simplicity, I've merged the smallest region—Valle d'Aosta—in with Piedmont, which nearly surrounds it).

Within each region are a variety of provinces. These are typically administered by and named for the biggest city or town. Because Italian specialties are so intensely local, sometimes I've called out not just the region, but also the province or even the town where you'll find it. (Don't count on finding it in the next town over.)

Each of the following chapters begins with an **introduction**

ITALY'S REGIONS

describing the geography, history, and character of the region—designed to give you a primer on how all those factors have shaped the food and wine.

Here you'll also find a handy **Foods and Drinks to Sample** section—a "must-try" list for food lovers. Of all the specialties, these are the items to prioritize seeking out—the ones that, for Italians, are synonymous with that region.

Then I've listed the region's top **Cities, Towns, and Places.** Some are popular tourist destinations; others are undiscovered gems; and still others are notable mainly, or entirely,

for their role in local food production. (If you couldn't care less about rice production, there's no reason to visit Piedmont's Vercelli; but if you're curious about this industry, it's a fascinating place.)

In his travels, Fred has discovered a favorite town in each region where the local food culture is best expressed. These are often not the big, famous, marquee destinations, so we've called them out as **"Fred's favorites"** for aficionados.

From there, I list the **foods** of that region—course by course—followed by the local **wine** scene.

You may find some repetition

Italy Almanac

Official Name: Repubblica Italiana (Italian Republic).

Locals Call It: Italia.

Size: 116,000 square miles (about the size of New Mexico), including the islands of Sicily, Sardinia, and others. Population is 62 million.

Geography: Italy is shaped like a boot, 850 miles long and 150 miles wide, jutting into the central Mediterranean. (By comparison, the state of Florida is 500 miles long.) The terrain is generally mountainous or hilly, with the Alps in the north and a north-south "spine" of the Apennine Mountains. The highest point is Mont Blanc (15,771 feet), on the border with France. Outside the Alps, the highest point on the peninsula is Corno Grande, in the Apennine Mountains of Abruzzo (9,554 feet). Italy has 5,000 miles of coastline; it's surrounded by the Ligurian Sea to the northwest, the Tyrrhenian Sea to the southwest, the Ionian Sea to the south, and the Adriatic Sea to the east (all sub-sections of the Mediterranean). Major rivers include the Po (the longest at 400 miles), Arno, Adige, and Tiber. Italy has three active volcanoes: Vesuvius, Etna, and Stromboli.

Latitude and Longitude: 43°N and 12°E (similar to Oregon and Maine).

Regions: Italy's 20 regions are subdivided into 107 provinces. At the local level, there are some 8,200 "communes," each with a community council and mayor.

Major Cities: Rome (the capital, 2.8 million), Milan (1.3 million), and Naples (1 million).

Economy: The gross domestic product is $2.3 trillion; the GDP per capita is $38,200. (By comparison, the USA's GDP is around $20 trillion, or $60,000

per capita.) About 74 percent of the economy consists of service jobs (especially tourism), 24 percent is industry (textiles, chemicals), and 2 percent is agriculture (fruit, vegetables, olives, wine, and fishing). There are 12,500 miles of train lines (mostly government-run) and 4,300 miles of expressway *(autostrada)*.

Government: Italy is a republic, with three branches of government. The chief executive is the prime minister. The bicameral legislature is elected by (mostly) direct voting. Since World War II, the fragmented country has had more than 65 national governments.

Italian Inventions: Opera, cologne, thermometer, barometer, pizza, wireless telegraph, espresso machine, typewriter, batteries, nitroglycerin, and yo-yos.

Museums: 3,800.

The Average Gio: The average Italian is 46 years old, has 1.2 kids, is nominally Roman Catholic, and will live to the ripe old age of 82 (1 in 5 Italians is older than 65). Every day, they consume two servings of pasta, a half-pound of bread, and two glasses of wine. Despite Italian cuisine, Gio isn't fat—only 20 percent of Italians are considered obese.

in adjoining regions. For instance, *bollito misto*—a sampler of boiled meats—is common throughout the North, but each region brings its own variations, flavors, and sauces. And in the South, spicy sausages (such as *capocollo* and *soppressata*) and milky cheeses (such as mozzarella, *burrata, scamorza,* and *caciocavallo*) cross regional borders, though each area brings its own flourishes. For these, I've described the dish in the place where it originated, or the place it's most associated with.

By browsing through these chapters, you'll assemble a more complete understanding of the astonishing diversity of food and drink in this one country. And you'll be armed with practical instructions for how to really eat like an Italian. I hope these descriptions will inspire you to go beyond the generic "Italian" dishes that you can always find wherever you go (and, often, even at home)—and venture out to try something you can only find in the place you're visiting.

One last tip: I know how hard it is to destroy a perfectly good book. But if you're traveling with a print edition of this book, please consider **tearing out the pages** of each region as you arrive there and tucking them in your back pocket to help navigate local menus. Why carry around heavy material on Venice, Florence, and Rome when you're out to dinner in Sicily? This book (and especially these regional sections) is a practical tool designed to take your tastebuds on the trip of a lifetime. Use it!

Northern Italy
Piedmont & the Valle d'Aosta

Piemonte

Of all the fine qualities Italy is known for, working hard may not be the first thing that comes to mind. But Italians find great satisfaction in a job well done; in fact, the opening words of the Italian constitution are "Italy is a nation founded and based on work." And Piedmont is Italy's workhorse. This land of factories and laborers is home to automotive, aviation, electronics, manufacturing, and many other industries. From the powerful Agnellis (who own FIAT) to the humblest farmers, the people of Piedmont work hard, save, invest, build, and create; they take great but quiet pride in their endeavors.

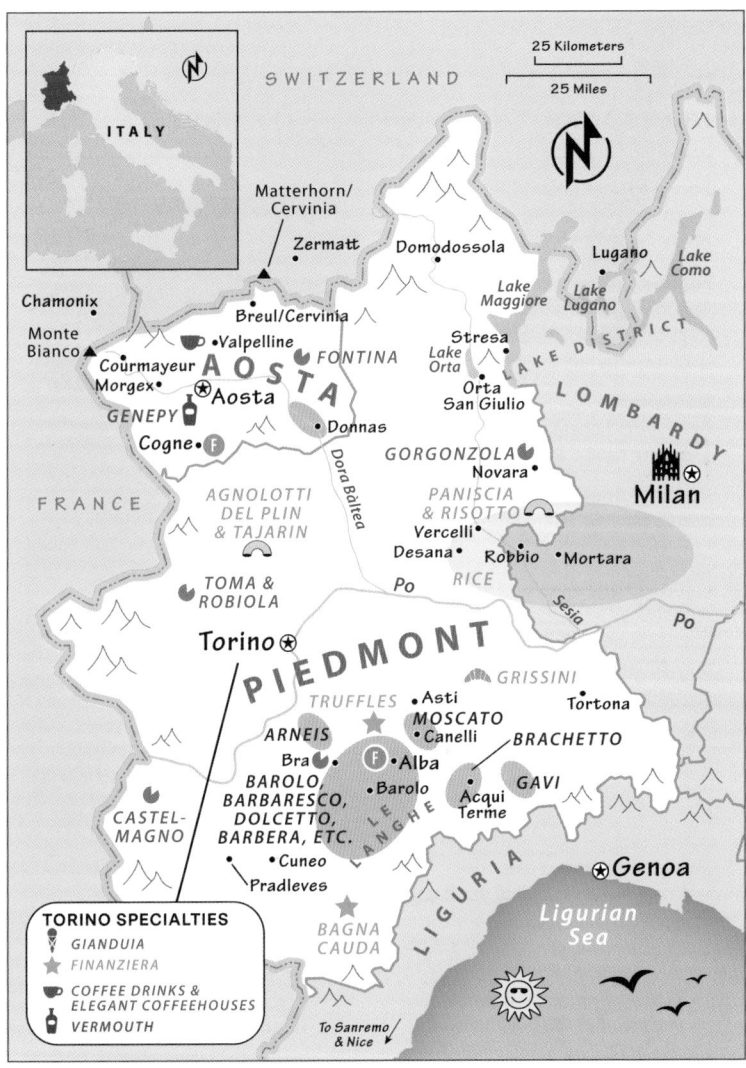

Yes, the *piemontesi* have a reputation among Italians for being workaholics, but that's incomplete: They also know how to derive pleasure from life. The wines of the region are among the best in the world. The terrain yields magnificent truffles and superb fruits and vegetables. The coffee, chocolates, and baked goods of Piedmont are as good as anywhere in Italy. And Piedmont was the birthplace of the now-global Slow Food movement. But because the *piemontesi* do not go out of their way to beat their own drums, Piedmont remains one of this country's least discovered regions—only recently beginning to attract food and wine pilgrims.

🍲 Foods and Drinks to Sample in Piedmont and the Valle d'Aosta

Bagna cauda
Fresh vegetables dipped in olive oil heated with garlic and anchovies.

Fontina
Decadent, buttery-nutty cheese—from the mountains of the Valle d'Aosta—that melts luxuriously.

Gorgonzola
Blue-veined cheese with a powerful, exquisite flavor.

White Truffles
Tartufi bianchi, the most precious (and expensive) truffles, are found near Alba.

Grissini
Italy's satisfyingly crunchy breadsticks originate in Piedmont.

Cioccolatini
Chocolates are a Piedmont forté; look for *gianduia,* a mix of chocolate and hazelnut paste.

Piemontese chocolates

Barolo and Barbaresco
These outstanding red wines—made with the native nebbiolo grape—are two of Italy's very best.

Moscato
This straw-colored grape makes a wonderful sparkling wine *(spumante)* with a fruity bouquet.

Piedmont is Italy's second-largest region (after Sicily). It sits at Italy's northwest corner, where the Alps of France and Switzerland fade into the hills and plains of northern Italy; in fact, "Piemonte" means "foot of the mountains." This variation in terrain creates a diversity of landscapes—but no coastline. (Looking at a map, it appears as if Liguria hogs what should be the Piedmont Riviera.) But no matter; Piedmont is blessed with an abundance of other resources.

The big name in this region's history is Savoy—the royal house that ruled here from the 15th century until 1861, when the Savoys became

the kings of a unified Italy. (Torino was, for a very brief time, the capital of Italy.) The Savoy lands extended from the Monferrato in the eastern part of the region well into territory on the opposite side of the French Alps. Even long after they departed, the Savoys left behind some French taste and style. And, as a royal seat, Torino developed a taste for elegant and elaborate cuisine and presentation that's still evident in restaurants and food stores today.

The other important strain in *piemontese* cuisine is the strong agricultural tradition that gives people an innate understanding of ingredients and their uses. The *piemontesi* produce magnificent wines, of course, and also wheat, corn, rice, and rye; beef, veal, and rabbit; and superb fruits and vegetables. Frogs in the canals that flood the rice paddies are prized in local cooking, and snails are also popular (especially delicious when cooked with Gorgonzola cheese). And the northernmost reaches of the region—and the neighboring Valle d'Aosta—are alpine and full of game.

The provinces of Alba and Asti are rich in white truffles, one of the world's most expensive and luxurious ingredients. (For more on truffles, see page 84.) Hazelnuts, walnuts, and chestnuts are abundant and play a central role in the cuisine of Piedmont, especially in its wonderful desserts. Chocolate and coffee are used with great skill, especially in Torino and Alba.

This chapter also includes the Valle d'Aosta. The smallest and least populous of Italy's 20 regions, this high alpine valley is tucked between Piedmont, France, and Switzerland. The Valle d'Aosta is the rooftop of

Europe, formed by chains of snow-capped Alps—Monte Bianco (Mont Blanc), Cervinia (the Matterhorn), and Monte Rosa tower over the region. Much of Aosta is occupied by the nation's largest natural reserve, Gran Paradiso National Park, which was once the Savoys' royal hunting ground. Aosta is fully bilingual; the culture is a mix of Italian and French, while the cuisine takes on a mountain flavor—best represented by the luxurious Fontina cheese that's beloved throughout Piedmont and northern Italy.

Courmayeur, in the Valle d'Aosta

🗺 CITIES, TOWNS, AND PLACES

Torino (pop. 840,000, with a metro area of over two million; sometimes called Turin in English) is Piedmont's capital and biggest city. While it briefly entered the world's awareness as host of the 2006 Winter Olympics, Torino flies surprisingly under the radar for such a big and beautiful Italian metropolis—it rivals Bologna as Italy's most underrated big city. Torino blossomed much later than most other Italian cities, in the 19th century (as the Savoy capital), which gives it a certain Parisian or Viennese feel. To this day, Torino's elegant coffeehouses set the standard for Italy, and the city is also known for its chocolates. And yet, Torino is also unmistakably modern. Its factories have attracted "internal immigrants" from throughout Italy, not to mention migrant workers from farther afield, giving it an urban eclecticism.

For an enticing look at Torino's food scene, go for a stroll down Via Lagrange, not far from the train station. While this was once almost exclusively a food thoroughfare, now many storefronts host clothing boutiques and trendy shops. For a more classic part of town—offering a peek into Torino from a century ago—browse the old shops along Via San Tommaso and Via Barbaroux, near Piazza Castello.

Alba (pop. 30,000) is Fred's favorite in Piedmont. This is the principal town of the Langhe, an

Above: Piazza San Carlo, Torino; **Below:** Torino skyline

area with sweetly rolling slopes that produce excellent wine, cheese, and truffles in a beautiful setting. Alba is home to Italy's largest truffle market, but otherwise it remains a contented small community that conserves much of the best of Piedmont. Make a point to wander down the Via Vittorio Emanuele, with an assortment of characteristic shops; if you can't hit your truffle quota here, you're truly insatiable.

Cuneo (pop. 55,000) is the leading town of the zone that many aficionados believe produces Italy's very best wines. And it has great charm and real gastronomic interest in its own right. Cuneo has lively markets, top-quality food stores, excellent produce (including peppers and other vegetables), and warm, easygoing locals who buck the Piedmont trend for being a bit reserved and formal.

Between Cuneo and Torino— easy for a day trip by train—is **Bra** (pop. 30,000), with the home offices of the Slow Food movement, plus a delicious namesake cheese and a delicate sausage.

Asti (pop. 75,000) is synonymous with Italy's most famous sparkling wine, Asti Spumante, and it also has an outstanding market. On Wednesday and Saturday mornings, the Campo del Palio and adjoining squares fill with hundreds of vendors of all kinds of food, seeds, flowers, clothes, shoes, housewares, and just about anything you can carry home. The city is also known for the Palio di Asti, a spirited horse race dripping with pageantry held each September (it's even older than Siena's more famous Palio).

Vercelli (pop. 45,000) is Europe's largest rice market and home to the commodity exchange for rice in Europe. On Tuesday and Friday mornings on the Piazza Ernesto Zumaglini, rice farmers gather to buy and sell machinery, seeds, and other rice-related products. Leaving town, look out across the flat landscape to see the rice fields that locals call the *mare a quadretti*—"sea divided into squares." Those squares change through the seasons: dry land is flooded, then produces green spouts that eventually grow tall and golden. Then, in the autumn, fog enshrouds the area, giving way to a winter stillness before the cycle begins again.

Midway between Torino and Milan, **Novara** (pop. 105,000) is a good example of a provincial capital whose citizens live quietly and well. Local chefs do excellent *risotti* and a similar local dish, *paniscia*. And Novara has become the chief production center for Gorgonzola cheese—invented in Lombardy, but perfected here.

To the north of Piedmont, the Valle d'Aosta only has one real city, **Aosta** (pop. 35,000). Aosta is a hub for the various lifts, hiking trails, ski runs, and mountain sports in the surrounding region, with a few Roman ruins to boot.

To get out of the city, **Courmayeur** is a small ski resort on the sunny side of Mont Blanc— Europe's highest mountain—and a popular stopover on the Tour de Mont Blanc hiking route around its base. While it has gone upscale, that means it has high-end food stores and a good selection for curious tourists. For a more characteristic spot, head to **Cogne,** a smaller, friendly former mining town in the middle of Gran Paradiso National Park, the former hunting grounds of the royal family of Savoy. With many good restaurants and ample charm, Cogne is a good place to unwind in nature.

🍴 FOODS OF PIEDMONT

Owing to its historic connections to France and its temperate climate, Piedmont's cuisine tends to be elevated, dairy-forward, and decadent. Think lots of creamy sauces and the liberal use of butter instead of olive oil. Cheeses are a local forté (especially Gorgonzola and, from nearby Valle d'Aosta, Fontina); the aroma of truffles hangs in the air; and all kinds of vegetables are served raw, cooked, or preserved in oil or vinegar. Similar to other northern regions, Piedmont's food also tends to make ample use of rice from paddies found along the border with Lombardy.

ANTIPASTI (APPETIZERS)

Bagna cauda (or **bagna caoda**)	In this classic *antipasto,* olive oil is heated with garlic, anchovies, and occasionally a bit of truffle, and used as a dip for fresh vegetables (especially artichoke-like cardoons, fennel, and sweet red and yellow peppers).
Caponet	Zucchini flowers or cabbage stuffed with ground beef, sausage, eggs, parsley, garlic, and Parmigiano-Reggiano, then dipped in eggs and sautéed in butter.
Carne cruda	Raw veal that is sliced very thin or chopped, and served with oil, salt, pepper, and lemon.
Grissini	Italy's famous breadsticks are native to Piedmont. They're traditionally hand-rolled. If you expect stubby little sticks, you're in for a surprise; *grissini* made in bakeries or homes can be the length of a small table.
Insalata di riso	"Rice salad" with chopped fresh vegetables, and usually meat and cheese, that's served cold and is popular in summer.
Lardo	Delicately sliced, herb-scented lard.

Left: *Bagna cauda;* **Right:** *Grissini*

Left: *Agnolotti* being freshly made; **Right:** *Tajarin*

Salame della duia (or ***salame d'la doja***)	A soft *salame* that is preserved in lard, a specialty of Novara.
Tortini	Vegetables combined with cheese and baked as little cakes.

PRIMI (PASTAS AND OTHER FIRST COURSES)

Agnolotti	Folded and filled pasta, typically stuffed with meat, but also sometimes with vegetables or cheese. ***Agnolotti del plin,*** from Alba and the Langhe, are tiny and often served with melted butter and truffles.
Cisrà	Chickpea soup.
Gnocchi alla bava	Potato dumplings with melted cheese.
Paniscia (or ***panissa***)	Typical of Novara and Vercelli, this is a rice dish that's drier than *risotto* and contains sausages, beans, and vegetables—whatever's in the pantry. In the Valle d'Aosta, this combination appears in a more souplike form.
Risotto	Various Piedmont versions come with numerous ingredients, such as saffron or mushrooms, vegetables, fish, frogs, cheeses (including Gorgonzola), or wine (including Barolo). (For more on *risotto,* see page 75.)
Tajarin (or ***taglierini***)	Very thin noodles made with egg yolk, giving them a distinct yellow hue and a rich flavor.
Tofeja	Pork-rind-and-bean soup.

Fontina: The Mountain Cheese of the Valle d'Aosta

Fontina is not only the most famous product of the Valle d'Aosta, but it's also one of the finest cheeses made in Italy—with an addictive, unique, buttery-nutty flavor and a smooth, easy-melting texture. Fontina, which has been made for seven centuries, is excellent eaten by itself, and it's also melted to make fondue *(fonduta)* and all sorts of sauces.

Each year, the Valle d'Aosta produces about eight million pounds of Fontina, 97 percent of which is consumed in Italy (mostly in the North and center). "Fontina" found internationally (including in the United States) is often an imitation made elsewhere, particularly in Scandinavia. (Scandinavian cheese has a red rind, while real Fontina has a light brown rind.)

The cheese has a subtly different flavor depending on when it was produced. From June to early October, the cows graze in high meadows, giving the cheese slightly higher fat content; the rest of the year, the cows are barned in the valley and eat hay.

The people of the Valle d'Aosta like fresh, young cheese that still tastes of milk. Fontina typically matures for three months, then is eaten quickly. A local saying goes: *Il formaggio fresco ha tre fondamentali qualità: toglie la fame, la sete, e lava i denti.* ("Fresh cheese has three fundamental qualities: It cuts hunger, it cuts thirst, and it washes the teeth.") But some older locals do age Fontina and use it for grating.

Left: *Brasato* with polenta; **Right:** *Vitello tonnato*

SECONDI (MAIN DISHES)

Bollito misto	In this classic dish of the North, a variety of meats—up to seven types—are boiled and served with local sauces (see below).
Brasato	Beef or veal that's braised in wine over a small flame for many hours. Usually one of Piedmont's fine wines is used (such as **brasato al Barolo**).
Fassona	This local Piedmont cow produces a tender beef that's much prized, and often featured in local recipes.
Finanziera	This sauce, a specialty of Torino, was named for bankers and financiers. It's made with chicken livers and gizzards, cockscombs, *porcini* mushrooms, minced veal, and Marsala wine, and often served with soufflés.
Fritto misto (also called *fritto misto all'italiana*)	A platter of fried foods, including calf's liver, sweetbreads, brains, veal cutlet, baby lamb chops, sausage, zucchini, eggplant, artichokes, apples, pears, bananas, grapes, and semolina fritters.
Grive	Meatballs made with calf's brains, pork liver, nutmeg, breadcrumbs, cheeses, eggs, and juniper berries.
Sauces	Piedmont often serves a sauce called **bagnet** with meats, eggs, or fish. A **bagnet verd** has a base of chopped parsley and includes olive oil, anchovies, breadcrumbs, garlic, and lemon or vinegar. A **bagnet ross** is made with tomatoes, basil, sweet red peppers, onions, and garlic. **Cognà** (or **cugnà**) is a sauce of pickled fruit, particularly grapes.
Stracotto	Very slowly cooked beef.
Vitello tonnato	Roast veal is chilled, sliced paper-thin, and topped with a sauce of puréed tuna, capers, and other flavors.

Left: Gorgonzola; **Right:** Tomini

FORMAGGI (CHEESES)

Bra	An ancient cheese, typical of the town of Bra, made with cow's milk, often mixed with sheep's and goat's milk. It can be eaten young or aged (and sharper).
Castelmagno	Cow's-milk cheese, produced in the village of Pradleves, that graced the tables of kings from Charlemagne to Vittorio Emanuele II. Its powerful flavor goes well with gnocchi, *risotto,* and in many other preparations.
Gorgonzola	This famous, blue-veined cheese has a powerful, exquisite flavor. The presence of mold may deter timid eaters, but that's a shame; that mold just adds to the complex taste. It comes either as the gold-colored *dolce* (sweet) or the sharper-tasting *piccante,* which is whiter. Gorgonzola pairs especially well with pears and walnuts, and a delicious *risotto* can be made using only these three ingredients. While it originated in Lombardy, now most Gorgonzola is produced in Novara, Piedmont.
Murazzano	A specialty of the Langhe, made either of sheep's milk or a blend of sheep's and cow's milk.
Raschera	An alpine cheese made of cow's milk, sometimes mixed with sheep's milk; it's sharp when aged.
Robiola	A cheese of ancient origins. There are a few varieties—in Piedmont, Valle d'Aosta, and Lombardy—each one wonderfully rich and creamy; when aged, it becomes firmer and a bit piquant.
Toma	A generic term for a whole group of cheeses that are made through-out Piedmont and the Valle d'Aosta, usually made with cow's or goat's milk and named for their place of origin—for example, ***toma della Val di Susa*** or ***toma di Pesio***. Many tend to be white to golden and have a gold crust.
Tomini	Little soft cheeses, often made with goat's milk and marinated in olive oil, pepper, and herbs.

DOLCI (SWEETS)

Torta di nocciola	Hazelnut cake.
Baci di dama	Sandwich cookies of almonds or hazelnuts with a chocolate filling. Some *baci* are made with red wine, too.
Amaretti, albesi, and *astigiane*	Macaroons, many flavored with wine, rum, or other liqueurs.
Pesche ripiene	Fabulously flavorful peaches filled with a stuffing of cocoa, sugar, eggs, and *amaretti*.
Pere cotte al vino	Pears cooked slowly in Barolo or another fine wine.
Cioccolatini	Piedmont makes a vast assortment of chocolates, but **gianduia** (a mix of chocolate with hazelnut paste) is the most famous. This combination originated in Napoleonic times, when chocolate was difficult to come by, so local chocolatiers mixed a paste of locally produced, high-quality hazelnut with their limited cocoa supply. **Gianduiotti** are little gold-wrapped pieces of *gianduia*.
Bonèt	A delicate custard or pudding usually containing chocolate, which may also feature flavors such as coffee, almond, or hazelnut.

Left: *Bonèt;* **Right:** *Baci di dama*

♀ WINES OF PIEDMONT

Piedmont's wines are known for their high quality and the fact that most are produced on small family estates. The region's compact wine-growing area boasts 42 DOC wines and a whopping 18 DOCG wines. Among Piedmont's outstanding wines, **Barolo** and **Barbaresco** are particularly revered. The best wines come from the hilly Le Langhe area, just south of Alba, where vineyards cover slopes crested by hill towns like Serralunga d'Alba. Piedmont's wines are shaped by altitude, exposure, soil type, and the morning fog that often blankets the hills—in fact, the name of the dominant grape, nebbiolo, comes from the Italian word for fog *(nebbia).*

Many Piedmont wines are named for the grapes from which they're made. Here are some to look for:

Barbera The most popular native grape in Piedmont, at least in terms of quantity. It's ruby red and can be quite acidic when young. As it ages, it smooths somewhat and develops orange glints in its color.

Dolcetto Another native grape (although Ligurians say it was originally theirs), dolcetto makes a very popular, fruity, slightly tannic, medium-weight red wine. Even though the name means "the little sweet one," it's decidedly not sweet.

Nebbiolo While sangiovese is the backbone of Chianti in Tuscany, nebbiolo is the grape that makes most of Piedmont's top wines—including famous wines like Barolo and Barbaresco. Both are produced in limited quantities and can be quite expensive. **Barolo**—which some consider Italy's very best red—is a "big" wine that can overwhelm lighter fare; it needs a hearty meat dish or strong cheese to stand up to its tannins. Aged a minimum of three years (18 months in oak barrels and 18 months in the bottle), this is a wine for a special occasion. Some prefer the more approachable **Barbaresco,** which is full-bodied but lighter and usually more affordable. Subregions in this area produce similar wines from nebbiolo grapes (sometimes called spanna), like Ghemme and Gattinara.

White Wines The three leading native white-grape wines are **Cortese di Gavi** (acidic and similar to pinot grigio); **Arneis di Roero,** a crisp, medium-body wine that pairs well with crab or lobster; and **Erbaluce.**

Sparkling Wines Moscato is a straw-colored sweet grape that yields the hugely popular sparkling wine (often called *spumante*) produced in Asti and Canelli. Unfortunately—as with Emilia-Romagna's over-production of low-quality Lambrusco— some sickly sweet "Asti Spumante" gave these wines a bad reputation, leaving the impression that spumante is just sugar water. But genuine moscato wine smells like a basket of flowers or a bowl of fresh peaches and apricots; it's a pleasing way to end a meal. **Brachetto** is a light, slightly red sparkling wine with strawberry notes from Acqui Terme that's popular as an *aperitivo*. It matches particularly well with chocolate—an unusual taste sensation.

Vermouth This native drink of Piedmont, originally produced for medicinal purposes, is an aromatic fortified wine flavored with a blend of herbs and spices including juniper, cloves, and cinnamon. The name comes from the German *Wermut* (wormwood)—one of the original ingredients, also used in absinthe. Vermouth ranges in taste from sweet to very dry and in color from clear (mainly French varieties like Noilly Prat) to the rosy hues of Italian vermouths (Cinzano, Carpano, and Martini & Rossi are major produc- ers). It can be consumed straight as an *aperitivo* on the rocks with a twist of lemon, but it's most often a building block for cocktails like the martini, Manhattan, or Negroni (an Italian classic made from equal parts gin, Campari, and vermouth).

Rustic polenta-making in the Valle d'Aosta

⽷ FOODS AND WINES OF THE VALLE D'AOSTA

This little mountain region's cuisine is simple. Milk from cows—who graze on high-altitude summer meadows—is used to make butter, cream, and various cheeses, particularly **Fontina** (described earlier in this chapter). These milky flavors form a soothing canvas on which other regional ingredients can play a leading role: wild mushrooms, game, beef, blueberries, raspberries, chestnuts, apples, pears, honey, and herbs. There's also good freshwater fish from rivers and lakes, and even these are sometimes cooked with cheese.

Antipasti Most common are hams and sausages: *mocetta* (leg of veal, chamois, moun-tain goat, or ibex, cured like prosciutto); *prosciutto di San Marcel* (made with 18 aro-matic alpine herbs); prosciutto from St-Rhémy-en-Bosses (sweet, delicious, and hard to come by); *lardo d'Arnad* (lard with herbs); *boudin* (blood sausage filled with beets, potato, lard, and spices; especially good from Morgex); *tetetta* or *teteun* (cow's udder, cooked and sliced thin); and typical sausages made of beef, pork, red wine, and garlic.

Primi More than in most Italian regions, soup (locally called *seuppa* or *seuppetta*) is an important first course. Most are made with bread, broth, vegetables, and cheese. *Zuppa di castagne*, made with chestnuts and rice boiled in milk, is popular in the autumn; in the winter, many soups are made with a milk base. There are also a few non-soup options: Fontina cheese is melted with crêpes or gnocchi, or it can be melted into polenta while it cooks *(polenta concia)*. The most popular pasta is the thin egg noodle called *tajarin* (or *taglierini*).

Secondi The classic local meat dish is *carbonada,* salted rump steak slow-cooked with onions, butter, bacon, cinnamon, salt, pepper, and wine, served with polenta. *Cotoletta alla valdostana* is a veal cutlet dipped in egg and breadcrumbs, fried in butter, and then finished with a slice of prosciutto and a layer of melted Fontina. Game is popular, including *capriolo* (venison) browned in grappa and cooked with fresh tomatoes. *Camoscio* (chamois) is ubiquitous, as is *capretto* (kid).

Other Flavors Apples, pears, and wild berries find their way into jams and desserts, and often serve as flavorings for the meat course. The region produces excellent honey, since the bees have quite a flavor palette to draw from: *millefiori* (a thousand flowers), raspberries, blueberries, and chestnuts. Speaking of chestnuts, these were once known as *il pane del bosco* (the bread of the forest) because the poor could forage them and grind them up to use as flour; it's still a predominant flavor in the region's cuisine. Mountain herbs are used sparingly in local cooking, but they do appear in omelets and are used for curing prosciutto. Rye flour is used to make various breads, usually designated as *pane nero* (black bread). In addition to Fontina, other cheeses include cow's-milk *toma* (easily digested and low in fat) and goat's-milk *robiola* and *tomini.* And walnut oil is considered a delicacy, both locally and when exported to neighboring France.

Wine At nearly 3,000 feet, the vineyards of the Valle d'Aosta are the highest in Europe. Local vintners *(vignerons)* have learned to grow grapes among stones arranged just so, to reflect light and heat toward the plants. But it's a tough place to cultivate grapes, and supply is limited, so prices are high. Red wines from near the border of Piedmont are often based on clones of nebbiolo. Donnas, Arvier, and Chambave are the leading towns for red wines, while Muscat de Chambave *(moscato bianco)* and Blanc de Morgex are the best-known whites. The most popular strong alcoholic beverage is Genepy, a juniper-berry distillate with a light gold color.

La Grolla The favorite après-ski custom is to sip a *caffè valdostano* (or *café à la valdôtaine*)—a combination of coffee, locally made grappa, and sugar, often served in a *grolla,* a wooden chalice with a spout. Historically this goes back to ancient times, when the hand-carved, maple-wood vessel might have two, four, six, or even eight spouts. Replicas of these are popular item in souvenir shops, and some bars and refuges in ski areas offer a multispouted *grolla* filled with spiked coffee.

Left: Various *salumi* from the Valle d'Aosta;
Right: Hiking above Courmayeur

Milan & Lombardy

Lombardia

Italy's most populous region is also its financial powerhouse. Not only does Lombardy make money through industrial production and banking, but also in agriculture, with by far the highest yields per acre of anywhere in Italy. And Milan—Italy's second city—is the de facto capital of the North and the trendsetter for the entire country. It's almost as if nobody bothered to tell Milan that it's not the capital of Italy... and it might not matter much if they did.

Milan is home to nearly all of Italy's major publishing houses and newspapers, such that Milanese opinion sets the terms of national debate. La Scala Opera House has been the Italian national stage since 1778, and in the 19th century, it was the place from where Verdi led the drive for Italian unification. Milan is the fashion and design capital of Italy (if not the world)—the place where innovators with names like Armani and Versace contribute to the ongoing effort to challenge

MILAN SPECIALTIES
- RISOTTO ALLA MILANESE
- COTOLETTA ALLA MILANESE & OSSOBUCO
- PANETTONE
- CAMPARI, APEROL & RAMAZZOTTI

perspective. Milan is also a great academic center, a pioneer in medicine, and a hotbed of political activity (not always a good thing; for a time in the 1990s, it became associated with Tangentopoli—"City of Bribes," a judicial investigation into political corruption). The city is a magnet for the best, the brightest, and the most elegant.

While only the fourth-biggest Italian region by area, Lombardy has more than 10 million residents—on par with entire countries (Hungary, Austria, two Irelands). One in six Italians is a Lombard. Within two hours of Milan in any direction is an amazing range of climates, terrains, foods, and cultural treasures. And yet, throughout, Lombardy has a

Foods to Sample in Lombardy

Bresaola
Air-dried fillet of beef, sliced
paper-thin.

Cheeses
A Lombard specialty, from
mascarpone (rich, sweet, creamy
dessert cheese) to Gorgonzola
(blue-veined and powerful) to
bitto (mountain cheese from the
Valtellina).

Risotto
This slow-cooked, creamy rice
dish comes in many forms, most
famously *alla milanese*—Milan-style,
with saffron.

Minestrone
Rich vegetable soup, often with
beans and pasta, that comes in
many variations.

Cotoletta alla milanese
Thin veal cutlet pan-fried in
clarified butter.

Ossobuco
Veal shank with lemony sauce; don't
skip the bone marrow.

Ossobuco with *risotto*

remarkable solidity, an inspiring
commitment to excellence, superb
food, and varied and beautiful
scenery. Its many cities are noble
and proud, and the Lombards are
industrious, creative, open, and kind.
The word "Germanic" is often applied
to Lombardy, particularly by other
Italians—who see Lombards as tidy,
organized, and efficiency-minded,
particularly compared to the South.

With so much going on in this
region, it helps to imagine Lombardy
in four horizontal bands:

The southern strip is the heart
of Padania, the rich agricultural
plain of the Po River (which, from
here, extends west to Piedmont, and
east through Emilia-Romagna and
Veneto). The broad fertile fields, the
big old stone houses, and the huge

disks of baled hay form a typical
Padania landscape that's beautiful
and soothing. Cuisine-wise, this is
the "white belt" of Italy, which favors
rice, butter, cheese, and cream.
Lombardy's cheeses are among the
best in Italy, and *risotto* is its classic
primo piatto. But Lombardy also has
many exquisite fresh pastas—including *tortelli di zucca, marubini, cason-
sei,* and *pizzoccheri*—second only to
those of Emilia-Romagna.

The band north of Padania—
through the center of Lombardy—
is the industrial plain that has Milan
as its center. But "industrial" doesn't
necessarily imply "ugly." While some
areas (including the pre-alpine valley
around Milan) suffer air pollution,
there's still much beauty here:
Milan has more green space than just

about any other Italian city. (This title is one of many that Milan vies with Rome to lay claim to.) Here rice transitions to polenta—usually served soft and creamy—as a typical *primo*.

The next band to the north is Italy's beautiful Lake District. Despite the northerly setting (at a latitude similar to that of Montreal), this area's climate is tempered by the lakes, so lemons, olives, and other heat-loving trees and plants make unexpected appearances. The Lombard portion of the district is the largest, including the eastern shore of Lake Maggiore, almost all of Lake Como, and the western shore of Lake Garda.

Finally comes the northernmost band, near the Swiss border, where the Alps ruggedly ripple across the upper fringe of Lombardy (and Italy). Much of this province is called the Valtellina, which feels a world apart from the rest of Lombardy. The *valtellinesi* have the genuine character of hardworking mountain folk—they more resemble people

Lake Como

from neighboring Trentino-Alto Adige than the dynamic Lombards to the south. And the Valtellina also has superb food, including *pizzoccheri, funghi porcini,* game, cheeses, mountain berries, and excellent red wines.

You could spend a week or two just in Lombardy and never tire of its terrain, its cuisine, its people, and its culture. It is economically rich, to be sure, but it's rich in many other ways, too.

CITIES, TOWNS, AND PLACES

Milan (Milano in Italian, pop. 1.3 million, with a metro area swelling to over three million) dominates Lombardy and all of Northern Italy. It boasts splendid architecture, one of Europe's great Gothic cathedrals, excellent museums with world-class artwork, beautiful window displays, elegant cafés, and classic restaurants serving a traditional cuisine. But considering its huge size, it's relatively untrampled by tourists; it's a city largely for the *milanesi.*

The city has several signature dishes that are worth trying, from the saffron-infused *risotto alla milanese* to *ossobuco,* heavenly veal shank. And, more than any other place

in Italy, Milan feels like an international, cosmopolitan city—one that looks beyond borders. That means you'll find a far wider variety of international foods here, as well as restaurants featuring regional cuisine from other parts of Italy (especially Tuscany, Sicily, and Piedmont) as if it were from a faraway land.

In general, it's smart to book ahead at Milan's restaurants. Sit-down restaurant prices are quite high, but Milan's hundreds of trendy bars, delis, and self-service cafeterias cater to people with taste who want an affordable, relatively quick meal. The *paninoteca*—a sandwich shop for office drones needing a bite on

The Frog Lady of Robbio

Many years ago, in the rice paddies *(risaie)* just outside the town of Robbio, Fred met a salt-of-the-earth elderly woman who called herself the Frog Lady of Robbio. On a steamy summer's day, she wore a broad straw hat and a large apron that she folded up around her waist. She carried a long pole with a short string that she dipped into the water. Imitating frog noises, she attracted her prey in short order, yanked it from the canal, and, as she sang a little song in dialect, broke its neck and dropped it into her apron. As her catch grew, so did her smile.

This is a prime example of *la civiltà contadina*—the disappearing world of rural peasant life. It's striking how quickly some of these centuries-old traditions have faded in recent years.

Once upon a time, rice cultivation was backbreaking work that required manual labor. Over the course of the rice-growing season, the paddies are periodically flooded, using a series of canals. This creates an ideal environment for gigantic mosquitoes, and one of the natural predators of the mosquito is the frog—which rice farmers were glad to have breeding in the canals. In the impoverished past, any source of protein was valuable, so naturally frogs were hunted and became an important part of the cuisine of Pavia province.

Over time, as the modern world reached places like Pavia, frog catching faded out of vogue. This led to a spike in the frog population so great that frogs would leave the crowded canals and wind up getting run over by cars at night. The next morning, ravens and other birds were frequently killed as they swooped down to eat flattened frogs, only to be run over by cars themselves.

But change comes on many fronts at once. And the frog problem solved itself as rice cultivation became more mechanized: Rice growers used more chemicals in their work, which in turn caused the frog population to decline at the same precipitous rate as the frog catchers. Now frogs are rare—not just squashed on roads, but even in the rice paddy canals. Meanwhile, as this supply dwindled, the culinary demand for frogs increased—not only in Pavia, but also on fancy tables in Milan and Torino. Frogs are harder than ever to find, and their prices have skyrocketed.

This is a story that repeats itself throughout Italy, particularly regarding its *cucina povera* ("cuisine of the poor") of ages past: A food that was once eaten as an inexpensive, abundant staple of the poor has now become a luxury item. Elsewhere in Italy, truffles and *bottarga* (tuna or mullet caviar) were originally eaten by poor people who had few alternatives for filling empty bellies.

The Frog Lady of Robbio did not know of fancy restaurants in big cities, but merely trudged out to her waterway out of centuries of tradition. It's unlikely that, all these years later, she's still out there catching frogs. And perhaps her methods have been lost, too. But who knows? Perhaps her grandchildren, or great-grandchildren, will rediscover the art of frog catching as a lucrative side hustle.

the run—was invented in Milan. The *milanesi* have refined tastes: Cheese comes gift-wrapped, upscale lunch spots manage to be both fast and elegant, and upscale *rosticcerie* cater to gourmet non-cooks rushing home with something exquisite to serve their family. The *milanesi* also adore their *aperitivo* custom of enjoying an après-work, pre-dinner cocktail with snacks. You'll see the *milanesi* hanging out, clutching their bright-orange glasses of Aperol *spritz* and Campari *spritz*. And, while Campari made its debut in Milan, a simple glass of vino bianco or Prosecco is nearly as popular.

There are so many other Lombard cities and towns—too many to cover thoroughly here. But here are a few highlights, with an emphasis on places that have their own distinctive cuisines.

In the Padania area south of Milan, **Pavia** (pop. 73,000) is home to one of Italy's top universities. There are two Pavias: the town center around Piazza Vittoria, where elegantly dressed people nurse cocktails and delicate finger sandwiches at genteel cafés; and the Borgo,

Top: Galleria Vittorio Emanuele II, Milan;
Bottom: Ponte Coperto, Pavia

across the Ticino River, where locals huddle in rustic *osterie* to dig into hearty plates of *risotto,* frogs, river fish, and meat. (For more on the culinary connection between rice and frogs in Pavia—and the nearby town of Robbio—see the sidebar.)

Mortara (pop. 15,000), near the Piedmont border, is a center of rice production. Its cuisine has been shaped by the influence of the Jewish people who lived here, who replaced pork in many recipes with goose.

Cremona (pop. 73,000), on the Po River facing Emilia-Romagna, is

Fred's favorite town in Lombardy. It has a rich musical tradition (home to great composers, pop stars, and Stradivarius violins), and is surrounded by remarkably fertile farm fields and pastures. Cows dot the countryside—raised both for meat and for dairy. Fitting for its name, Cremona is one of the country's most important milk producers; you could think of it as Italy's Wisconsin. Cremonese cuisine also makes liberal use of *mostarda* (fruits pickled with mustard seed), and it's one of the best places to try the nougat treat *torrone*.

Mantova (or Mantua in English, pop. 48,000) sits at the intersection of Lombardy, Veneto, and Emilia-Romagna. This Renaissance gem rises up from flat plains and wetlands, which have helped it produce a unique cuisine that mingles elements of the regions it straddles. A stroll down Via Pescherie—once lined with fish stalls, for which it's named—is a delightful way to experience the town's many fine food shops.

Moving north, you reach Italy's **Lake District.** In this land of lakes, the million-euro question is: Which one? For the best mix of accessibility, scenery, and offbeatness, **Lake Como** is hard to resist; the sleepy village of Varenna is mellow and user-friendly, but Bellagio and Menaggio

Above: Gardens of Villa del Balbianello, Lake Como; **Below:** Mantova

also have their charms (and crowds). **Lake Maggiore** and **Lake Garda** are other dreamy destinations where you can get a full dose of Italian-lakes wonder and aristocratic-old-days romance.

Farther north still is the high-alpine part of Lombardy, called the **Valtellina** (the "Valley of Teglio"). While Italy's Dolomites—to the east, in Trentino-Alto Adige—are better known, the Valtellina also has beautiful scenery; skiing in the winter and hiking in the summer are wonderful. Lombardy's Alps have been blessed with natural splendor but assaulted by mud slides, avalanches, and a soil much less generous than in the rest of the region. **Sondrio** (pop. 22,000) is the capital of the Valtellina, but Fred favors **Chiavenna** (pop. 7,000), a historic town scenically situated along the Mera River. From here, a bus runs up to the delightful small town of **Madesimo,** high in the mountains at the Swiss border.

🍴 FOODS OF LOMBARDY

Depending on exactly where you are in Lombardy, dominant components include dairy (especially cheese), rice, polenta, big flavors, and rich sauces. But given the region's size and variety, you'll find many different cuisines in its various pockets. Milan is where many of these elements come together, along with a hearty serving of flavors from across Italy and around the world—and some local specialties all its own.

ANTIPASTI (APPETIZERS)

Bresaola	Air-dried fillet of beef, a mountain specialty from the Valtellina. It's sliced paper-thin and often served with shards of Parmigiano-Reggiano and chopped greens such as arugula.
Oca	Goose is a specialty of the rice-producing city of Mortara. It can be made as a *salame* or prosciutto; goose breast can also be smoked.
Salame	Lombardy has various *salame* specialties, including **salame mantovano** (from Mantova; lightly garlicky, crumbly, delicious in *risotto*), **salame di Varzi** (from the Staffora Valley in Pavia province; sweet, long-aged, and often infused with red wine), and **salame milanese** (from Milan; fine-grained, made of pork, garlic, and spices).
Sciatt	Folded buckwheat fritters filled with *bitto* cheese, then cooked with butter and grappa (from the Valtellina).
Violino di capra/ camoscio	Similar to *bresaola,* but made with goat/chamois.

Left: *Bresaola;* **Right:** *Salame*

Left: *Pizzoccheri;* **Right:** *Casoncelli*

PRIMI (PASTAS AND OTHER FIRST COURSES)

In most regions, one of the four main *primi*—pasta, *risotto*, polenta, soup—dominates. But in Lombardy, you'll find all four. In general, *risotto* is found in the central, southern, and western areas (naturally, close to the rice paddies), while polenta predominates in the east and north. Polenta can be served either as a *primo* or as a *contorno;* **polenta taragna** is soft polenta with melted cheese and butter.

Agnoli	Meat-filled pasta typical of Mantova.
Busecca	Milanese tripe soup, with vegetables, tomato sauce, butter, and white beans, topped with grated Parmigiano-Reggiano.
Casoncelli (also *casonsei* or *casunsei*)	Folded pasta filled with beef, veal, pork, or sausage plus spinach, potatoes, *mortadella,* and Parmigiano-Reggiano or *grana.* Served either in rich broth or with melted butter, these are found mainly in eastern Lombardy.
Insalata di riso	This "rice salad" with vegetables—and occasionally meat—is served cold and popular in the summer; it's eaten across the North, but it's especially popular here.
Marubini	*Tortelli* filled with braised beef, roast pork, roast veal, *grana* cheese, and eggs (from Cremona).
Minestrone	A rich vegetable soup with greens, beans, legumes, and pasta. There are seasonal variations, but it's always satisfying, because the cooks of Lombardy emphasize variety as well as freshness in selecting the ingredients.
Pizzoccheri	A pasta dish from the Valtellina made with buckwheat noodles, boiled potatoes, Savoy cabbage, garlic, and lots of melty *bitto* cheese.
Ris e verz	Rice-and-cabbage soup.

Riso al salto	Leftover *risotto alla milanese* (see below) is pan-fried with butter to make a tasty, crunchy *primo*.
Risotto alla certosina	This specialty from Certosa (near Pavia) is made with frog's legs, perch fillets, and vegetables.
Risotto alla milanese	Classic *risotto* flavored with saffron, which gives it an intense yellow color. The subtle flavor of the saffron pairs nicely with the veal shanks of *ossobuco* (see later).
Tortelli	Folded pasta filled with different ingredients depending on the town you're in and the preferences of the cook. Many *tortelli* are filled with meat, cheese, potatoes, or green vegetables. Typically, *tortelli* are served with melted sweet butter, grated Parmigiano-Reggiano or *grana,* and occasionally a few sage leaves. The particularly exquisite **tortelli di zucca** are a specialty of Mantova and Cremona. They are made with pumpkin or orange squash (Mantova has its own special pumpkin, called *zucca mantovana*), plus ground *amaretti* cookies and *mostarda.*
Zuppa pavese	Broth with toast floating on top; a raw egg is cracked on the toast and gradually cooks in the broth. This soup was created in 1525 to give strength to Francis I in the Battle of Pavia, which was under French rule. The French lost to Spain, but the soup survived.

SECONDI (MAIN DISHES)

Asparagi alla milanese	Boiled asparagus topped with a fried egg and grated Parmigiano-Reggiano.
Bocconcini di vitello	Chunks of veal cooked in white wine with onions, peas, and sometimes mushrooms.
Bollito misto	A cart of assorted boiled meats, usually including beef, veal, tongue, pork, and sausages. Served with *mostarda* (see later) and various sauces, and common throughout the North.
Cassoeula	A hearty, stew-like Milanese dish of pork (typically spareribs, pork belly sausage, and other parts), Savoy cabbage, and vegetables. It's served with polenta.
Cotoletta (or *costoletta*) *alla milanese*	A thin, delicate veal cutlet (or sometimes chop) dipped in egg and bread crumbs and sautéed in clarified butter. While this is often imitated throughout Italy, the genuine article in Milan is delicious. Some places have supersized it and call it *orecchia di elefante,* an "elephant's ear" (large enough to share).
Lavarello	A lake whitefish, popular on menus in the Lake District.
Luccio in salsa	Pike in a piquant green herb sauce, a specialty of Mantova.
Lumache	Snails, prepared in many ways.

Left: *Cassoeula;* **Right:** *Ossobuco* with *gremolata*

Missoltino (or ***missultitt***)	This Lake Como specialty is made from salted little dried fish (typically shad), often served with pasta or local-style polenta (buckwheat is mixed in with the corn).
Mondeghili	Cabbage filled with minced veal, potatoes, Parmigiano-Reggiano, and nutmeg.
Nervetti	Chilled, boiled calf's foot—a rustic specialty.
Ossobuco	Veal shank (shin) cooked very slowly and served with ***gremolata*** (a sauce of lemon peel, garlic, and parsley). The name translates to "hole in the bone"—the prized marrow, extracted with special little forks, is considered the best part of the meal. Save it for last.
Rane	Frogs. More precisely, this refers to frog's legs, often called *cosce di rana.*
Rostín Negàa	Veal chops and potatoes baked for four hours in white wine.

FORMAGGI (CHEESES)

If I had to choose just one region as the source for all my cheese, it would be Lombardy. The exquisite richness and variety of Lombardy's cheeses give special flavor and character to its cuisine.

Bel Paese	This very mild cheese, widely used throughout Italy and internationally, has been industrially made in Lombardy since 1906. Mild and creamy, it's a good snacking cheese and can be used in place of mozzarella.
Bitto	A cow's-milk cheese (sometimes blended with goat's milk) from the Valtellina. When young, it melts beautifully and is used in *pizzoccheri* and *polenta taragna*. When aged, it's used for grating.

Gorgonzola	The famous blue-veined cheese originally came from a town of the same name just outside Milan. Most Gorgonzola is now made in Piedmont, but it remains very popular in Lombard cuisine. It can be smeared onto raw vegetables as an *antipasto,* melted and tossed with pasta, sprinkled over polenta as a *primo,* or served with pears and walnuts as a dessert. There are two types of Gorgonzola: *dolce* (a slightly sweet version that's golden yellow) and *piccante* (a sharper version that's white).
Grana	This granular cheese is the (lesser) Lombard version of Parmigiano-Reggiano; fine versions are made in Lodi and Cremona.
Mascarpone	A sinfully rich, wonderfully sweet and creamy dessert cheese, available only in cooler months. It's one of the prime ingredients in *tiramisù,* but can also be eaten straight or blended with a bit of brandy.
Panerone (or *pannerone*)	A slightly bitter cheese typical of Mantova and found only in the winter.
Parmigiano-Reggiano	Although this divine cheese is primarily produced in Emilia-Romagna (see description on page 211), part of the delimited production zone is in the province of Mantova.
Robiola	This rich, creamy mountain cheese, also found in Piedmont, has several varieties in Lombardy.
Stracchino	The word derives from *stracco,* or "exhausted." Cows who made long journeys for grazing would be milked at the end of these travels; that milk produced a cheese that's soft, creamy, straw-yellow, and rich. **Crescenza** is similar.
Taleggio	A rich, creamy cheese similar to *stracchino,* found primarily in the province of Bergamo.

Left: *Parmigiano-Reggiano;* **Right:** *Robiola*

DOLCI (SWEETS)

Amaretti	Bitter macaroons, typically made with almond.
Crema del Lario	A mixture of cream, lemon, and dry liqueur popular at Lake Como.
Miascia	A cake made with milk, stale bread, butter, sugar, eggs, pears, apples, lemon peel, grapes, raisins, and rosemary.
Mostaccini	Spicy biscuits from the town of Crema.
Mostarda	Whole fruit pickled with mustard seed, most associated with Cremona and Mantova. Some of the fruits used are cherries, quince, plums, figs, and watermelon. There are slight variations in *mostarda,* depending on the type of fruit and whether it's cut or left intact. *Mostarda* is served with sliced *salumi* or with *bollito misto,* or it's minced and blended into the filling of *tortelli di zucca.*
Panettone	The classic, scrumptious yeast cake of Milan, with egg, saffron, raisins, and sometimes candied fruit. It's popular during the Christmas period, starting on December 7—the feast day of San Ambrogio, patron of Milan—and often accompanied by sparkling wine. But these days you can usually find it at other times, as well.
Torrone	Nougat, a dessert made of almonds, honey, and egg whites. This specialty of Cremona dates back at least to 1441, and possibly to Roman times. While there are many legends as to its origin, Lombards say it's shaped like the *torrazzo*—the gigantic bell tower next to Cremona's cathedral, one of Italy's tallest.
Torta di tagliatelle	A crunchy, unusual dessert made with thin egg noodles and almonds (from Mantova).
Torta sbrisolona	A wonderful crumbly and crispy cake (in fact, the name means "crunchy") made with cornmeal, flour, almonds, wine, and lots of butter (from Mantova).

Left: *Torrone;* **Right:** *Panettone*

♀ WINES OF LOMBARDY

With Piedmont and Veneto just next door, you might expect that Lombardy, too, would be a formidable winemaker. In truth, there are some good wines made here, but this region's strength is its food rather than its wine. There are six main wine-producing zones, three of which are notable:

Valtellina This northern valley, near Switzerland, is perhaps Lombardy's best wine-producing area. They use the nebbiolo grape (here sometimes called chiavennasca), which is used in some of the famous reds from neighboring Piedmont. Look for the DOC called Valtellina or Valtellina Superiore, often denoted by the district in which it is grown: Grumello, Sassella, Valgella, and Inferno. All are delicious.

Oltrepò Pavese The district "beyond the Po River," in the province of Pavia, makes good wine that has often been underrated because it was traditionally sold at low prices in *osterie* along the banks of the Po and the Ticino. But now it has finally begun to be justly recognized. Good reds include barbera and the slightly fizzy bonarda. Many white varieties are also planted here, most successfully the Riesling Italico. The Oltrepò area is best regarded for its sparkling wines, which are delicious. Towns such as Broni and Stradella produce outstanding moscato that holds its own in comparison with the more famous wines from Asti (in Piedmont).

Franciacorta This zone, in eastern Lombardy, produces excellent reds and whites and an outstanding sparkling wine. The foremost producer of reds and table whites is Ca' del Bosco, and the best sparkling wine (often called Italy's best) comes from Berlucchi. Closer to the city of Brescia, you'll find charming DOC reds called Cellatica, Botticino, and Capriano del Colle. Along the shores of Lake Garda are wines reminiscent of the light, agreeable ones produced across the lake in the province of Verona. Ever more popular is the white trebbiano di Lugana, produced on the southern shores of the lake.

Others The **Valcalepio** DOC near Bergamo results in a good red. The area south of Mantova produces a good **Lambrusco** that rivals the one made across the border in Emilia. And there's a tiny DOC in the province of Milan called **San Colombano** that makes a nice little red.

The Italian Riviera: Liguria

On Italy's Riviera—in the Italian region of Liguria— little mountain towns perch high over the stunning blue Mediterranean. The 220-mile coastline is dotted with romantic fishing villages, rocky cliffs, and pebbly beaches. And Liguria smells as good as it looks: One of the most important local industries is flower cultivation; the mountain valleys are draped in basil, rosemary, thyme, and marjoram; and garlic *(aglio)*—otherwise largely ignored in the North—is a major player in local dishes. (A garlic sauce called *agliata* is close at hand whenever fish, meat, or vegetables are served.)

Geographically, Liguria is a skinny crescent that hugs the coastline of the Ligurian Sea, bordered on its inland side by the Alps and the Apennines. Among Italians, Ligurians are known for their frugality. If that stereotype contains a kernel of truth, it's only because subsistence has always been challenging in this rugged terrain where mountains meet sea. The waters here don't abound with fish and seafood, compared to areas to the south and west. Flat land is at a premium, making every arable patch valuable and every Ligurian farmer an expert in making the most of limited resources.

As great seafarers, Ligurians developed clever methods for preserving food to be consumed on long voyages. Dried ravioli were the pasta of choice on Genovese vessels of the late Middle Ages. Dehydrated codfish—much of it imported from Norway—has been a staple of Ligurian sailors for half a millennium. And anchovies and sardines preserved in olive oil are revered.

All of this dried and preserved food could become tiresome quickly. So it's striking that Ligurian cuisine is some of the most fragrant and delicate in all of Italy. The combination of pasta, vegetables, fruit, oil, wine, herbs, bread, fish, and small amounts of meat and cheese makes Ligurian cooking both delicious and healthy. Watching robust octogenarians pedaling their bicycles up and down hills, you'll appreciate the Ligurian devotion to fresh fruits and vegetables. A visit to a bustling Ligurian market offers a lesson in how extraordinary local produce can be.

When seeking definitive local flavors, note that Liguria is the birthplace of pesto. Basil, which loves the temperate Ligurian climate, is pounded with cheese (half Parmigiano-Reggiano and half

pecorino), garlic, olive oil, pine nuts, and coarse salt to create a creamy green paste or sauce, which is then tossed with pasta. Two distinctive local noodles are designed specifically for pesto to cling to: *trenette* (similar to linguine) and *trofie* (short, dense twists). Or simply have pesto over gnocchi, or a pesto *lasagne*. While the phrase *alla genovese* ("Genoa-style") can indicate a number of things, it often means "with pesto sauce." Buy a little jar of pesto to bring home, or to enliven picnics and happy hours throughout your trip.

Top: Vernazza, Cinque Terre; **Bottom:** Making pesto

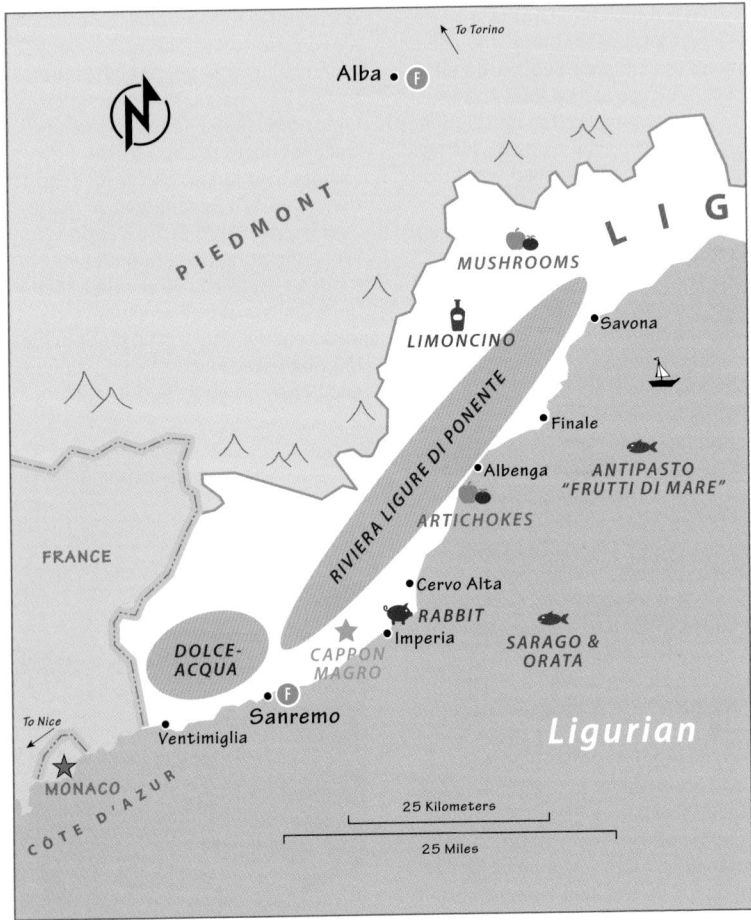

🗺 CITIES, TOWNS, AND PLACES

For many travelers, the highlight of the Italian Riviera is the **Cinque Terre:** five traffic-free villages carving a good life out of difficult terrain (with a healthy boost from tourism). The "five lands"—as the name means—line up along a six-mile stretch of Ligurian coastline, connected by a train line, a hiking path, and boats. Each of the villages

(resorty Monterosso, cover-girl Vernazza, hilltop Corniglia, photogenic Manarola, and amiable Riomaggiore) fills a ravine with a lazy hive of human activity. Overhead are steep wine-growing terraces, where locals have mastered the art of using the rugged terrain to produce wine. While the Cinque Terre isn't the most representative place to sample

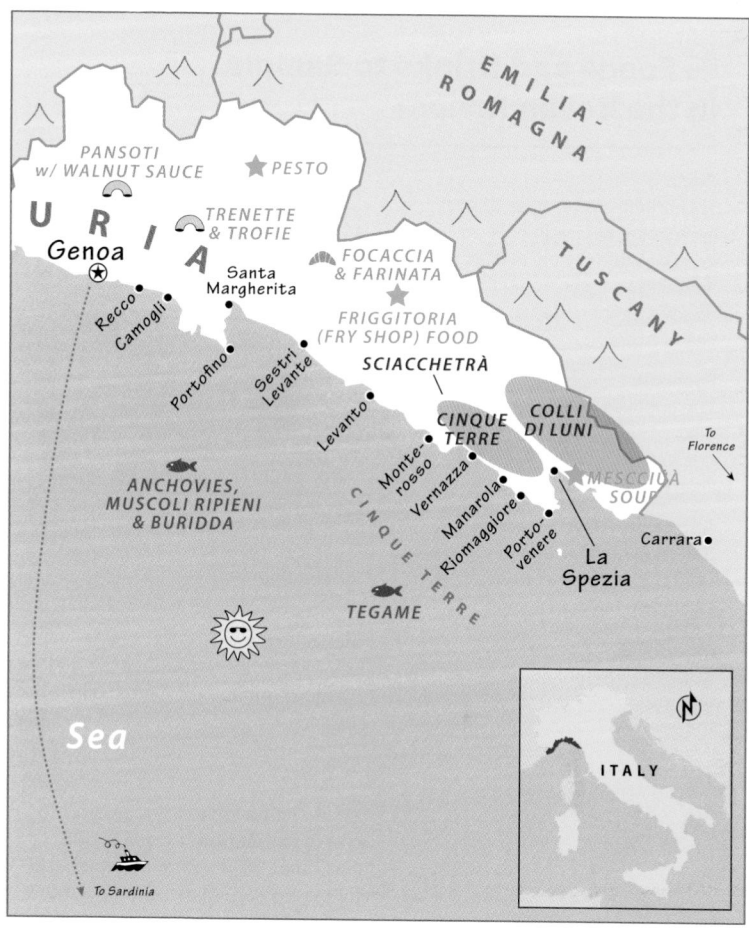

Ligurian cuisine, it offers a handy cross-section to give day-trippers and sunburned hikers a taste of the Riviera—and is one of Rick's favorite places in Italy.

The Cinque Terre has been discovered. But several nearby towns—bigger, more mainstream, and a bit less overrun in high season—offer a similar experience. To the north are **Levanto,** the gateway to the Cinque Terre; **Sestri Levante,** stunningly situated on a narrow peninsula flanked by two beaches; and **Santa Margherita Ligure,** a thriving city of about 9,000 with an active waterfront and easy connections to yacht-happy **Portofino.** At the south end of the Cinque Terre, around the bluff toward La Spezia, is the pretty pastel town of **Porto Venere.**

The Cinque Terre is flanked by two big industrial ports. **La Spezia,** to the south, has a population of 93,000, a gritty harbor, a busy train station, a nondescript grid of streets, a fine selection of mostly untouristy restaurants, and a lively *passeggiata*

🍽 Foods and Drinks to Sample in the Italian Riviera

Pesto
This bright-green sauce of basil, garlic, pine nuts, and cheese goes wonderfully on, over, or with anything—most commonly *trenette* noodles or short, dense pasta twists called *trofie.*

Focaccia
The famous Ligurian bread is pillowy, salty, and generously drizzled with olive oil—ideal for snacking or a light meal.

Antipasto ai frutti di mare
Start your meal with a mixed plate of "fruits of the sea"—the perfect showcase for local seafood.

Anchovies
Prepared a variety of ways, Ligurian anchovies *(acciughe)*—especially the very fresh ones *(alici)*—taste

Pasta with pesto

totally different than the harsh, smelly, salty ones back home.

Sciacchetrà
This sweet dessert wine of the Cinque Terre is ideal for dunking *biscotti.*

scene along Via del Prione. And to the north, **Genoa** (pop. 600,000) has been the leading city of Liguria since the Republic of Genoa was established in the 11th century. While few travelers linger in Genoa (which they consider a transit hub and not much else), food lovers might enjoy perusing its Mercato Orientale.

Between the Cinque Terre and Genoa is humble **Recco** (pop. 10,000), which was badly bombed in World War II and lacks the charm of most nearby towns. But locals have compensated by preserving its food heritage, making it the culinary citadel of Liguria. Recco is also known for its *focaccia col formaggio,* a crispy amalgam of flour, cheese, and olive oil.

Rooftops of Sanremo

Fred's favorite Ligurian town is **Sanremo** (pop. 55,000), sitting just over the border from France—a quick side-trip from places like Monaco and Nice. Sanremo rose to fame in the 19th century, when British and Continental aristocrats made it their winter resort of choice. From 1860 until the 1930s, elegant hotels, villas, and a glittering casino were built, along with a beautiful Russian Orthodox cathedral to comfort the many émigrés who arrived after the Russian Revolution. But in the postwar era, Sanremo was no longer chic. Although someone at the turn of the 20th century never would have believed it, today Sanremo has been eclipsed as a tourist hotspot by the tiny towns of the Cinque Terre.

But Sanremo's elegant decline has made it a delightful place to explore. Its winter song festival and thriving flower market are both big draws. (It's best to wander the flower market bright and early, starting at 6 a.m.) Locals shop for food and meet up in bakeries, bars, and along such popular thoroughfares as the Via Palazzo. And Sanremo's Mercato Comunale (near Piazza Eroi

Top: Recco's *focaccia col formaggio,* fresh from the oven; **Bottom:** Narrow lanes of Sanremo

Sanremesi) provides insights into the way people shop, eat, and live in Liguria. Fred ranks it among Italy's best markets.

La Pigna ("The Pinecone"), the ancient neighborhood that stands above Sanremo's market, is a hill with labyrinthine streets and alleyways that evoke a Liguria of centuries past. Walls crumble, and steps are worn away. Sounds and smells of cooking issue from kitchens. Voices speak in Italian, in local dialect, and occasionally in Arabic—immigrants from North Africa. If nothing else, this ramble is a great way to burn off calories from all that fine Ligurian food.

🍽 FOODS OF THE ITALIAN RIVIERA

While this section is organized as in other regions—course by course—Ligurian cuisine is unusual in that many dishes aren't eaten at a table. For example, one Ligurian fixture is the *friggitoria* (fry shop), which produces Liguria's answer to fast food; you'll also see shops labeled *focacceria,* selling focaccia bread and other on-the-go snacks.

ANTIPASTI (APPETIZERS)

Acciughe	Anchovies are ideally served the day they're caught. If you've always hated anchovies (the slimy, salty kind), try them fresh here. They're particularly good when very fresh, in which case they might be called **alici.** They can be prepared in a dizzying variety of ways: marinated in lemon juice *(acciughe marinate),* salted, butterflied, and deep-fried (sometimes with that tasty garlic sauce called *agliata*), and so on.
Antipasto ai frutti di mare (or simply *antipasti misti*)	While in most of Italy, *antipasti* means *salumi* and cheese, in Liguria you'll get a plate of mixed "fruits of the sea." Many restaurants are proud of their *frutti di mare*—it's how they show off. For two diners, splitting one of these and a pasta dish can be plenty.
Cappon magro	Traditionally served on non-meat feast days (such as during Lent), this elaborate dish is a salad composed of various cooked fishes, vegetables, and assorted greens. The ingredients are stacked in layers in a bowl lined with vinegar-soaked crackers. The salad is then dressed with a sauce made of anchovies, garlic, pine nuts, capers, olives, olive oil, and parsley, and then decorated with hard-boiled eggs and pieces of lobster and shrimp. **Capponada** is a less elaborate version.
Frisceu	Fish-and-vegetable fritters.
Gianchetti (or **bianchetti**)	Whitebait (tiny anchovies or sardines), boiled or fried.
Muscoli ripieni	Mussels stuffed with breadcrumbs, herbs, pork, and cheese.

Left: *Antipasto ai frutti di mare;*
Right: *Muscoli ripieni*

Left: Ligurian fish soup; **Right:** *Trofie* with pesto

PRIMI (PASTAS AND OTHER FIRST COURSES)

Remember: The key topping here is **pesto,** which goes with *lasagne,* gnocchi, *trenette,* or *trofie.*

Corzetti (or **croxetti**)	An ancient Ligurian pasta with a figure-8 shape modeled after a coin used in the medieval Republic of Genoa. It also comes in disks, with the imprint of a decorative stamp.
Fish soup	There are various kinds in Liguria, called *ciuppin, brodetto,* or simply *zuppa di pesce.* This resembles the Italian American dish cioppino.
Gattafin	Greens and herbs stuffed into pastry and deep-fried.
Mescciüà	The special soup of La Spezia is made with chickpeas, white beans, *farro* (spelt), olive oil, and pepper.
Minestrone alla genovese	Vegetable soup spiked with pesto.
Pansoti (or **pansotti**)	Ravioli-like triangles of pasta filled with greens (often *borragine,* borage) or herbs, as well as *ricotta* or another soft cheese; it's typically topped with a walnut sauce that has a hint of curdled milk (called **tocco di noci** or **salsa di noci**).
Picagge (con salsa di carciofi)	Wide *tagliatelle,* often served with an artichoke sauce.
Ravioli	Typically served filled with herbs **(con preboggion),** ricotta **(di magro),** fish **(pesce),** or meat **(carne).**
Trenette	Long, flat noodles similar to linguine, typically served with pesto.
Trofie	A Genovese pasta—dense, toothsome twists—tossed with string beans, boiled potatoes, and pesto.

SECONDI (MAIN DISHES)

Seafood is abundant on local menus. *Pesce* (fish) might include **sarago** and **orata** (both are white fish, similar to bream); served grilled or broiled, these are central to Ligurian cooking. As for land food, rabbit is popular, using various preparations.

Ligurians stuff all sorts of vegetables (zucchini, lettuce leaves, cabbage leaves, tomatoes, eggplants, artichokes, peppers, etc.) with all kinds of fillings, including meat, herbs, cheeses, nuts, and other vegetables. If you see the words *ripieno, ripieni,* or *farcito* following the name of a vegetable, it's stuffed.

Buridda	A stew made with the best local fish, tomatoes, and vegetables.
Cima ripiena (or *cima alla genovese*)	Veal breast stuffed with organ meats, herbs, cheeses, vegetables, pine nuts, and pâté. It's rolled, boiled, chilled, and sliced thin.
Condiggion (or *condjon*)	A salad made with vegetables, rusks, and *bottarga* (dried roe).
Coniglio con le olive	Rabbit cooked with olives and herbs; a specialty of Imperia.
Funghi	The inland areas of Liguria are full of wild mushrooms that are prepared in many ways, often as a main course. When prepared **alla genovese,** the mushrooms are cooked with potatoes, garlic, and parsley.
Scabecio	Small fish are fried and then pickled in vinegar, wine, onions, and spices.
Tegame alla vernazzana	The most typical main course in Vernazza (and its four sister towns in the Cinque Terre) is a layered, casserole-like dish of whole anchovies, potatoes, tomatoes, white wine, oil, and herbs.
Tomaxelle	Veal rolls filled with marjoram, parsley, garlic, wild mushrooms, pine nuts, cheese, and egg.

Left: *Torta pasqualina;* **Right:** *Pandolce genovese*

Torta pasqualina	An Easter dish made with 33 layers—of pastry, vegetables, cheeses, and eggs—one for each year in the life of Christ.
Triglie alla genovese	Red mullet baked in white wine, fennel seeds, capers, and tomatoes.

PANE (BREAD)

Farinata	This humble flatbread snack (also popular over the border in the French Rivera, where it's called *socca*) is sold at pizza and focaccia places. It's made from chickpea flour, water, oil, and pepper, and baked on a copper tray in a wood-burning oven. Made throughout the day and sold hot in wedges, it's dense, filling, and more delicate than focaccia.
Focaccia	Liguria's famous bread—pillowy, flat, salty, and olive-oily. The baker roughs up the dough with finger holes, sprinkles it with salt water, then bakes it. Focaccia comes plain or with flavorings (such as onion, sage, rosemary, cheese, or olives) and is a favorite for a snack on the beach. Bakeries sell it in rounds or slices by weight (a portion is about 100 grams, or *un etto*). The town of Recco, between the Cinque Terre and Genoa, is famous for a delicious crispy/cheesy variation called **focaccia col formaggio.**
Sardenaira (also called **pissadella**)	A flat tart topped with tomatoes, olives, onions, and anchovies.

DOLCI (SWEETS)

Dessert is often accompanied by a sweet *digestivo*. Sciacchetrà wine, from the Cinque Terre, is commonly served with dry cookies for munching or dunking. And Liguria loves its locally grown lemons: They produce a lemon liqueur called *limoncino*, similar to *limoncello* from the South.

Marrons glacés	Candied chestnuts, which some say were invented in Genoa around 1790, when the city was under French domination.
Quaresimali	Marzipan confections served during Lent, made with almond paste, cocoa, vanilla, and mint.
Pandolce genovese	The local equivalent of Milan's famous yeast cake includes currants and pine nuts.
Pane del marinaio (or **del pescatore**)	This "sailor's" (or "fisherman's") bread is sweet and soft yet crumbly. It's served in bars and is tasty at breakfast.
Pasta genoise (or **genovese**)	What we call genoise—an airy sponge cake made with butter.

♀ WINES OF THE ITALIAN RIVIERA

Although Liguria's steep slopes and difficult soil aren't ideal for growing grapes, wine has always been present here—largely due to Liguria's proximity to Piedmont and Tuscany, two of Italy's top wine regions. The small vineyards of Liguria are home to about a hundred grape varieties (the leading ones are pigato, vermentino, and rossese). Northern and western Liguria tend to make wine from a single grape (dolcetto or nebbiolo, for example), as in Piedmont, while in eastern Liguria, wines tend to be blends of several grapes, as in Tuscany.

Ligurian wines marry perfectly with the region's delicate cuisine. Many recipes feature a splash of wine, and locals insist on drinking white wine while munching on a fresh focaccia. Only a few Ligurian wines (the red Rossese di Dolceacqua, whites from pigato and vermentino grapes, and the whites of the Cinque Terre) have achieved fame beyond the region, but because of limited production, they are hard to find and often pricey.

One traditional symbol of Liguria is the *pirone,* a wine bottle with an unusually long, skinny neck—allowing drinkers to pour the wine straight into their mouths. This was designed for fishermen to pass around while waiting for the fish to bite.

There are four principal wine-producing zones in Liguria:

Riviera Ligure di Ponente The provinces closest to France (Imperia and Savona) produce most of the top wines in Liguria. Pigato is made of a grape of the same name; it's a lightly fragrant white with a slightly bitter almond taste, which goes beautifully with Ligurian seafood dishes and savory baked goods (the best, called Pigato Albenganese, is from near Albenga). Vermentino from this area is slightly more fragrant and fruitier than its cousin in Colli di Luni (described later). The Rossese Ligure di Ponente, a light ruby red, is dry and quite drinkable; a fuller red is Ormeasco di Pornassio, similar to the Dolcetto wines of Piemonte, made of a grape that has been grown in a small area of the province of Imperia since 1300. Ormeasco Sciac-trà is a lighter, rosé version.

Rossese di Dolceacqua This wine is often referred to simply as Dolceacqua. The name (meaning "sweet water") refers not to the taste of the wine, but to the town it comes from, which sits a stone's throw from the French border. This flavorful, full-bodied DOC red goes well with local rabbit dishes. When aged for at least a year, the wine can be called Rossese Superiore.

Cinque Terre The wines of the Cinque Terre require great effort to produce. Tiny vineyards dot the steep slopes, and grapes are collected by hand and placed in small baskets that were traditionally carried by workers (sometimes on their heads) or on the backs of donkeys. (These days, a cute miniature train called the *trenino* does most of the work.) Wines are typically blends, predominantly using the bosco grape, found only here. A delicate, straw-colored DOC white wine called Bianco delle Cinque Terre is made using bosco, albarola, and vermentino grapes. This flows cheap and easy throughout the region; it's crisp and refreshing, ideal with seafood.

For a sweet but potent dessert wine, **Sciacchetrà** is worth a try. While 10 kilos of grapes yield 7 liters of Cinque Terre wine, Sciacchetrà is made from near-raisins: 10 kilos make only 1.5 liters of the wine (with 18 percent alcohol). The name (pronounced shah-keh-TRAH) means "push and pull"—push in lots of grapes, pull out the best wine…then age it a year. It's often served with dunkable cookies.

Colli di Luni (or **Lunigiana**) This zone, whose wines were well regarded even in Roman times, is a mountainous area covering the point where Liguria, Tuscany, and Emilia-Romagna meet. A ruby-colored fragrant red, Rosso dei Colli di Luni, is made of sangiovese and other grapes, including canaiolo, pollera nera, and ciliegiolo. The area's white *(bianco)* is made of Ligurian vermentino, trebbiano, and other grapes. Vermentino, a wine made entirely of the grape of that name, is a delicious, dry white with a slightly almond taste.

The Dolomites: Trentino-Alto Adige/Südtirol

At Italy's rooftop, tucked between the soaring peaks of the Dolomites, you'll find a region of divided loyalties and identities. To most Italians, this is a cool, mountainous place that produces white wine and is populated by Germanic people. Germans and Austrians think of it as a sunny place where Italians produce red wine. And the strange thing is…both are correct.

While officially a single region, Trentino-Alto Adige is in practice two separate provinces, each with its own character. Alto Adige, close to Austria, owns some of Italy's most dramatic Alps and is predominantly German-speaking—and those residents call it Südtirol. Trentino, while still quite mountainous, feels like a transition—in terms of landscape, climate, culture, and language—between the Alps and flat, humid Veneto. Trentino's towns and cities are predominantly Austrian

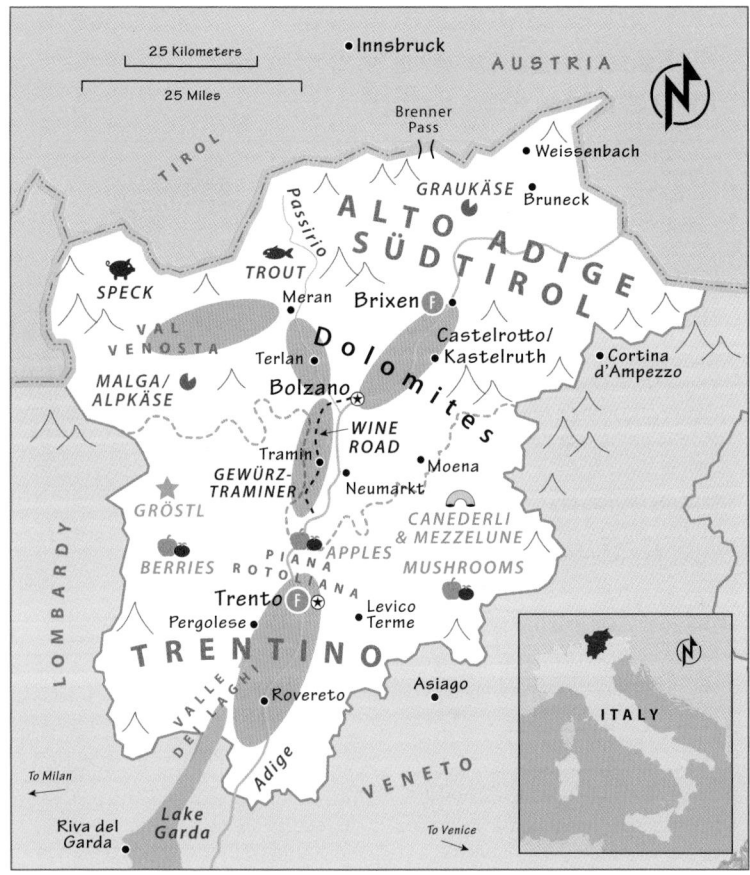

in style, but most residents speak Italian first.

In the Middle Ages, as part of the Holy Roman Empire, this territory faced north. Later, it was firmly in the Austrian Habsburg realm. When Austria lost World War I, their Südtirol became Italy's Alto Adige. Mussolini did what he could to Italianize the region, including giving each town an Italian name. But for decades, German-speaking secessionist groups agitated for more autonomy. Finally, Italy's 2001 constitution gave Alto Adige a measure of independence—both from Trentino and from Italy. While it's still officially tied to Trentino, Alto Adige's roads, water, electricity, communications, and schools are under provincial control.

Let's handle each part of this region in turn. **Alto Adige** is named for the upper reaches of the Adige River (Italy's second-longest). Its German name, **Südtirol,** refers to the southern reaches of Austria's Tirol region. German is the first language of nearly two-thirds of the population, and television, radio, and the press are primarily in German, as are most signs. (Some include a third language, Ladin—an ancient Romance

🍽 Foods and Drinks to Sample in Trentino-Alto Adige

Speck
Bacon that's cured, smoked, aged, then thin-sliced.

Funghi
The mountains abound with wild mushrooms.

Canederli
These big bread dumplings are hearty and filling—ideal mountain food to carbo-load for a day of hiking.

Mountain cheese

Mountain cheeses
Buttery, aged wheels of alpine cheese, sometimes called *Alpkäse* or *formaggio di malga*.

Apfelstrudel
The best you'll find this side of Austria—which, after all, isn't far away.

Gewürztraminer (or traminer aromatico)
This dry white wine has a spicy, fruity flavor.

language still spoken in a few traditional areas.) Only in the provincial capital, Bolzano/Bozen, will you hear much Italian spoken. You'll notice that in this chapter, when discussing Alto Adige, I list town names and foods using both German and Italian.

Meanwhile, **Trentino** feels like a hybrid of the Germanic (Alto Adige)

and the Italianate (the rest of Italy). Its Dolomite peaks and chalet-filled ski resorts are strictly alpine, while the southern part of the region has a strong Venetian influence, with locals strolling the *passeggiata* amidst pastel-painted townhomes. In the middle of the region is the Piana Rotoliana, a vast plain framed by mountains—an important agricultural zone, especially for wine.

A distinct feature of Trentino is the *maso,* an archaic term referring to a landed estate cultivated by a family. Many of these now offer food and lodging for travelers. While traditionally rustic and budget-friendly, today some *masi* have gone upscale. Local tourist offices can provide a list of all types. And while Alto Adige doesn't have quite the same tradition, it has many farms where you can dine on country cooking while gazing at cows resting on tranquil hillsides.

One thing that unites Alto Adige/Südtirol and Trentino is geography. Especially for travelers, this region is synonymous with the Dolomites—an alpine range famous for its fantastically jagged peaks. These differ from the rest of the Alps because of their dominant rock type, dolomite, which forms sheer vertical walls of white, gray, and pink that rise abruptly from green valleys and meadows. The terrain of Trentino-Alto Adige is also distinguished by tranquil high-altitude meadows, deep valleys filled with picturesque towns and cities,

and air that's fresh and clean. These mountains enjoy a great deal of sunshine—much more, for example, than in the Lake District farther south and west.

Within Trentino-Alto Adige, the many mountain ranges, valleys, and rivers tend to create further linguistic and gastronomic boundaries; some areas are more remote, traditional, and Germanic, while others are better connected to the Italian mainstream. Because of this terrain, and the region's unique history and cultural heritage, you'll find a great variation in food specialties from place to place. But that's part of the joy of the mountains.

 CITIES, TOWNS, AND PLACES

Bolzano (or **Bozen** in German) is the capital of Alto Adige/Südtirol, with 107,000 people. Because it sits in a valley facing Trentino, it's the most Italian-feeling place in Italy's most Germanic corner. But really, it's a happy hybrid: The locals are warm

and friendly, but organized. One person greets you in Italian, the next in German. Its lively shopping arcades and food-and-flower market are more bustling than anything north of the border in Austria, and it's the one town in Alto Adige with a distinct

Street markets of Bolzano

Top: Castelrotto/Kastelruth; **Bottom:** Brixen/
Bressanone

a day of hiking at nearby mountain meadows (the Alpi di Siusi and Seceda lifts are both very close by).

Brixen/Bressanone (pop. 20,000), Fred's favorite Alto Adige town, sits on the highway connecting Italy to Austria. With an illustrious history of powerful bishops—and a sleepy present—Brixen feels like a charming mini-Bolzano. The people of Brixen seem preoccupied with health and well-being; they sip herbal teas, drink mineral water from a source just outside of town, and go on long walks in the nearby hills.

Meran/Merano (pop. 40,000)—onetime Habsburg retreat and genteel spa town—is a popular destination for Austrians and Germans. Everyone from Sigmund Freud to Franz Kafka to the Habsburg Princess Sisi came here to breathe the clean mountain air. It's ideally set up for those who enjoy strolling in nature; there are even two different paths—one for summer, the other for winter—on opposite sides of the Passirio River through town. And in the fall, during the grape harvest, people flock here to take the "grape cure" (cura dell'uva/Traubenkur): drinking several glasses of fresh-squeezed grape juice to cleanse the system.

Wine lovers enjoy driving the **Weinstrasse/Strada del Vino**—a wine road that begins in Bolzano and meanders south toward Trentino. It passes through the village of **Tramin,** the home of the Gewürztraminer grape. If visiting during the fall harvest, look for Buschenschank signs, announcing that new wine is ready to be tasted.

Farther down the valley toward Trentino, but still in Alto Adige, little **Neumarkt/Egna**—with just 5,000 residents—feels less touristy. It's a hub for local apple orchards and has a charming small-town market on Tuesday mornings.

passeggiata tradition. The town has only one museum worth entering, but it's world-class, offering the chance to see Ötzi the Iceman—a 5,300-year-old Tirolean found frozen in a glacier.

Venturing beyond Bolzano deeper into Alto Adige/Südtirol, you'll enter a more fully Germanic world. Of the many charming mountain towns, Rick's favorite is **Castelrotto**—or **Kastelruth** to its residents, 95 percent of whom are native German speakers. With just over 2,000 people, it's a combination of real town, ski resort, and administrative center for surrounding villages. Situated at 3,475 feet, it's an ideal home base for

The capital of Trentino—the city of **Trento** (pop. 118,000)—has a long tradition of learning and government. In the 16th century, it hosted the famous Council of Trent (1545-1563), which changed the course of religious history: As the cultural midpoint between Germany and Italy, Trento represented an opportunity for finding middle ground between Lutherans and Catholics. The reforms established here created a context from which a more enlightened, modern Catholic Church could emerge. Today Trento is simply an enjoyable town to explore (and Fred's favorite in Trentino), with a fortress-like church, traffic-free streets lined by stately townhouses, and a lively mushroom market; if visiting in the autumn, try to attend the mushroom fair.

Stretching west and south of Trento is the **Valle dei Laghi** (Valley of Lakes); the largest and most famous of these is **Lake Garda,** which is shared with neighboring Lombardy and Veneto. While Trentino is thought of as a chilly alpine region, the microclimate along the northern shore of Garda—toward Trento—is warm enough to produce the northernmost olives in the world. Also in the Valley of the Lakes is **Pergolese,** a town that produces outstanding Vin Santo from the nosiola grape.

🍴 FOODS OF TRENTINO-ALTO ADIGE

Altoatesino cuisine is largely German, with some Italian (specifically Venetian) influence that grows stronger as you move south into Trentino. The region is famous for its fruits and vegetables, especially apples, which turn up in dishes from *antipasto* through dessert. Other produce of note includes grapes, berries, plums, and chestnuts.

In Alto Adige/Südtirol, *Wurst* and sauerkraut are the Tirolean clichés. With its many dairy cows, contentedly mooing on grassy slopes and meadows, it's no surprise that the local fare goes heavy on milk, cream, butter, and cheese. And the cooking here is distinguished by the use of herbs and spices—fresh

ones that flourish during alpine spring (horseradish, garlic, chive, dill) and more exotic ones that were imported when this was part of the Habsburg Empire (cinnamon, poppy seeds). *Altoatesino* bakers also make excellent breads, often with seeds such as poppy or caraway, and flavorings such as onion, garlic, and herbs.

In Trentino, the flavors go heavier on Italian and lighter on Germanic. Demonstrating the Venetian influence, polenta is the principal staple of Trentino.

In general, the dishes on this list with German names predominate in Alto Adige, while the Italian-named dishes are more common in Trentino.

ANTIPASTI (APPETIZERS)

In Alto Adige, a **merenda** (or **merenda altoatesina**) is a platter of cured meats and hard cheeses, often including *speck*.

Carne salada (or **carne salà**)	Raw beef cured in vinegar and spices and served paper-thin, or sometimes cooked as a *secondo*.
Funghi	Everyone in Trentino seems to be an expert on mushrooms. Following a rainfall, the woods are full of people gathering *funghi,* and special inspectors called *micologi* (mushroom experts) monitor mushrooms in the market to ensure they're safe and edible. **Finferli** are small, delicious wild mushrooms found high in the mountains.
Probusto	This traditional sausage from Rovereto (Trentino), made with a mixture of pork and beef, is smoked over a beechwood fire before being cooked.
Speck	This is an Alto Adige staple. Bacon is cured, and then smoked for a few hours, before being aged for about six months. It's then sliced thin and served as an *antipasto* or on a sandwich.
Tortel di patate	Crispy potato pancakes served with *salumi* in some parts of Trentino.

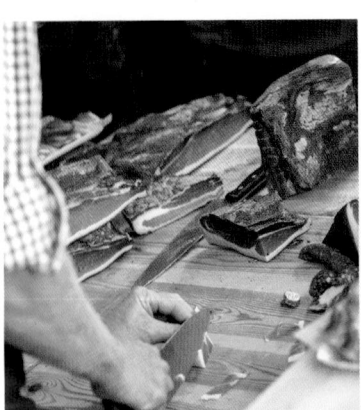

Left: *Speck;* **Right:** *Canederli* in stew

PRIMI (PASTAS AND OTHER FIRST COURSES)

Canederli (or *Knödel*)	These large, dense dumplings—which can be as big as a tennis ball—evoke a time when poor people needed to fill hungry bellies inexpensively. *Canederli* are made of bread and flour, and some are flavored with *speck,* liver, cheese, herbs, spinach, beets, or other meat. (Tourist-oriented restaurants offer a sampler plate of three or four different kinds of *canederli.*) They're served as a *primo,* either in broth or topped with butter and cheese; or they can accompany main courses such as *gulasch.* There are also soups that feature them, including **Speckknödelsuppe** (with *canederli* studded with *speck*) and **Leberknödelsuppe** (with liver-flavored *canederli*).
Filled pastas	Most commonly seen are **mezzelune** (ravioli shaped like a "half-moon"), **Tirtlen** (little fried pasta, which often contain vegetables or cheese), and the larger **Schlutzkrapfen,** which are ravioli filled with either sauerkraut, potatoes and herbs, or cheese. In Trentino, **ravioli alla trentina** can be filled with meat or potatoes.
Polenta	In Trentino, a popular *primo* is polenta with melted cheese and sautéed mushrooms.
Smacafam	Literally "hunger killer," this Trentino Eastertime dish is a casse-role of polenta, sausages, and cheese.
Soups	Alto Adige has a wide variety of hearty soups (beyond the *canederli* options noted above). **Zuppa di vino/ Weinsuppe** is a wonderful soup with a white-wine base. **Meraner Schneckensuppe** is a snail soup typical of Meran. **Bauernbrotsuppe** is a rye-bread soup from the Val Venosta. And there's also **minestra di orzo** (barley), **crema di castagne** (chestnut), and **Sauerkrautsuppe.**
Strangolapreti	In Trentino, gnocchi are made of spinach and stiff bread, and called "priest stranglers."

SECONDI (MAIN DISHES)

The people of both Alto Adige and Trentino are enthusiastic meat eaters: Game, poul-try, pork, and beef are all popular. Unlike traditional Italian *secondi,* these are nearly always served with side dishes of *canederli,* potatoes, vegetables, or **crauti rossi** (a.k.a. **Rotkohl,** a sweet-and-sour sauerkraut made from red cabbage).

Biroldo	Blood sausage made with chestnuts, pine nuts, and walnuts.
Bollito misto	As in much of northern Italy, you'll find this combination of boiled meats and sauces here—especially in Trentino.
Carrè affumicato	Pork shank that is first smoked, then boiled.

Gröstl	Similar to Swiss *Rösti,* this is a hash of potatoes and onions to which either *speck,* beef, or occasionally poultry is added. While garlic is often the dominant flavor, other variations rely on oregano, cumin, or chives.
Gulasch (or *Goulasch*)	Spicy meat stew, which can be made with beef, veal, or sometimes pork.
Luganega	While this sausage originates in Basilicata and is usually associated with Lombardy, it's also found all over the Trentino; each butcher shop has its own secret recipe, and most restaurants feature *luganega* with polenta on their menus.
Polenta smalzada	Polenta served with butter that has been browned with a bit of anchovy; originally a main course, this is now more commonly seen as a side dish.
Sauerer Kalbskopf (or *testina di vitello all'agro*)	Thin slices of cooked calf's head served with a vinegar sauce and onions. Sounds weird; tastes delicious.
Stinco di maiale	Roasted pork shank, usually garnished with potatoes.
Trout (*Forelle/trota*)	Typically from the Passirio River, the leading fish of Alto Adige is served smoked, boiled, or sautéed.
Wiener Schnitzel	Delicate breaded veal cutlets, cooked in butter.
Wild Game (*Wildfleisch/ selvaggina*)	This comes in the form of *Hirsch/cervo* (venison), *Reh/capriolo* (fawn), *Gämse/camoscio* (chamois/antelope), or *Hasen/lepre* (hare). Game can be smoked and thinly sliced as an *antipasto,* in meat sauce *(ragù)* with fresh pasta or as ravioli stuffing, or as a *secondo,* as tender chunks grilled or roasted in a rich sauce *(spezzatino).*

Left: *Gröstl* with potatoes; **Right:** *Graukäse*

FORMAGGI (CHEESES)

This is a region of formidable cheese production, most of it based on cow's milk. Some are what we might broadly think of as an alpine or Swiss-style cheese: big wheels of aged mountain cheese, often with tiny bubbles. It's tricky to give specific recommendations because specialties change so much from town to town and valley to valley; many are simply called *nostrano* (literally "ours"). But here are a few to look for.

Asiago	This is produced near the Veneto border, and—atypical of other Asiago variations—is sometimes aged.
Bela Badia	This sweet, *caciotta*-like cheese from Alto Adige is soft and buttery.
Formaggio di malga	This is the generic name for a category of mountain cheeses made with the summer milk from cows that graze in the highest valleys of the region—what German speakers would call **Alpkäse.** It's made by *malgari,* farmhands who live in little huts at high-altitude meadows to tend, herd, and milk the cows through the summer months, and make the cheese right there on the premises.
Graukäse	Despite its unappealing name ("gray cheese"), this low-fat cow's-milk cheese (made with what's left after the richest part of the milk is used to make butter) is an anchor of *Altoatesino* cooking. Through aging, it builds up a dark-colored mold on the rind and has a tangy finish.
Puzzone di Moena	*Puzzone,* loosely translated, means "big and smelly"; this cheese, which ripens in humid caves, is not so big, but it does have a distinct odor. If you can get past that, it's worth trying.
Tilsit	This cheese of German origin is found in the areas near the border.
Trentigrana	Trentino's version of Lombardy's aged grating cheese *(grana padano);* it's formed into giant wheels and ages for 22 months.
Vezzena	This mountain cheese is lovingly made, expertly aged, and carries the flavors of high-mountain herbs the cows graze on; it's prized by cheese connoisseurs throughout Italy.

DOLCI (SWEETS)

Given the Alto Adige's proximity to Germany and Austria, it's no surprise that they do excellent cakes and pies—loaded with locally grown fruits (especially apples), *mirtilli* (berries), raisins, and nuts. Chestnuts also find their way into many desserts. In Trentino, the ubiquitous polenta even turns up at dessert—topped with raisins or other fruit that has been soaked in grappa.

Apfelstrudel	You may get a bit tired of apple strudel, which is served everywhere. The crust here is thicker than the flaky ones in Vienna, but in good bakeries the quality of the apple filling is first-rate.

Left: *Kaiserschmarrn;* **Right:** *Apfelstrudel*

Karottenkuchen (or *torta con le carote*)	Often made with ground almonds or pine nuts, the local carrot cake is light and delicious—it bears no resemblance to its heavy, dark American cousin.
Kaiserschmarrn (or *Schmarrn*)	This dessert of Austrian origin is a thick, fluffy, caramelized crêpe that's pulled apart into pieces; it's usually prepared with raisins and topped with powdered sugar and red-currant jam.
Mirtilli	This is a generic term for berries, which are used widely in local desserts (and other dishes). Some variations don't quite have a North American equivalent: ***Mirtilli rossi*** look like cranberries, and ***mirtilli neri*** are a darker version of American blueberries, but in each case the flavor is different.
Mohrenköpfe	Chestnuts boiled in spiced milk and then served with cream and cherries; the unfortunate name, meaning "Moors' heads," has aged poorly.
Torta di fregoloti	A dry, crunchy cake made with butter, flour, walnuts, and almonds—a perfect match for Trentino's many dessert wines.
Torta di grano saraceno con mirtilli rossi	Buckwheat cake with red berries.
Zelten	This traditional Germanic Christmas cake is made with candied fruit, nuts, and a fair amount of grappa. Some bakeries make these only in the winter, but a few sell it year-round.

♀ WINES OF TRENTINO-ALTO ADIGE

There are important differences between the wines of Alto Adige and those of Trentino. Alto Adige has mainly small family producers, and most of the wine is drunk locally or exported to Austria and Germany, whereas Trentino has more industrial production, which is sent throughout Italy. I've covered the basics for each province below.

ALTO ADIGE

This is an area where red meets white. In fact, traditionally locals drink light white wine until noon, then switch to red wine through the evening. Two-thirds of production is red, but whites here are exceptional—some of Italy's very best. While we often think of Germanic whites as being sweet, most here are dry.

Whites Gewürztraminer/traminer aromatico, a dry white wine with a spicy fruit flavor, is now found throughout the world. But it's native to this area and is much celebrated. Other major whites include Goldmuskateller/moscato giallo, Müller-Thurgau, Rulander/ pinot grigio, Sylvaner, Terlano (a blend of pinot bianco, chardonnay, Riesling Italico, sauvignon, Sylvaner, and Müller-Thurgau), and Weissburgunder/pinot bianco.

Reds A pleasing light red is made primarily from the Vernatsch/schiava grape; a commonly seen red house wine is called **St. Magdalener/Santa Maddalena. Lagrein scuro** is a full-bodied, dry and fruity red, similar to a cabernet sauvignon or merlot. You'll also find cabernet franc, cabernet sauvignon, and Blauburgunder/pinot nero.

Hard Drinks For a local *aperitivo,* try the popular and refreshing **Hugo,** made with sparkling wine, elderflower syrup, sparkling water, and a sprig of mint. While popular all over Italy, it's particularly beloved in this land of elderflowers. For something stronger, consider grappa made from Williams pears (and served with a wedge of fresh pear). At Christmas markets, look for **Parampampoli**—a brew of coffee, grappa, wine, and caramelized sugar served flambé.

TRENTINO

There's a Trentino saying: *Pane e vino fanno un bel bambino* ("Bread and wine make a beautiful baby"). While obstetricians would beg to differ, this speaks to the deeply ingrained belief in wine and bread as fundamental sources of nourishment and well-being.

Teroldego Rotoliano is a wonderful medium-bodied red, made from a native grape that takes its name from the Piana Rotoliana plain in the heart of Trentino. While not as well known internationally, it's a good all-purpose red at a good price. Other native grapes are the red **marzemino** and the white **nosiola,** which makes an outstanding Vin Santo (sweet dessert wine made with withered, noble-rot grapes). You'll also find the major international grapes such as chardonnay, cabernet, merlot, moscato, pinot nero, and especially pinot grigio.

Hard Drinks While Trentino produces only about 1 percent of Italy's wine, it makes 10 percent of its grappa, and the abundant fruit is transformed into tasty *acquavite. Amaro* in this region, like local favorite **Cappelletti,** is made with a blend of local alpine botanicals.

Venice & Veneto

Most visitors to Veneto (VEH-neh-toh) never venture beyond the regional capital, Venice. That's understandable—Venice is one of the great destinations of the world. It's unique, legendary, and so enchanting it's known as La Serenissima (The Most Serene One). But for travelers who do go beyond Venice, a special region awaits. The "California of Italy" has a remarkably diverse terrain and economy—from the beaches of the Adriatic; to the hills in the provinces of Padua, Vicenza, and Treviso; to the beautiful, if overbuilt, eastern shore of Lake Garda; through zones of intense viticulture; past some of the world's most magnificent villas; to the heights of Belluno and Cortina d'Ampezzo for alpine fare and Olympics-quality skiing.

VENICE SPECIALTIES

- BACCALÀ, SARDE IN SAOR, & OTHER LAGOON SPECIALTIES
- FEGATO ALLA VENEZIANA
- CICCHETTI
- SPRITZ & OTHER COCKTAILS

Throughout Veneto, polenta is the starch of choice—so much so that other Italians have dubbed the *veneti* and their neighbors "polenta-eaters" *(polentoni)*—although rice and pasta dishes also abound. Inland, the people are meat eaters, while at the shore, fish and seafood are preferred. The many provincial capitals of Veneto—Padua, Verona, Vicenza, Treviso, and others—each have their own identity and culinary specialties.

On the one hand, variety is a Veneto hallmark. On the other, the region's character and cuisine have been undoubtedly shaped by its leading city. Most of today's Veneto was the inland, *terra firma* part of Venice's empire. With ample capital, plenty of traders with ready ships, and a strong military, Venice peaked as a commercial powerhouse from roughly 1100 to 1500. While the city-state didn't have vast land holdings, it was a mighty trading empire—built upon a network of Mediterranean ports and a mastery of the sea. If you needed gold from Egypt, silk from

🍴 Foods and Drinks to Sample in Veneto

Cicchetti
These tapas-like Venetian bar snacks are fun to assemble into a memorable, progressive meal.

Bigoli in salsa
Long wheat noodles in anchovy sauce.

Spaghetti or risotto al nero di seppia
Cooked with cuttlefish ink, with a black color and the flavor of the Adriatic.

Asiago
Cow's-milk cheese that's either young (creamy) or aged (pungent).

Tiramisù
"Pick-me-up" layer dessert of coffee-soaked ladyfingers, mascarpone cheese, bitter chocolate, and often Marsala wine.

Tiramisù

Amarone
Intense, velvety, full-bodied red wine, usually made from dried (passito) grapes.

Prosecco
Refreshing, floral, fruity, sparkling white wine, often used to make famous Venetian cocktails such as a Bellini.

Byzantium, or a fleet of ships for the Crusades, Venice delivered.

As the main commercial city of the Italian Renaissance, Venice was the center of the world spice trade—a place where coffee and cinnamon were common back when they seemed exotic to much of Italy. Venetian (and Veneto) cooking is a combination of three sources: the bounty of both the sea and the land, and that subtle influence of the East—sweet-and-sour fish with raisins, nutmeg or cinnamon in pasta sauces, pastries perfumed with rose-water, and so on. Unfortunately, most Venetian restaurants cater to the hordes of tourists, so they skip these dishes in favor of crowd-pleasing, generic "Italian" food. But savvy food lovers seek them out.

Venice is proud of its unique-ness—and not just its canal-lined, slowly sinking cityscape. Venice is also one of the only important Italian cities that was not founded by the Romans. When Aquileia in Friuli was destroyed by Attila the Hun in the fifth century, refugees fled to about

a hundred inhospitable islands in a lagoon north of the Adriatic Sea. Through sheer will, energy, and genius, they not only survived, but created a glorious city that was one of the zeniths of world civilization. Everything had to be brought to the city by boat. (The road bridge from the mainland was not built until 1846.)

Venice is also unique in being entirely car-free. Pay special attention to the acoustics: If you take a moment to listen, really listen, it's possible to hear things you wouldn't in other cities. Footsteps become audible, as does the sound of raindrops hitting pavement. Speaking voices carry much farther, and so does music—a singing gondolier's baritone echoing off the brick houses and the shimmering surface of the canal. The sounds of cooking, of clattering dishes, of popping corks and clinking glasses, are all more palpable in Venice. Here, you can hear the sounds of daily life on a human scale.

Perhaps at odds with its most famous cities, Veneto embraces rusticity. For all of the elegance of Venice, and the economic strength of Padua and Verona, Veneto is still a society that has close links to the land, to farm traditions, to "poor" cuisine such as polenta and codfish, and to sharing *un'ombra* (a glass of red wine) and *due chiacchiere* (a chat) with a friend old or new. It was the Venetians who coined the word *ciao,* as a salutation to say hello or goodbye. You will hear *Ciao!* wherever you go, and that word really says something about the buoyant, flirtatious, direct, and intriguing people of Veneto.

🗺 CITIES, TOWNS, AND PLACES

Engineers love **Venice** (home to about 55,000 people, but the mainland parts of the city grow the population to 270,000)—a completely man-made environment rising from the sea, with no visible means of support. Romantics revel in its elegant decay, seeing the peeling plaster and seaweed-covered stairs as a metaphor for beauty in decline. And first-time visitors are often stirred deeply, awaking from their ordinary lives to a fantasy world unlike anything they've experienced before. Venice can seem like one giant amusement park for grown-ups, centuries in the making.

Frankly, Venice can also be an overcrowded, prepackaged, tacky tourist trap. But even the most jaded visitors can't deny its specialness. The longer you're here—and the more you explore its back streets, especially after hours—the clearer it becomes that this is also a real, living town, with its own personality and challenges. Fred, a native New Yorker, is struck by the similarities between his home city and Venice. Both are island cities that have been seats of empires. As economic capitals, they had large mercantile classes and citizens who looked to the world beyond their mainland nation, and who continue to adore art, theater, and spectacle. These are cities where people are valued for genius and creativity, not merely for the ability to seize power and wealth. New Yorkers and Venetians are pragmatic and have chosen to live where they do in the face of adversity.

During the day, visitors ogle the big landmarks: St. Mark's Square and Basilica, the Doge's Palace, the

Venice's Grand Canal

Rialto Bridge over the Grand Canal, the mirage-like San Giorgio Maggiore and the towering La Salute Church, and world-class museums such as the Accademia, Correr, and Peggy Guggenheim. Venice's calm lagoon harbors the islands of glassmaking Murano, colorful Burano, and the city's birthplace, Torcello, all connected by *vaporetti* water buses. And late in the day, when the day-trippers have gone, crowds disperse and another Venice appears.

Frustratingly for food lovers, looking for an "untouristy restaurant" in Venice is like looking for the same thing at Disneyland. A restaurateur once confided in me that no restaurant in Venice can be truly untouristy: They all want and need the tourist euro. But while some cater to groups and sloppy big spenders, others respect their clientele—both locals and travelers. You can just give in and enjoy a relaxing dinner in a romantic canalside or piazza setting, without worrying too much about authenticity. Or you can go on a scavenger hunt for those elusive and rewarding

places that attempt to be actually "Venetian." And yet another great option—which is also quite local—is a *cicchetti* bar crawl (see sidebar).

Padua (Padova in Italian, pop. 210,000) is the region's economic center and the seat of one of Italy's foremost universities. Nicknamed the "brain of Veneto," Padua is full of art treasures (including the Scrovegni Chapel, with its 38 Giotto frescoes) and hosts one of the best food markets in all of Italy (on Piazza delle Erbe and Piazza della Frutta, every morning and all day Saturday). Both Padua and the little-visited neighboring province of Rovigo—sandwiched between Emilia-Romagna and the rest of Veneto—draw characteristics from both regions.

Verona (pop. 260,000) is the home of Romeo and Juliet, Italy's most famous opera festival, and some of the most intensive wine production in the country. The varieties produced here read like a list of great Italian wines: Bardolino, Valpolicella, Amarone, Bianco di Custoza, Soave, and so on. Verona is full of delightful

The Stand-Up Progressive Venetian Pub-Crawl Dinner

Rick's favorite Venetian dinner is a pub crawl, or *giro d'ombra. Giro* means stroll, and *ombra*—local slang for a glass of wine—means "shade," from the old days when a portable wine bar scooted with the shadow of the Campanile bell tower across St. Mark's Square.

Venice's residential back streets hide plenty of characteristic bars *(bacari),* which display countless trays of interesting toothpick munchies called *cicchetti* (chi-KEH-tee). Blackboards list the wines that are uncorked and served by the glass. Dropping in on a *cicchetti* bar—or several—is an ideal way to mingle with the Venetians. Bars don't stay open very late, and the *cicchetti* selection is best early, so start your evening by 6 p.m. Many bars are closed on Sunday. (For a description of one specific area, see page 365.)

Cicchetti bars have a social stand-up zone and a cozy gaggle of tables where you can generally sit down with your *cicchetti* or order from a simple menu. In popular places, crowds happily spill out into the street. Food generally costs the same price whether you stand or sit.

Look for a place that's more "bar" than "restaurant." Make sure they have *cicchetti* on display. Sip your drink and make the scene while standing at the bar. Next, order a *cicchetto* or two by pointing. Hang out, munch, and sip. Then order another one (or two). If there's a free stool or table, take a seat. Pay when you're ready to leave. And then move on to the next place for another drink with *cicchetti*.

Try deep-fried mozzarella cheese, Gorgonzola, calamari, artichoke hearts, and anything ugly on a toothpick. *Crostini* (small toasted bread with a topping) are popular, as are marinated seafood, olives, and prosciutto with melon. Meat and fish munchies can be expensive; veggies are cheap, at about €3 for a meal-sized plate. In many places, there's a set price per food item (for example, €1.50). Breadsticks *(grissini)* are free for the asking.

For drinks, start with an *aperitivo:* Order a Bellini, an Aperol *spritz,* or a Prosecco. Then enjoy the house wines with the food. House wine, served from a jug, is cheap: *un'ombra* (small glass of red wine), *un bianchetto* (small glass of white wine), or *un birrino* (small glass of beer) costs about €1. *Vin bon,* Venetian for fine wine, may run you €2 to €6 per little glass. A good final drink is *fragolino,* the local sweet wine—*bianco* or *rosso;* it often comes with a little cookie *(biscotto)* for dipping.

Top: Piazza dei Signori, Vicenza; **Above:** Treviso;
Below: Piazza degli Scacchi ("Chess Square"),
Marostica

enoteche and each April is the site of Vinitaly, the largest wine exposition in Italy.

In Verona province, **Valeggio sul Mincio** (pop. 14,000) is full of fine restaurants that make excellent *tortellini* and other fresh pasta to rival Bologna. There aren't enough locals to support them by themselves, so Valeggio is a food destination attracting people from nearby Mantua, Verona, and Brescia, as well as in-the-know travelers. The town also specializes in cooked or preserved fruit, including peaches, apricots, cherries, and grapes.

Vicenza (pop. 111,000) is best known as the hometown of Andrea Palladio (1508-1580), one of the most influential architects of the last several centuries; his work is everywhere in and around Vicenza and has been hugely impactful on

stately Neoclassical works, from Buckingham Palace to Thomas Jefferson's Monticello. Vicenza also has Italy's finest library of food history, with volumes dating back hundreds of years. Strangely, among the *veneti,* the people of Vicenza (nicknamed *magnagati*) are famous for eating cats. This unusual hardship food—now illegal in Italy—dates back to a tale from the 15th century, when Venice loaned Vicenza an army of cats to deal with an infestation of mice. Once the mouse population declined, the Venetians asked for their cats back. They were told, "Sorry! We ate them." (Today's locals favor codfish and Asiago cheese.)

The province that surrounds Vicenza is—like neighboring Verona—full of wine. Notable towns include **Marostica,** which produces delicious cherries and hosts a famous biannual "human chess match" on its piazza; and **Bassano del Grappa,** a lovely town with a historic wooden covered bridge. Locals make excellent grappa and ceramics, and gorgeous white asparagus grows here each spring.

Even with so many contenders, Fred's favorite Veneto town is **Treviso** (pop. 86,000), a 30-minute drive or train ride inland from Venice.

With its canals and resolutely under-stated chic, Treviso is a pleasant place to escape the hubbub of Venice for a day. And the city captures the full variety that Veneto offers: It's both industrial and agricultural, hardworking yet charming, and the surrounding province contains beaches, Venetian-type canals, plains, and pre-alpine hills. Fish and meat are both part of the diet, as are polenta and rice. Treviso's most famous vegetable, red-leaf radic-chio (which they call *trevigiano*), is now prized around the world, and arguably Italy's most famous dessert, *tiramisù,* was invented here in the 1950s. The *trevisani* are both indus-trious and fun-loving, stylish and rustic, and they speak in the lilting accent (and dialect) that so quickly identifies someone as a *veneto*. The province of Treviso also includes the charming small city of **Asolo** (pop. 9,000) and many rustic towns with a variety of excellent restaurants and Palladian villas.

And finally, the mountains. **Lake Garda**—one of the gems of Italy's Lake District—is shared by Veneto,

Bardolino, Lake Garda

Lombardy, and Trentino-Alto Adige. Along the shores of Lake Garda, lemons grow not far from snow-covered mountains, and above Garda they produce excellent olive oil. Several towns on the Veneto shores of Garda are worth a visit—including **Bardolino,** known for its excellent red wines. And higher up, the 1956 Winter Olympics in **Cortina d'Am-pezzo** (in the province of Belluno) briefly alerted the world to Veneto's stunning mountains; now the 2026 Winter Olympics—shared between Cortina and Milan—are set to do it all over again.

🍴 FOODS OF VENETO

Because of Veneto's remarkable variety of terrain, it has more types of food than most Italian regions. Many of the specialties listed here are specific to a city or province; because many travelers will be going to Venice, I've focused on that cuisine, but have also included some dishes from other places.

In Venice and other areas near the Adriatic, along rivers, and on the shores of Lake Garda, fish and seafood are common as *antipasti,* with pasta, and as main courses. Veneto has a long tradition of eating cod *(baccalà),* in numerous preparations. Especially inland, the *veneti* also eat a wide variety of meat: beef, pork, horse (particularly in Verona and Padua), calf's liver (in Venice espe-cially), poultry, and many types of small game birds.

The countryside of Veneto produces a range of high-quality fruits and vegetables, including *radicchio* from Treviso, asparagus from Bassano and Cavaion Veronese, many wonderful lettuces, beans, and other delights. The apples, pears, cherries, and peaches that grow near Verona are made into juices and jams that are consumed throughout Italy.

ANTIPASTI (APPETIZERS)

Antipasto di mare	Marinated mix of chilled fish and shellfish. While available anywhere in coastal Italy, this can be a particularly interesting choice in Venice.
Radicchio	This bitter, red-leaf lettuce from Treviso is now known globally. Internationally, we think of it as a tight little ball. But in Treviso (where they call it *trevigiano*), they also have a long-stalk version shaped like romaine lettuce.
Sarde in saor	Sardines marinated in a tangy, acidic mixture of vinegar, onions, raisins, and pine nuts. Other fish marinated this way—*in saor*—is a Venetian specialty.
Sopa cauda	A soup made of layers of bread and squab, topped with broth.

PRIMI (PASTAS AND OTHER FIRST COURSES)

Remember, **polenta** (described on page 76) is beloved in Veneto. It's usually served soft, and what's left over hardens to be served later cold or grilled. Rice and *risotto* are also popular, and there are several notable pasta dishes, mostly involving seafood. Veneto's alpine area features foods more typical of Trentino-Alto Adige, including the giant dumplings called *canederli* and filled pastas that contain sauerkraut, beets, cabbage, or potatoes.

Brodetto di pesce	Fish soup.
Bigoli in salsa	Long, fat, whole-wheat noodles, served in a sauce of anchovies and oil; it can also be served **col'arna,** with duck sauce.
Pasta allo scorfano	Pasta with a sauce made of fish (typically scorpion fish, *scorfano*), tomato, carrot, celery, onion, and parsley.

Left: *Sarde in saor;* **Right:** *Antipasto di mare* with anchovies and octopus

Left: *Pasta e fagioli;* **Right:** *Spaghetti al nero di seppia*

Pasta e fagioli (or ***pasta e faxioí***)	This bean-and-pasta soup is outstanding in Venice.
Risi e bisi	A classic dish of rice, peas, and sometimes *pancetta*.
Risotto or ***spaghetti al nero di seppia***	This "black *risotto*/spaghetti" is made with cuttlefish in its own ink and tastes of the sea.
Spaghetti alla busara	In a rich seafood-tomato sauce, generally with shrimp and garlic.
Spaghetti alle vongole	With clams.

SECONDI (MAIN DISHES)

In Venice and along the Adriatic, menus are dominated by fish and seafood—including some you won't commonly find elsewhere in Italy.

Anguilla	Eel, typically fried or roasted.
Baccalà	Preserved Atlantic salt cod that's rehydrated and served with polenta. If there is one classic dish that locals associate with Veneto, this is it. *Baccalà* can also be whipped with olive oil as a *cicchetti* topping called **baccalà mantecato.** Vicenza has **baccalà alla vicentina,** which is cooked in milk.
Bollito misto	This dish of boiled meats, common in the North, comes with local sauces—such as ***pearà,*** a marrow-based sauce served in Verona and nearby. In local dialect, a Veronese *bollito misto* is called **lesso con la pearà.**
Branzino	Sea bass, grilled and served whole.
Brasato all'Amarone	From Verona, this is beef braised in rich Amarone wine.

Left: Grilled fish; **Right:** *Spaghetti alle vongole*

Calamari	Squid, often cut into rings and deep-fried or marinated.
Coda di rospo	Monkfish tail, a Venetian specialty.
Cozze	Mussels, often steamed in an herb broth with tomato.
Fegato alla veneziana	This "Venetian-style liver" is strips of calf's liver sautéed with caramelized onions and sometimes wine, often served with polenta or mashed potatoes.
Gamberi	Shrimp (*gamberetti* are small, and *gamberoni* are large).
Gò	Goby, a small, fatty, bottom-dwelling fish found in the mud of the Venetian lagoon, often cooked in a *risotto*.
Moleche (or *moeche*) *col pien*	Fried soft-shell crabs from the Venetian lagoon.
Orata	Sea bream, a white fish.
Pesce fritto misto (or *frittura di pesce*)	Deep-fried seafood, often calamari and prawns.
Pesce spada	Swordfish.
Peverada (or *salsa peverada*)	This sauce for poultry is made with anchovy fillets, chicken livers, pickles, parsley, garlic, grated cheese, vinegar, and olive oil.
Rombo	Turbot, a flatfish similar to flounder.
Rospo (or *rana pescatrice*)	Frogfish, a small fish that's often grilled.
Schie	Small, gray shrimp from the Venetian lagoon.
Seppia	Cuttlefish, a squid-like creature. **Nero di seppia** is the squid served in its own ink, often over spaghetti (see earlier).

Sogliola	Sole, served poached or oven-roasted.
Vitello di mare	"Sea veal," like swordfish—firm, mild, and grilled.
Vongole	Clams, often steamed with fresh herbs and wine, or served with pasta (see earlier).
Zuppa di pesce	Seafood stew.

FORMAGGI (CHEESES)

Veneto's top cheese is **Asiago,** a cow's-milk product that comes from the province of Vicenza. It's either *mezzano* (young, firm, creamy) or *stravecchio* (aged, pungent, granular). Asiago is delicious—one of Italy's top cheeses—and it goes well with cherries. Veneto's alpine valleys produce many good mountain cheeses.

DOLCI (SWEETS)

Many factors combine to make desserts a big deal in Veneto: the abundance of good fruit and spices, the Venetian love of festive food, and the cake-loving Austrians who once ruled the uplands.

Baicoli	Dry cookies shaped like sea bass (for which they're named), originally designed to take on long nautical journeys, now often served with coffee.
Bisse	Seahorse-shaped cookies.
Bussolai	Ring-shaped cookies made for Easter, typical of Burano.
Crema fritta	Fried custard dessert popular in Venice.
Croccante	Toasted almond confection, similar to peanut brittle.

Left: *Pandoro* from Verona; **Right:** *Tiramisù*

Offalle	Soft round or oval cakes, often associated with Vicenza.
Pandoro	A yeasty cake from Verona that many Italians eat at Christmastime.
Pinza	Rustic cornmeal-and-wheat-flour cake filled with figs and/or dried fruit; made for Epiphany, January 6.
Tiramisù	Literally "pick-me-up," this is spongy ladyfingers soaked in coffee (and often Marsala or another sweet wine), layered with mascarpone cheese and bitter chocolate. While it's found all over Italy (often in disappointing, bastardized forms), it originated in Treviso, and many purists believe it still tastes best in and near its birthplace.

♀ WINES OF VENETO

In many years, Veneto produces the most wine of any Italian region. And with 29 DOC zones and an impressive 14 DOCGs, it's known as much for quality as for quantity. Grapes from the Valpolicella appellation are blended to make the fruity, red table wine called simply **Valpolicella** (found everywhere). The same grapes are also the basis for the full-bodied red Amarone and the sweet dessert wine Recioto. Connoisseurs love the high-quality wines of the Verona area: The hills to the east are covered with grapes to make Soave, to the north is Valpolicella country, and Bardolino comes from vineyards to the west.

Here are some wines to look for:

Amarone Literally "big bitter one," this intense red wine is made from dried *(passito)* corvina, rondinella, and other grapes from Valpolicella, then aged for a minimum of four years in oak casks. The result is a rich, velvety, full-bodied red that's high in alcohol—often around 15 percent.

Bardolino Made with the same grapes used for Valpolicella in vineyards near Lake Garda, this is a light, fruity, fragrant, exuberant red wine—similar to a French Beaujolais. It's a perfect picnic wine. Bardolino used to appear on tables around the world. When demand increased, so did production, and by the early 1980s, quality had slipped. But the delicious young wine consumed locally offers an opportunity to try Bardolino in its finest form.

Fragolino A sweet, slightly fizzy dessert wine made from a strawberry-flavored grape.

Prosecco The generic term "prosecco" is mistakenly used abroad to describe any sparkling white from Italy. But capital-P Prosecco originated in northeastern Italy, where Veneto and Friuli each have DOC zones. And Prosecco is the name of a town near Trieste. Prosecco is produced using the Charmat bulk method, with the second fermentation occurring in large tanks. (This is different from French Champagne, where the second fermentation takes place in the bottle.) True Prosecco must be made from 85 percent glera grapes, distinguished by their sweetness and aroma, and ranges from dry to sweet. Beyond its effervescence, this sparkling wine is known for its refreshing floral and fruity (citrus, apple) notes. The Prosecco from Conegliano, in Treviso province, is particularly worth seeking out.

Recioto Meaning "ears" in local dialect, this sweet dessert wine uses only the grapes from the top of the cluster (so they sort of look like the "ears" of the cluster's "head"). Because these grapes get the most sun, they mature the fastest and have the highest concentration of sugar. Before pressing, the grapes are dried for months; the wine is then aged for one to three years.

Soave One of Italy's best-known white wines is crisp and dry; it goes well with seafood and *risotto*. Like Bardolino, Soave was overproduced for many years, which blemished its reputation. While Soave can vary widely in quality, the best—called Soave Classico—comes from the heart of the region, near Soave Castle. Soave is sometimes aged in oak casks, giving it a mellow, rounded flavor.

Other White Wines Bianco di Custoza is a lesser-known but still good-quality white. And the often-seen **Lugana** pairs well with artichokes.

Cocktails

Venice, with its many expensive grand cafés facing stage-set piazzas, has some cocktails for which it's particularly known. For other cocktail options, see page 98.

Bellini Prosecco and white-peach puree, invented at the famous Harry's American Bar near St. Mark's Square.

Sgroppino Traditional after-dinner drink of squeezed lemon juice, lemon gelato, and vodka.

Spritz Prosecco or white wine and soda mixed with **Campari** (bitter) or **Aperol** (sweeter), over ice.

Tintoretto Prosecco and pomegranate juice.

Tiziano Prosecco and grape juice.

Left: Vineyards; **Right:** *Sgroppino*

Friuli-Venezia Giulia

Friuli-Venezia Giulia may well be the great undiscovered region of Italy (especially now that Piedmont and Emilia-Romagna are becoming more known to food lovers). This region has beautiful Adriatic beaches, the untrampled Carnic Alps, idyllic scenery in the Collio vineyards, vibrant and handsome cities such as Udine and Trieste, towns with ancient roots, wonderful food and wine, great coffee, and, above all, some of the warmest, most welcoming people in Italy (and that's saying something).

Friuli-Venezia Giulia—which, for simplicity, I'll refer to as "FVG"—is tucked in the northeast corner of Italy—squeezed between the burly Dolomites, Austria, Slovenia, and the humid crook of the Adriatic. For such a small region, the geographic, cultural, and culinary variety here is remarkable. You'll even find unusual-in-Italy flavors such as nutmeg, which date back to when Trieste and Venice were ports for transporting exotic

spices—by way of Udine—to Vienna and Budapest.

This part of Italy has long been a crossroads. The Romans had major settlements here (including today's Cividale del Friuli and Aquileia), and the region's convoluted name reflects the fact that large swathes once belonged to the Venetian Empire, and still carry that cultural and culinary influence. Later, much of Friuli—most notably Trieste—became part of the Austrian Empire. And to

this day, the borderlands with neighboring Slovenia are marked by a cross-cultural mingling, where dishes with distinctly Slavic names turn up on Italian menus, and vice versa. People here remind themselves that humans invented borders that nature disregards and, with the first glass of new wine, often drink to the well-being of their friends and neighbors "over there."

South of its mountains, FVG opens up into a broad, flat,

🍴 Foods and Drinks to Sample in Friuli-Venezia Giulia

Prosciutto di San Daniele
Rivals Parma's ham as Italy's very best *prosciutto crudo*.

Cjarsons
Decadent ravioli, traditionally made with more than 40 ingredients, from the Carnic Alps.

Frico
Mountain fritter made of Montasio cheese and sometimes potatoes.

Frico

Jota
Thick, hearty soup with cabbage, beans, and sometimes pork, popular near the Slovenian border.

Ribolla gialla (white) or pignolo (red)
Two of the many distinctly Friulian wines—among Italy's best and most underrated.

easily traversable plain that leads to important ports on the Adriatic. This geography has invited great sorrow: Every northern invader from Attila the Hun to the Nazis passed through here, and FVG (along with nearby parts of Slovenia) witnessed some of the most gruesome battles of World War I—especially on the mountaintops high above the Isonzo River, which is called the Soča upriver in Slovenia. It was here where a young Ernest Hemingway drove an ambulance, and where his protagonist recovered from his wounds in *A Farewell to Arms*.

Even in peaceful times, much of FVG suffered through grinding poverty and hunger—known locally as *La Miseria*. From the late 1800s through World War II, many *friulani* emigrated to the Americas (including a contingent who became winemakers in Argentina). But then,

starting in the mid-20th century, the region reversed its fortunes through sheer hard work, bringing about an economic miracle. The *friulani* transformed the area around Manzano into the chair-making capital of the world—following the logic that everyone has to sit somewhere, so there will always be demand. And much of FVG became a world-class vineyard, producing some of Italy's top wines.

FVG is a melting pot of cultures, cuisines, and languages: Attentive travelers may notice that they hear Slovene, German, or Croatian spoken in the eastern provinces, near the border. And in much of FVG, people are especially proud to speak their own language, called Friulano (or Furlan). This isn't a dialect of Italian, but its own tongue with Latin, Slavic, and Teutonic influences. Even when speaking Italian, the *friulani* tend to add a very soft *g* after an *n*—so "good"—*bon*—becomes "bong," and "wine" becomes "vihng."

As you travel around the region, try to eat in places where the people eat: the *osteria* in Udine, the *buffet* in Trieste, the *gostilna* in Collio, and, in the western part of Friuli, the *frasca*—a place where wine is produced and food is served. In the past, this was a sort of private *osteria* for peasants and farmworkers that would have a seasonal permit to serve food. When a *frasca* was opened, a tree branch with leaves would be hung over the portal. The rule was that food could be sold until the leaves

dried (usually by the end of the summer). Now anyone can eat at a *frasca* (called a *privada* in Gorizia and an *osmizza* in Trieste).

Whatever you call it, the *osteria* is central to the social and spiritual life of FVG. Everyone who enters—whether an architect or a bricklayer, a doctor or a bread baker—is equally welcome. Titles are cast aside, unlike in southern Italy, where one's station in life is brought to bear on every social situation. Once seated, order a *tajùt* (pronounced "tie-YOOT")—a small glass of wine, typically Tocai (a.k.a. Friulano)—and dig into earthy but delicious food such as polenta, *risotto,* gnocchi, cheeses, braised meats, omelets made with wild herbs, and good baked desserts.

As people eat and drink, they often sing the *villotta friulana,* a mournful song sung in dialect that recalls the beauty and tragedy of a little region that's had more than its share of challenge. Despite the hardships they have endured, the *friulani* and *giuliani* remain markedly sweet and good-natured.

🗺 CITIES, TOWNS, AND PLACES

Trieste (pronounced tree-EHS-tay in Italian, pop. 200,000), the biggest city in FVG, was once the principal port of the Habsburg Empire. As the foods and flavors of the world passed through its harbor, they influenced the local cuisine and culture. Between the world wars, Trieste was a "Free Territory," only becoming part of Italy in 1954. Consequently, the *triestini* are a mix of Slavic, Mediterranean, and Central European stock, and when speaking Italian, they have a distinct, lilting cadence. Trieste has few major sights, but the elegant

architecture along the harborfront is striking.

As the onetime shipping hub for a sprawling realm, Trieste's cuisine makes use of flavors less familiar elsewhere in Italy—from cinnamon to dill—and coffee is a big deal here. (When you consider how much the Viennese love coffee, and then how much of that coffee passed through here on its way to those grand cafés, Trieste's coffee addiction is understandable.) Trieste is home to the headquarters of Illy, one of Italy's premium coffee brands, and the city has its own distinct coffee culture:

Above: Canal Grande, Trieste; **Below:** Udine

A *cappuccino triestino* comes in an espresso cup, has less foamed milk, and is often topped with whipped cream. (If you want a more typical cappuccino, order a *cappuccino grande.*)

Trieste also excels at baked goods, cakes, and pastries—another holdover from the Habsburg days, considering the Austrian and Hungarian affection for *Kaffee und Küchen* (afternoon coffee with decadent treats). One special option is *putizza* (similar to Slovenian *potice*): a rum-soaked layer cake with walnuts and melted chocolate. You'll also find other classic cakes from Central Europe, including the chocolate-bomb *Sachertorte* (from Vienna) and *torta Dobos,* a delicate layer cake of chocolate, buttercream, and caramel (from Budapest).

Triestine cooking is a blend of land and sea, with Italian, Slavic, Germanic, and Greek influences. It features dishes of Slovenian origin, such as *jota* (a hearty, earthy soup) and *persuto* (the Slovenian/Triestine version of prosciutto). For classic

local cuisine, locals also go to small country restaurants in the Carso, the rural district that surrounds the city.

On the flat interior plain, **Udine** (OO-dee-neh, pop. 100,000) is Fred's favorite Friuli town. It thrived during the Renaissance, and today it has a lively market district (near Piazza della Libertà), a wonderful assortment of *osterie,* a coffee scene very nearly as enjoyable as Trieste's, and more than its share of Austrian tourists (who drive across the border for great food and clothing). The *udinesi* are elegant: They enjoy dressing up

for the *passeggiata,* and people-watching here is a delight.

North of Udine, just before the alpine foothills, the town of **San Daniele** is synonymous with *prosciutto crudo*—it produces some of Italy's best. Nearby, **Maniago** is known for its knives and scissors, as well as for its local pork and game specialties.

Friuli has a pair of towns that are of interest to those who enjoy ancient sites: **Aquileia,** founded in 181 BC, was for a long time the second most important city in the Roman Empire; it has a fine museum and an early-Christian basilica with outstanding mosaics. **Cividale del**

Friuli—founded in 50 BC by Julius Caesar—was the site of an ancient market when it was a stopping point on the trade route from the Adriatic to the Alps. It remains a market town today.

In the province of **Gorizia,** along the border with Slovenia, you'll find names and flavors that bear a Slavic influence: simple restaurants called *gostilna* and specialties made with buckwheat and turnip.

To the north, bordering Austria, the **Carnic Alps** are rugged and scenic. One fine spa town in this area, **Arta Terme,** is an ideal spot to try the luxurious mountain ravioli called *cjarsons.*

🍴 FOODS OF FRIULI-VENEZIA GIULIA

Remember: FVG has a great deal of internal variety—in landscape, history, culture, and even language. While I've lumped everything together in this section, you'll find dishes are highly localized.

ANTIPASTI (APPETIZERS)	
Cevapcici (or *čevapčiči*)	Little grilled minced-meat sausages, savory and spicy, which migrated to FVG through Habsburg lands from deep in the Balkans.
Frico	A sensational fritter made of Montasio cheese (described later). There can be variations on this general theme. It's usually crunchy, but sometimes has a crunchy top and a runny, cheesy interior. Even larger versions (sometimes called *frico morbido,* "soft") can have potato and onion mixed in with the cheese; in this case, it's big enough to be a *primo,* or even a meal in itself. (The biggest can resemble a very cheesy hash-brown *Rösti* from Switzerland, or a *Gröstl* from Alto Adige.) And there's a smaller version, sometimes called *frico friabile*—just small, lacy wisps of cheese heated on a grill until crispy.
Frittata alle erbe	Omelet with fresh herbs (traditionally seven or more types), often served cool.
Musetto (or *musèt*)	Highly spiced pork sausage that often includes cinnamon.
Prosciutto affumicato	Smoked raw ham, a specialty in the Carnic Alps.

Left: *Frico;* Right: *Jota*

Prosciutto di San Daniele	An exquisite air-cured ham whose flavor rivals the famous stuff in Parma (in Emilia-Romagna). The flavors of Italy's two top prosciuttos are worth tasting and comparing. *Prosciutto di San Daniele* is customarily sliced very thin and served as an *antipasto,* but is also used in pasta sauces, omelets, sandwiches, and in combination with cheeses and other meats.
Speck	Smoked bacon from the Carnic Alps.

PRIMI (PASTAS AND OTHER FIRST COURSES)

Brodetto alla gradese	This fish-and-seafood soup, flavored with garlic and vinegar, is a specialty of the seaside resort Grado.
Cjarsons (also **cjalsons** or **cialzons**)	These ravioli from the Carnic Alps, traditionally made with more than 40 ingredients—including bitter chocolate, lemon, cinnamon, mint, onions, dried figs, potatoes, eggs, raisins, marjoram, flour, parsley, and smoked *ricotta*—are simply amazing.
Frico	The crispy Montasio cheese fritter (described under *"Antipasti,"* earlier) can also show up as a *primo.*
Gnocchi di susine	Meltingly delicious gnocchi that enclose a piece of ripe plum (or sometimes apricot) that softens as the pasta cooks.
Gnocchi di zucca con ricotta affumicata	This *friulano* classic is squash-flavored gnocchi served with melted butter and fragrant smoked *ricotta.*
Gulasch (or **goulasch**)	Spicy meat stew, a holdover from the Austro-Hungarian Empire.
Jota	A thick soup of Slovenian origin, made with beans, cabbage or sauerkraut (or sometimes turnip), onions, sage, and garlic; sometimes pork is added, as well. It's popular in Trieste, Gorizia, and other areas in the borderlands.

Lasagne ai semi di papavero	*Lasagne* with poppy seeds.
Paparot	Spinach-and-cornmeal soup.
Toç	A generic term for a soup that's fortified with polenta and then diluted with milk. ***Toç in braide*** is a simple but nourishing soup, traditionally consumed by peasants working in the fields: White flour and polenta are cooked until they have the texture of a biscuit. A little water or wine is then added, resulting in a thick soup, and it's finished with soft cheese and butter. ***Toç de pur-cit*** is a pork version stewed with white wine, cinnamon, cloves, and other flavorings.

SECONDI (MAIN DISHES)

Many dishes listed under *"Antipasti"*—such as **cevapcici, musetto, frittata alle erbe, and toç**—are also served as *secondi*. In addition, the *friulani* and *giuliani* enjoy all sorts of fish and seafood from the Adriatic, as well as grilled meats and game.

Brovada	Turnips marinated with grape skins and cooked with pork sausage.
Stinco	Meaning "shin," this can be applied either to pork *(maiale)* or veal *(vitello)*; either way, it's typically roasted or braised.

FORMAGGI (CHEESES)

Formaggio di malga	Fresh cheese made in the high Alps from the milk of cows that graze on mountain grass and herbs.
Montasio	A deceptively unpretentious cow's-milk cheese that has grand flavor. It's the essential ingredient for a *frico* (see *"Antipasti,"* earlier).

Left: *Ricotta affumicata;* **Right:** *Gubana*

Ricotta affumicata	Smoked *ricotta,* the preferred grating cheese for most local pasta dishes.

DOLCI (SWEETS)

Gubana	An exquisite, fragrant, bread-like cake filled with ground nuts, pine nuts, dried raisins and figs, and other ingredients. It's a specialty of Cividale del Friuli (where it's made with puff pastry) and the Natisone Valley (where it's made with a yeast dough).
Pinza, presnitz, and putizza	Three special cakes typical of Trieste and the surrounding area.
Strudel	Another holdover of the Austro-Hungarian Empire, local strudel can be made with apples, *ricotta,* or other fillings.

♀ WINES OF FRIULI-VENEZIA GIULIA

The wines of this region represent only 2 percent of Italy's output, yet they are among the most outstanding in the country. Because of their high quality and relatively limited supply, FVG wines (especially whites) command high prices. Local wines are remarkable not only for quality, but also for the number of grape varieties that are used—both native varieties and grapes imported from many lands.

    Zones: FVG has seven DOC zones, all of them excellent. About half of this region's wines come from the Grave del Friuli, high plains with a fair amount of gravel in the soil (hence the name). The emphasis is on medium-weight reds, such as merlot, and the whites are also good. Nearby zones include Latisana, Aquileia, and the Carso (around Trieste); all produce wines that are tasty and drinkable. The Isonzo area is a transitional zone between the coastal/plain areas and the mountains. And along the Slovenian border are two outstanding zones called Collio ("hills"): Collio Goriziano and Colli Orientali. These produce excellent whites such as Friulano (formerly Tocai), pinot bianco, pinot grigio, sauvignon blanc, malvasia, and chardonnay, as well as reds including pignolo.

WHITE WINES
Ribolla gialla grapes produce a pleasing wine that's bright, fruity, lightly floral, and acidic. Especially across the border in Slovenia, the same grapes can be fermented with their skins to produce the unusual "orange" or "amber" wine. While this

is recently quite trendy, it dates back to ancient times.

Another well-known white is what used to be called Tocai Friulano. But, after the EU made Tokaji unique to Hungary in 2006, a new name was required. They went with the accurate yet generic and uninspiring Bianco Friulano, or **Friulano** for short.

Other whites produced in FVG include chardonnay, malvasia istriana (a light, slightly metallic white that marries beautifully with Adriatic seafood—not to not be confused with the amber malvasia produced in Sicily), Müller-Thurgau, pinot bianco, pinot grigio, Riesling Italico, Riesling Renano (the type used in Germany), sauvignon blanc, traminer aromatico (like Gewürztraminer), and verduzzo (a native variety that can also be produced as a dessert wine).

RED WINES

While FVG is known mainly for its whites, there are many fine reds as well. One of the best is **pignolo,** named for the "pinecone" *(pigno)*-like density of its very dark-colored grapes. (*Pignolo* also means something like "finicky" or "fussy," and it's true that these grapes are challenging to cultivate and have low yields.) Often aged in oak, pignolo is rich and full-bodied, beautifully balancing tannic and acidic notes. It goes well with heavy meats.

Also look for **Terrano,** which is typical of the Carso (the area surrounding Trieste, with a particular limestone terrain that imbues wines with a high mineral content). Terrano is made with the refosco grape and grows in red soil, with high iron content. Since Roman times, people have sought out Terrano medicinally: Its high acids are thought to be beneficial for digestive problems, and it's still given to anemic patients needing supplemental iron. A wine road stretches from Opicina to Visogliano, connecting wineries and restaurants that serve Terrano. The wine is also popular in neighboring areas of Slovenia, where it's called Teran.

Other FVG reds include cabernet franc, cabernet sauvignon, Collio (a blend of cabernet franc, cabernet sauvignon, and merlot), Collio Cabernet (a blend of franc and sauvignon, as is also done in Bordeaux), merlot, pinot nero, and native varieties including Refosco dal Peduncolo Rosso, schioppettino, and tazzelenghe (literally "Tongue Cutter"—because of its high acidic content, it's usually consumed in winter with pork and game).

OTHER DRINKS

Dessert Wines: FVG has three excellent dessert wines: picolit (from the native, difficult-to-grow grape) that, at its best, is an ambrosial nectar; Ramandolo, a delicious, little-seen white; and the dessert version of verduzzo.

Grappa: And finally, don't overlook this region's fine grappa—made with leftover grape skins from all that winemaking. The Nonino family, in the Colli Orientali, elevated production of grappa to an art and make some of Italy's best.

Central Italy
Emilia-Romagna

Emilia-Romagna (eh-MEEL-yah roh-MAHN-yah) is an odd duck. Despite sitting just between major touristic draws to the north (Venice and Milan) and the south (Florence and Tuscany), it's largely ignored by sightseers. And yet, for food lovers, Emilia-Romagna is simply the best that Italy has to offer. For Italians and gourmands, the region is synonymous with classic flavors such as the ultimate Italian cheese, Parmigiano-Reggiano; the world's best balsamic vinegar *(aceto balsamico tradizionale);* melt-in-your-mouth *prosciutto di Parma* (not to mention *culatello* and *mortadella);* delicate *tortellini* and other filled pastas; and much, much more.

🍲 Foods to Sample in Emilia-Romagna

Parmigiano-Reggiano
Sets the global standard for crumbly, sweet, nutty, aged cheese.

Balsamic vinegar
At its very best *(aceto balsamico tradizionale)*, this luscious, complex, thick, black liquid is nothing like what you can get back home.

Tortellini in brodo
Handmade, filled pasta traditionally served in poultry broth.

Culatello
Extremely lean, cured pork—prosciutto's overachieving cousin.

Mortadella
The original inspiration for "baloney"...but so much better.

Mortadella

Emilia-Romagna's culinary tradition is rooted in a rich local culture. This region has produced great opera stars (Luciano Pavarotti and Mirella Freni), filmmakers (Federico Fellini), fashion icons (Giorgio Armani), sports-car pioneers (Enzo Ferrari), and so on. The *emiliani* and *romagnoli* are hardworking, but they also devote time to pleasure and enlightenment. Emilia-Romagna's cities routinely rank near the top of national listings for quality of life.

Most of all, the people of Emilia-Romagna specialize in eating well. Italians almost universally acknowledge this region's cuisine to be the country's best. There's no doubt it's the richest. I suspect that the relaxed quality of life combined with excellent medical care mean that locals can enjoy enviable life expectancies despite eating more than their share of cheese, pork, butter, and cream. (*Besciamella*, sometimes called *balsamella*, is rich Béchamel sauce.)

A favorite regional pastime is debating which city has the best food. Each location, big and small, has its own specialties. One reason is that the great ancient cities of this region were independent duchies and city-states, each with its own identity. Those distinct cuisines and personalities persevere to this day: Locals report, for example, that the people of Parma are more reserved, while those from Modena are more vivacious.

Geographically, Emilia-Romagna fills the fertile plain of the Po River, which cuts diagonally across the middle of Italy, between the Alps and the Apennines. Most of its important towns line up like breadcrumbs along the Via Emilia, a road dating to Roman times (roughly aligned with today's E-35 highway): From the Milan area, it crosses the regional border and heads southeast to Parma, Reggio Emilia, Modena, Bologna, Faenza, Forli, and all the way to Rimini on the Adriatic.

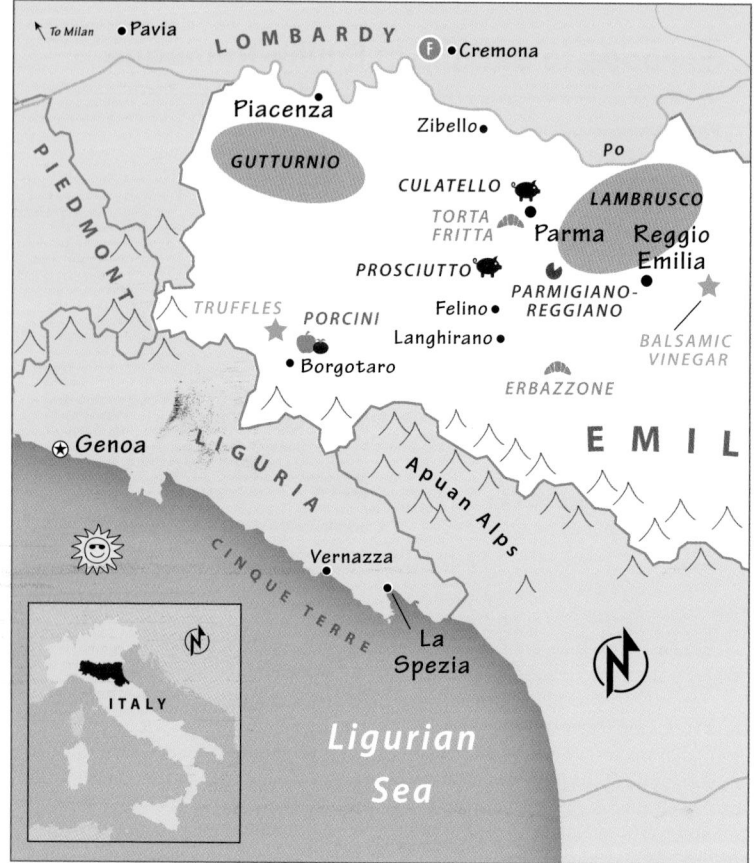

Many say the secret to Emilia-Romagna's abundance of quality ingredients is the thick fog that blankets this central plain (especially in the autumn)—creating an ambience that can be alternately gloomy, nostalgic, or cozy. The fogs and mists are especially beautiful in the cities, where people walk under porticoes and encounter one another at occasional spots of illumination. It's said this evocative aura inspired Fellini (who was born in Rimini).

Within this region, the area from Bologna to the north and west (including Parma and Modena) is Emilia; to the south and east is Romagna. Italians say that the *emiliani* are more sophisticated and the *romagnoli* more rustic, but that's an oversimplification—Ravenna, for one, is a great example of how classy *romagnolo* cities can be. And yet, the people of Romagna do have a wonderful brio and love of life.

One part of Emilia-Romagna has been discovered by tourists, mainly ones from Italy and Europe: the Adriatic coastline, called the Riviera di Romagna, centered on Rimini. The many beach towns here specialize in affordable, filling meals for

vacationing families. This land is less fertile than the higher-yielding soil inland, so was traditionally the terrain of poor farmers—who, as beach tourism flourished after World War II, sold out and got a huge payout. Some *romagnoli* still think of food and wine in terms of quantity over quality, giving the cuisine a bit less refinement than Emilia's.

While all of Italy has the *passeggiata,* in Emilia-Romagna they call it *andiamo in piazza* ("let's go to the main square")—much as the Romans did 2,000 years ago. Each day, central piazzas in towns large and small

are filled with people who gather for conversation and fun. And no square in the region is more animated and engaging than Bologna's Piazza Maggiore. Throughout the day and night, it bustles with conversation, music, old friends reconnecting, parents nurturing kids, couples cultivating young romances, and much more.

Although Emilia-Romagna lacks the spectacular sightseeing gems of Tuscany, Venice, or Rome, that's part of its charm: It's a fine place not only to eat amazing food, but also to settle in and get a taste of real, everyday life in Italy that's less trampled by tourism.

📍 CITIES, TOWNS, AND PLACES

Bologna is the leading city (pop. 400,000) and culinary hub of Emilia-Romagna. Come with an expectation to melt into the city—and to dig into its fabled food scene—rather than to be wowed by great architecture and art. For aficionados, Bologna is a sensual paradise of fragrances, flavors, and smiling people who love life. It's a living textbook of food culture, fashion, style, perspective, and taste. The city cultivates a sense of a civic whole in which everything is in its place. (Can you tell this is Fred's favorite city in Italy and adopted Italian hometown?)

The *bolognesi* are a mix of elegant and fun: openhearted, fun-loving, intellectual, and sensuous. They adore good food and wine and have the best markets in Italy. Bologna's university, founded in 1069, is the world's oldest and the best in the country. The city's architecture is largely medieval; its trademark are the porticoes that line most of the streets. These arcades provide shade from the sun and shelter from the rain, all while funneling pedestrians to mix, mingle, and socialize.

And, of course, Bologna specializes in food. Restaurants are practically a religion here: Debating each one's pros and cons, and tracking their shifting fortunes, is the most popular topic of heated local debate. (If you have your heart set on a particular place, it's essential to reserve ahead—even more so here than elsewhere in Italy.) But don't miss the chance to also explore the city's many markets and food shops. Vendors obsess over educating their customers about the intricacies of their ingredients. And they do it with an evangelical zeal.

The streets east of Bologna's main piazza teem with food stores. The venerable choice is Tamburini (Via Caprarie 1), in business since 1932 and still approaching local ingredients with reverence. The streets behind Tamburini are filled with additional markets and stalls (especially on Via Drapperie, Via Caprarie, Via Pescherie Vecchie, and Via Clavature). To continue exploring, carry on west a few blocks from the main square on Ugo Bassi to the Mercato delle Erbe, a covered market that also has places for casual dining.

Top: Piazza Maggiore, Bologna; **Bottom:** Castello Estense, Ferrara

Parma, a noble city of 200,000, is preoccupied with food, hospitality, and elegance. The *parmigiani* are thought of as trendsetters, dating back to the Farnese family (ruled 1513-1727), who lured artists and scholars here. When the Bourbons took over in the 1730s, they carried on this tradition and imported French tastes, leaving the local dialect (and cuisine) with a distinctly French accent. The legacy of these rulers is grand palaces and stately gardens. Parma province was also home to Italy's top composer, Giuseppe Verdi (whom they affectionately call "Peppino"), and its greatest conductor, Arturo Toscanini.

A huge part of Parma's sterling reputation is its food. The city is world-famous for Parmigiano-Reggiano—the king of cheeses—as well as for *culatello* (lean cured pork), sublime prosciutto, all sorts of dairy products, and excellent vegetables. And it's the home of Barilla, Italy's largest producer of dry pasta.

Many of Parma's public buildings are painted an egg-yolk hue (called "Parma yellow") that take on a particular luster in the sun and project a welcoming warmth on the misty days that enshroud Parma in late autumn. The city's Piazza del Duomo has a beautiful cathedral that's overshadowed by a massive, octagonal baptistery completed in 1196. From here, the streets toward the river are filled with the fruit-and-vegetable markets of Piazza Ghiaia. And don't miss the *passeggiata* along Via Cavour and Via Garibaldi. You'll see elegant women walking arm in arm and clusters of men standing under an arcade discussing politics, sports, or, more likely, what's for dinner.

Racecars, opera singers, rich Lambrusco, sensational food, and adorable people. What more can be said about **Modena**? *Aceto balsamico tradizionale,* that's what. This city (pop. 190,000) is the birthplace of Italy's "black gold." It's also home to Osteria Francescana, which has been repeatedly listed as the world's top restaurant. Its owner, the animated Massimo Bottura, has become the ubiquitous ambassador for the

Byzantine mosaic-slathered church in Ravenna

Balsamic Vinegar

Top-quality balsamic vinegar is an extraordinary ingredient. But, like many great food products, it is little understood and often misused. *Aceto balsamico tradizionale* isn't just a brown vinegar used to make salad dressing or marinate vegetables; it's a luxuriously thick, ambrosial liquid that stands on its own as the ultimate condiment. A drop or two of *aceto balsamico tradizionale* exalts almost anything it touches: Parmigiano-Reggiano cheese, potatoes, meat, poultry, strawberries. Expensive as caviar or a fine aged wine, a small bottle is worth investing in to bring home and use sparingly to impress your gourmand friends.

The vinegar is made only from the juice of trebbiano grapes, and—unlike with many vinegars—a "mother" is never used to start the process. Real *aceto balsamico tradizionale* goes through up to 12 years of fining: absorbing the essences of various woods as the vinegar is moved to different barrels from year to year. The consortium that governs the quality of *aceto balsamico tradizionale* grades the product, rejecting 80 percent as unacceptable. (To assure fairness, they erect tall boards between tasters so they can't read each other's facial expressions.) The provinces of Modena and Reggio Emilia are the only places where *aceto balsamico tradizionale* can be produced.

foods of Emilia-Romagna. If you've watched a trendy TV show about the Italian food scene, you've surely seen him. Whether you think Bottura is overrated, there's no question he has attracted many food pilgrims to Modena—who, once here, realize what a beautiful, enjoyable, and livable place this is, and are very glad they came.

Reggio Emilia (pop. 171,000), which sits between Parma and Modena, is one of the most unjustifiably ignored cities in Italy—and not just by travelers. Even most Italians pass it by, opting for its more famous neighbors. And yet, only Reggio can claim to share its name with Parma on Parmigiano-Reggiano cheese, and also be part of the very small zone (including Modena) where the real, traditional balsamic vinegar can be made. Its handmade pasta rivals what's made in Bologna, to boot.

Ferrara (pop. 132,000) was a

Modena

leading city of the Renaissance and once had one of Italy's foremost Jewish communities. Its centerpiece is a stately, walled-and-moated fortress, Castello Estense, with a cathedral and fine, elongated piazza just steps away. Today it's a great place to dine on pumpkin-filled *cappellacci con la zucca,* the delicious *salama da sugo, pampepato,* and some of the best pears anywhere.

Borgotaro is famous for its truffles and its porcini mushrooms; be sure to try *minestra dei carbonai* (a mushroom-and-potato soup from a historic recipe)—or, really, anything with *funghi porcini.* The town of **Felino** makes some of the finest salami in Italy. And **Faenza** is famous not for food, but for its ceramics (known abroad as "faience").

For sightseers, **Ravenna** (pop. 160,000) is the most interesting place in Emilia-Romagna for one reason: its 1,500-year-old churches, decorated with best-in-the-West Byzantine mosaics, dating from the time (c. AD 400-600) when Ravenna was the center of Western civilization—a civilization in transition, from Roman to barbarian to Byzantine to medieval.

🍴 FOODS OF EMILIA-ROMAGNA

Locals have a saying, paraphrased from a Bertolucci film: *A Parma si mangia due volte. Prima si mangia, poi si parla.* ("In Parma, one eats twice. First you eat, then you talk.") The people of Emilia-Romagna love to endlessly discuss and debate the quality and virtues of food. Use this list as a starting point, but once you're on the road, be prepared to encounter many new teachers offering deep insights into the local cuisine.

ANTIPASTI (APPETIZERS)

Salumi (Cold Cuts)

At the heart of Emilia-Romagna's cuisine are its many pork products. Parma has another saying: *Il maiale è come la musica di Verdi—tutto buono, niente da buttar via.* ("The pig is like the music of Verdi—it's all good, with nothing to throw away.")

Culatello	Outsiders think of Parma for its *prosciutto crudo* (described later). But the *parmigiani* are cultists of the cured pork product called *culatello.* This comes from the leanest part of the hind leg of the pig—and specifically the *right* leg, which the pig curls under itself as it sits. (The left leg, used for standing, builds up muscle and is not considered lean enough.) The pigs used for *culatello* can only come from the flat, moist zone between Parma and the Po River—where the humidity results in a moist cure. The *culatello* is then aged for 15 to 18 months. It's traditional to eat *culatello* as an appetizer combined with *torta fritta* (see *"Pane,"* later).

Left: *Salumi;* **Right:** Parmigiano-Reggiano

Mortadella	For most Americans, Bologna is synonymous with a bastard-ized meat product that, adding insult to injury, is sometimes anglicized to "baloney." But that's baloney: The delicious sausage indigenous to Bologna is called *mortadella*—a combination of pork, sometimes pork liver, spices, bits of fat, and sometimes slivers of pistachio. The best ones come in large form—some more than three feet wide—because small *mortadelle* dry out too easily. Other *salumi* are at their best when sliced thin, but *mortadella* works well in thin slices or in chunks.
Prosciutto cotto	Excellent boiled ham, a specialty of Parma.
Prosciutto crudo	Usually called **prosciutto di Parma** (or, in English, "Parma ham"), this is actually produced in the town of Langhirano, in the Apennines above Parma, which has air and humidity ideal for curing. It's thought that much of the flavor of *prosciutto di Parma* comes from the whey (a by-product of cheesemaking) that's fed to the pigs. Many people believe it's best to eat sliced prosciutto by hand, rather than cutting it with a knife; *prosciutto di Parma* will invariably tear in the right place.
Salame all'aglio	Ferrara's special *salame* is laced with garlic.
Salame di Felino	Some of Italy's best *salame* is not made of felines—it's from the town of Felino, in the province of Parma.

Formaggi (Cheeses)

Formaggio di fossa	This cheese, with a complex flavor that mixes sweet and sharp, is aged in a straw-lined pit *(fossa)* for three months.
Mascarpone	A sweet, buttery cheese that is often swirled with a liqueur and served as a dessert.

Parmigiano-Reggiano	This is what Americans mistakenly call "Parmesan," and much of what's sold abroad is a poor imitation. But once you taste the real thing—sweet and nutty, perfect for eating in little chunks or for grating over pasta like a dusting of gold—you'll accept no substitutes. Parmigiano-Reggiano has been produced for more than 700 years and is regarded with reverence by the *emiliani*. It's among the first foods given to local babies, and Parma's soccer team considers it their secret weapon.

This cheese—exclusively made by hundreds of small producers in the provinces of Parma, Reggio Emilia, Modena, Bologna, and Mantua (in Lombardy)—deliciously illustrates the old saying that "cheese is milk's leap to immortality." To make one 75-pound wheel of cheese, they use more than 150 gallons of milk (five each from thirty cows). Every cheese is made by hand and then aged in carefully controlled rooms for at least one year, and usually for two years. (Because it takes time to mature the cheese, banks lend local cheesemakers a certain amount per wheel, which is repaid with interest when the cheese is sold; one big wheel can go for close to $1,000.)

Most local restaurants have a beautiful cart with a glass dome covering a wedge of cheese, as if it were a mystical object or an ancient jewel. The cart is rolled to your table, and a piece of the cheese is served with great flourish.

Better stores in the region will vacuum-pack *(sotto vuoto)* a wedge of Parmigiano-Reggiano for you to take home; be sure it has the official seal stamped on the wheel.

Squacquerone	Literally "shapeless," this soft, young, white, easy-eating cheese is popular in Romagna, and often, by necessity, served in a bowl.

Pane (Bread)

Erbazzone	This specialty of Reggio Emilia is a flattish bread filled with Swiss chard, spinach, or beet tops.

Left: *Piadina* sandwich; **Right:** *Torta fritta*

Pane bolognese and ***pane ferrarese***	In Bologna and Ferrara, people often eat very dry breads; while strange at first, these are an ideal match for the rich dishes of these two cities.
Piadina	The famous flatbread of Romagna, often wrapped around a filling (from vegetables to cheese to meat, or even chocolate or fruit). The dough is made into thin disks about six inches wide and cooked on a tile. This has become known throughout much of Italy as the perfect platform for a wrap-like sandwich.
Torta fritta (or ***gnocco fritto***)	Made simply of flour, water, and lard, this delicate little fried bread is the perfect match for *culatello* and prosciutto—especially in Parma. Sometimes a little vinegar is added to the batter to reduce the richness of the lard.

PRIMI (PASTAS)

The range of pasta courses in Emilia-Romagna is unmatched for both quantity and quality. Local pasta is made with flour, water, and egg, giving it a golden color. In Romagna, meals often include more than one pasta course. It's not uncommon to be served a *tris*—a platter containing three different pasta courses, such as *lasagne verdi, tagliatelle al ragù,* and *tortelloni al pomodoro.*

Tortellini and **other filled pastas**	These can contain meat, cheese, vegetables (*zucca*/pumpkin, *patate*/potato, or *bietola*/chard), or occasionally fish. **Tortellini** is the most famous, and fillings differ from town to town. For example, in Modena, tortellini are filled with minced chicken, pork, veal, a little beef, butter, *prosciutto crudo,* and Parmigiano-Reggiano. In Bologna, they contain turkey, veal, ground pork, *mortadella, prosciutto crudo,* Parmigiano- Reggiano, and nutmeg.
	There are few simpler joys here than going from town to town comparing the delicate flavors of tortellini. Filled pastas also change names as you move through the region; in addition to tortellini, you may see **anolini, cappelletti, cappellacci, tortelli d'erbette, tortelloni,** and **balanzoni** (with spinach in the dough).

Left: *Tortellini in brodo;* **Right:** *Cannelloni* filled with meat

Other pastas	Large sheets of pasta *(sfoglie)* are cut into noodles such as ***tagliatelle*** and ***taglierini,*** along with sheets to make ***lasagne*** and ***cannelloni*** (filled cylindrical pasta tubes). You'll also find ***gnocchi,*** ***caramelle*** (shaped like a candy in a twisted wrapper), ***garganelli*** (flat egg pasta rolled into a tube), ***gramigna*** (hollow coils), and especially ***passatelli,*** which are made with breadcrumbs, lemon, egg, and nutmeg, and served *in brodo* (see next).
In brodo	Many filled pastas are served *in brodo* (in broth), which at its best is a sublime broth made of capon (a neutered rooster).
Other pasta preparations	Pasta is also commonly served ***alla panna*** (in cream), ***al ragù*** (a divine meat sauce), ***burro e oro*** (thin tomato sauce with butter), ***alla salsiccia*** (sausage sauce, usually served with *gramigna* noodles), and, of course, ***al pomodoro*** (tomato).

SECONDI (MAIN DISHES)

Cotechino	A spicy minced sausage, often served with lentils, cabbage, or pureed potatoes. It's frequently part of a *bollito misto,* in which case it's boiled and sliced.
Cotoletta alla bolognese	A breaded veal cutlet topped with prosciutto, Parmigiano-Reggiano, and, often, mozzarella and a slice of truffle.
Salama da sugo (or ***salamaina da sugo***)	This specialty of Ferrara is a form of sausage that crumbles when cooked and is ideally matched with *purè* (mashed potatoes). In the summer, it's cooked for a shorter time and served with slices of cantaloupe.
Tacchino al cardinale	Turkey breast with prosciutto and Parmigiano-Reggiano, often with a slice of truffle.
Zampone con le lenticche	Pig's trotter filled with minced pork and spices, then sliced thin. This specialty of Modena is usually served with lentils, especially at New Year's, when it is thought to bring wealth in the coming year.

CONTORNI (SIDE DISHES)

Verdure gratinate (or ***gratte in Romagna***)	Vegetables such as zucchini are cut open and baked with oil, spices, and breadcrumbs—but, unlike a typical *au gratin* preparation, no cheese.

Left: *Castagnole con la crema;* **Right:** *Torta srbisolona*

DOLCI (SWEETS)

Castagnole con la crema	Shaped like chestnuts, these cream-filled fritters are eaten during Carnival, particularly in Romagna.
Cherries *(ciliegie)*	While Romagna produces excellent fruit of all kinds, the cherries from Vignola (near Modena) are among the best anywhere. Sour cherries *(amarene)* are another local specialty, especially in Bologna and Modena.
Chiacchiere delle monache	"Nuns' chatter," the same pasta as *tagliatelle,* is cut in various shapes and then fried and covered with sugar. These are Carnival sweets found in many parts of Italy, especially in Romagna.
Pampepato	The origins of this Ferrara delicacy go back to the Renaissance. This "pepper bread" is actually made with spices, chocolate, nuts, and sometimes wine.
Torta di riso	A rice cake, from Reggio Emilia.
Torta di tagliatelle	A dry cake baked with thin strands of pasta; it's moist and crunchy.
Torta sbrisolona	A crumbly, buttery, dry cake perfect with dessert wine.

♀ WINES OF EMILIA-ROMAGNA

For such a culinary hotspot, Emilia-Romagna's wines are not particularly well regarded. The reputation of local wines was partly blemished by the Lambrusco craze of the 1970s, when it became an international favorite for a cheap buzz. This bubbly wine can be subtle and tasty when well made, but what was sent abroad was generic and designed to be inexpensive. Give it another chance—look for Lambrusco di Sorbara.

Sangiovese, from the red grape that provides the foundation of Chianti, Brunello, and other great Tuscan wines, is made in abundance in Romagna and, at its best, is a fine still wine. Gutturnio, from Piacenza, is another good red. Pagadebit is a hearty grape that produces a reliable if unremarkable red. The name (literally "pay the debts") derives from the fact that growing the grape would give dependable yields.

Albana was once a dusky, amber-colored white wine. It's now vinified in a much more refined way, resulting in a charming straw-colored wine. Albana is also made as *passito,* a sweet dessert wine.

Pignoletto is a charming white produced in the province of Bologna. Trebbiano is a dependable white from Romagna, and malvasia grapes are used often in the wines of Parma.

Hard Drinks: Made in Bologna from a secret formula of over 40 ingredients, **Montenegro,** Italy's most popular *amaro,* is lighter and sweeter than others, making it a good entry-level *digestivo.* This *amaro*—in its distinctive green bottle—came to prominence in 1894 at the royal wedding between King Victor Emmanuel III of Italy and his bride, a princess from Montenegro. Also look for the delicious quince liqueur called ***sburlon;*** this can be tricky to find, but worth the effort.

Tuscany

Toscana

Whether you've been to Tuscany many times, or merely dreamed of going there, this region is high on anyone's list of Italy's highlights. Tuscany was the cradle of the Renaissance, and the place that gave us Leonardo da Vinci, Michelangelo, Amerigo Vespucci (America's namesake), Puccini, Gucci, and so many other artists, inventors, designers, and geniuses. It's a land of superb red wines, magnificent art, silent hill towns, gorgeous leather bags and shoes, and neat lines of cypress trees that crown hilltops or run along roadsides like so many exclamation points.

While people flock here primarily for the art and architecture—the Renaissance treasures of the Uffizi, the cathedrals of Florence and Siena, Pisa's Field of Miracles with its Leaning Tower, Michelangelo's *David* in the Accademia—Tuscany also has hearty and satisfying food. Tuscan

cuisine, even more than elsewhere in Italy, is deeply rooted to the land. "Zero-kilometer" dining—a meal consisting of ingredients sourced within one kilometer of where you're eating it—is especially popular here. For some food lovers, that makes Tuscan cooking a bit one-note, with less variety. But at least that one note is delicious and satisfying. This is simple, meaty, home-style comfort food.

Tuscany is big—larger than New Jersey. While neighboring Emilia-Romagna, to the north, has most of its cities lined up in a flat basin, Tuscany is more rugged; two-thirds of it is rippled with hills and mountains. (The Apennines hem in its eastern edge.) So, while Tuscany has

🍴 Foods and Drinks to Sample in Tuscany

Panzanella
Day-old bread, tomatoes, and olive oil. Is it a starter, a soup, a salad? Who cares? It's delicious.

Pici and Pappardelle
These two local noodles are quite different—the first round and chewy, the other wide ribbons—but equally typical; try them with meat sauce, preferably *cinghiale* (wild boar) or a simple *ragù*.

Bistecca alla fiorentina

Bistecca alla fiorentina
Gigantic T-bone, from top-quality local Chianina beef, grilled rare.

Brunello di Montalcino and Vino Nobile di Montepulciano
Two of Italy's top red wines, full-bodied and luscious, both made in the Val d'Orcia.

Chianti Classico
Yet another top-quality red wine from this region that specializes in them.

fine cities and towns in abundance, they are scattered across an undulating landscape; this region feels dominated by farms, pastures, and vineyards.

Tuscany also has a long coastline (nearly 150 miles) that's often overlooked by visitors more interested in hill towns. The main maritime city, Livorno, has a culture all its own. And

Tuscany also has several offshore islands, the biggest of which, Elba, is best known for being the place to which Napoleon was exiled in 1814. Along Tuscany's coast and on the islands, seafood can be prepared as an *antipasto,* with pasta, or as a main course.

The Tuscan diet is straightforward and genuine, with abundant, top-quality olive oil and vegetables. And yet, just as they adorn their workaday towns with glorious facades, Tuscans also appreciate extravagance: Tuscans eat a lot of meat, especially beef (to be specific, top-quality Chianina beef), but also pork, wild boar, rabbit, lamb, liver, tripe, spleen, prosciutto, and *salame.* (That said, Tuscan food is still less rich than the cuisine in neighboring Emilia-Romagna.)

The various towns of Tuscany—so

popular among travelers today—have historically been fierce rivals. For instance, the Florentines and the Sienese have been at each other's throats for centuries. Pisa, Lucca, Arezzo, Livorno—each has its own independent identity, which is often reflected in the local cuisine. And that's one delightful aspect of Tuscany: We expect the heirs of Dante, Galileo, and Machiavelli to be clever and reasoned. But these were also tormented people who raged as they created art and ideas. For them Tuscany was as much a battleground as a paradise. And over many visits, you come to know and love the Tuscans not for their presumed perfection but for their brilliant idiosyncrasy.

 CITIES, TOWNS, AND PLACES

Florence (Firenze), with 380,000 people, is Tuscany's capital and biggest touristic draw. As the home of the Renaissance and the birthplace of the modern world, Florence practiced the art of civilized living back when the rest of Europe was rural and crude. It boasts some of the top Renaissance sightseeing in all of Europe: the Uffizi Gallery (greatest collection of Florentine paintings anywhere), the Accademia (with Michelangelo's *David*), the Bargello (sculptures), the Duomo (pajama-striped cathedral), and myriad other churches, museums, palazzos, and piazzas.

From a culinary standpoint, however, Florence can be a victim of its own success. While there are some excellent restaurants geared to Florentines, the city center is overwhelmed with tourist traps. You can settle for decent food at high prices. Or you can make a point to avoid the *menù turistico* at all costs and invest a little time and energy in finding better restaurants. (Even with that, food

Duomo, Florence

Florentine Food Carts
for Those with Guts

While on a lunch break from chipping trapped statues out of blocks of marble, Michelangelo would swing by the market and dig into a bun stuffed with stewed organs. Offal sandwiches originated as an affordable source of protein for working-class Florentines. While this tradition had nearly faded away, the recent worldwide foodie trend for "nose-to-tail" eating has kicked off a renaissance of food carts and shops selling this local delicacy. As in centuries past, offal vendors are commonly found at or near markets.

Tourists may find it hard to stomach, but Florentines' favorite quick lunch is a *panino* (sandwich) of *trippa* or *lampredotto*—the second and fourth stomach of a cow, respectively—slow-boiled to tender perfection. Less common variations include *tettina* (udder) and *nervetti* (tendons). While these are worth trying (be brave), most carts also offer the less-challenging *bollito* (stewed beef) and the always-delicious *porchetta* (roast pork with herbs). When you order, the food-cart proprietor pulls the lid from a gently simmering pot, forks out some tender meat, and—if you're lucky—dips the bun in the broth. Your sandwich comes topped with *salsa piccante* (spicy red sauce) and/or *salsa verde* (tangy parsley sauce).

Come on, have some guts!

---

lovers may find more memorable, better-value meals in smaller towns and the countryside.)

One fine feature of Florence is its many covered market halls—even the most central of which remain at least partly for locals. The biggest is the Mercato Centrale. In its cavernous downstairs, you can enjoy free samples, watch pasta being made, and take your pick of fun eateries sloshing out cheap lunches for locals. The upstairs has been converted into a modern food court; it's touristy and the prices are high, but most of the counters are operated by respected Florentine restaurateurs. Or you could go extremely local and try an offal sandwich (see sidebar).

Siena (pop. 53,000), the ultimate hill town, is famous for its Palio horse race, which takes over the city twice each summer. At other times, this longtime Florentine rival is simply a delightful place to visit—with one of Italy's most inviting piazzas (Il Campo), vibrant street life, and beautifully decorated churches and civic buildings. On the food front, Siena is known mainly for its dense fruitcake, *panforte,* but the nearby countryside is the source of some of Italy's best olive oil, red wine, and other top-quality ingredients.

South of Siena is the **Val d'Orcia**—the heartland of rustic Tuscan cuisine, bookended by two of Italy's best winemaking towns:

Montalcino and Montepulciano. Wine tasting in this zone is a special treat. In the countryside near **Montalcino,** you'll twist up curvy roads to the high-altitude vineyards of Brunello country. Then you'll explore the hill town of **Montepulciano,** sampling its Vino Nobile in cellars burrowed deep beneath its main piazza. Between those towns is Renaissance-flavored **Pienza,** a hub of *pecorino* cheese production. Wherever you go here, the scenery is sublime: The Val d'Orcia is the location of many of the classic Tuscan views you'll see on postcard racks and calendars.

North of Siena is another of Italy's most esteemed wine zones, **Chianti.** While the towns and scenery of Chianti fall just shy of the Val d'Orcia's soaring standards, a good excuse for a scenic joyride is to follow the Strada Chiantigiana (road 222 between Florence and Siena) and visit wineries in the Chianti Classico zone.

Just west of Chianti are a pair of visit-worthy towns: **San Gimignano**—a hilltop community spiny with 14 medieval towers—is, per square mile, perhaps the most touristy town in Tuscany. It also has a strong culinary tradition, especially for *cinghiale* (wild boar) and the excellent white wine Vernaccia di San Gimignano. (To enjoy these flavors without the crowds, consider arriving late in the day, having dinner, savoring the twilit town all to yourself, and leaving at dawn.) **Volterra,** just a half-hour's drive away, is less overrun and more atmospheric, with Etruscan roots.

At Tuscany's northwest edge, closer to Liguria, sits a trio of visit-worthy cities. The big draw in **Pisa** (pop. 90,000) is its glorious Field of Miracles; while a few locals-oriented restaurants hide out in its urban streets, you'll have to get past the tourist traps near the Leaning Tower

Top: Duomo di Siena; **Bottom:** Quiet back lanes of Pienza

first. **Lucca** (pop. 88,000) is less discovered; its lack of famous monuments and museums is a plus, and it enjoys an array of good restaurants. And **Livorno,** a hardworking port city of 160,000 with a long history, has a personality all its own. In addition to being the natural place in Tuscany to opt for seafood over land food (especially *cacciucco,* fish-and-seafood stew), Livorno has a strong Jewish tradition that influences its food—particularly its desserts.

North of Livorno, almost to Liguria, is the mountainous landscape surrounding **Carrara** (pop. 63,000)—famous for its marble quarries (which supplied Michelangelo) and for the luscious herbed-lard delicacy *lardo di Colonnata.*

🍴 FOODS OF TUSCANY

Tuscan food matches many visitors' expectation of eating well in Italy. It's hearty, rustic, and delicious. Admittedly, it lacks the elegance of the North—less refined than the rich, buttery, complex meals you might have in Piedmont or Emilia-Romagna. But you really feel that you're in Italy's heartland, with an abundance of fresh ingredients and a country-cooking esthetic. Tuscan steaks are famously gigantic and rare, and even the prosciutto is cut thicker here. Tuscany also has some deposits of truffles, which flavor many dishes (for more on truffles, see page 84).

ANTIPASTI (APPETIZERS)

Pane (Bread) and Bread-Based Dishes

Tuscan bread, called **pane toscano,** is distinctive in that it's made without salt—dating back to a tax on salt in the 12th century. While this can be an acquired taste for visitors, Tuscans believe the bread is a platform for other ingredients and shouldn't overwhelm them. (It's the same reason, they say, that Asian cuisines don't salt their rice.) Tuscans also have many uses for stale bread, including some listed here.

Bruschetta	Bread that's sliced, toasted, and topped with olive oil and a bit of garlic; sometimes it's further topped with chopped tomato, mushroom, or whatever else sounds good. A very simple version of this—just toasted bread and olive oil—is called **fettunta,** regional dialect for "oily slice."
Crostini	Toasted bread rounds topped with meat or vegetable pastes (such as a puree of olives or artichokes); **alla toscana** generally means with chicken liver pâté, maybe some spleen, and a hint of caper.
Panzanella	Leftover bread soaked in vinegar, combined with chopped tomato, onion, and basil, and dressed with oil. Many people consider *panzanella* a soup, others a salad, and still others an *antipasto.* Whatever it is, it's delicious.

Left: *Crostini;* **Right:** *Panzanella*

Left: *Lardo di Colonnata;* **Right:** Thick-cut Tuscan prosciutto

Schiacciata	A thin, crispy, "squashed" bread sprinkled with sea salt and olive oil (similar to a focaccia), often used to make sandwiches.
Torta di ceci or cecina	A savory, crêpe-like, garbanzo-bean flatbread that's served at many *pizzerie.*

Salumi

Finocchiona	This classic Tuscan *salame* is embedded with flavorful fennel seed. A less aged, crumbly version is called **sbriciolona.**
Lardo di Colonnata	Seasoned lard is a popular type of *salumi* throughout Italy, but the best is from the town of Colonnata, near the famous marble quarries of Carrara. This *lardo* is seasoned, herbed, spiced, and cured for six months in basins made of the marble. Then it's sliced very thinly, with a silky, melt-in-your-mouth texture.
Prosciutto	Tuscans tend to cut theirs thicker than elsewhere in Italy. Purists claim that the best comes from *cinta senese* (Sienese-branded) pigs, with black hooves, who range freely through the forests, munching on acorns.
Soppressata toscana	Headcheese-like gelatinous brick of pork trimmings, in which pieces of pig's head and tongue are pressed with spices and pistachio nuts. (Don't confuse this with *soppressata* from the South, which is a spicy salami.)

PRIMI (FIRST COURSES)

Pastas

For the most part, Tuscan pasta is simple but flavorful. *Penne* are popular throughout the region, often served with a sauce of vegetables or meat *(ragù)*. Tuscans particularly like wild boar *(cinghiale)*, duck *(anatra)*, and hare *(lepre)* in their meat sauces.

A few regional noodles to watch for:

Pici	In southern Tuscany—especially near Siena—you'll find this long, chewy, often hand-rolled pasta. While more rustic than sophisticated, it's addictive.
Filled pastas	In northern Tuscany are filled pastas such as **tortelloni** (with cheese) or **ravioli,** representing the influence of neighboring Emilia and Liguria, respectively. For example, in Lucca you'll find **tordelli** (the Lucchesi version of *tortelli*), traditionally stuffed with meat and served with more meat sauce.
Pappardelle	The most classic fresh pasta in Tuscany are these very long, flat, wide noodles (not unlike *lasagne*) that cling luxuriously to meat sauces.

Soups

Tuscany also has a strong tradition for soups, including **pasta e fagioli** (pasta and beans), **minestrone** (vegetable soup), and **zuppa di farro** (with spelt—hulled wheat), along with some unique options:

Acquacotta	A thin vegetable soup (literally "cooked water"), most common in southern coastal Tuscany, containing a few greens, leftover bread, and olive oil. In Arezzo, *acquacotta* is much more elaborate, including mushrooms, tomatoes, garlic, wild mint, Parmigiano-Reggiano, eggs, bread, and oil.
Carabaccia	Onion soup.

Left: *Pappa col pomodoro;* **Right:** *Ribollita*

Left: *Pappardelle con ragù;* **Right:** Grilling steaks

Fagioli all'uccelletto	Beans slow-cooked with tomato and sage.
Pappa col pomodoro	A combination of fresh tomatoes, stale bread, and olive oil.
Ribollita	This popular soup has local variations throughout Tuscany. It usually has beans, cabbage, onions, and sometimes layers of day-old bread—and, as its name suggests, is twice cooked (literally "boiled again") to give it more depth of texture and flavor.
Zuppa alla volterrana	A variation on *ribollita,* from the town of Volterra, but with fresh bread instead of day-old.
Zuppa lombarda	"Lombard soup," a hearty bean dish, originated to fortify transplants from Milan who were working in Tuscany.

SECONDI (MAIN DISHES)

Tuscans are enthusiastic carnivores. They love all sorts of meat, whether *alla griglia* (grilled), *arrosto* (roasted), or *bollito* (boiled). They might choose just one, or have a platter of mixed meats (**arrosto misto** is an assortment of roasted meats, sometimes served on a skewer, *spiedino*). Tripe *(trippa)* is best washed down with Chianti.

Anatra in porchetta	Duck stuffed with prosciutto, duck liver, rosemary, fennel seed, and garlic.
Bistecca alla fiorentina	The most characteristic Tuscan main course is this thick T-bone from local Chianina cattle—the perfect match for the region's superb red wines. It's grilled exceedingly rare (by American standards), sprinkled with coarse sea salt, served in huge portions, and typically priced by the *etto* (100 grams). Because it can add up to a giant bill, ask for a price estimate before ordering. And bring famished friends.

Left: *Cinghiale* (wild boar) sauce on pasta;
Right: *Peposo*

Cacciucco	This fish-and-seafood stew from Livorno is the most famous Tuscan seaside dish. It usually includes *triglia* (red mullet), shellfish, and tomatoes. Tradition has it that there should be at least five kinds of fish in this stew—one for each C in the name.
Cinghiale	Wild boar, common in many parts of Italy, is especially prevalent here. If you haven't had boar before, make a point to try it—it's similar to pork, but with a much richer, even spicier flavor. Boar is eaten in a variety of ways: roasted, braised, in pasta sauces, or air-dried in the manner of prosciutto.
Fegatelli	Pork liver wrapped in caul fat, flavored with herbs, and cooked in lard.
Game birds	Squab *(piccione),* pheasant *(fagiano),* and guinea hen *(faraona)* are popular.
Peposo	Highly peppered beef stew made with abundant red wine.
Trippa alla fiorentina	Tripe and vegetables cooked in tomato sauce, sometimes baked with Parmigiano-Reggiano.

VERDURE (VEGETABLES)

Tuscan vegetables are top-quality. You may associate this region with spinach (because dishes abroad called "Florentine" usually have spinach). But beans, of all types, are even more abundant. When cooked and topped with olive oil, they're delicious. White beans *(cannellini)* are often combined with tuna, onions, and olive oil for a nice light lunch. In Tuscany, fava beans are called **bacelli.**

Olives (raw and cured) are also a staple and can be combined with many meats, especially chicken and rabbit. Tuscan olive oil is considered some of the world's best; there's great dispute within Tuscany about which area owns the title (most favor the provinces of Lucca or Siena).

FORMAGGI (CHEESES)

There is excellent cheese in Tuscany, most of it **pecorino,** made from the milk of ewes *(pecore)*. If sheep seem a strange fit for the grassy, rolling countryside here, it's interesting to know that Tuscan *pecorino* production was introduced by Sardinian transplants after the birth of the Second Italian Republic in 1946. Tuscan sheep cheese tends to be creamy and soft, or firm without being granular. Some of the best is sold in Pienza. You'll find both fresh *(fresco)* and aged *(stagionato),* sometimes embedded or infused with additional flavors, such as truffles or cayenne pepper. Look on menus for warm *pecorino* (*al forno* or *alla griglia*), often topped with honey and pine nuts or pears and served with bread. Sheep cheeses can also be called *cacio* or *caciotta.*

DOLCI (SWEETS)

Except for the Sienese, Tuscans don't go for sweet or elaborate desserts. Instead, they opt for fruit, or dry cookies to accompany sweet dessert wine (see "Vin Santo," at the end of this chapter). And, of course, Tuscany (especially Florence) is revered for its gelato.

Bollo	This onetime specialty of Livorno—now difficult to find—is a dessert made with leavened dough, orange-flower water, eggs, sugar, and anise. It's influenced by Livorno's deep Jewish roots.
Brigidini	Popular anise cakes from Pistoia.
Buccellato	A traditional doughy cake from Lucca that's dotted with raisins, lightly flavored with anise, and often shaped like a wreath. It's sold only in large quantities, but luckily it keeps for a few days (and it also pairs well with Vin Santo, fortified Tuscan dessert wine).
Cantuccini or **biscotti di Prato**	Dry almond cookies, typically eaten alongside (or dunked in) Vin Santo or another sweet wine.

Left: *Pecorino;* Right: *Cannellini*

Left: *Cantuccini* with Vin Santo; **Right:** *Panforte* from Siena

Castagnaccio	A muddy pudding, popular in Lucca and Florence, that's made with chestnut flour, olive oil, rosemary, and pine nuts; it's an acquired taste.
Monte Sinai	Another Livorno dessert from the Jewish tradition, this one made with almonds.
Necci	Chestnut-flour galettes often rolled like a *cannolo* and stuffed with *ricotta,* candied fruit, or chocolate chips.
Ossa dei morti	Cookies named for "bones of the dead," eaten on All Saints' Day.
Panforte	Dense, sweet cake made with honey, candied fruit, almonds, and other nuts. This is best in Siena, where it's softer, fresher, and has a broader range of flavors than what is sent to other cities. There are a few varieties: **panforte Margherita,** dusted in powdered sugar, is fruitier, while **panpepato** has a spicy, peppery crust.
Ricciarelli	Delicate, chewy, macaroon-and-almond cookies from Siena.
Schiacciata alla fiorentina	Sweet, orange-flavored flatbread popular at Carnival time.

♀ WINES OF TUSCANY

Wine is a Tuscan forte. Tuscany and Piedmont have an eternal argument—Bordeaux-versus-Burgundy-style—as to which region produces the best red wine in Italy. Ultimately it's a matter of personal taste. Most Piedmont reds are made with the nebbiolo grape, while most Tuscan wines use sangiovese—literally "blood of Jupiter." Sangiovese makes dry, food-friendly, medium-bodied wines with moderate tannins and high acidity. Consumed young, it has a fruity (cherry notes) and sometimes spicy quality; aged in oak, it mellows and takes on other flavors. Many Tuscan wines blend sangiovese with small amounts of cabernet sauvignon, canaiolo, ciliegiolo, and other grapes.

While you could spend a lifetime deepening your appreciation of Tuscan wines, I'll cover just the highlights here—focusing on the major classic reds, plus a bold new entrant, followed by whites and a dessert wine.

Brunello di Montalcino In 1888, the Biondi Santi family created a fine, dark red wine, calling it "the little brunette of Montalcino"—named for the color of the grapes before harvest. Made from 100 percent sangiovese grosso (a.k.a. brunello) grapes, it's smooth, dry, and aged for a minimum of two years in wood casks, plus an additional four months in the bottle. *Riserva* wines are aged an additional year. Brunello is designed to cellar for 10 years or longer. It pairs well with hearty, meaty food. Today, there are around 240 mostly small producers of Brunello in the Montalcino area.

Rosso di Montalcino This is a lighter, less-aged version of Brunello—sometimes called "baby Brunello" or "poor man's Brunello"—that lacks Brunello's depth of flavor and complexity. But it's still an excellent wine at half the price. In lesser-quality harvest years, only Rosso di Montalcino is produced.

Carmignano Made in the town of the same name in the province of Prato, this wine was the forerunner of Chianti. It was first described in 1716, and, because the production is limited and the growers are very protective, Carmignano maintains its cachet even in a region that makes so much fine wine. It's made with 45 percent to 65 percent sangiovese, 10 percent to 20 percent canaiolo nero, and the balance is other varieties.

Chianti This is the generic name for what is probably Italy's most famous wine. It has been saddled by its past reputation (through about the 1970s) as a cheap wine sold in straw-covered flasks. It's important to distinguish run-of-the-mill Chianti from Chianti Classico, which means something more specific and regulated (described next). Still, there are good non-Classico Chiantis made in the provinces of Pisa, Florence, Lucca, Arezzo, Pistoia, Prato, and Siena. Deserving special mention are the wines made in Rufina, in the rolling hills northeast of Florence, where the cooler weather gives the wine a distinct, more austere flavor. Chianti is made with 70 percent sangiovese, with the remaining grapes a blend of canaiolo, ciliegiolo, malvasia, trebbiano, and sometimes some cabernet sauvignon.

The very best is **Chianti Classico.** This is the zone, in the provinces of Florence and Siena, that has a delimited growing area, stringent DOCG rules, and meticulous wine-making methods. The consortium of Chianti Classico producers, like good Tuscans, find many things to argue about over how their wine should be made and promoted. Chianti Classico has a distinctive pink DOCG label around its neck and the symbol of a black rooster (called *il gallo nero* in Italian).

Morellino di Scansano This little-known wine from the province of Grosseto has a devoted following. While made primarily with sangiovese, it's often more aromatic than other sangiovese wines and goes very well with wild boar and other game found in the Maremma zone of southern and coastal Tuscany.

Vino Nobile di Montepulciano This luxurious, dry, ruby-red wine is made in the hill town of Montepulciano, mostly with the prugnolo gentile variety of sangiovese (70 percent), plus other varieties including mammolo (30 percent). Aged two years (or three for a *riserva*)—one year of which must be in oak casks—it's more full-bodied than a typical Chianti and less tannic than a Brunello. It pairs well with meat, especially roasted lamb with rosemary, rabbit or boar *ragù* over pasta, grilled portobello mushrooms, and local cheeses like *pecorino*. Several large wineries produce and age their

Vino Nobile in the sprawling cellars beneath the town of Montepulciano. The oldest described red wine in Tuscany, Vino Nobile has been produced since the late 1500s. And yet, because it's made just up the road from Brunello di Montalcino, this wine gets tragically overlooked—but it's worth discovering. (Don't mistake this for the lesser-quality montelpulciano d'Abruzzo, where montepulciano is the name of the grape.)

Super Tuscans In the 1970s and 1980s, a new breed of winemakers who felt confined by the DOC rules created a new wine that they modestly called *vino da tavola* (table wine)—but that wine experts call the Super Tuscans. These extremely expensive wines feature blends of grapes that reflect the taste of the enologist rather than the dictates of DOC/DOCG law. In fact, the arrival of Super Tuscans and other international-style wines spurred the creation of a new designation of quality—IGT—that doesn't fit traditional methods but still indicates a top-quality wine. If your budget permits, you should sample a few Super Tuscans in restaurants and *enoteche*.

White Wines Tuscany also produces a few whites, the most notable being **Vernaccia di San Gimignano.** This bright, golden-yellow, fruity, medium-dry wine, at its best, pairs beautifully with food. Other white wines to look for are Grattamacco, Bianco di Elba, Bianco di Bolgheri, Belcaro (by San Felice), vermentino, Bianco della Val di Nievole, galestro, and Bianco di Pitigliano.

Vin Santo This sweet dessert wine is usually made of white trebbiano grapes that are harvested in the fall, then dried until Holy Week in the spring (most wines are made in September and October). The dry grapes have more concentrated sugars, and it requires a greater quantity to produce each bottle—making this sweet wine very precious. Vin Santo has a variety of flavors as minor notes in the taste: honey, chestnut, vanilla, cinnamon, and pepper. You can drink Vin Santo on its own or—far more enjoyable—dunk dry almond cookies (*cantuccini* or *biscotti di Prato*) into the wine. This is, in fact, Rick's favorite Tuscan dessert of all.

Umbria

Umbria is often described with words like "mystical," "serene," and "enchanted." Although it's between mega-popular Tuscany and bustling Rome, most of Umbria remains quiet and somewhat set apart. The mystery of Umbria is how it retains its mellow otherworldliness; only Perugia, the capital, seems at all immersed in the Italian mainstream. While Umbria gets some of the touristic spillover from chic Tuscany, the region still feels less wealthy and refined than its famous neighbor. But Umbria also has hill towns, olive oil, young *pecorino* cheese, limpid light, and medieval and Renaissance art.

Landlocked Umbria is often called the "Green Heart of Italy." Geographically, it's a combination of mountains (some soaring to over 8,000 feet), hills, and flat valleys in the middle. The Tiber River (Tevere) begins just over the border in Tuscany and gurgles through Umbria toward Rome, then meets the sea near Ostia Antica. The Tiber nourishes a fertile agricultural zone called the Alto Tevere, and its tributaries course through Umbria's high-mountain valleys. But the region's main body of water, by far, is the huge Lake Trasimeno, Italy's largest lake south of the alpine foothills. Trasimeno—which provides a moderating influence on much of Umbria's climate—is so vast (about 50 square miles) that when you're standing on the northern shore you can't even see all the way across.

The eastern part of Umbria has lofty Apennine peaks. The forests and dales of this zone are full of truffles and wild boars, two of the signature flavors of the Umbrian kitchen. And above all those trees are high pastures where cattle and sheep graze on pure grass in fresh air.

🍽 Foods and Drinks to Sample in Umbria

Black truffles
Some of Italy's best *tartufi neri* are
unearthed right here.

Umbricelli
The region's namesake pasta are
hearty, toothsome noodles.

La ghiotta
Rich, flavorful local sauce, used in
various preparations.

Umbricelli

Baci
Foil-wrapped "kiss" chocolate-
hazelnut treats from Perugia.

Orvieto Classico
One of Italy's best white wines, with varieties ranging from bone-dry to
intensely sweet.

🗺 CITIES, TOWNS, AND PLACES

Umbria is full of abbeys, monasteries,
and convents in tranquil towns such
as **Assisi** (pop. 30,000). Saint Francis
of Assisi (1182-1226) is the most
famous Umbrian, and to this day,
many local children are christened
Francesco or Francesca. Umbria's
character derives from many of St.
Francis' values: Simplicity is considered a virtue, nature is regarded with
wonder, and, yes, a hint of mysticism
is in the air. Umbrians are among the
most environmentally conscious of all
Italians, and much of Italy's "health
food" is grown here.

Assisi still looks much as it did
since St. Francis' time, 700 years ago.
These days, tourists and pilgrims—
flocking to the Basilica of St. Francis,
slathered in glorious art celebrating
the town's favorite son—greatly outnumber monks and nuns. But even

at its most crowded, it feels peaceful...especially after dark, when the
day-trippers have departed.

Another Umbrian highlight is
Orvieto (pop. 20,000), which perches
on its high, flat plateau of *tufo* rock
overlooking the central valleys. It's
a big, sprawling, fun-to-explore hill
town with a dazzling Duomo (inside
and out), more than its share of
history, and a wonderful culinary tradition. The surrounding vineyards are
famous for producing one of Italy's
best white wines, Orvieto Classico.

A visit to the regional capital of
Perugia (pop. 165,000) offers a different sense of Umbria. Its Università
per Stranieri is a popular place for
people from around the world to
come study Italian (and many decide
to stay). Perugia, which was always
an intellectual citadel, grew into a

major cultural and business center; today, it hosts Italy's biggest jazz festival and is known to Italians both for pasta production (Buitoni) and chocolate making (Perugina). The chocolate Easter eggs of Perugia are eaten the world over, and you'll see *Baci* ("kiss" chocolates) at food shops all over Italy.

To discover what Perugia was like before it became cosmopolitan, go to smaller towns such as **Gubbio, Spello, Todi,** and **Spoleto** (known for its olive oil and black truffles). **Montefalco** is a fortified hill town of 5,600 people with views over Umbria;

Above: Franciscan monk in Assisi; **Below:** Back streets of Assisi

its hillsides are planted with grapes that are used to create decadent and powerful wines. Lovers of Italian ceramics know the name **Deruta,** a hill town south of Perugia that has produced lovely, colorful *maiolica* pottery for centuries. Exploring the Umbrian countryside in autumn or winter, you'll inhale the toasty smell of burning wood—used both for heating homes and for cooking.

Norcia, tucked in a remote valley near the Marche border called Valnerina, was damaged by an earthquake in 2016. It's known to Italians as the birthplace of St. Benedict, for its exquisite black truffles *(tartufi neri),* and for its excellent pork butchers. The term *norcino* ("person from Norcia") doesn't refer to just anyone from this town of about 5,000, but exclusively to its butchers. (Everyone else is called *nursini,* from the town's Latin name.) Norcia's abundant butcher shops are fragrant with sausages, *salame,* and prosciutto. The town is also known for its delicate lentils, fresh river trout, and famously pure drinking water (which makes everything here—pasta, coffee, baked goods—taste that much better).

🍴 FOODS OF UMBRIA

Umbria's cuisine is rustic, hearty, and satisfying. You'll find many features resembling Tuscan cuisine, including meats grilled and used to make pasta sauces. The area around Norcia and Spoleto is known throughout Italy for its black truffles (***tartufi neri;*** for more on truffles, see page 84). And the local olive oil—often jade green, fragrant, fruity, and sometimes very lusty—is among the finest in Italy.

ANTIPASTI (APPETIZERS)

Bruschetta	These classic, rustic toasts are served with olive oil and sometimes truffles.
Pizza di pasqua	A bread flavored with *pecorino,* originally served only at Easter.
Torta sul testo (or **crescia umbra**)	Flatbread cooked on hot stones, often made into a sandwich with *salumi.*

PRIMI (PASTAS AND OTHER FIRST COURSES)

One grain you'll find around Italy—but especially in Umbria—is **farro,** which in English is called spelt, emmer, or hulled wheat. This was a staple in ancient times; part of the wedding rites of ancient Roman nobility was that the bride and groom sacrificed a *farro* cake to Jupiter Farreus. Their marital state was called *confarreatio,* and a divorce was termed *disfarreatio.*

Minestra di farro	Soup made with *farro* and cooked with a ham bone.
Pasta alla norcina	This term is used to describe two different types of pasta topping: a sauce of black truffles, oil, and anchovies; or a sauce made with sausage and cream.

Left: *Pizza di pasqua;* **Right:** *Minestra di farro*

Left: *Stringozzi;* **Right:** *Porchetta*

Spaghetti col rancetto	A Spoleto specialty, made with *pancetta* and marjoram.
Stringozzi (or **strangozzi**)	Long pasta strands made with hand-milled flour. It's named for a long leather cord *(strangozzo)* that was, in the Middle Ages, used to strangle unwanted tax collectors from the pope.
Umbricelli	This is a thick, chewy strand pasta, very suitable to robust pasta sauces or oil with garlic or herbs.

SECONDI (MAIN DISHES)

Pork is the most popular meat in Umbria, although there's good veal and lamb, too. Umbrians like poultry and fowl such as chicken, duck, squab, guinea fowl *(faraona),* and pheasant *(fagiano).*

Anguilla	Eel from Lake Trasimeno, served either grilled **(alla griglia)** or braised in wine, tomatoes, onions, and garlic **(in umido).**
Fagiano all'uva	Pheasant cooked with grapes.
La ghiotta	A popular sauce made of cooking juices from meat or fowl, plus olive oil, vinegar, anchovies, olives, lemon peel, sage, salt, and pepper.
Palombacci	Wild pigeon, often served *la ghiotta* (see above).
Piccione alla perugina	Squab cooked with olives.
Porchetta	Roast suckling pig with garlic, rosemary, and other herbs.
Salsiccia all'uva	Fresh pork sausage cooked with grapes.
Tegamaccio	A stew of carp, pike, trout, and other fish from Lake Trasimeno.

CONTORNI (SIDE DISHES)

Agretti	This delicate, delicious, grass-like vegetable has a very brief season in late spring.
Fave	Fava beans appear in soups, as a *contorno,* or on *crostini.*
Lenticchie	Many gourmets consider the lentils from Castelluccio the best in Italy; they're especially small and have a delicate but palpable flavor (the lentils, not the gourmets).

DOLCI (SWEETS)

Attorta	A typical Spoleto cake made with apples and a soft crust.
Baci	These walnut-sized, foil-wrapped chocolates from Perugia consist of a dark chocolate shell encasing a ball of creamy milk chocolate and chopped hazelnuts, all surrounding a whole hazelnut center. Inside each wrapper is a multilingual message of love (*bacio* means "kiss").
Cicerchiata	Traditional cake, with a hole in the center, made of deep-fried dough, candied fruit, almonds, honey, and pine nuts, and typically eaten at Carnival time.
Fichi	Excellent figs come from Amelia, near Orvieto.
Pan nociato	A rich dessert from Todi, made of bread, *pecorino,* raisins, walnuts, cloves, and red wine, all wrapped and baked in grape leaves.
Pinoccate	Cookies made with pine nuts, lemon peel, orange peel, sugar, and sometimes chocolate.
Rocciata	Apple strudel with raisins.
Torcolo	A sweet roll that contains pine nuts, raisins, anise seed, and candied fruit. This is a specialty of the Capuchin nuns of Perugia. The dough is shaped in a coil form, so that it looks like a sleeping snake; it's sometimes called *il serpentone* (the big snake).

Left: *Agretti;* **Right:** *Pinoccate*

♀ WINES OF UMBRIA

Umbria produces both reds and whites, made in zones such as the Colli del Trasimeno (near the lake), Colli Perugini (near Perugia), and Altotiberini (near the source of the Tiber River). Here are some special ones to look for:

Orvieto Classico This is the most famous wine in the region, a pleasant white that can range from bone-dry to buttery creaminess. It's a blend of five grapes, primarily procanico (trebbiano toscano), verdello, and grecchetto. Most of the production is **Orvieto Secco,** the dry variety, although the dryness varies from one producer to another. And make a point to try **Orvieto Abboccato**—a hard-to-classify but delightfully round wine; while not as sweet as dessert wines, it can overwhelm most foods. Still, true to its name (*abbocato* means, roughly, "full mouth"), it's pleasurable.

Rosso di Montefalco Good with stews and red meats thanks to its particular richness, this wine is made of approximately 65 percent sangiovese, 15 to 20 percent trebbiano toscano, and 5 to 10 percent sagrantino grapes.

Sagrantino di Montefalco This red is Umbria's answer to Tuscany's Brunello (although local wine lovers would say that it's vice versa). It comes in two types, each made with at least 95 percent sagrantino grapes and perhaps a few trebbiano toscano grapes to lighten its intensity. The traditional version can often reach 14 percent alcohol (just below dessert wines like port); it goes with meat, cheese, or a rich pasta.

Sagrantino di Montefalco Passito In this very sweet variation, the grapes are dried to shrivel before pressing, which produces a very intense and fragrant wine to sip at the end of a meal or for meditation (it has been used as a sacramental wine in the hill town of Montefalco).

Torgiano From a town of the same name, where wine has been made since Etruscan times. One fine producer is Lungarotti, with a particularly attractive red called Rubesco Riserva. The town of Torgiano also has a good wine museum.

Vin Santo As in Tuscany, an amber-colored sweet wine made of dried white-wine grapes (typically trebbiano) is often consumed at the end of a meal, typically with dry cookies.

Marche

Le Marche

Few travelers make it to Marche (MAR-kay; Italians call it Le Marche, and it's sometimes called "The Marches" in English). And even for Italians, it can be an afterthought: a place sandwiched between Umbria and Tuscany on one side and the Adriatic on the other. But, likely because of this, there's something about Marche that promotes peace and tranquility.

Marche has a rugged landscape—one-third mountains, two-thirds hills, with flat land essentially limited to the coastline. The *marchigiane* towns on the coast have attractive beaches (popular with overflow from the Riviera Romagnola in Emilia-Romagna), lush green vegetation nearby, and a delightful climate. And in the interior are many quiet hill towns that stand tall and seem immersed in green—unlike the typically brown (or, at best, sparsely green) surroundings of their Umbrian and Tuscan counterparts.

Why is Marche so little known? The Apennines seal it off from the rest of Italy. Most access is along the coast; the only major inland city with roads to Marche is Bologna. You only

go to Marche *on purpose;* it's not "on the way" between much of anything.

Despite the region's relative obscurity, many prominent *marchigiani* are household names in Italy: artists such as Raphael and Bramante; Leopardi, one of Italy's great poets; and composers such as Pergolesi, Rossini, and Spontini.

Marchigiani are considered among the friendliest of Italians. It's said they are blessed with good looks and a long life; statistically, they're among the longest-lived of all

Italians (which typically ranks as one of the top countries in the world). The friendliness of the *marchigiani* is only exaggerated by the relative lack of tourism here; as the place isn't overrun (aside from a few beach towns), people are genuinely pleased, even surprised, to see you. And they go out of their way to welcome you. Because the towns are small (the biggest, Ancona, barely cracks 100,000), they tend to be built on a human scale, with nature always close at hand.

🍳 Foods and Drinks to Sample in Marche

Casciotta
Michelangelo's favorite cheese,
made of a mix of sheep's and cow's
milk.

Ciauscolo
Soft, spreadable smoked *salame.*

Brodetto
A rich seafood stew, found all over
Italy, but excellent in Marche.

Brodetto

Verdicchio
Light white wine, at one time
overproduced, and now returning to its original quality.

🗺 CITIES, TOWNS, AND PLACES

Ancona (pop. 100,000), the capital
and biggest city, is situated on an
elbow-shaped peninsula ("Ancona"
comes from the ancient Greek word
for "elbow"). The peninsula's layout
blocks winds from blowing south,
so the part of Marche to the south
is much warmer than that to the
north. The city is a hub of transit and
commerce, but most visitors simply
pass through.

Urbino (pop. 15,000) is more
worth a lingering visit. During the
Renaissance, Urbino had one of the
most refined courts in Italy, full of
artists and scholars in the service
of Federico da Montelfetro (whose
famous hook-nosed portrait hangs
in Florence's Uffizi Gallery). And
the province was home to three
Renaissance greats: Raffaello Sanzio
da Urbino, a.k.a. simply "Raphael";
the lesser-known but also talented
Federico Barocci; and Donato
Bramante, the architect who first

designed the new St. Peter's in
Rome. (The National Gallery of
Marche is a surprise treasure trove of
Renaissance art. If it were in a bigger
Italian city, it would be famous and
crowded. But it isn't...so it's not.) The
town's streets are alternately steep
and narrow, culminating in views of
undulating green fields under blue
skies. And the local student population helps give Urbino a youthful vibe.

The most attractive part of
the Marche is in the **Montefeltro**
area, which spreads north from
Urbino, tucked into the border areas
of Tuscany and Emilia-Romagna.
Carpegna produces top-quality,
salty, melt-in-your-mouth *prosciutto
crudo,* and the surrounding woods
abound with game.

The coastline is mainly tourist-
oriented beach towns (such as
big **Pesaro,** pop. 95,000). One fine
town here—close to the border with
Romagna—is **Gabicce Mare,** less

Left: Loreto; **Right:** Urbino

overrun than many of its neighbors; in the mountains just above is its uphill sister town, **Gabicce Monte,** which was a trendy artistic community in the 1960s (Fellini used to hang out here) and has now settled into a quieter existence.

Macerata (pop. 42,000), inland from the coast and away from the beach crowd, is Fred's favorite Marche town. It has an important art museum, a university, a wonderful summer opera festival in the Sferisterio, beautiful public buildings, and excellent food. Other interesting towns in the southern part of the region are **Loreto** and **Ascoli Piceno.** On the border with Umbria, **Visso** has a cuisine with Umbrian influences and is known for its soft *salame,* called *ciauscolo*, and for its lamb.

🍴 FOODS OF MARCHE

Marche's combination of sea, hills, and mountains provides various environments for cultivating and harvesting ingredients. *Marchigiano* cuisine features superb seafood as well as excellent truffles, mushrooms, meats, olives, grapes, and especially cheeses. Charcoal-grilled meats are popular.

ANTIPASTI (APPETIZERS)

Ciauscolo (or *ciavuscolo*)	While technically a *salame,* this pork product from the province of Macerata (specifically Visso) is so soft that it's spreadable—giving it a texture more like pâté. Fatty pork is finely ground, spiced with pepper and garlic, encased, smoked over juniper, and typically eaten within a couple of weeks.
Lonza	A *salame* made of meat from a pig's neck or cheek.
Olive all'ascolane	Large stuffed olives, breaded and deep-fried, from the town of Ascoli Piceno.
Tartufo	Truffles are a specialty in Montefeltro, north of Urbino. They appear in *antipasti*, with pastas, and in *secondi*. For more on truffles, see page 84.

PRIMI (PASTAS AND OTHER FIRST COURSES)

Maccheroncini di Campofilone	Thin egg noodles, often served with a pork-and-veal sauce. This dates back to medieval times, in the town of Campofilone.
Tacconi allo sgagg	A pasta made of fava-bean flour, from Mondavio.
Vincisgrassi	A very rich *lasagne* that contains cream, a dense veal *ragù*, chicken giblets, black truffles, fresh tomatoes, butter, Parmigiano-Reggiano, mozzarella, and other ingredients. This Macerata specialty is named for Austrian Field Marshal Alfred von Windisch-Grätz, who helped defend Ancona from the French during the Napoleonic Wars.

SECONDI (MAIN DISHES)

Brodetto	Although *brodetto* is the name of a rich fish stew all over the Adriatic, it reaches its apex in Marche, where every little seaside town seems to have its distinct version. Classic *brodetto* uses only fish (usually including sole and red and gray mullet), but no seafood. It also includes onions, garlic, herbs, and olive oil, and is served over slices of bread. Regional variations are exactingly specific: In the north (including Ancona), they use thirteen types of fish, untoasted bread rubbed with garlic, and a dash of vinegar. South of the town of Numana, it's made with nine types of fish, which are floured, plus saffron and toasted bread that has not been rubbed with garlic.
Coniglio in coccio	Rabbit first marinated in white wine, then cooked in milk and spices, then browned in the oven.
Coniglio in porchetta	Roast rabbit stuffed with wild fennel.
Garagoli	Cone-shaped mollusks cooked with wild fennel, available May through August.

Left: *Ciauscolo* and other *salumi* from Norcia;
Right: White truffles

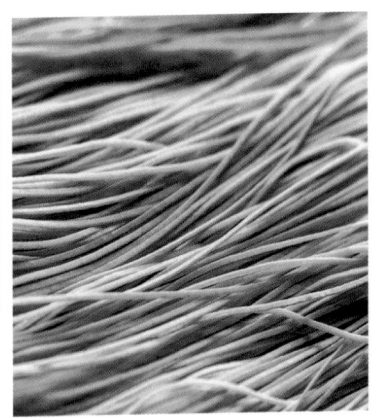

Left: *Vincisgrassi;* **Right:** *Maccheroncini di Campofilone*

Lumache alle erbe	Snails cooked with herbs, a specialty of northern Marche.
Oca in potacchio	Braised goose cooked in white wine, olive oil, garlic, tomatoes, and rosemary.
Olivette	Thin rolls of meat, usually veal, that are stuffed or spread with different flavors. For example, **olivette alla pesarese** are thin veal rolls with a caper spread.
Porchetta	Roast suckling pig stuffed with herbs and garlic.
Sarde alla marchigiana	Sardines baked with breadcrumbs, rosemary, parsley, and lemon.

FORMAGGI (CHEESES)

Casciotta	This cheese—made of 70 percent sheep's milk and 30 percent cow's milk—was Michelangelo's favorite. His letters note that he preferred *casciotta* that was made in the spring when the sheep grazed on tender grass. He always had a large supply of *casciotta,* which he nibbled on while sculpting. And when he became wealthy, he bought a flock of sheep and a tract of land near Urbino to guarantee a steady supply.
Formaggio di fossa (or *formaggio di tufo*)	*Pecorino* cheese that is stored in caves, which causes it to lose 20 percent of its fat and concentrates its flavor. The origin of this process came when barbarians invaded the region centuries ago, and the shepherds hid their cheeses in caves, covering them with leafy branches. This atmosphere fostered a second fermentation, which led to the cheese's unique flavor and, as it aged, its distorted shape.

Left: *Porchetta;* **Right:** *Crescia sfogliata*

Pecorino di Monte Rinaldo	Sheep's-milk cheese flavored with herbs.
Pecorino sotto foglie di noci	*Pecorino* cheese wrapped in leaves from a walnut tree, so it takes on a hint of nut flavor (a specialty of Carpegna).

PANE (BREAD)

Crescia sfogliata	A popular food with students at the University of Urbino, this is flatbread filled with cheese, eggs, or vegetables.
Piadina	This flatbread, typical of Emilia-Romagna, is also found in northern Marche.

DOLCI (SWEETS)

Beccute	Little cookies from Ancona made with almonds, raisins, dried figs, olive oil, and cornmeal.
Cicerchiata	This Carnival honey cake might be topped with cinnamon and almonds.
Frustignolo marchigiano	Christmas cake from Ascoli Piceno with nuts, figs, honey, and candied fruit.

🍷 WINES OF MARCHE

Verdicchio This light white from Jesi became famous because it was sold in an amphora-shaped bottle with a little scroll attached that told the story of the wine. Heavy plantings followed, and the wine boomed in the 1960s and 1970s. Mass production led to a decline in quality, but more recently local vintners have been working on improving it. The wine is made with the verdicchio grape, although DOC rules permit using up to 15 percent trebbiano or malvasia grapes.

Bianco dei Colli Maceratesi Made primarily of trebbiano grapes, sometimes with the addition of maceratino, malvasia toscana, and verdicchio.

Bianchello del Metauro The local white wine of Urbino.

Rosso Cònero and Rosso Piceno Two excellent DOC reds. Rosso Cònero is made with montepulciano grapes with a bit of sangiovese. Rosso Piceno is 60 percent sangiovese and 40 percent montepulciano, sometimes with a bit of trebbiano added.

Sangiovese dei Colli Pesaresi A lesser-known and less forceful red.

Hard Drinks

Anisette A clear, anise-flavored *digestivo* popular in Ascoli Piceno. Ask for it *con la mosca* and they'll add a coffee bean (meant to resemble a drowned fly). The coffee flavor infuses the *anisette* with delicious results.

Merletti This flavorful local *amaro* is made from a 150-year-old recipe, which includes cinnamon and anise.

Mistrà An anise-based after-dinner drink.

Moretta Typical of the town of Fano, this unique cocktail is made of one part *anisette*, one part rum, and one part cognac. It's heated, a bit of sugar is melted in, coffee is added, and then it's finished with a curl of lemon peel.

Rome & Lazio

Roma

Two thousand years ago, the word "Rome" meant—to the people who lived there—civilization itself; everything was considered either civilized (part of the Roman world) or barbarian. And today, Rome is Italy's political capital, the spiritual home of a billion Catholics, and an open-air museum of the evocative remains of the leading city of what was the greatest empire in the history of humanity.

You can take the "Roma" out of "romance," but you can't take the romance out of Rome. There's just something so sensual (in the most expansive sense) about this city. Romans derive pleasure from human interaction and all activities: food, fashion, flirtation, politics, driving, arguing, and making up. In most of Italy, people call the evening stroll *passeggiata;* here they use a coarser term, *struscio*—which roughly translates to "rubbing." You'll see Romans walking down the street arm in arm, deep in conversation, stopping occasionally to add emphasis. Once that point is made, they resume the gentle cadence of their stroll, rocking gently

To Florence

UMBRIA
MARCHE
Adriatic Sea

Norcia

•Orvieto

EEL
Lake Bolsena
•Civita di Bag.

EST! EST!! EST!!! •Viterbo

Rieti

ABRUZZO

Tiber

LAMB & PORCHETTA

PECORINO ROMANO

LAZIO

Lido di Tarquinia•
Civitavecchia

Lake Bracciano

Sulmona

Santa Marinella

To Sardinia

VATICAN CITY

Rome

•Tivoli

•Olevano Romano

Fregene •
Lido di Ostia

FRASCATI

CASTELLI ROMANI

Castel Gandolfo

TORRE ERCOLANA

Cassino

CIOCIARIA

SUPPLÌ & FRITTI MISTI

CAMPANIA

Tyrrhenian Sea

•Latina

Anzio• •Nettuno

PUNTARELLE

Terracina •

Gaeta•
•Formia

To Naples

ROME SPECIALTIES

SPAGHETTI ALLA CARBONARA, CACIO E PEPE, FETTUCCINE, ARRABBIATA & AMATRICIANA

CARCIOFI

"QUINTO QUARTO" & SALTIMBOCCA

GRATTACHECCA

SAMBUCA

Ponza

ITALY

50 Kilometers

50 Miles

right, then left, as they promenade down the street. They blow kisses to one another from motor scooters, shouting *Shau!*—the local pronunciation of *ciao*.

Simply being in Rome—whether as a resident or as a visitor—feels like an indulgence, considering the city's visual delights, luxuriant fountains and gardens with erotic statuary, and the cooling *venticelli*—special

breezes that blow through the city on even the hottest day.

Even the food of Rome—and, by extension, the surrounding region of Lazio—has a certain lustiness. While other cuisines (such as that of Emilia-Romagna) can be rich and substantial, *laziale* cooking is characterized by an astonishing amount of fat from pork, lamb, cheese, eggs, and organ meats. At the same time, the region

Foods and Drinks to Sample in Lazio

Carciofi
Artichokes, either *alla romana* ("Roman-style," simmered with garlic and mint) or *alla giudìa* ("Jewish-style," flattened and deep-fried).

Pecorino romano
Delectable ewe's-milk cheese, aged and grated over just about everything.

Supplì
Deep-fried balls of rice, mozzarella, meat, and tomato sauce.

Spaghetti cacio e pepe

Pastas
Decadent Roman classics include **spaghetti alla carbonara** (with egg, *guanciale,* black pepper, and *pecorino romano*), **cacio e pepe** (simply fresh-ground black pepper and *pecorino romano*), **amatriciana** and **arrabbiata** (different sauces of tomato, *guanciale,* onions, garlic, and *peperoncino*), **fettuccine al burro** (a.k.a. "fettuccine Alfredo," with a butter-and-Parmigiano-Reggiano sauce), and many more.

Frascati
This refreshing, drinkable local white accompanies many memorable meals.

produces some of the sweetest, most exquisite vegetables anywhere. At the seashore you'll find good-quality fish and seafood, and Rome's ancient Jewish community has contributed many dishes to the local cuisine, as well. All of this food is swept up with dark, fragrant, crusty bread called *pane casareccio* and washed down with unpretentious, earthy, easy-to-drink white wine.

Since most people's first (and often only) contact with Lazio is in Rome, it's easy to forget that this region's cuisine is a pastoral one—born of shepherds. Lamb is the foremost meat, the ewe's-milk cheese *pecorino* is preferred to cow's-milk varieties, and practically every part

of the animal is used. This also helps explain the Romans' fondness for meats known as the quinto quarto ("fifth quarter"), such as tripe, tail, brain, and pig's feet, as well as their interest in natural preservatives like chili peppers and garlic.

Roman food also goes very heavy on the salt. In ancient times, salt was priced at a premium for its food-preservation qualities, so its liberal use was considered a sign of generosity or even extravagance. (The English words "sauce," "salad," and "sausage"—not to mention "salary"—all derive from the Latin *salsus,* or "salted.") To this day, in many Roman homes and a few restaurants, rather than a shaker you'll find a special

days. Tuesday often sees either fish or *bollito misto*. On Thursday, there are always gnocchi. Friday brings cod and *pasta coi ceci* (with chickpeas). Saturday means tripe, usually cooked with mint and *pecorino*. And Sunday is the day for pork or lamb.

salt bowl called a *saliera*. Sometimes richly decorated with gold, silver, glass, crystal, or ceramic, the *saliera* might be handed down over the generations and occupy a place of honor in the home. (If you're watching your salt consumption, you can request *niente sale,* no salt; or *poco sale,* just a little salt.)

The people of Lazio, prodded by centuries of tradition that even they don't always fully understand, tend to eat certain foods on certain

An age-old tension exists within Italy between the South and the North, and specifically between its two biggest cities, Rome and Milan. The *milanesi* pride themselves on doing all of the work, while complaining that Rome expends the nation's resources. If there's a kernel of truth there, it's that for Romans, pleasure trumps work. (Put another way: If the *milanesi* work hard and play hard, the Romans play hard…and play harder.) The Romans sometimes come off a bit entitled, even arrogant, in their status as the capital city—as if that endows them with special privileges. And sure enough, this magnificent city sometimes seems as if it were designed to be their enormous, beautiful playground.

🗺 CITIES, TOWNS, AND PLACES

Rome, with nearly three million people, is magnificent and overwhelming at the same time. It's a showcase of Western civilization, with astonishingly ancient sights and a modern vibrancy.

Tourists see Rome as a bucket list of great attractions: the Pantheon, Colosseum, and Forum. The Vatican, with St. Peter's Basilica, the Vatican Museums, and the Sistine Chapel. Piazza Navona, Campo dei Fiori, and other grand squares. Famous landmarks like the Trevi Fountain and the Spanish Steps. World-class museums, from the National Museum of Rome to the Borghese Gallery. But food lovers could spend a marvelous

day, week, or month in Rome and never step through a turnstile.

As in Venice and Florence, it's all too easy to get sucked into tourist-baiting eateries where you'll pay far too much for lower-quality food and indifferent service. Unlike those other two cities, however, Rome is big enough that—with a little homework, a sense of adventure, and a willingness to venture beyond the touristy core—it's not too difficult to find truly local restaurants where you can savor quality food among Romans.

Food lovers enjoy exploring Testaccio, the former slaughterhouse district south of the city center. In ancient times, 90 percent of the

Above: Skyline of Rome; **Below:** One of Frascati's many villas

city's food came through this area's wharves; later, it was known for its gigantic slaughterhouse. These days, Testaccio chefs are still renowned for their ability to cook up the animals' least palatable parts...the *quinto quarto*. The covered, unpretentious Testaccio Market is typically Italian and a focal point of the neighborhood. The many produce stands display a glorious array of colorful, fragrant, top-quality ingredients, and there are also cheap and delicious stand-up food counters, cafés, and clothing and housewares sections (open mornings through about lunchtime, closed Sundays).

Rome is so all-encompassing that it's easy to overlook the rest of the region. Lazio has beautiful areas for recreation, many within an hour of the capital. Romans head for picnics in the *campagna* (the nearby countryside) or to the **Castelli Romani,** where much of the region's wine is produced. About 20 miles southeast of Rome, this is a land of limpid air, deep lakes, sloping hills, and rustic cuisine. In addition to restaurants,

trattorie, and *osterie,* Romans enjoy stopping at roadside stands for *porchetta* (roasted pork) on crusty *pane casareccio* with a glass of white wine. Or they head here for a big Sunday meal that begins with homemade fettuccine and continues with *abbacchio* (lamb) or *porchetta* accompanied by roast potatoes and green vegetables...and, of course, rivers of white wine. The area's main town, **Frascati,** is blessed with villas and gardens and is the birthplace and namesake of the most popular Lazio wine.

Farther south of Rome is

Ciociaria, famous for its vegetables, pasta, and hill towns.

Viterbo (pop. 68,000) is a beautiful medieval city an hour north of Rome. It's immersed in a zone dating back to Etruscan times. Farther north is one of Italy's largest lakes, **Lake Bolsena**—famous for recreation and for its eels. Not far from there is one of Rick's favorite little hill towns in Italy, **Civita di Bagnoregio**—now a near-ghost town, clustered at the top of a giant *tufo* rock and tethered to the modern world only by a steep footbridge. (It's easiest to visit Civita from Orvieto, in neighboring Umbria.)

On the Lazio coastline, Rome's own beaches at Ostia and Fregene are unappealingly crowded and built-up. But quieter options still exist at **Tarquinia.** Or head south to **Anzio** and **Nettuno,** two beach towns that were also the sites of Allied landings that led to some of the most ferocious Italian battles of World War II. (Nettuno has an American military cemetery, and Anzio has a British

Civita di Bagnoregio

one.) The train ride to this area takes you through a beautiful cross-section of Lazio terrain: After leaving the ugly sprawl of Rome, you'll begin to spot sheep grazing on green slopes, then olive groves and hills covered with grape trellises. Finally, you carry on along the coast, with sea breezes on one side and mountain breezes on the other. The food here—just 30 or so miles south of Rome—begins to take on a more Neapolitan character.

🍽 FOODS OF LAZIO

The cuisine of Lazio is robust and strongly flavored, with lots of fatty meats (lamb, pork), eggs, cheese (especially *pecorino romano*), and a nose-to-tail approach to using every part of the animal. Fried foods are also popular. Simple, fresh, seasonal ingredients dominate; Lazio's farm fields produce sweet, delectable vegetables and white wine. You'll often see dishes described as ***alla romana***—"Roman-style." The exact meaning of this varies by dish.

ANTIPASTI (APPETIZERS)	
Bruschetta	Toasted bread brushed with olive oil and garlic, sometimes topped with chopped tomatoes, mushrooms, or other tidbits.
Carciofi alla giudia	Originally a classic in the Roman Jewish kitchen, these are artichokes that are flattened and then deep-fried until golden.
Carciofi alla romana	These "Roman-style" artichokes are stuffed with mint and garlic and slow-cooked in olive oil.

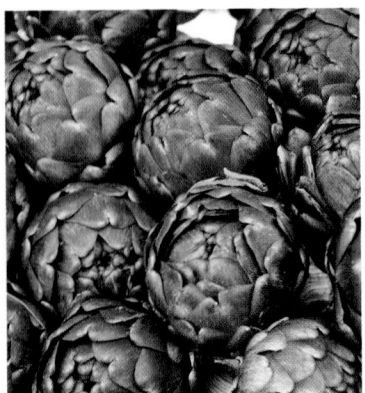

Left: Fresh artichokes; **Right:** *Carciofi alla giudia*

Fave con il pecorino	Raw fava beans served with a slice of cheese.
Fritti misti	Battered or breaded fried snacks—often olives stuffed with meat, potato croquettes, and mozzarella balls. Other fried goodies include **fiori di zucca** (squash blossoms filled with mozzarella and anchovies, then deep-fried) and *supplì* (see next). Don't confuse this with **fritto misto alla romana**—described later—which is an assortment of deep-fried organ meats.
Supplì	Rice balls made with mozzarella, chopped meat, tomato sauce, and sometimes other fillings, then deep-fried. When you bite into one, the cheese stretches all the way to your mouth. (They're sometimes called *supplì al telefono* for the way the cheese hangs like a telephone wire.) *Supplì* are a Roman specialty, but a similar item called *arancina* (bigger, with the filling contained inside the rice rather than mixed up) is found in much of the South and Sicily.

PRIMI (PASTAS AND OTHER FIRST COURSES)

Pasta preparations are a Roman forte; many "Italian" classics—particularly the rich and decadent ones—originated here in the capital.

Bucatini all'amatriciana	Thin pasta tubes, served with a sauce made with *guanciale* (pork cheek), tomatoes, onions, garlic, *pecorino romano*, and *peperoncino*. The name comes from Amatrice, the Lazio town where it originated.
Fettuccine alla papalina	"Papal" fettuccine with eggs, prosciutto, and peas.
Fettuccine alla romana	Sauce of prosciutto, chicken giblets, and tomatoes.

Fettuccine al burro	Commonly called "fettuccine Alfredo," the original version is made with lots of sweet butter and Parmigiano-Reggiano (but no cream). This is so lavish, it's sometimes called *fettuccine maestose*—"majestic"—*al burro*.
Gnocchi alla romana	Disks of semolina baked with cheese and butter—quite different from the *other* (non-Roman) version of gnocchi, little pillowy potato pellets.
Pasta cacio e pepe	With grated *pecorino romano* and freshly ground pepper. Simple and delicious.
Pasta alla ciociara	Sauce of tomatoes, mozzarella, *pecorino romano,* olive oil, and oregano, named for the fertile agricultural zone south of Rome.
Pasta alla gricia	A classic shepherd dish, made with *pancetta,* olive oil, pepper, and grated *pecorino romano*.
Pasta coi ceci	With a sauce of chickpeas and tomatoes.
Penne all'arrabbiata	"Angry penne" has a flavor profile similar to *amatriciana,* except it has more tomatoes and *peperoncino* and less pork and onions.
Rigatoni alla pajata	Pasta topped with a stew of calf's or lamb's intestines cooked in a piquant tomato sauce. This is an old Roman dish that is still served in Testaccio and other traditional neighborhoods.
Spaghetti alla carbonara	Thick spaghetti tossed with beaten egg, sautéed *guanciale,* grated *pecorino romano,* and copious amounts of freshly ground pepper.
Spaghetti alle vongole veraci	Pasta served with small clams in the shell.
Stracciatella alla romana	An egg-drop soup made with chicken or meat broth, topped with grated cheese.

Left: *Stracciatella alla romana;* **Right:** *Pasta alla gricia*

SECONDI (MAIN DISHES)

Abbacchio al forno	Oven-roasted, milk-fed baby lamb made with garlic and rosemary.
Abbacchio allo scottadito	Thin strips of baby lamb that are quickly cooked in a frying pan. *Scottadito* means "scorched fingers"—either referring to the overwhelming desire to grab and eat them before they've cooled off, or because the chef turns them over manually.
Anguille	Eels—mainly from Lake Bolsena—are customarily cooked in wine (often Est! Est!! Est!!! or vernaccia).
Coda alla vaccinara	A stew of oxtail braised with garlic, wine, tomato, and celery.
Coratella	The old-fashioned English word for this is "pluck," which implies the heart, liver, lungs, and windpipe of an animal. In Lazio, those of the lamb are used. They are minced and fried as *fritto misto alla romana* (see below), cooked with lots of onions and pepper, or braised in wine-and-tomato sauce.
Filetti di baccalà	Battered and fried salt cod (like fish-and-chips minus the chips).
Fritto misto alla romana	Fried meats, organ meats, and vegetables.
Involtini di vitello al sugo	Veal cutlets rolled with prosciutto, celery, and cheese in a tomato sauce.
Pizza romana	Roman-style pizza is made with a very thin and crispy dough called **scrocchiarella** (less chewy than Neapolitan-style pizza). In Rome, **pizza bianca** (white pizza) can mean a pizza made without tomato sauce, but can also simply mean a chunk of flat, crispy bread, or a sandwich made with that bread.
Porchetta	Delicious boned suckling pig roasted with rosemary, garlic, and lots of pepper. It's served as the centerpiece of a meal—especially on Sunday—and is also sold in sandwiches at roadside stands. While this is popular throughout central Italy (and beyond), many believe it originated in Lazio.
Saltimbocca (alla romana)	Thinly sliced veal cutlets layered with fresh sage and *prosciutto crudo,* then lightly sautéed. The name means "jump in your mouth."
Trippa alla romana	Tripe braised with onions, carrots, and mint.

Left: Roman-style pizza; **Right:** *Saltimbocca alla romana*

CONTORNI (SIDE DISHES)

Romans go out of their way to select the freshest, most flavorful vegetables possible. They are attuned to the seasons and look forward to the annual arrival of each ingredient. Roman peas are remarkably sweet, and artichokes, asparagus, spinach, and all sorts of greens are outstanding.

Fave al guanciale	Fava beans simmered with cured pork cheek and onion.
Misticanza	Mixed green salad.
Puntarelle	A popular dark-green Roman version of chicory found in winter and spring. They are plunged in ice water to make them curl and then served with a dressing of oil, vinegar, and anchovy. They have a nice crispy crunch and are addictive.
Spinaci	Spinach is often served cold with a squeeze of fresh lemon juice.

FORMAGGI (CHEESES)

Pecorino romano	While you'll find versions of *pecorino* elsewhere (including Tuscany), the most popular is the slightly salty grating cheese that is often called *pecorino romano* or *pecorino stagionato*. These days, much of it is actually made in Sardinia; classic *pecorino romano* from Lazio has a greenish tinge, while the one from Sardinia is whiter. (The green tinge comes when the cheese is aged in *tufo* caves.) The first taste of aged *pecorino romano* is salty, but then other flavors emerge, including milk and herbs. The cheese has a very long finish. It tastes different depending on when the milk was gathered: A one-year-old *pecorino romano* that was made in the spring will taste younger and fresher than one made in summer or fall, because the sheep eat more tender grass in the spring. A cheese made in June, when the grass is harder, will taste stronger after a year.

Left: *Bignè;* **Right:** *Crostata di ricotta*

Ricotta romana	This smooth, fresh, creamy cheese is one of the simplest and most addictive in all of Italy. It's made of milk curds (cow's or sheep's) that are twice cooked, and then cooled; it goes well with cut fruit.

DOLCI (SWEETS)

Perhaps the best desserts in Lazio are simply fresh, seasonal fruits: an orange in February, cherries in June, a peach in July, and moscato or regina grapes in September.

Bignè	Cream puff-like pastries filled with *zabaione* (egg yolks, sugar, and Marsala wine). ***Bignè di San Giuseppe*** is a variation that's popular on Father's Day, March 19 (the feast of St. Joseph)—cream puffs that are fried or baked, then coated with sugar.
Baked goods	Bakeries in the Castelli Romani make nice cookies and *ciambelline al vino* (rings made with wine).
Crostate	These tarts of fruit or jam can be very good in Lazio when local fruits are used.
Crostata di ricotta	A cheesecake-like dessert with *ricotta,* sweet Marsala wine, cinnamon, and bits of chocolate.
Grattachecca	Sweetened shaved ice. Vendors at little booths scrape *(gratta)* shavings off ice blocks (*checca* in Roman dialect) into a cup, then flavor them with syrups, such as *limoncocco* (lemon and coconut with fresh chunks of coconut). Eat it quickly, before it loses its unique "snowy" texture and flavor.
Other *ricotta* desserts	*Ricotta romana* cheese can be very good in a light cheesecake **(*torta di ricotta*),** in a mousse, or simply by itself with a little sugar or cocoa powder.

🍷 WINES OF LAZIO

Lazio's wine (mostly white) is pleasant but generally not exceptional. That's because Rome is a huge market that consumes most of it and wants it at a low cost—so there's little incentive to produce anything better than a solid table wine. If you'd like something better, order a bottle from a different region.

Castelli Romani This is the name of the zone southeast of the capital (also called the Colli Albani) where most Lazio wine is produced. A wine called Castelli Romani, made with trebbiano grapes, is light and fairly dry and is similar to Marino, Colli Albani, and Velletri wines. The best known of these is Frascati (see below).

Est! Est!! Est!!! This acidic white wine from Montefiascone can come either dry or semisweet, and goes well with fried foods. As you might imagine from the over-the-top name, it comes with a silly legend: Around the year 1100, a German bigwig journeyed to Rome. He sent his cupbearer ahead to scout places to stop for a rest, with instructions to mark the word *est* (Latin for "it is") in chalk on the doors of inns that had good wine. In Montefiascone, the cupbearer found a wine so outstanding that it warranted more than just an *est*—he marked it as *Est! Est!! Est!!!* The bigwig was so pleased with the wine that he spent three days enjoying it before reaching Rome—and on his way back, he decided to stay in Montefiascone, where he's still buried today.

Frascati This is Lazio's best-known wine. Centuries ago, Frascati owners effectively captured the Roman market by opening *osterie* that were leased to local franchisers, much like fast-food restaurants today. Frascati is an amiable young wine made of 70 percent malvasia bianca di Candia and/or trebbiano toscano, plus 30 percent greco and/or malvasia di Lazio.

Sambuca This ouzo-like anise liqueur, from Civitavecchia, is now found throughout Italy. Drink it neat or with water, which makes it cloudy. Ordering it *con la mosca* (with the fly) adds a coffee bean (or a few) at the bottom of your glass. Some bartenders add the gimmick of lighting the drink on fire to "toast" the coffee beans.

Torre Ercolana While most Lazio wines are whites, this is a dense, balanced, medium-bodied red that's considered Lazio's best. It's made from the regional cesanese grape, as well as cabernet and merlot, then aged for at least five years.

Left: *Salute!* **Right:** *Sambuca con la mosca* ("with flies"—with coffee beans)

Southern Italy
Naples &
Campania

Napoli

If you like Italy as far south as Rome, go farther—it gets better. If Italy is getting on your nerves, stop at Rome. Italy intensifies as you plunge deeper. And Naples is Italy in the extreme—its best (birthplace of pizza) and its worst (petty and organized crime).

When most Americans think of "Italian" food, they're thinking of the cuisine of Naples and the surrounding region of Campania: pizza, spaghetti with tomato sauce, gooey mozzarella cheese, stuffed eggplant, seafood salad, San Marzano tomatoes, honest wine, steaming-hot espresso, crunchy pastries, and ices made of lemon or coffee. Before Italy unified in the 19th century, Naples was the wealthiest Italian city. But when the capital of modern Italy was established in Rome, Naples' fortunes plummeted, and the people of Campania fled poverty and harsh conditions—relocating to North America and bringing these dishes

along with them. If you enjoy these flavors back home, you may be surprised by how they taste even better in their place of origin.

Naples has had a complicated history, forever passing between hands of powerful rulers. The period of Spanish (Aragonese) rule, which began in the early 16th century and lasted two centuries, left a huge impact on both Neapolitan and Italian cuisine. New ingredients from the Spanish colonies in the Americas—tomatoes, potatoes, peppers, beans, and so on—were introduced here in Naples, then spread throughout the peninsula, becoming Italian staples. At other times, Arab, Norman, and French rulers also left their marks.

Campania is largely mountainous, with a rugged landscape punctuated by wide valleys where fruits, vegetables, and livestock flourish. Naples, facing the Tyrrhenian Sea, has about a million residents, making it Italy's third-biggest city. The rest of Campania seems to radiate out from the Bay of Naples—where an estimated five million people live in the shadow of a sleeping, yet very much alive, volcano. It's a congested, complicated knot of humanity: the second-biggest metro area in Italy,

🍽 Foods and Drinks to Sample in Campania

Real Neapolitan pizza
The world's favorite food is best in its birthplace; try a classic *pizza Margherita,* with mozzarella, San Marzano tomatoes, basil, and olive oil.

Pasta
In Campania, it's usually dry pasta topped with a simple sauce, such as *alla puttanesca* (tomato sauce with anchovies and/or tuna, black olives, capers, and garlic), *alla pizzaiola* (tomatoes, oregano, garlic, white wine), or *alle vongole* (with clams).

Mozzarella
Fresh, milky, soft, and chewy, the best version is *mozzarella di bufala,* made with milk from water buffalos—giving it a unique, pungent, slightly sour flavor.

Insalata caprese
"Capri salad" of tomatoes, mozzarella, and basil, drizzled with olive oil.

Mozzarella

Sfogliatelle
Crunchy pastry dough filled with *ricotta* cheese, cream, and/or candied fruit.

Limoncello
This sweet lemon liqueur comes from the Amalfi Coast, where products made with lemons abound.

after Milan's; one of Italy's poorest corners; and the most densely populated place in all of Europe. And, with all that density and poverty, the Neapolitan sprawl comes with its own distinct culture and personality—so much so that it often feels "foreign" even to fellow Italians.

Speaking of that volcano, it's difficult to overstate the influence of Mount Vesuvius (Vesuvio) on the history, culture, and cuisine of Campania. Its slopes were home to a thriving civilization in ancient times, until the infamous eruption in AD 79 that instantly killed thousands and

left much of the area under a blanket of ash. People eventually resettled those same places, although Vesuvius still smoldered on (the last eruption, a small one, was in 1944). The volcanic soil gives incredible flavor to fruits and vegetables; everything from peaches to tomatoes to potatoes and lemons just seem to taste better. And with an abundance of such fine produce, local chefs are adept at keeping things simple and respecting the integrity of their ingredients.

Even so, there's also a long tradition of elaborate cooking and baking

for the royal families and the nobles who have been part of the scene since antiquity (the Roman Emperor Tiberius made Capri his playground). There are also, as in most of Italy, special foods for the frequent religious and pagan festivals. But the highlight for food lovers is pizza—invented right here, and still at its finest expression in its place of birth. Friends and families gather at humble Neapolitan *pizzerie* for an evening of delicious, inexpensive conviviality.

The people of Naples, and of Campania, are by turns courteous, festive, pensive, despondent, calculating, and joyous…but always vibrantly *alive*. People in Campania love to gather and spend time together, to drink wine, to sing, to race cars, to shout to each other from balconies, to fight, to flirt. People are everywhere, and there's constant motion. Motor scooters speed by on the street while people walk in erratic patterns, hands flying in wild gestures, mouths opening to receive food or make a pronouncement. Hips shake to music, pockets are deftly picked, fingers scratch private areas, eyes dart. Babies are being coddled, fed, burped, powdered, diapered, and passed from one loving embrace to another. Neapolitans may at first

strike you as a bit presumptuous—perhaps too intimate—but they thrive on human interaction and living in the moment.

It's unfortunate that Naples has a sinister reputation: organized and petty crime, pollution, chaos, and grinding urban problems. While these exist, Naples is also a city of beauty, excitement, and drama. The city has produced great scholars, doctors, painters, composers, musicians, sex symbols, and a population that is innately theatrical and resourceful.

📍 CITIES, TOWNS, AND PLACES

While in many ways it feels like an urban jungle, **Naples** surprises the observant traveler with its impressive knack for living, eating, and raising children with good humor and decency. Overcome your fear of being run down or ripped off long enough to talk with people. Enjoy a few smiles and jokes with the shopkeeper running the neighborhood tripe shop, or the teacher taking a daycare class on a stroll through the traffic. Walking through Naples' colorful old streets is one of my favorite experiences anywhere in Europe.

And enjoy some sightseeing: Naples has one of Europe's top archaeological museums, fascinating churches that convey the city's unique personality and powerful devotion, an underground warren of Greek and Roman ruins, fine works of art (including pieces by Caravaggio, who lived here for a time), and evocative Nativity scenes (called *presepi*).

The ancient artery of Naples is called the Spaccanapoli—literally "split Naples"—which runs straight through the heart of town from roughly the train station to the Spanish Quarter, just uphill from the old royal palace and port. But the Spaccanapoli isn't a broad boulevard; it's narrow, crowded, and claustrophobic, a canyon framed by towering, rickety old apartment houses. Along the way, keep an eye out for the many fragrant fruit stands, selling produce from the fertile volcanic soil. Or stop by the fish market, under the Porta Nolana, which still squirts and stinks as it has for centuries.

Neapolitans also love their coffee, which ranks with the best in Italy. Once upon a time, the *caffettiera alla napoletana* (Neapolitan coffee pot) was a fixture in every house and bar. It's a cylinder designed to be turned upside-down once the water has boiled, so that it filters through the canister containing ground coffee (rather than relying on steam pressure, as with the more typical Moka pot). A few smaller restaurants still prepare coffee this way.

Just south of Naples are two towns that were stopped in their tracks by the eruption of Mount Vesuvius in AD 79: **Pompeii** (once a thriving, middle-class port town of 20,000) and **Herculaneum** (smaller, less crowded, and less ruined). These give you the best look anywhere at what life in the Roman Empire must have been like around 2,000 years ago: ancient kitchens, bakeries, theaters, and brothels.

The islands offshore from Naples are also tempting. **Capri** (KAH-pree) was made famous as the vacation hideaway of Roman emperors Augustus and Tiberius; in the 19th century, it was the haunt of Romantic Age aristocrats on their Grand Tour of Europe. These days, while undoubtedly gorgeous, the island is a world-class tourist trap that still rewards a thoughtful visit.

The isle of **Ischia** is one of Italy's most important spa destinations, particularly famous for its mud cures. While the port is ugly, take the loop drive to sample the volcanic island's beauty and explore appealing towns like Forio and Lacco Ameno. Nearby, the lesser-known isle of **Procida** is quieter and has a sleepy pastel charm.

San Marzano sul Sarno, a nondescript small town of about 10,000 in the Sarno Valley behind Vesuvius, is unexceptional aside from one thing: It's the hometown of the San Marzano tomato, some of the world's best. These long, skinny tomatoes, which culminate in a little point, have a rich, sweet flavor that's delicious eaten fresh and ideal for sauces and pastes.

Just an hour south of Naples— facing the city from across its bay— sits serene **Sorrento.** Wedged on a ledge under the mountains and over the Mediterranean, spritzed by lemon and olive groves, Sorrento is an attractive resort of 16,000 residents and, in summer, just as many tourists. It's as well located for regional sightseeing as it is a fine place to stay and stroll.

Around the bluff from Sorrento begins the **Amalfi Coast,** with stunning scenery, hill- and harbor-hugging towns, and historic ruins. Cantilevered garages, hotels, and villas cling to the vertical terrain, and beautiful but out-of-reach coves tease from far below.

The coast has three major towns. **Positano** (pop. 4,000), built on a series of man-made terraces, is like a living Gucci ad. Its beach is inviting, its prices are high, and its rooftops

Left: Pompeii; **Right:** Sorrento

Amalfi

tell its story: a mix of Roman-style, red terra-cotta tiles and white domes inspired by the Saracens.

Amalfi (pop. 5,000) is Fred's favorite town in the region. The sun; the sea; the flavors of lemon, tomatoes, mozzarella, and herbs; the beautiful church; and the playful spirit of the place all make Amalfi emblematic of the pleasures of Campania. The city shows Moorish influence in its flavors and its architecture. Amalfi thrived as a maritime republic (like Venice or Genoa) after Rome fell. But a 1343 tsunami and devastating plagues left Amalfi a humble backwater. To this day, it's less pretentious and more interesting than other Amalfi Coast towns, with a real-life feel and a vivacious bustle.

The Amalfi Coast's version of a hill town, **Ravello** (pop. 2,500), sits atop a lofty perch 1,000 feet above the sea. It feels like a lush and peaceful garden floating in a world all its own. It seems to be made entirely of cafés, stonework, old villas-turned-luxury hotels, tourists, and grand views. Ravello feels like a place to convalesce.

Salerno (pop. 135,000) is a big city that most travelers see simply as a transit point between Naples, the Amalfi Cost, and Paestum. It has one of Italy's oldest universities and a long tradition of commercial pastamaking, and its *lungomare* (seafront prome-nade) is a delightful place to stroll.

At **Paestum,** you can see one of the world's best collections of 2,500-year-old Greek temples. And farther south, **Battipaglia** (pop. 50,000) is the center of *mozzarella di bufala* production; approaching town, you'll see white water buffalo grazing.

🍴 FOODS OF CAMPANIA

The unique volcanic soil produces outstanding vegetables and fruits (especially tomatoes), which give Campania's food a pop of powerful flavor. Chefs combine these with cheeses, dry pastas, deep-frying methods, locally caught fish and seafood, and delicate pastries to create a cuisine that's simple, tasty, and satisfying.

ANTIPASTI (APPETIZERS)

Arancina (or *arancino*)	A breaded, deep-fried rice ball filled with meat sauce or other ingredients. Neapolitans have been eating fried street foods since Roman times. Others include *frittatine* (balls of mac-and-cheese plus sausage) and *crocché* (croquettes).

Frittura di paranza	In Naples slang, *paranza* means a gang of criminals. That's a strange name for a seafood dish, but it makes sense: These are the small, less desirable fish that are still left after the prime catch are sold...so they're fried up and eaten.
Frittura di pesce	A bit fancier than *frittura di paranza,* this is a selection of fried seafood that typically includes fish, squid, octopus, and perhaps a few shrimp.
Insalata caprese	This "Capri salad" is an addictive combination of perfect mozzarella, tomatoes, and basil, with a few drops of olive oil.
Insalata di mare	Boiled seafood, served cool with oil, vinegar or lemon juice, and pepper.
Melanzane ripiene	Stuffed eggplants.
Mozzarella in carrozza	Mozzarella is placed in squares of bread ("in a carriage"), dipped in egg, and deep-fried.
Peperoni imbottiti	Sweet peppers filled with capers, olives, anchovies, breadcrumbs, basil, garlic, and parsley.
Pomodori ripieni	Stuffed tomatoes.

PRIMI (PASTAS AND OTHER FIRST COURSES)

Gnocchi alla sorrentina	This "Sorrento-style" gnocchi dish is baked with tomato sauce, mozzarella, and occasionally eggplant.
Minestra maritata	Popular in wintertime, this simple, nourishing "married soup" celebrates the marriage of meat and vegetables.

Left: *Melanzane ripiene;* **Right:** *Insalata caprese*

Pasta	Campania is the heartland of dry pasta. It has given the world spaghetti, *maccheroni,* vermicelli, *ziti,* and many other shapes. Traditionally, the poor could not afford *secondi,* so they made do just with a *primo* and simple sauce, such as **alla pummarola** (San Marzano tomatoes, a bit of garlic, and a pinch of oregano), **alla puttanesca** (literally "prostitute-style"—tomato sauce with ancho-vies and/or tuna, black olives, capers, and garlic), **alla pizzaiola** ("pizza-maker," with tomatoes, oregano, garlic, and white wine), or **alla genovese** (sauce of onions, carrots, celery, and often meat). For something a bit higher-end, **alle vongole** (with clams) is popular.
Pasta al forno	Baked pasta comes in several forms, ranging from *lasagne* to cylin-drical pastas such as *maccheroni* or *ziti.* The noodles are combined with tomato sauce, mozzarella, and a variety of other ingredients that can include boiled eggs, tiny meatballs, sausage, assorted vege-tables, and other cheese.
Pasta e fagioli	Some of the best pasta-and-bean soup is made in Campania.
Risotto alla pescatora	This "fisherman's *risotto*" has shellfish, shrimp, and seafood stock.
Sartù di riso	An elaborate Neapolitan rice tart made with mozzarella, sausage, peas, *ragù,* mushrooms, hard-boiled eggs, and chicken livers.

SECONDI (MAIN DISHES)

The endless variety of fish and seafood is the primary choice for a *secondo.* In Campania, certain specialties are eaten only on Sunday or religious holidays.

Baccalà	Salt cod often comes **alla napoletana** (also known as **in casse-ruola**)—with tomatoes, olives, capers, and pine nuts. You might also see **baccalà con peperoni,** cooked with sweet peppers (also popular in Basilicata).

Left: *Risotto alla pescatora;* **Right:** *Gnocchi alla sorrentina*

Left: *Braciola;* **Right:** *Polpette*

Braciola	A slice of beef that's rolled with chopped prosciutto, grated provolone cheese, eggs, and sultanas. It's tightly tied and cooked in tomatoes.
Capitone	Saltwater eel, traditionally eaten in Naples at Christmastime, cooked in tomato sauce.
Costata alla pizzaiola	Anything *alla pizzaiola*—in this case, veal—has a sauce of tomatoes, oregano, garlic, and white wine.
Friarielli	These tender greens (tips of *broccoletti*) grow only in the province of Salerno. They are sautéed with oil, garlic, and *peperoncino* and are often eaten as a *secondo*, paired with sausages.
Genovese	This is a sauce of onions, carrots, and celery that tops many meat dishes and sometimes pasta. (Confusingly, *genovese* can also mean "pesto," especially in the North.)
Impepata di cozze	Peppered mussels.
Parmigiana di melanzane	What we'd call "eggplant parmesan," this is a casserole of thin-sliced eggplant, breaded and fried, then baked with tomatoes and cheese (mozzarella, *fior di latte,* Parmigiano-Reggiano, or a combination).
Polpette	Meatballs in a tomato sauce. Note that these are eaten by themselves as a *secondo,* rather than—as in Italian American cooking—with pasta.
Polpi alla luciana	A Neapolitan favorite, made with baby octopus, tomatoes, garlic, and olive oil.
Totani e patate	Red squid that's sautéed with onions and garlic, and served with potatoes (sometimes in a tomato sauce); a specialty of the Amalfi Coast.

Naples: Birthplace of Pizza

Pizza—Naples' great culinary creation—has been exported around the world. And yet, it still tastes best in its birthplace. If this sounds like hyperbole...come to Naples and find out for yourself.

The origins of pizza date back 2,500 years, to when flatbreads were dressed with oil, salt, herbs, and sometimes cheese. Tomatoes only arrived in Campania after Columbus' journeys to the Americas, and were not routinely used with flatbread until the early 19th century.

But once they figured out this recipe, the Neapolitans perfected it. An ideal pizza must have a light crust. Neapolitan *pizzerie* often make the crust the day before, using very little yeast, and then they let it rise for 12 to 15 hours. (Lesser *pizzerie*—especially outside of Campania—use ample yeast to affect a quicker rise, but this toughens the crust and gives it a yeasty flavor.) The *pizzaiolo* (pizza maker) makes an individual pie for each diner, and bakes it in a very hot wood-burning oven for about three minutes.

In Naples, you can head for the famous, venerable places, but these can have long lines stretching out the door, and half-hour waits for a table.

As an alternative, there are plenty of simple neighborhood places offering a tasty pie. Most *pizzerie* offer both takeout and eat-in, and pizza is often the only thing on the menu.

In Campania, a classic pizza uses very few toppings, and the ones they use are of the best possible quality. For example, a classic **pizza Margherita** uses fresh *mozzarella di bufala* (made from the milk of water buffaloes—or, in a pinch, absolutely fresh mozzarella made of cow's milk). To this are added the incomparable San Marzano tomatoes. A basil leaf and a few drops of good olive oil finish the perfect pizza.

A **pizza marinara** contains tomato sauce, garlic, and oregano, but no cheese. On Christmas Eve, it's traditional to eat **pizza alla scarola,** topped with chopped escarole, black olives, sultanas, pine nuts, and capers.

Another kind of pizza is the **calzone,** in which the crust is folded over to enclose the ingredients. The result looks like a big shoe, which is what the word means.

Most Neapolitans drink beer or mineral water with pizza—rarely wine—but one classic pizza wine is Asprinio di Aversa.

Locals prize their method so highly, they've created a certification for "True Neapolitan Pizza" (the Associazione Verace Pizza Napoletana). Would-be *pizzaioli* from around the world travel great distances to learn the precise methods for making a real Naples pizza. You can find the red, yellow, and black logo for the AVPN around the world—perhaps even in your own neighborhood.

Left: *Struffoli* (top shelf) and *sfogliatelle* (bottom shelf); **Right:** *Babà al rum*

FORMAGGI (CHEESES)

Mozzarella	This cheese—with its fresh milkiness and soft, chewy texture—is adored around the globe, but nowhere is it made better than in Campania. Other nearby regions, such as Abruzzo and Molise, also make good mozzarella, but the very best comes from the area around Battipaglia, south of Salerno. The finest is ***mozzarella di bufala,*** made with milk from water buffaloes, which is higher in fat, richer, and sweeter than cow's milk. The result is pungent, slightly sour, and uniquely flavorful. Because buffalo milk is hard to come by, many mozzarellas are made with a mixture of cow's (70 percent) and buffalo's (30 percent) milk. The cheese is best eaten very young (unless it has been smoked) and should be stored in cool water to keep it fresh. A mozzarella made only from cow's milk might be called ***fior di latte.*** And ***burrata***—basically a mozzarella shell around a gooey center—originates in Puglia (see page 303) but is also popular in Campania and throughout the South (and, increasingly, stateside).

DOLCI (SWEETS)

The dominant tastes in most local desserts are cream, *ricotta,* and citrus fruits; other fruits and nuts are also featured.

Babà al rum	A pear-shaped sponge cake drowned in rum.
Frutta	The excellent fruit of Campania is a fine way to end a meal. The peaches in particular are wonderfully flavorful. A traditional way to eat them is to cut them into a glass of wine and then take a swig, letting a piece of peach roll into your mouth.
Frutta secca	Nuts and dried fruits are also special in Campania. The best hazelnuts come from Avellino, almonds from Nola, and walnuts from Sorrento. These nuts find their way into many special baked goods.

Pasta reale	Neapolitan marzipan cakes served at Christmas.
Pastiera	A special Easter cake made with flour (sometimes barley flour), *ricotta,* eggs, orange blossom water, and candied orange or lemon peel.
Sfogliatelle	In this delectable Naples treat, pastry dough is filled with *ricotta* cheese, pastry cream, and/or candied fruit, then baked until crunchy. It's eaten for breakfast, to accompany your morning coffee. A variation is the **coda d'aragosta** ("lobster's tail"), a longer *sfogliatella* filled with pastry cream and cherries.
Struffoli	This Neapolitan Christmas treat is tiny, crunchy fried balls of dough with honey.
Susamielli	Pastries made with sesame seeds and honey.
Zeppole	These Campanian "doughnut holes"—spongy and soft compared to the similar **struffoli**—are especially popular on March 19, the feast day of St. Joseph (Giuseppe), Italy's Father's Day.

♀ WINES OF CAMPANIA

Wine has been made in Campania at least since the 13th century BC. Like so much else in the region, the wines are designed for immediate pleasure rather than commercialization and sales abroad. Even so, the quality of Campania wines has soared in recent years. The **Taurasi** made by Antonio Mastroberardini is one of the best red wines in Italy, sometimes called the "Barbaresco of the South."

Campania has several native grape varieties, which give the wines some unusual qualities:

Fiano The Romans called this delicate white grape *Vitis apiana* because its particular fragrance is very attractive to bees. Grape pickers today still cover themselves to avoid being stung.

Greco A white grape that was introduced by the Greeks.

Coda di Volpe Named for the foxtail shape of the grape clusters.

Piedirosso Literally "red feet," the red stems resemble the feet of doves.

Lemons

In Campania—and especially on the Amalfi Coast—*limoni* are ubiquitous: screaming yellow painted on ceramics, dainty bottles of *limoncello,* and lemons the size of softballs at the fruit stand. Souvenir shops sell lemon biscuits, lemon pasta, lemon drops, lemon chocolate, lemon perfume, lemon soap, and on and on.

The Amalfi Coast and Sorrento area produce several different kinds of lemons. The gigantic, bumpy ones are actually citrons, called **cedri,** which are more pulpy than they are juicy, and make a good marmalade. The juicy **sfusato sorrentino,** grown only in Sorrento, is shaped like an American football, while the **sfusato amalfitano,** with knobby points on both ends, is less juicy but equally aromatic. These two kinds of luscious lemons are used in sweets such as *granita* (shaved ice doused in lemonade), *delizia al limone* (a dome of fluffy cake filled and slathered with a thick whipped lemon cream), *spremuta di limone* (fresh-squeezed lemon juice), and, of course, gelato or *sorbetto al limone.*

The ultimate lemon product is the classic after-dinner drink called

limoncello (or sometimes **limoncino**): a sweet, almost candy-like lemon-infused liqueur. At its best, *limoncello* manages to capture all the freshness and sunshine of Campania in a glass. The best *limoncello* has only lemon juice, alcohol, and sugar, with the canary color coming from the rind of the lemon. Some say the top limoncello is made with *sfusato amalfitano,* from the Amalfi Coast. Unfortunately, the drink's popularity has made producers take shortcuts in order to capitalize on the demand. Read the label before buying to assure that there are no artificial colors or flavorings; at many places, you can even taste it before purchasing.

Some of the best wines in Campania are named for the places they come from: Capri, Ischia, Procida, Solopaca, and Ravello, for example. The small community of Furore on the Amalfi Coast produces a wine called **Gran Vino del Furore,** which is a hyperbolic name for a nice little wine. Many good, more substantial wines of ancient pedigree are produced inland in the provinces of Benevento and Avellino; **Fiano di Avellino** is one of the best white wines in southern Italy. Also look for distinct wines such as Cilento, Greco di Tufo, and Vesuvio.

The most famous wine of Campania, **Lacryma Cristi** or Lacrima Christi ("Tears of Christ"), is usually a white wine, though occasionally red. It used to be good-quality, but it has become so overproduced and denatured that its reputation was nearly ruined. Producers have now conscientiously made an effort to restore the wine to its former stature.

In terms of hard drinks, beyond *limoncello* (see earlier), there's **Liquore Strega,** a delicious saffron-colored liqueur from Benevento made with 70 herbs and spices. Keep an eye out for Strega gelato, a real delicacy.

Abruzzo

The story of Abruzzo (ah-BROOT-soh) is shaped by its landscape. This is true of every Italian region, of course, but even more so here: Abruzzo is among Italy's most mountainous regions, and virtually everything that isn't covered in mountains is hilly. Abruzzo has the highest peak in the Apennines, the Corno Grande (9,554 feet), and Europe's southernmost glacier (Calderone). Its high elevations result in snow and cold that are among the most severe in Italy.

The many lofty mountain passes, in the days before modern tunnels and telecommunications, meant that the *abruzzesi* were cut off from one another. In some places, this isolation continued all the way through the mid-1960s. Going even further back, Abruzzo's seclusion meant that Christianity arrived here later than in most of Italy—and when it did, it blended with pagan traditions rather than replacing them. (If this

makes Abruzzo sound "less Italian" than more mainline Catholic regions, keep in mind that the name "Italia" derives from the ancient *italici* people who lived in today's Chieti province. No one is more Italian than the *abruzzesi*.)

For all of these reasons, despite Abruzzo's seemingly dead-central location (bordering Lazio, Umbria, the Marche, Molise, and the Adriatic), it has its own cuisine and culture. And, while geographically in the center of Italy, culturally and culinarily it's closer to the South.

Traditions are long-lasting here.

A town-wide celebration called the *panarda* can carry on for days, featuring many customs that betray its pagan roots (see the sidebar). Another example: Traditionally, young women learned how to weave blankets, create lace, and embroider cloths, all in order to help prepare their dowry. And these handicrafts remain an important part of *abruzzese* culture (especially in Sulmona). Even the colorful *confetti* candies (sugar-coated almonds) come with a complicated color-coding system that hints at the *abruzzese* propensity for superstition.

🍴 Foods to Sample in Abruzzo

Maccheroni alla chitarra
Fresh egg pasta cut into noodles on a guitar-shaped box, topped with a tomato or meat sauce.

Scrippelle
Crêpes served with sauce, in a broth, or baked with cheese.

Confetti
Sugar-coated almonds that are color-coded to celebrate various special occasions.

Confetti

The *abruzzesi* place great importance on nature. The mountains are a popular ski destination for southern Italians, and it has the highest percentage of land dedicated to national parks of any Italian region. The Parco Nazionale d'Abruzzo is a preserve full of bears, wolves, chamois, and eagles (the *aquila,* meaning eagle, gave its name to the region's capital, L'Aquila). The Gran Sasso d'Italia, closer to the coast, is another set of towering peaks that afford magnificent views of the sea. The region has had a tradition of environmentalism, animal preservation, and organic farming methods since long before those became trendy throughout Italy.

Agriculture is still the main source of income. Produce includes potatoes (the ones from Avezzano are considered the best in Italy), wheat, corn, olives, wine, many vegetables, oregano, and excellent saffron. Cattle, sheep, and goats are raised, and shepherding has, since ancient times, been an important part of life. The *transumanza*—an annual migration of sheep and people through Molise to Puglia—begins

here (for more on this, see page 288 in the Molise chapter).

All of this makes Abruzzo sound hopelessly isolated. But in our modern times, it's well connected and, given its close proximity to Rome, worth a visit by curious travelers interested in getting away from the big tourist areas and finding a pocket of traditional life. Not only will you gain a more well-rounded understanding of Italy as a whole...but you'll also eat and drink very well.

🗺️ CITIES, TOWNS, AND PLACES

Sulmona (pop. 25,000) is Fred's favorite *abruzzese* town. It combines excellent food, rich folklore, a cultured populace, and natural beauty in a way that feels quintessentially Abruzzo. It also has grand medieval and Renaissance architecture and a lovely, if somewhat formal-feeling, *passeggiata*. This was the birthplace of Ovid (in 43 BC), one of the literary giants of the Roman Empire. Sulmona also has shops selling wonderful blankets, shawls, and sweaters, all handmade with local wool, and it's one of the production centers for *confetti*—colorful sugar-coated almonds. Sulmona's food has some distinct flavors as well, such as the unique red garlic *(aglio rosso)* found nearby.

L'Aquila, the capital of Abruzzo, is scenically situated on a hill surrounded by mountain peaks. It's small for a regional capital (just 70,000 residents), largely due to a devastating 2009 earthquake from which the town is still recovering.

Pescara (pop. 120,000), on the Adriatic coast, is Abruzzo's biggest town. It's a modern city built upon ancient foundations, and it presents a very different Abruzzo from what you'll find inland. Compared to the interior, Pescara is less conservative; the *passeggiata* (on Corso Umberto I) is particularly vibrant, and there's a busy beach scene, lively nightlife, and, of course, excellent seafood.

Other *abruzzese* towns have their own claims to fame. **Rivisondoli** is a popular mountain resort known for its cheesemaking, and also for a special ham dish cooked with pepper, cloves, cinnamon, and sugar served at wedding lunches. **Calascio** is the place to find a good sheep's-milk cheese, *cacio marcetto,* with a

Top: Sulmona; **Bottom:** Pacentro, one of many striking *abruzzese* villages

sharp flavor and a soft texture that's ideal for spreading on good bread. The potatoes grown near **Avezzano** are very floury and make delicate gnocchi. **Navelli** produces some of the best saffron *(zafferano)* in Italy—considered to be in a class by itself. And **Villa Santa Maria** is home to a world-famous culinary institute with roots dating back to the 16th century: La Scuola Alberghiera, whose students gained fame and fortune cooking for czars, presidents, kings, and dictators.

The *Panarda:*
An Epic *Abruzzese* Feast

Abruzzo feels unusually rooted in its distant past, with pagan features that persist even in modern times. One of the best examples of this are the feast days *(sagre e feste)* for each town, as well as the elaborate weddings and other celebrations. Some of these include a remarkable tradition called the *panarda*—a meal with unbridled feasting and partying that can last hours, or even days, with up to 30 courses.

At a traditional, elaborate *panarda,* the first part (or the first night)—called *magro* (lean)—features multiple courses of fish and vegetables, all washed down with rosé wine. After midnight (or, sometimes, the next day), the dishes become *grasso* (fat): sausages and *salumi* of many types, then soups and pastas, followed by boiled meats, fried sweetbreads and brains, and roast meats. Many dishes in the *panarda* are flavored with *peperoncino* (hot red chili pepper, called *pepedinie* in local dialect). The grand finale is roast kid, followed by cheeses, sweets, coffee, and liqueurs.

The number seven is a prime example of the *panarda*'s melding of pagan superstition and Christian belief. Often there are seven *minestre,* one of them a soup from Teramo called *le virtù*—referring to the seven virtues taught in religious instruction. This soup was originally prepared by seven maidens and includes seven types of legumes, seven types of pasta, seven types of vegetable, seven types of meat, and seven seasonings, and the soup was slow-cooked for seven hours.

If all of this sounds extravagant, keep in mind that the specter of poverty hung over inland Abruzzo until very recently. Feasting was an act of defiance against famine, born of fear that hunger may soon return. Harvest festivals were intended to give thanks to pagan gods for providing food. If you have the opportunity to experience a festival, try to notice how the rituals you observe aren't just "folklore," but something that is felt very deeply.

🍴 FOODS OF ABRUZZO

Abruzzese cuisine makes ample use of produce, livestock, and seafood that abounds in its territory. There are very good *salumi* made of pork or lamb, particularly in the province of L'Aquila. Like neighboring Molise, Abruzzo isn't afraid of heat—often using *peperoncino* (hot pepper) in its dishes. And saffron (from the town of Navelli) shows up regularly in recipes, as well. Figs and grapes are especially good here, and licorice *(liquirizia)* often appears in desserts and drinks. Many *abruzzese* dishes come with an elaborate preparation, perhaps reflecting the same pagan intricacies that inform the *panarda* feasts.

ANTIPASTI (APPETIZERS)

Frutti di Mare	The coastal provinces enjoy all sorts of shellfish raw, cooked in wine and herbs, or boiled and dressed with oil and vinegar to make *insalata di mare.*
Mortadella di Campotosto	Large, round *salumi* with soft pulp, from Campotosto. They're nicknamed "mule's balls," and traditionally they're bought in pairs—never just one.
Salsiccie di fegato	These delicious sausages are made with pork liver and come either spicy *(pazza)* or sweet *(dolce).*
Ventricina	A *salame* from the province of Chieti made with pork, *peperoncino,* fennel, and orange peel.

PRIMI (PASTAS AND OTHER FIRST COURSES)

Some of Italy's best commercial pasta is made in Abruzzo by producers such as De Cecco and Del Verde, both in the town of Fara San Martino; the excellent-quality water gives the pasta a special purity of flavor.

Le virtù	A rich minestrone with legumes, vegetables, meat, seasonings, and pastas. (For the full story, see the *panarda* sidebar.)

Left: *Salsiccie di fegato;* **Right:** *Mortadella di Campotosto*

Left: *Timballo;* **Right:** *Scrippelle*

Maccheroni alla chitarra	In this famous dish, fresh egg pasta is cut into strips by pressing dough through steel wires anchored in a wooden box that looks like a guitar (as the name means). It's served with a tomato sauce, or with a *ragù* of either lamb or beef. In northern Abruzzo, it's served with a sauce of tomato and bite-sized meatballs (***alla teramana*** or ***con le pallottine***).
Pasta all'abruzzese	Abruzzo's classic sauce is made of chopped *pancetta,* saffron, parsley, *pecorino romano,* and onions.
Ravioli abruzzesi	These stuffed pasta are sweet (filled with *ricotta*) and served with tomato sauce.
Scrippelle (also called ***crespelle***)	Crêpes made with flour and sometimes egg. They can be served with many types of sauce, baked with cheese and sauce, or served as ***scrippelle 'mbusse,*** in a rich chicken broth. According to legend, this originated when Bourbon troops occupied the province of Teramo. The captains' crêpes accidentally slipped into the privates' broth, and a new dish was born.
Timballo	Meaning roughly "casserole," this *lasagne*-like dish usually features pasta, but sometimes *scrippelle* or potatoes are used instead. Other ingredients might include lamb or pork. A ***timballo bianco*** usually has cheese but no meat. ***Timballo alla teramana*** contains lamb, pork, eggs, and *scrippelle.*

SECONDI (MAIN DISHES)

Agnello al cotturo (also called ***pecora a lu cuttur***)	Lamb that is boiled for many hours, defatted, and then cooked in wine, parsley, carrots, celery, onions, sage, salt, *peperoncino,* tomatoes, and garlic.

Agnello all'uovo e limone (or *cacio e ova*)	Lamb flavored with egg and lemon—an Easter favorite.
Brodetto	The most highly regarded *abruzzese* version of this Adriatic fish stew is served in Vasto (Chieti); meanwhile, **brodetto alla pescarese** has more *peperoncino* than most preparations. Unfortunately, it's difficult to find a classic *brodetto*, which was made by fishermen on their boats, who tossed together just-caught fish, dried sweet red pepper, oil, garlic, and *peperoncino*. These days, the sweet pepper has been replaced by tomato.
'Ndocca 'ndocca	Marinated braised pork offal.
Tacchino alla canzanese	This dish, a specialty of Canzano, requires 48 hours of preparation. A large turkey is slowly defatted with baths of hot water, and this, plus material from the turkey bones, is used to make a gelatin that dresses slices of the turkey, which has been cooked with garlic and bay leaves. It's finished by topping with pomegranate seeds.

FORMAGGIO (CHEESE)

Scamorza	A pear-shaped shepherd's cheese. When served **ai ferri,** it has been grilled.

DOLCI (SWEETS)

Cassata abruzzese	This Sulmona specialty is made of sponge cake and custard, flavored with chocolate, nougat, and candied roasted nuts (*croccante*).

Left: *Parrozzo;* **Right:** *Ferratelle*

Confetti	These colorful, sugar-coated almonds are central to every sort of celebration in Abruzzo and all over Italy. Whenever you attend a wedding, anniversary party, birthday, saint's day, christening, first communion, or graduation, you'll be handed a tiny package of *confetti*. Most *confetti* are still handmade and decorated in Sulmona, with a tradition dating back centuries. The specific colors of the *confetti* are highly symbolic. For instance, white is for first communions and weddings; for an anniversary, you might get silver (25th) or gold (50th); and graduates are celebrated with red. At one time, the almonds were coated in real gold to celebrate weddings and coronations, and to bring good fortune. And one more superstition: *Confetti* are always given in odd numbers (usually five, sometimes three or seven)—it's bad luck to give someone an even number.
Ferratelle	Anise cakes stamped with patterns.
Parrozzo	A specialty of Pescara, this is an almond cake rich in butter and covered with bitter chocolate. Each box comes with a copy of a poem by Gabriele D'Annunzio extolling the virtues of the *parrozzo* in *abruzzese* dialect.
Pepatelli	These white-pepper-and-honey cookies are a Christmas specialty from Teramo.
Torrone ai fichi secchi	From Chieti, a delicious nougat laced with dried figs.
Torrone al cioccolato	Chocolate-covered nougat, a specialty of L'Aquila.

Torrone al cioccolato

♀ WINES OF ABRUZZO

Abruzzo has only a few DOC wines (including Montepulciano, Cerasuolo, and Trebbiano), but they produce many others that are also worth tasting.

Montepulciano d'Abruzzo In Abruzzo, "montepulciano" refers not to the Tuscan town (the namesake of Vino Nobile di Montepulciano), but rather to a specific grape. The many varieties of montepulciano d'Abruzzo can range from gutsy, direct red wine good for basic drinking to examples of real class and sophistication. It's also a popular export wine because it represents a good value at a moderate price. The only DOCG in Abruzzo is **Montepulciano d'Abruzzo Colline Teramane,** from the hills of Teramo between the mountains and the Adriatic. Aged two years, it's robust and earthy, but still smooth.

Cerasuolo This special wine made from montepulciano grapes can appear as a delicate, sometimes-fragrant rosé.

Trebbiano d'Abruzzo A serviceable-to-good white wine made largely of the trebbiano grape, although sometimes other grapes are blended in. The best is from the province of Chieti.

Hard Drinks

Centerba A delicious *digestivo* that's supposedly made with one hundred herbs.

Genziana Slightly bitter liqueur made from the roots of the gentian flower, a popular *digestivo*.

Ratafià This liqueur, made in June from bitter cherries, must stand in the sun before being bottled.

Molise

Molise (moh-LEE-zay) is the region nobody knows. Even most Italians have never been there and might be hard-pressed to locate it on a map. All the way until 1963, it was simply folded into the larger region of Abruzzo to the north—largely forgotten even by the *abruzzesi*.

And yet, Molise is special: It preserves much of the culture of southern Italy at a time when other areas are assimilating with the materialism and affluence of the rest of the country. The *molisani* still feel, in many ways, removed from the currents of modern life. It's a land where basic foods are cultivated in a beautiful but often-unyielding soil.

Historically, Molise was along the route of *la transumanza*—annual migrations of shepherds and their flocks, up and down this part of the Italian Peninsula, seeking suitable grazing land (see sidebar). And *molisana* cuisine, too, is a legacy of *la transumanza:* Many dishes are prepared rapidly and simply, as by people on the move. The *molisani* had to eat a broader range of vegetables and greens than do most Italians; these would be gathered in fields and on the fringes of the

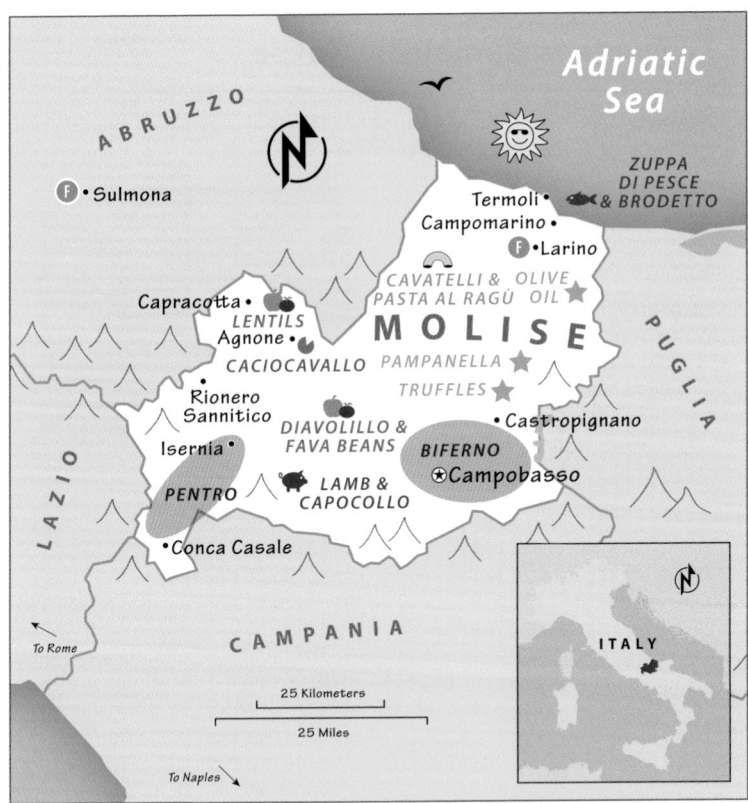

tratturi (migration paths), then boiled and topped with olive oil. Pasta is simply cooked and sauced.

Meat was a luxury in old Molise, because animals taken on la transumanza were meant to be sold. As in much of the South, a sheep was a complete resource: Its wool provided warmth; its milk and cheese provided nutrition. Pigs were a prized commodity—a family would slaughter one in early December, and every usable piece of it would become food: ham, bacon, sausage, salame, and so on. When a piece of meat was available, it would be cooked in tomatoes, oil, and herbs to create a pasta sauce called ragù. Then the meat itself was removed, cut into smaller pieces, and served with vegetables.

Another kind of transumanza was the emigration of thousands of molisani to the US (notably to Cleveland), Canada (Montreal and Toronto), Argentina (Buenos Aires and the winegrowing regions), and cities in northern Italy, Germany, Switzerland, and Belgium. A recent agricultural revival has improved conditions, but Molise remains unmistakably poor compared to most of Italy. Many people live in narrow, two-story houses that huddle together in small towns. Until not too long ago, the family lived on the upper floor and the animals were kept below.

🍲 Foods to Sample in Molise

Diavolillo
Intensely hot red pepper used to add a kick to many dishes.

Caciocavallo
Misnamed "horse cheese" (but made with cow's milk)—soft, rich, and shaped like a giant pear.

Pasta al ragù
With a simple sauce of tomato, flavored with herbs and a small amount of meat.

Agnello
Lamb is grilled, roasted, or stewed; its organ meats are also popular.

Caciocavallo

Molise also has an Albanian-speaking minority—people who migrated from across the Adriatic centuries ago and barely assimilated into the local population. More arrived when Albania opened up at the end of communism. Even today, it can be unusual to hear Italian in some Molise towns.

As in much of the rural South, the land is both a friend and a tormentor. When it's generous, it provides sustenance. But it also can be stubborn

and difficult. Water scarcity—less critical than it once was—remains a concern.

The leading agricultural products of Molise are excellent pastas and olive oil. La Molisana is considered one of Italy's best pasta brands. Colavita is the largest olive-oil producer and one of Italy's biggest exporters. Other products include corn, potatoes, tomatoes, and fava beans. And Molise has also, fairly recently, discovered a cache of black truffles; these figure very little in traditional *molisano* cooking, and are mainly being sent farther north. (For more on truffles, see page 84.)

Considering how efficiently most of Italy handles its hordes of visitors, it's striking how undeveloped Molise remains. If you go, you'll be venturing into uncharted terrain. Outsiders are received with a mixture of watchfulness and cordial hospitality. Here you can sample real flavors, real fragrances, and a genuine slice of life that is hard to find anywhere else. In Molise, the fascination of the new comes in the discovery of the old.

Campobasso

🗺 CITIES, TOWNS, AND PLACES

Campobasso (pop. 50,000) is Molise's capital and nerve center—though considering that the region has only been independent since 1963, it still lacks the pride and self-assurance of most regional capitals. For a good sense of the old town, visit the market and explore the shops on Via Marconi. **Castropignano,** just outside of the capital, is the hub for Molise's fairly recent truffle industry.

Larino (pop. 8,000), between Campobasso and the Adriatic, is Fred's favorite Molise town. It's most appealing in its historic, lower old town, filling a valley; the upper area, with most tourist services and some Roman ruins, is less interesting. In the old town in particular, everyone seems to know one another and interacts as if one large, extended family. The largest piazza is home to the ninth-century Norman *municipio,* the hub of social life; behind it, near

a small public fountain, are a few fruit-and-vegetable sellers. Scenes like this capture the southern Italy of yore—like a sepia-toned postcard of the "Old Country."

To the northwest, **Agnone** (pop. 5,000), perched on a hill surrounded by dense oak woods, is one of the most beautiful and important towns in Molise. Its claim to fame is bells: Many of the church bells you hear throughout Italy were made right here. You can visit the Pontifica Fonderia Marinelli, a bell foundry that dates back nearly 1,000 years—making it (some believe) the oldest business in Italy. The museum contains examples from that long history. The town also produces excellent copper pots and pans, and some of the best cheeses in the South.

Termoli (pop. 32,000) is Molise's relaxed and cheerful seaport. Swing by the Mercato Ittico by the port to see the morning catch.

La Transumanza

La transumanza (roughly translated as "transhumance") is a unique phenomenon that has shaped every aspect of Molise's culture, cuisine, and history. Essentially this describes a huge human migration of shepherds moving with the weather, on an annual basis, seeking suitable grazing terrain for their cattle and sheep. *La transumanza* took place each and every September, starting in the uplands of Abruzzo and Molise, and working their way south to the town of Foggia (in Puglia). There are traces of *transumanza* dating back to the fourth century BC, and it continued on a massive scale until only about a century ago.

The routes that these shepherds tracked were called *tratturi:* broad green highways of antiquity. (*Tratturi,* with its implication of plowing, is the origin of *trattore,* the word for tractor.) Along the sides of the *tratturi* developed a whole civilization: Toll stations collected money or goods to permit passage. A fee was paid to the local landowner for every head of sheep that passed through. Taverns opened to receive traveling shepherds. *Masserie* (ancient estates that provided food and rest for animals and humans) also became plantations where indentured peasants raised crops.

Religiosity became a deep part of these migrations. Pagan festivals coincided with the arrival of harvest-time or the prayer for a safe journey. With the arrival of Christianity, these events took on a different tone, but the sentiment remained. Many ancient churches in Molise have a series of hooks and rings, where animals could be tied while the humans worshiped. Religious observances were not necessarily linked to the calendar used in Rome; rather, they coincided with the times of the year when the travelers were passing through.

After World War II, in a conscious effort to eradicate this antiquated lifestyle, the Italian government enacted a policy of building over the *tratturi.* Yet in your travels through this sparsely populated region, you can still find segments of *tratturi* that remain as they were centuries ago. Look for a wide, flattened path that's unusually broad (some can be as wide as 600 feet). And even though there are no longer mass migrations, you'll still spot shepherds and their flocks who wander for hundreds of miles each year.

🍴 FOODS OF MOLISE

The *molisani* eat a simple, heart-healthy diet: pasta, grains, fruits, vegetables, olive oil, wine, and small amounts of meat (primarily lamb) and animal fat.

ANTIPASTI (APPETIZERS)

Capocollo	Sausage made from the head and tail of a pig.
Signora di Conca Casale	From the village of Conca Casale in Isernia province, this is a special type of *salume* prepared using high-quality cuts of pork and spices (especially fennel), which was used to show appreciation for professionals (such as physicians) who came to the aid of locals.
Pampanella	More a street-food snack than an *antipasto,* this is a chunk of pork rubbed with both hot and sweet red pepper and then roasted. They're bright-red, spicy, and delicious.
Prosciutto crudo affumicato	Smoked ham, from Rionero Sannitico.
Salsiccia al finocchio	Fennel sausage.
Soppressata (salame)	The spicy *salame* popular in the South is also found in Molise.

PRIMI (PASTAS AND OTHER FIRST COURSES)

The standard pasta option is *cavatelli, lasagne,* or *maccheroni* served with *ragù* of lamb or goat. Fusilli—short pasta twists—originally came from Molise.

Brodosini	Tagliatelle in broth with *guanciale.*

Left: *Capocollo;* **Right:** *Pampanella*

Left: *Cavatelli;* **Right:** Hot pepper

Calcioni di ricotta	Fried pasta stuffed with *ricotta,* provolone, prosciutto, and parsley, sometimes served with a *frittura mista* of artichokes, cauliflower, brains, sweetbreads, potato croquettes, and *scamorza* cheese. This is a specialty of Campobasso.
Cavatelli	Gnocchi-like pasta (sometimes made with potatoes) served in a tomato-and-meat sauce.
Diavolillo	This small, intensely hot *peperoncino rosso* (red pepper) is a staple of Molise (and much of the South). It's often minced and mixed into olive oil, or it might be dried and ground to use as a powder. In its oil infusion, *il diavolillo* is tossed with spaghetti as a popular dish. Or it can be added to other sauces, to boiled eggs and omelets, or to vegetables, fish, or meat.
Pasta e fagioli	Pasta-and-bean soup cooked with pig's feet and pork rinds.
Polenta di Capracotta (or *p'lenta d'iragn*)	"White polenta," actually made of wheat and potatoes, sauced with raw tomatoes and *pecorino romano.*
Ragù	Quite different from the meat-heavy *ragù* common in Emilia-Romagna and Tuscany, a Molise *ragù* begins with an inexpensive cut of meat that's cooked in tomatoes, oil, and herbs to create a pasta sauce. The meat itself is removed and eaten separately.
Zuppa di cardi	Soup of cardoons (similar to artichokes), tomatoes, onions, *pancetta,* and olive oil.
Zuppa di ortiche	Soup of nettle stems, tomatoes, onions, *pancetta,* and olive oil.

SECONDI (MAIN DISHES)

Agnello	Lamb might be served **alla griglia** (grilled), **arrosto** (roasted), or **in umido** (stewed). **Ragù d'agnello** is braised lamb with sweet peppers, a specialty of Isernia. Many organ meats of lamb, especially tripe, are popular; **torcinelli** are rolled strips of lamb tripe, sweetbreads, and liver, while **mazzarelle** are tightly wrapped rolls made with lung and tripe of lamb.
Brodetto	Molise's local fish-and-seafood soup comes from Termoli.
Carciofi ripieni	Artichokes stuffed with anchovies and capers.
Cipollaci con pecorino	Fried strong onions with *pecorino romano* cheese.
Coniglio alla molisana	Rabbit pieces skewered with sausage and herbs, then grilled.
Frittata con basilico e cipolle	Omelet with basil and onions.
Zuppa di pesce	Fish stew; a specialty of Termoli.

CONTORNI (SIDE DISHES)

Fave	The *molisani* eat fresh fava beans and also dry them, so they become nutlike and can provide nourishment through the winter. Similar beans, called **cicerchie,** are soaked overnight, boiled, and seasoned, and are popular as a snack.
Lenticchie	The lentils from Capracotta are considered among the best in Italy, rivaling those of Castelluccio in Umbria.
Tortalalli	This unusual *molisano* fruit is technically a melon but looks more like a giant cucumber; it's often eaten in salads or with other raw produce, such as tomatoes.

FORMAGGI (CHEESES)

Burrino	Soft, delicious, buttery cow's-milk cheese.
Caciocavallo	This cheese, which is typically cow's milk in Molise, is shaped like a giant pear; it's soft and rich, and has a thin, edible rind. The strange name ("horse cheese") refers not to the source of the milk, but because two of these cheeses are tied at the top with a string and hung to dry, like saddle bags. As it ages, it acquires spicy notes. While this cheese is found in various parts of the South—including Abruzzo and Puglia—the one from Agnone is particularly revered.

Left: *Caciocavallo;* Right: *Crostata di ricotta*

Manteca	Similar to *burrino.*
Scamorza	Bland cow's-milk cheese, often served grilled.

DOLCI (SWEETS)

Caucuoni	This Christmas treat is *ravioli* filled with chestnuts, almonds, chocolate, vanilla, cooked wine musts, and cinnamon, and then fried.
Ciambelline	Ring-shaped cakes made in the country. They may be *all'olio* (with olive oil) or *al vino rosso* (with red wine).
Crostata di ricotta (or **ricotta a mo' di pizza**)	A cake pan filled with a blend of *ricotta* cheese, sugar, flour, butter, maraschino liqueur, and chocolate chips.
Ferratelle	Anise cakes made in metal molds and stamped with special patterns. These are similar to *pizzelle,* which are popular in many Italian-American communities.
Ostie ripiene di Agnone	A wafer-like sandwich with walnuts, almonds, and honey, and flavored with cinnamon and orange.
Uccelletti	These "little birds," a specialty of Larino, get their name from their birdlike shape. They're soft cookies filled either with cooked cherries or *mosto cotto,* grape skins used in winemaking that are cooked until reduced to an intense, winey jam.

🍷 WINES OF MOLISE

Oil production and winemaking, which often go hand in hand, date back to ancient times in Molise. Archaeological digs have revealed Greek and Roman amphorae and jars as well as coins that show oil and wine activity. More than in most of Italy, wine in Molise tastes as it did years ago; modern techniques have yet to catch on in a big way (with a few exceptions—Di Majo Norante makes a good line of wines). That means that it likely wouldn't fare well on the international market, but it does have an honest native character that makes it distinct from the more polished product from the big wine regions. It's also perfectly suited to the flavors of the local cuisine.

Three-quarters of Molise wine is produced in the province of Campobasso; the rest is from the province of Isernia. The region has only three DOC wines: **Biferno,** which comes in red, white, and rosé (from Campobasso); **Pentro** (white, also red and rosé, from Isernia); and **Tintilia del Molise** (made throughout Molise, with the local grape tintilia, ruby-red and full-bodied).

Non-DOC varieties planted in Molise include the reds aglianico, barbera, bovale grande, cabernet franc, ciliegiolo, montepulciano, pinot nero, and sangiovese; and the whites bombino bianco, garganega, malvasia del Chianti, moscato, pinot bianco, pinot grigio, Riesling Italico, Riesling Renano, sauvignon blanc, Traminer aromatico, trebbiano, and Veltliner.

Puglia

Puglia (pronounced POOL-yah, sometimes called Apulia in English)—the region that occupies the heel and spur of the Italian boot—is awash in sunshine that produces abundant wheat, powerful wines, and radiant fruits and vegetables with intense flavor. And the *pugliese* people are also sunny and friendly, particularly in the smaller cities and towns.

While the preceding several chapters describe hilly and mountainous areas, Puglia is Italy's flattest region: More than half is plains, and the rest is lowlands and low plateaus, with just a small fringe of mountains. This lends a consistency to both the culture and the cuisine throughout the region: Communication and transport have never been difficult,

easing distribution of ideas and ingredients to all corners.

Even so, there is one major division in Puglia: Its northernmost province, Foggia, is starkly different from the other four (Bari, Brindisi, Taranto, and Lecce). There are many reasons for this. One is historical: The market town of Foggia was, for centuries (if not millennia), the destination of

🍲 Foods to Sample in Puglia

Capocollo
Tender, spicy *salame* made with wine and peppercorns.

Burrata
Milky cheese with a round, shiny, firm exterior and a luxuriously rich cream inside.

'Ncapriata
Delicious fava-bean puree, served with cooked chicory.

Panzerotti
Deep-fried mini-calzone filled with vegetables, cheese, or meats.

Panzerotti

Orecchiette
Puglia's ubiquitous ear-shaped pasta, often served with *cime di rapa* (broccoli rabe).

thousands of people—and even more sheep—during the annual *transumanza* migrations (see page 288).

Foggia is also the mainland Italian city with the hottest weather. It sits at the heart of a formidable wheat-growing zone (called the Tavoliere, Italy's largest plain south of the Po River) that has kept Puglia well fed even as other southern regions went hungry. Rivers flow down from the Apennines in Molise and Campania, keeping the wheat fields well irrigated. And this flat expanse (especially near the town of San Severo) was a landing zone for Allied planes that did battle in Campania, Lazio, and elsewhere farther west during World War II.

Foggia is essentially a meat-and-cheese town, while the rest of the region relies more on fish and seafood. This dates back 2,500 years to when a community of shepherds was driven out of Arcadia in Greece and eventually sailed to Foggia.

The hardship of the crossing turned them off from fishing forever, and instead they developed a distinctive meat-eating tradition. To this day, certain dishes—including *gnemeridde* and *quagghiaride*—are strikingly similar to dishes served in Arcadia. (In contrast, the native peoples of Puglia, called the Apuli, adeptly exploited the sea for food.)

Foggia is also different because it uses abundant garlic in its kitchen; farther south, this is gradually replaced by onion. There are two types of onion in Puglia's cuisine: the familiar sweet ones, and smaller, bitter *lampasciuni* (which are technically hyacinth bulbs).

In the southern provinces, the soil is rich in limestone, which gives particular flavor to fruits, vegetables, and legumes. And the abundant sunshine serves a special function in the local cuisine: Everywhere you look during the hot months, people set out wooden boards loaded up

with fruits and vegetables to dry in the sun. Many are stored dry, while others are packed in oil *(sott'olio)* or vinegar *(sott'aceto).*

The *sagre*—festivals celebrating the arrival of a new seasonal food—are celebrated with a special verve here in Puglia. When tomatoes are in season, families gather to chop them and make sauce, which they preserve in jars with a few leaves of basil. Sometimes they also spread tomato sauce on wooden boards in the sun, creating tomato concentrate for later

use. The boards are also used to roll out *orecchiette* or one of the other shapes of pasta that Puglia is famous for.

Olives and almonds (both likely introduced by those ancient Greeks) are central to *pugliese* agriculture and cuisine. Puglia is responsible for 40 percent of Italian olive-oil production, with oil that ranges from dense and rich in flavor to quite delicate. In the 19th century, much of the olive oil produced in Puglia was shipped to England and elsewhere in northern

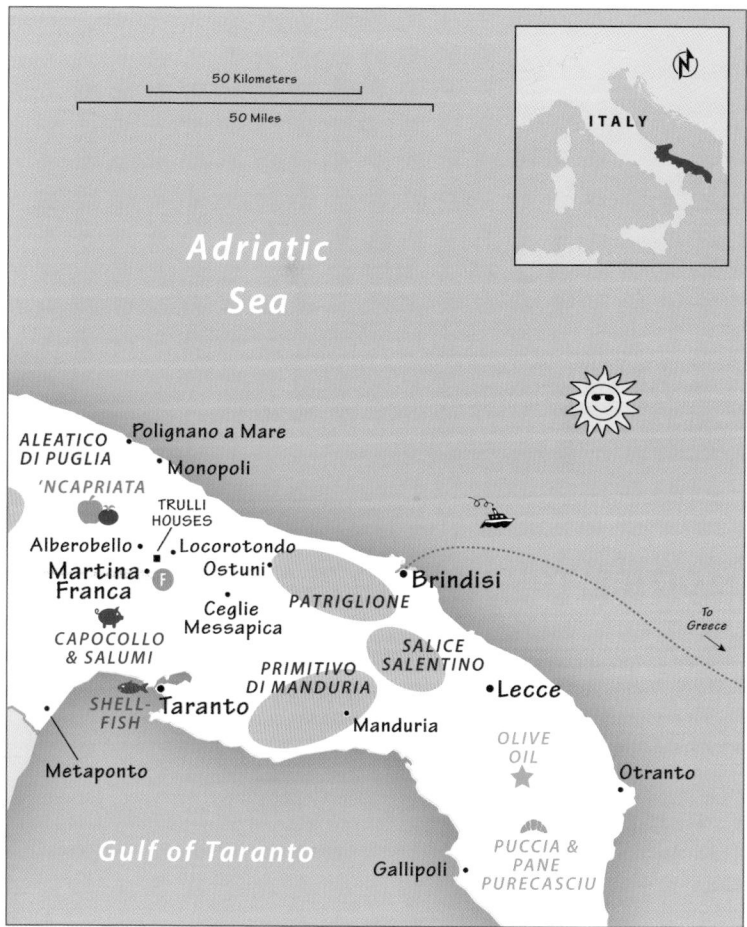

Europe to power oil lamps and to grease the machines of the Industrial Revolution.

The long Puglia coastline yields a remarkable bounty of fish and seafood—the region's primary sources of protein. Taranto has excellent oysters, mussels, and clams (although pollution has taken a toll).

Of Italy's southernmost regions, Puglia has had the most success in pulling itself out of poverty. And in recent years, it has become newly trendy as a tourist destination. Most visitors find their way to the *trulli,* the old, conical structures in and around Alberobello, and to coastal resorts along the coastline. Lovers of Baroque make a pilgrimage to Lecce. And many travelers begin or end their trips in Brindisi, with overnight ferry connections to Greece. Even aside from these tangible draws, Puglia—with its friendly people, delicious food, and abundant history—is well worth visiting for its own merits.

Peshcici, Foggia province

🗺️ CITIES, TOWNS, AND PLACES

As already described, **Foggia** (pop. 151,000)—with its hot temperatures, abundant wheat fields, meat-loving ancestors, and *transumanza* legacy—is something apart from the rest of Puglia.

The **Gargano Peninsula** is a rugged little knob that forms the spur on Italy's boot, on the Adriatic northeast of Foggia. It's quite hilly—in contrast to the flatness of most of Puglia—with fine beaches, picture-perfect coves, hidden grottos, and unusual rock formations. The beach town of **Vieste** (pop. 14,000), perched on sea cliffs at the peninsula's apex, is a handy home base.

Martina Franca (pop. 49,000) is Fred's favorite Puglia town—and in many ways, it embodies much of what's fun, joyous, beautiful, and timeless about all of Italy. It's handy to the famous *trulli* described next, but just far enough away not to feel like a tourist trap. Martina Franca is a

delightful place simply to explore—from its centerpiece, the triangular Piazza Roma, fronted by the Palazzo Ducale with its dramatic Baroque facade; to Piazza Plebiscito, with a richly Baroque church that serves as the spiritual center of the city; to the pleasant, unexplored backstreets of its lovely *centro storico*. The town is also known for its excellent meats, especially all manner of *salumi*.

Martina Franca is also a natural home base for side-tripping to **Alberobello** (pop. 11,000), which is the best place to see *trulli*—those iconic, traditional dry-stone houses with conical roofs. You can round out the day with a visit to **Locorotondo,** with views on both towns.

Lecce (pop. 95,000) is a deservedly popular tourist town and simply a beautiful place. Most of its great buildings were built between 1660 and 1720 in High Baroque style using a golden stone called *pietra di Lecce*.

The city is nicknamed "the Florence of the South" because of its architectural harmony.

Two big, industrial port cities are seen by travelers mainly as transit points: Bari and Brindisi. **Bari,** Puglia's capital and biggest city (pop. 320,000, with 750,000 in the urban area), is a busy place with broad boulevards, brazen pickpockets, and a labyrinthine old quarter called Città Vecchia. **Brindisi** (pop. 87,000) is known mainly as the place from where backpackers can catch the overnight ferry to Greece. And **Taranto** (pop. 200,000), on the gulf of Italy's "instep," is mainly a grimy, industrial town; it has some of the largest oil refineries and steel mills in the country, and is one of the chief ports of the Italian navy, but it also provides many of the region's better oysters, mussels, and clams.

Other notable towns near Bari: **Bitonto** produces excellent almonds, candies, and pastries, while **Corato** has some of the best *burrata* cheese.

Top: Vieste, on the Gargano Peninsula;
Bottom: Martina Franca

🍴 EATING IN PUGLIA

Pugliese cuisine has abundant wheat (pastas and breads), excellent fruits and vegetables (which are often used with pasta), a wide variety of fish and seafood, a strong tradition of *salumi* (especially in Martina Franca), elaborate casseroles, and luscious cheeses.

ANTIPASTI (APPETIZERS)

Puglia has an amazing variety of *antipasti*—it ranks alongside Piedmont and Emilia-Romagna in its mastery of this course. There are all sorts of baked, grilled, fried, or stuffed vegetables and seafood, as well as delicious *salumi* from Martina Franca.

Benedetto	This Easter *antipasto* in Foggia contains hard-boiled eggs (which are blessed by a priest), *ricotta, salame,* boiled asparagus, and sometimes oranges.

Capocollo	A tender, spicy *salame* from Martina Franca made with wine and peppercorns. Its name (meaning "head-neck") suggests the part of the pig that's used—specifically, a muscle that runs down the animal's neck.
Cervellata	A slender sausage made either with veal and pork or just pork, and seasoned with red wine and pepper.
Frisella	A small, hard, round roll with a hole in the middle (like a bagel). These can be strung together to dry and have a long shelf life. When it's time to eat, the roll is soaked in water, then dressed with olive oil, salt, and fresh tomatoes.
Panzerotti	These fried turnovers—sort of a deep-fried mini-calzone—are filled with vegetables, cheese, or meats. The name (from *panza*, belly) suggests its bulging shape.
Tarantello	Salted, preserved tuna.

PRIMI (PASTAS AND OTHER FIRST COURSES)

There are many styles and shapes of pasta that are peculiar to Puglia. In addition to the ones listed below, look for *lagane* and *laganelle* (wide noodles from sheets of pasta), *strascinati* and *pociacche* (both variations on *orecchiette*), *cavatelli* (a.k.a, *cavateddi*, also popular in much of the South), lesser-known types like *mignuicchie* and *fenesecche,* and many others. Some local noodles are made without eggs—during times of hardship, they were considered too valuable for this use.

Vegetables are the most popular ingredients for pasta sauces. These include *cime di rapa* or *broccoletti* (bitter greens along the lines of broccoli rabe or rapini), cauliflower, eggplant, arugula, chickpeas, chicory, and fava beans.

Left: *Capocollo* from Martina Franca;
Right: *Panzerotti*

Left: *Troccoli* pasta from Foggia; **Right:** *Orecchiette* with *cime di rapa*

Ciambotto	This vegetable-and-fish stew, often used to sauce pasta, is a specialty of Bari.
Ciceri e tria	Strips of fried pasta, served with chickpeas; this Lecce specialty dates back to ancient times.
'Ncapriata (or **fave e cicoria**)	This addictive dish is a combination of cooked chicory and pureed fava beans, all flavored with olive oil. The *pugliesi* say that Hercules drew strength for his labors from fava-bean puree, but it's just as likely that he ate it because it was so delicious. In the variation called **'ncapriata alla martinese,** the fava-bean puree is served with boiled *lampasciuni* (bitter onions) instead of chicory.
Orecchiette (or **recchietelle**)	This little ear-shaped pasta is Puglia's dominant type outside of Foggia. *Orecchiette* ("little ears") are made of 80 percent semolina and 20 percent winter wheat, often from Canada. Large pasta factories make them by machine, but many people in Puglia make them by hand on a wooden board. (You'll likely see people making these out on the street while enjoying the sunshine.) *Orecchiette* are slightly concave so that they can contain cheese or sauce. A common preparation for *orecchiette* is with **cime di rapa** (bitter greens).
Rosmarina	Pasta shaped like a large grain of rice.
Sagne 'ncannulate	A long pasta with sauce and very strong *ricotta* (a specialty of Lecce).
Troccoli	Foggia eats this distinctive pasta, which resembles the *maccheroni alla chitarra* of Abruzzo (see page 280). They probably arrived by way of the annual *transumanza* migrations from that area.

Left: *Ricci di mare;* **Right:** *Taralli*

SECONDI (MAIN DISHES)

Cozze arraganate	Mussels cooked with breadcrumbs, garlic, oil, parsley, and tomato; a specialty of Taranto.
Gnemeridde	Lamb innards cut into strips or balls and cooked with *pecorino romano* and various spices.
Quagghiaride	An ancient shepherd dish found mostly in Foggia, made with sheep's stomach filled with chicken giblets, *scamorza* cheese, eggs, and *salame*. It's baked and then served with boiled arugula or raw celery.
Polipetti alla barese	In Bari, when baby octopi are caught, they are immediately beaten against rocks and then shaken in a basket to make their tentacles curl. Then they're boiled and served with oil and lemon or cooked in a spicy tomato sauce. When the dish is called **casseruola di polipetti,** it has a special sauce of olive oil, onions, white wine, pepper, parsley, and fresh tomatoes.
Ricci di mare	Sea urchins appear in April.
Spiedo martinese	Skewers with lamb, goat, veal, and sausage cooked over a fire of oak logs; a specialty of Martina Franca.
Tiella (or **tiedd**)	This is usually a casserole (the name means "baking dish"), and it comes in many variations. It can be layered with some combination of meat or fish, vegetables, potatoes, and/or sometimes cheese. Try some local versions; in Bari, for example, a *tiella* is made with rice, potatoes, and mussels.
Triglie di scoglio	Rock mullet, a fish much prized in Polignano. When grilled, its skin dissolves into a red liquid, creating an unusual natural sauce.
Turcinieddhri	Rolls of lamb's liver, heart, and lung.

CONTORNI (SIDE DISHES)

In addition to all the usual vegetables found in the southern Italian kitchen, Puglia specializes in *fenecchiedde* (boiled baby fennel cooked with oil, garlic, and anchovy fillets), *lampasciuni* (tiny, bitter hyacinth bulbs), *marasciuoli* (or *marsciùle*, bitter greens), *paparuli* (peppery mushrooms), and *senape selvatica* (or *sanàpi*, mustard greens).

PANE (BREAD)

The hearty loaves of Puglia, especially of the town of Altamura, use mainly durum wheat and are justifiably famous. *Grano arso*—literally, burned wheat—is one of those hardship foods that has become trendy. Originally it was gathered after the wheat fields were razed to end the season; today it's used to make earthy-flavored breads and pastas. In a *pugliese* home, the bread is treated with respect and occupies a central place in the kitchen. One superstition—common throughout the South—dictates that a loaf must always be right-side up; turning it upside-down is unlucky and disrespectful.

Focaccia barese	Bari has a tradition of focaccia bread (more associated with Liguria), typically topped with cherry tomatoes, olives, and oregano.
Pane purecasciu	A bread from Lecce made with oil, onions, and tomatoes.
Puccia	A bread from Lecce made with pitted black olives.
Puddica	A focaccia-type bread served with tomatoes, garlic, oil, and oregano.
Taralli	Little round breads with a hole in the middle. They can be as tiny as crackers or the size of a small loaf. They're frequently flavored with pepper or wild fennel, or for dessert, with cinnamon.

FORMAGGI (CHEESES)

This region makes excellent cheeses, including *ricotta, scamorza,* provolone, *pecorino romano,* and *caciocavallo* (the misnamed "horse cheese" described on page 395); mozzarella from water-buffalo milk can sometimes be found in the north, especially Andria.

Burrata	This must-try, soft, sweet, milky cheese is round, with a shiny exterior. It's essentially a casing of mozzarella filled with a rich, gooey cream called *stracciatella*. Handle it with care—once you cut into it, the *stracciatella* comes running out. For the best results, dip the skin into the *stracciatella* and pop it into your mouth. Supposedly the shah of Iran would send jets to Puglia just to bring *burrate* back to Tehran; the best are said to come from Castel del Monte.
Cacioricotta	This aged *ricotta* is used for grating.
Canestrato	Cave-aged sheep's-milk cheese used for grating.

Left: *Pettole;* **Right:** *Cartellate*

DOLCI (SWEETS)

Although Puglia produces good fruit, especially grapes, the people of this region tend not to eat them for dessert. Instead, they opt for a plate of raw vegetables, including radishes, fennel, carrots, and celery. The one fruit that is a popular dessert is the **barattiere**—a very sweet watermelon native to the region.

Cartellate (called *carteddate* in Bari)	A Christmas sweet made of strips of dough soaked in white wine and olive oil and then topped with honey and cinnamon.
Cotognata	A specialty of Lecce, this sweet is made by cooking quinces down to their pulp to form a concentrate that is placed into molds to cool into a jelly.
Pasticciotti	Custard-and-cherry tartlets from Lecce.
Pettole	These fried dough balls, also available in savory versions, are a sweet Christmas treat.
U grane cuotte	On All Saints' Day, a sweet is made with flour, chopped almonds and walnuts, chocolate, citron, cinnamon, pomegranate seeds, and small sugar-coated almonds, all cooked in wine; in Bari, this is called **colva.**

🍷 WINES OF PUGLIA

Puglia is one of Italy's biggest wine-producing regions, rivaling Veneto. The ancient Greeks recognized how Puglia's fertile soil, hilly topography, and hot climate (moderated by cool sea breezes) provided excellent grape-growing conditions. Historically, much of the local wine—rich in grape flavor, high in alcohol content, and low in acidity—was sent north to Torino to make vermouth or to France, where it was blended to give structure to French wines in years with thin output. But more recently, *pugliese* vintners (and some savvy transplants from the North) are prioritizing wines suitable for drinking with food. These contemporary wines more effectively balance sweetness, acidity, alcohol content, and density.

About four-fifths of Puglia's production is red; the rest is white, with a bit of rosé. Red wines are known for their deep color, high alcohol content, and intense flavor. Commonly used red grapes include primitivo (similar to zinfandel—originally from Croatia, and later brought by Italian immigrants to California), negroamaro, nero di Troia, and malvasia nera. White wines, which are generally not memorable, use grapes including verdeca, bombino bianco, and Greco bianco. Negroamaro is the grape commonly used for rosé.

Most of Puglia's 29 DOC wines are named for the town where they're grown—including Castel del Monte and Gioia del Colle (these two are among the nicest), Brindisi, Locorotondo, Martina Franca (a rather charming white wine from *trulli* country), Ostuni, and San Severo.

Salice Salentino is an excellent value for a quality red wine on a budget. It comes from the heel of Italy's boot—the Salentine Peninsula, in the province of Lecce—and it's made primarily with the negroamaro grape. **Patriglione,** from Brindisi, is one of the best reds in southern Italy. And **Primitivo di Manduria** is well known internationally.

The most famous dessert wine is **Aleatico di Puglia,** most of which is made in the province of Bari; *dolce naturale* indicates moderate sweetness, while *liquoroso* is made of grapes that have been dried to concentrate the sugars.

Basilicata

Basilicata occupies the "instep" of Italy's boot, at the farthest reaches of the Italian Peninsula. Many Italians (essentially from Rome northward) feel more kinship with Milan, Paris, or Vienna than they do to this distant outpost. In literature, and simply in the cultural conversation, Basilicata is thought of as a faraway and backward netherworld—disconnected from the currents of modern life that most Italians enjoy.

This is both fair and an oversimplification. It's true that Basilicata is remote and—unlike flat Puglia—rugged, with a landscape of mostly hills and mountains that have always cut it off from the Italian mainstream. The land is parched and unyielding, and the people are quite poor.

But even in this distant outpost of Italy, the history is unusually rich. The original name of the region is "Lucania," which might be a reference to the Latin *lucus* (woods) or the Greek *lukus* or *lykos* (wolf). The original inhabitants were called *Lyki*, who came from Anatolia (today's Turkey)

to settle here around 1300 BC; they lived inland and developed a civilized democratic society. About five centuries later, the Greeks arrived and set up colonies. They were succeeded by the Romans, and after the fall of Rome, the region fell into the hands of the Byzantine Empire.

The name "Basilicata" was thought to come from *basileus,* the title of the Byzantine functionary who was posted here. Or it may refer specifically to the basilica in the town of Acerenza. Either way, Mussolini—so

obsessed with the glorious ancient origins of the land he conquered—ordered that the region go by its original, historic name of Lucania. Even after they reverted back to "Basilicata" in 1947, people from here are still called *lucani*.

Needless to say, the cuisine of Basilicata is *cucina povera.* But "poor" does not equal bad. The cooks of the region took what meager ingredients they had and created delicious dishes. The region produces a great deal of grain, especially wheat, which

🍴 Foods and Drinks to Sample in Basilicata

Lucanica
Spiced sausage named after the region's ancient iteration, Lucania.

Lagane
Broad, flat noodles, typically tossed with tomato sauce or with chickpeas.

Cutturiedd'
Slow-cooked lamb.

Aglianico del Vulture
Excellent red wine—which rivals any in Italy—from an ancient Greek grape.

Lucanica

is used to bake excellent bread and create a variety of interesting pasta shapes. (Basilicata eats more pasta per capita than anywhere in Italy—an indication, perhaps, of the slim pickings when it comes to ingredients.) And the *lucani* produce an exceptionally fine wine: aglianico, one of the great red wines made south of Tuscany.

Historically, meat was eaten only on Christmas and Easter, at weddings, and on a town's patron-saint day. Typically the meat was chicken or rabbit; sheep were only eaten when they died of old age, and they were cooked very slowly in a container called a *cutturiedd'* to try to eliminate some of the toughness. Every family had one pig each year. If they were too poor to own it outright, they would raise it for a wealthier family and then, after slaughter, keep half of it (usually the less desirable cuts). Since ancient times, locals have been skilled at making their meat last as long as possible in different

The basilica of Acerenza

forms—in other words, they were masters of *salumi*.

Not surprisingly when you consider the hardship of simply existing here, Basilicata has had the highest per-capita level of emigration of any Italian region. From the 19th well into the 20th century, mass migration left some towns practically empty; an astonishing 270,000 *lucani* left between 1945 and 1955 alone. Today the region has about 575,000 people (rivaling Valle d'Aosta as the least densely populated region, despite its relatively large size)—with Potenza and Matera being the only towns with more than 50,000 residents.

This gives Basilicata an empty feeling. You can travel long distances without seeing another person. While this isolation might sound off-putting, the empty spaces can be starkly beautiful and come as quite a change in a nation with high population density. Visiting Basilicata—especially outside of Matera, which has become somewhat touristy—you feel like a pioneer exploring a new land. For the right kind of traveler, Basilicata is a unique destination that warrants the long journey.

🗺️ CITIES, TOWNS, AND PLACES

In **Matera** (pop. 60,000)—Fred's favorite Basilicata town—travelers are struck by a unique landscape. The center of the city is a giant bowl surrounded by a newer city. That bowl is made of soft rock in which caves called *sassi* were hollowed out 9,000 years ago and used for habitation. These were cleared out during the Fascist and postwar era, partly to combat the diseases that spread in such close quarters. But in recent years, people have begun to return to the *sassi*. With electrification and indoor plumbing, some of these *sassi* are now desirable places to live. There are also 120 *chiese rupestri,* cave churches carved into the stone. The *sassi* and churches are connected by narrow paths and form a labyrinth. It's a place where it's extremely easy to get lost (and can be quite disorienting after dark). Matera also has an excellent *passeggiata,* bakes breads that are famously excellent, and is the only place in all of Basilicata that has any sort of touristic metabolism.

While Matera is the spiritual and cultural heart of Basilicata, its official capital is **Potenza** (pop. 67,000), deep inland. In fact, the occupying French only made it the capital in 1806 because it was closer to Naples. Much of the town was destroyed in a 1980 earthquake, and its high altitude (2,700 feet) can lead to harsh winters despite its southern latitude. The city has evocative Good Friday observances, and its Via Pretoria is one of the oldest thoroughfares in Italy.

Left: Matera; **Right:** Traditional Basilicata home

🍴 FOODS OF BASILICATA

Basilicata cuisine is classic *cucina povera* ("food of the poor"): limited meat, lovingly preserved and prepared to coax out maximum nutrition. Pastas are a major staple, and cooking techniques make the most of humble cuts of meat. Like other cuisines of the South, the *lucani* aren't afraid of spice; *diavolicchio* and other hot peppers are widely used. As an alternative, watch for sweet Senise peppers, which are lashed into necklace-like wreaths and hung out to dry to create a flavoring called **peperone crusco** (in dialect, it means "crunchy peppers"—describing the dry texture). Horseradish *(rafano),* sometimes called "poor-man's truffle," also appears.

ANTIPASTI (APPETIZERS)

Once upon a time, cured meats were the principal source of animal protein and were eaten in small amounts to make them last as long as possible. Today they are *antipasti* staples.

Lucanica (a.k.a. **luganiga, luganica,** or **luganega**)	The most famous food product of Basilicata, this spiced sausage is renowned throughout Italy. Named for the region's ancient name, Lucania, it has long since been copied in many other areas (including Lombardy and Trentino)—but is nowhere near as delicious as in its homeland. This is a *salame* with history: The ancient Roman writer Varro described it being consumed by Roman soldiers stationed in Lucania, and it's quite possible that Longobards who occupied this region in the mid-ninth century brought the recipe back north.
Pezzente	Literally "beggars," this *salame* is made of the less desirable parts of the pig that are otherwise unused—in other words, the bits and pieces that would be given to panhandlers. They are finely minced and mixed with *peperone crusco,* making a tasty *salame.*
Soppressata	This spicy dry *salame,* common throughout the South, is also found here (and, some say, originated in Basilicata).
Sugna piccante	Lard flavored with *peperoncino rosso,* stored in jars and used to cook or to spread on bread.

Left: *Salame;* **Right:** *Grano e ceci*

Left: *Pasta mollicata;* **Right:** *Orecchiette*

PRIMI (PASTAS AND OTHER FIRST COURSES)

Basilicata produces ample grain and has many types of pastas—some of them, as in Puglia, made without eggs. In addition to the ones listed below, look for snail-shaped *cavatelli* (also known as *rascatelli*), *bucatini* (a long, hollow noodle), supersized *orecchiete* variations such as *tapparelle* and *strascinati,* and *fusilli* (also known as *ferretti* or *frizzuli* here).

Grano e ceci	A soup made with chickpeas, barley, and wheat with a touch of oil, tomato, and rosemary.
Lagane (or **lacane**)	Broad, flat noodles resembling extra-wide (but short) tagliatelle. The word's root is related to *lasagne,* but here they're usually tossed with tomato sauce or with lentils and beans rather than being baked. **Lagane con lenticchie e fagioli** is always eaten on March 19, Saint Joseph's Day, and is offered to the poor.
Maccheroni di fuoco	This fiery dish is made with *bucatini* tossed with red-hot *diavolicchio.*
Minestra strascinata	A specialty of Potenza, this square pasta is tossed with tomato sauce and aged *pecorino romano.*
Minuich	Short spaghetti with a hole running through them that are served either with tomato and *cima di cola* (boiled green cauliflower) or with oil and *peperoncino.*
Orecchiette	Matera has these ear-shaped pastas (also typical of Puglia—see page 301), but the ones here are larger and sometimes called **scorze di mandorla** (almond skins).
Pasta mollicata (or **ammuddicata**)	With a simple sauce of tomato, onion, red wine, crumbs *(molliche)* from yesterday's bread, and sometimes a bit of anchovy.

Left: *Funghi cardoncelli;* **Right:** *Calzone*

Rafanata	A sort of frittata or quiche-like egg dish with potato, *pecorino romano,* and occasionally sausage, and flavored with horseradish *(rafano);* this is especially popular at Carnival time.
Zuppa di legumi	A soup of various beans, peas, and chickpeas.

CONTORNI (SIDE DISHES)

In Basilicata, it was once common to serve vegetables after the *primo* instead of with or after the *secondo.* This is largely because—until recently—there often *was* no *secondo,* as meat dishes were reserved for special occasions. These days the *contorni* follow the more typical Italian order. Look for **lampasciuoli** (onion-like, bitter hyacinth bulbs); unusual bright-red eggplants (which resemble tomatoes, or red persimmons) called **melanzane rosse;** and many local mushrooms, particularly **funghi cardoncelli.**

Calzone	Dough folded around cooked vegetables, then baked.
Ciammotta	A stew of seasonal local vegetables, flavored with sweet and smoky *peperone crusco.*
Ciaudedda	Fava beans, onions, artichokes, potatoes, and sometimes a bit of *pancetta* cooked in olive oil.
Mandorlata di peperoni	A stew of peppers, almonds, and *peperoncino.*

SECONDI (MAIN DISHES)

As in much of the rural South, the standard diet is pasta and vegetables. As affluence has begun to reach even this poor region, lamb and goat now are eaten periodically. Fish and seafood are available primarily near the coast.

Agnello con funghi cardoncelli	Lamb and mushrooms sautéed or stewed; a specialty of Matera.
Beccacce in salmì	Jugged snipe (woodcock) with prosciutto, capers, and dry Marsala wine; a specialty of Potenza.
Ciammaruchedde	Pan-cooked snails with mint, garlic, *peperoncino,* and tomatoes.
Cutturiedd'	Slow-cooked lamb flavored with numerous herbs, onions, and potatoes; this might also be called **spezzatino di agnello.**
Pasticcio (or *u pastizz*)	A half-moon-shape calzone filled with meat (pork, kid, or lamb).
Pigneti	A stew made with chunks of kid, lamb, or mutton with sliced *salame,* tomatoes, onions, potatoes, celery, carrots, aged *pecorino romano* cheese, *peperoncino,* and wine, cooked over a tiny flame all night.
Scapice	Fresh anchovies fried and flavored with mint.
Zuppa di pesce	A stew of mixed fish, spiked with spicy *diavolicchio.*

FORMAGGI (CHEESES)

Burrata, burrino, and mozzarella are delicious soft cow's-milk cheeses, and you'll also find *pecorino* (ewe's cheese), both soft and aged. And Basilicata has its own version of *caciocavallo* (see page 395), flavored by the sparse herbs the cows graze on. **Canestrato di Moliterno** is a cheese of both sheep's and goat's milk, which can be eaten fresh or aged and grated.

Left: *Pasticcio*; **Right:** *Canestrato di Moliterno*

DOLCI (SWEETS)

In addition to local sweets, people in Basilicata eat a lot of fruit; its oranges and lemons are flavorful.

Calzoncelli	Pastries filled with quince jam.
Focaccia al miele	A dessert dough drenched in honey.
Linguette	Flour, sugar, wine, and yeast.
Mandorle atter-rate (or *mennu'l atturat'*)	Toasted almonds.
Paparotta	A sweet made with wine must during harvest time.
Rococò	Filled with a mixture of flour, almonds, and sugar.
Stozze	Filled with a mixture of flour, eggs, almonds, and sugar.
Strazzate	Chocolate-almond cookies.
Torta di latticini alla lucana	"Cake of cheeses" is the literal translation of this unusual pastry, which is often served as a sweet but is more of a savory. A sweet crust is filled with *ricotta,* grated *pecorino romano,* mozzarella, egg, prosciutto, salt, and pepper.

A variety of sweet pastries

♀ WINES OF BASILICATA

Basilicata wines aren't very well known, but there is one excellent exception: **aglianico.** The grape's name is a corruption of the word "Hellenic." Aglianico was planted by the Greeks long ago (seventh to sixth century BC), giving it a longer tradition than many proudly "native" grapes of the North. The Greeks planted many vines near Monte Vulture, an extinct volcano in northern Basilicata, and that's still where most of the best wine is produced today (called **Aglianico del Vulture**). The aglianico harvest, in late October to early November, is one of the latest in Italy. For its first two years, the wine tastes closed and often harsh. But when it finally opens up, it displays pleasing flavor, color, character, and persistence; try to pick up notes of cherry and choco-late. It's sometimes called the "Barolo of the South."

The most prominent non-DOC wines are called **colli lucani,** which are made in both white and red.

White wine production in Basilicata is modest in quality and quantity.

For hard drinks, the local *amaro*—called **Lucano**—is one of the more popular *digestivi* in the South, with a well-balanced blend of herbs and spices (for more on *amaro,* see page 99). **Vena** is a licorice-flavored cordial.

Calabria

Calabria—the toe of the Italian boot—remains one of the poorest and most isolated regions of the country, but that makes it no less appealing. Many travelers—just passing through—see only the dull corridor to Sicily via Reggio Calabria. But there's so much more to experience, both in the interior and along Calabria's 500-mile coastline (which is far less developed than farther north—gracing it with some of the cleanest coastal waters in Italy). The Ionian (east) coast in particular has vast expanses of virgin beach and scrub and a fertile agricultural plain that yields sublime produce, especially figs.

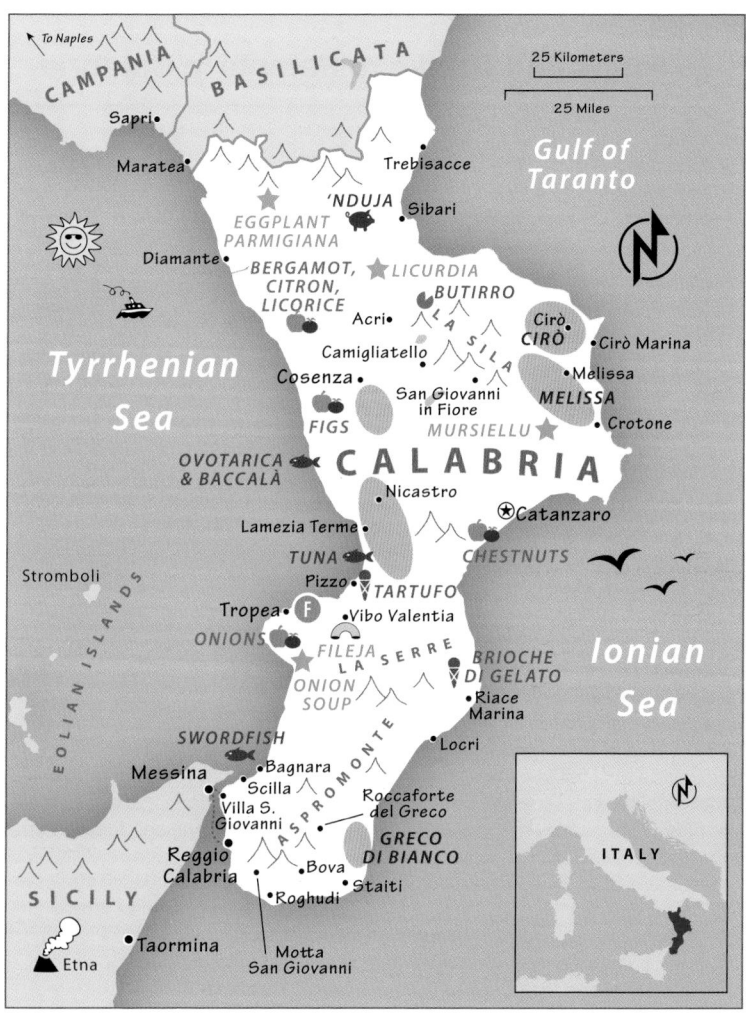

The story of Calabria can be told in its trees. Near the shore you find palm, lemon, oleander, and almond trees. In the low hills just above are citron and bergamot, along with date palms, magnolias, bananas, and even rubber trees. The higher hills beyond are where many of the important towns are—in centuries past, people did not live near the shore, fearing malaria and invasions. Here are

the vines and olive trees that have sustained Calabria since its earliest inhabitants. In fact, grape vines and olive trees are reminiscent of the *calabresi* themselves: They've been bent and twisted by the elements, yet they endure and produce and never break.

In the center of the region are the Calabrese Apennines, three ranges of high peaks and plateaus known as the Sila, Serre, and Aspromonte. Their

🍴 Foods and Drinks to Sample in Calabria

'Nduja
Spicy, smoky, spreadable pork sausage popular throughout Italy; also try the dry spicy *salame* called *capocollo*.

Licurdia
Simple, savory soup of sweet Tropea onions and other vegetables.

Pesce spada and tonno
Fresh-caught swordfish and tuna can be prepared a variety of ways.

'Nduja

Tartufo di Pizzo
A ball of gelato and various mix-ins, rolled in cocoa powder.

Cirò
Wine still produced near ancient vineyards, which comes in red, rosé, and white.

vast forests are sparsely inhabited and rarely visited; those who do venture there see beech, fir, oak, and pine trees, many green all year round and covered in snow in winter. The Serre has a distinct tree called the Calabria pine, with silvery scales on the bark that reach all the way up to the needles. This area looks more like Scandinavia than the southern tip of the Italian Peninsula.

The mountain people in Calabria have always been more self-sufficient than lowlanders. In the past, many of them worked as serfs (and, later, as peasants) on landed estates called *latifundia* in Latin (or *latifondi* in Italian). They toiled in abysmal conditions that often verged on starvation, while a few lords became wealthy on the backs of the poor. *Latifundia* existed as far back as the Roman era, and many lasted until the 1940s. In 1949, land reform brought bloody riots in the winemaking town of Melissa as it was being determined

how the valuable land would be parceled.

During the long winters, people in the Sila and other mountain areas create handicrafts that began as necessity, and have now become souvenirs. Traditionally, the men were adept woodcarvers, and the women wove beautiful blankets.

Like neighboring Basilicata, Calabria has an extremely long history. It was inhabited in Paleolithic times and, later, was an important chunk of Magna Graecia (the Greek Empire) as a supplier of foodstuffs and raw materials to Athens. Cities such as Sibari, Crotone, and Locri were founded on the Ionian Sea between 744 and 650 BC. Sibari was the home of the Sybarites, a group that understood pleasure in life; today's (rather obscure) word "sybaritic" carries on their spirit of hedonism. Pythagoras was the most famous resident of Crotone, which was a center of science and culture

Left: Aspromonte National Park; **Right:** Traditional dances

in the sixth century BC. (He also was influential in helping his city destroy the Sybarites.)

The Romans followed the Greeks, and then came centuries of foreign occupiers: Goths, Byzantines (who collected silkworms from mulberry trees, which were prized in Constantinople), Lombards, Saracens, the Catholic Church (which consolidated the *latifundia*), Normans, and Swabians, who tried to develop commerce and check the power of the *latifundia*. Jewish traders arrived and encouraged cultivation of citron and other crops. Then came the French and the Spanish, the kingdom of Naples, and the Austrians.

In effect, *calabresi* were seldom self-governing and never had a chance to develop civic institutions of their own. Over time, they came to believe they could only trust family members for protection against outsiders. So originated the 'Ndranghetta—Calabria's answer to the Sicilian Mafia. It's easy to overlook that the 'Ndranghetta emerged not to commit crime, but to protect people from it. And by providing protection, the 'Ndranghetta became a sort of counterbalance to the *latifundia*.

Rivalries between towns and interfamilial quarrels meant that local disputes could carry on for generations. And when *calabresi* emigrated to new lands, they tended to bring along those ancient feuds. In immigrant communities of North America, this gave new arrivals from rural southern Italy a bad reputation. Many *calabresi* seem more reserved in their dealings with visitors because of the defensiveness that has evolved over centuries.

For the visitor, Calabria's lack of polish, modernity, and development is part of its appeal. After all, underdevelopment means less desecration of the land. A city such as Cosenza remains notably old-fashioned— almost a living time warp compared to northern cities of similar size, such as Lucca in Tuscany or Treviso in Veneto. You get the sense that people cling to the old in Calabria because, in a changing world, what's old is what's comprehensible—and what's theirs alone. Anything introduced from the outside—even a genuine improvement—might be seen as a threat to a way of life that has stood tall, with roots deeply planted, like the trees that tell the story of Calabria.

CITIES, TOWNS, AND PLACES

Reggio Calabria (pop. 183,000) sits at the tip of Italy's (and Calabria's) toe. It's a gloomy city with two saving graces: an enjoyable seaside promenade and a good museum featuring objects from antiquity (including the Bronzes of Riace, discovered on the seafloor in 1972). For most, this city is merely a transit point on the journey to or from Sicily across the Strait of Messina.

Just up the coast, **Tropea** (pop. 7,000), facing the Tyrrhenian Sea, is Fred's favorite town in Calabria. Tropea is just away from the busier tourist areas—preserving its character—but still has enough commerce to feel vital and viable. Despite its small size, it has many food specialties, thanks to fertile land and a generous sea. It's best known for its decadently sweet red onions, and the eggplants, capers, and tomatoes are also excellent. This is a good place to try *fileja,* mini-macaroni in a spicy pork sauce; they also have good pasta with cuttlefish ink *(al nero di seppia)*.

Farther north, the regional capital of **Catanzaro** (pop. 91,000) is at the heart of an area famous for chestnuts and figs. The chestnuts are shipped all over Italy—to be served roasted in sidewalk kettles in the winter, to be turned into chestnut flour, and to be candied as *marrons glacés.* This part of Calabria is also known for its gutsy red and white wines, wild mushrooms, citrus fruits, tuna, vegetables

Above: Tropea; **Below:** Promenade in Reggio Calabria

preserved in oil and vinegar, and sausages spiked with *peperoncino rosso*.

Cosenza (pop. 68,000) has an old city center that feels trapped in the early 20th century—its Corso Telesio is an inviting place for a time-warp stroll. Cosenza is also the gateway for visiting the mountains of the **Sila** (for *silvia brutia,* "wild forest"). This area—in the inland heart of Calabria—has six rivers that flow into artificial lakes, and 500-year-old pine trees known as the "Giants of Sila" (Italy's answer to the giant redwoods of California). As you head up into the mountains from Cosenza, **Camigliatello** is a charming town; higher up is **San Giovanni in Fiore.** Roadside vendors sell mountain cheeses, *porcini* mushrooms, and other products. Cattle graze in high pastures of grass and purple, red, and yellow flowers that make a beautiful contrast to the deep lakes and towering trees beyond.

Cosenza

🍴 FOODS OF CALABRIA

Like the rest of the South, Calabrian cuisine was born in kitchens that had few ingredients and used them resourcefully. Pasta with vegetables is a staple, and it comes in many forms. *Peperoncino rosso* (hot red pepper) is a dominant flavor, including *diavolicchio* (super-spicy small red peppers, used to infuse oil or crushed into a powder). The land produces superb vegetables, especially eggplant, sweet peppers, artichokes, zucchini, onions, and mushrooms. People who live near the coasts feast on swordfish and seafood, while those inland get much of their protein from lamb, kid, pork sausage, and cheeses such as *caciocavallo* and provolone. Citrus flavors occasionally show up in different parts of the meal, including sauces for fish and for baking. And there's a hint of Sicilian influence (not surprising, since it's just a few miles away across the Strait of Messina).

ANTIPASTI (APPETIZERS)	
Capocollo (or **coppa**)	This spicy dry *salame*—common throughout the South—is also a Calabrian specialty. It appears in virtually all *antipasti*.
Lagrumuse	This *salame,* which weeps a drop of fat when you cut it, has a name that means "tearful" (or "lachrymose").

'Nduja	This soft pork sausage is heavily spiked with *peperoncino rosso,* giving it a fiery kick. It's smoked but retains a spreadable, pâté-like texture. Its name is a variation on the French *andouille,* which is similar. The powerful flavor of *'nduja* has made it popular throughout Italy and internationally.
Soppressata	Spicy dry *salame,* popular throughout the South.
Melanzane a scapece	Pickled eggplant.
Ovotarica	Dried tuna eggs, like the Sicilian or Sardinian *bottarga,* served on bread with olive oil and tomatoes.
Sardella	Fish fry (baby fish) of all types, minced with powdered *peperoncino* and olive oil and spread on bread; this specialty of Crotone is also known as **caviale calabrese,** Calabria caviar.

PRIMI (PASTAS AND OTHER FIRST COURSES)

Calabria has a wide variety of pastas; in centuries past, brides were expected to be able to make at least a dozen types. Look for *pizzicotti* (which are round), *ricci di donna* ("woman's curls"), *paternostri* (small cubes with holes in them), *raschiatelli* (long, thick-cut pasta), *cannaruozzoli* (bent canes), and *bucatini* (also called *perciatelli,* thick spaghetti with a hole running through it).

Bucatini con la mollica	*Bucatini* with olive oil, mashed anchovies, and breadcrumbs.
Fileja (or **filej**)	A pasta resembling a short macaroni, which gets its shape by being rolled around wire or sticks. This specialty of Vibo Valentia is typically served with a spicy pork sauce.
Lagane e cicciari	This pasta dish, also popular in Basilicata, is wide, short, flat noodles served with a light sauce of chickpeas, onions, garlic, parsley, and sometimes *peperoncino.*

Left: *Melanzane stupide;* **Right:** *'Nduja*

Left: *Lagane e cicciari;* **Right:** *Fileja*

Licurdia	This simple soup from Tropea has a base of sweet red onions, combined with potato and *peperoncino rosso,* and often other vegetables, including carrots, asparagus, or greens. It's frequently served with bread and a bit of *pecorino romano.*
Millecosedde	"A thousand things"—a soup with rigatoni, fava beans, chickpeas, red and white beans, and lentils.
Pasta e alici	A simple pasta preparation with anchovies *(alici)* and breadcrumbs in olive oil, sometimes with tomatoes and/or *peperoncino.*
Perciatelli con le marozze	*Bucatini*-like *perciatelli* (or sometimes a different pasta) with various types of snails.
Ravioli alla calabrese	Stuffed with cheese (typically provolone and *pecorino*) and *soppressata,* and served in a tomato sauce.
Rigatoni alla toranese	Rigatoni with onions, grated *pecorino romano,* and a touch of lard.
Sagne chine	*Lasagne* filled with different flavorings, including sausage, tiny meatballs, hard-boiled eggs, artichokes, cheeses, and fresh tomato sauce.
Zite	Served with lard, *prosciutto crudo,* parsley, tomatoes, garlic, and basil.

SECONDI (MAIN DISHES)

Alici a beccafico	Fresh anchovies stuffed and fried.
Baccalà	Rehydrated salted cod, so common in Veneto and the North, is also a fixture of Calabria.

Left: *Involtini di alici;* **Right:** *Melanzane alla parmigiana*

Frittole	Hot pig's skin eaten with warm bread, a specialty of Reggio Calabria.
Involtini di alici	Fresh anchovy fillets stuffed and rolled.
La ghiotta	The *calabrese* version of this sauce features tomatoes, eggplant, peppers, olives, capers, onion, garlic, anchovies, and often raisins and/or pine nuts. It's also commonly eaten at Christmastime, made with stockfish.
Melanzane alla parmigiana	Breaded, fried eggplant baked with tomatoes, mozzarella, and Parmigiano-Reggiano. This classic dish, common in the South and elsewhere, is particularly popular in Calabria.
Mursiellu (also *morsello,* *morzello,* or *murzeddhu*)	A slow-cooked stew made of tripe, tongue, spleen, and other organ meats, with red wine, tomatoes, *peperoncino,* and herbs (especially oregano). This Catanzaro specialty is typically served with a round bread called *pitta,* which has a hole in the middle for the stew. It's eaten in "little bites" *(mursiellu)*—the origin of the name.
Mustica	Sun-dried whitebait, peppered and preserved in oil.
Pesce spada	Swordfish, cooked in many ways. It can be served simply, with garlic, parsley, and olive oil *(riggitana);* with lemon and capers *(bagnarota);* or *alla ghiotta* (see above; especially common near Reggio Calabria). The best is caught at Bagnara and Scilla.
Tonno	Tuna steaks can be served *in agrodolce* (a sweet-and-sour preparation) or with *salsa verde,* a slightly sharp green herb sauce, or a variety of other ways. The best tuna is caught near the beautiful little town of Pizzo, just north of Tropea.

CONTORNI (SIDE DISHES)

The many *calabrese* vegetables—especially eggplant—are cooked in numerous ways, including grilling, frying, baking, stuffing, and stewing.

Cipolle di Tropea	This famous, sweet, red-purple onion hails from Tropea.
Insalata calabrese	A mix of boiled and raw greens, tossed and dressed with olive oil.
Melanzane stupide	These "stupid eggplants" are seasoned with oil, parsley, salt, and cheese, and then baked.

FORMAGGI (CHEESES)

Mozzarella, *scamorza, provola,* provolone, and *caciocavallo* are all excellent cow's-milk cheeses. **Butirro** is a creamy, buttery cheese from the Sila made with milk from cows that have not calved for a year. The region also is famous for goat's-milk cheeses (especially the towns of Bova, Roccaforte del Greco, Staiti, Motta San Giovanni, and Roghudi).

FRUTTA (FRUIT)

Bergamotto	Bergamot is a citrus fruit (closer to an orange than a lemon) that's prized for its spicy fragrance. It's exported to France for use in perfumery and to England, where it contributes a unique bouquet to Earl Grey tea.
Cedro	The citron is a large citrus fruit in the lemon family, harvested mainly for its skin—which is boiled and then candied, and winds up in fruitcake the world over, in Sicilian pastries, and in Milan's *panettone.* The skin is rough, with indentations called "Adam's bites." Legend has it that the citron was the forbidden fruit eaten by Adam and Eve in the Garden of Eden.

Left: *Caciocavallo;* **Right:** *Bergamotto*

Fichi	Calabria's excellent figs turn up everywhere. Eaten fresh, they're the perfect dessert. Or they might be dried and stuffed with almonds, chocolate, fruit, or other nuts.
Liquirizia	The licorice plant thrives in the clay soil of Calabria; you'll encounter this scent and flavor in many local foods.

DOLCI (SWEETS)

Calabria has all sorts of sweets, most of them originally connected with Easter and Christmas. This is because in the past, when the region was very poor, the luxury of sweets was only permitted for holidays. When sampling gelato flavors, look for *liquirizia* (licorice—found throughout Italy, but a specialty here) and **crema reggina** (a pink, rum-flavored gelato, often with chocolate bits and candied fruits).

Brioche con il gelato	In warm weather in Reggio Calabria, it's customary to fill a large roll with ice cream to have for breakfast with the morning coffee.
Cumpittu	Of Arab origin, this is a soft nougat with honey, sesame seeds, and almonds.
Fichi alla sibarita	From Sibari, these are dried figs filled with almonds, hazelnuts, cocoa powder, *sapa* (cooked wine must), sugar, cinnamon, and candied fruits.
Fichi ripieni	From Cosenza, these are dried figs with a single filling, such as one of the items listed above for *fichi alla sibarita*.
Mostaccioli	This specialty of Soriano Calabro is a dry cookie made of flour, honey, and almonds. They come in various shapes; some are pagan motifs called *babbaluti* or in the shape of early Christian fish and bird symbols. The similar *'nzuddi* are made with flour, white wine, honey, and spices.

Tartufo di Pizzo

Nacatula	Flour and spices, fried in olive oil. This was once a cake eaten at weddings and during Carnival.
Tartufo di Pizzo	This gelato-chocolate bomb, found throughout Italy, originated in the Calabrian town of Pizzo. It comes in various types, but it's essentially a ball of gelato and assorted mix-ins, all rolled up in decadent cocoa powder.
Torrone gelato	From Reggio Calabria, a cylinder made with candied tangerine, orange, and lime mixed with ground almonds and coated with chocolate. Despite the name, this is not an iced dessert.

♀ WINES OF CALABRIA

Most Calabria wine production is red, and it heavily uses the gaglioppo grape. There are 12 DOCs, but their output is limited. As in Puglia, production is focused mainly on quantity over quality; a good bit of wine is sent to the North, in order to be mixed in blends.

The Greeks brought grapes and winemaking techniques to Calabria, and the indigenous people took to it so well that, soon, the wine made here was considered better than what was produced in Greece proper. The Greek name for Italy—Enotria, "Land of Wine"—was first applied to Calabria before being expanded to refer to the entire peninsula. Wine was mostly produced around Sibari, and archaeologists have discovered an ancient vinoduct—a system of pipes that carried the wine from the producing areas to the thirsty Sybarites. In ancient times, Cremissa, a wine from Krimisa (between Sibari and Crotone), was used to toast victorious athletes at the Olympic Games.

Today, that same area—in the eastern foothills of the Sila, toward the Ionian Coast—produces a wine called **Cirò,** which likes to claim it's the "oldest wine in the world." Cirò—made in red, rosé, and white—is Calabria's best-known DOC wine. **Melissa,** another good DOC wine produced nearby, comes in white, red, and the better *rosso superiore*. **Greco di Bianco** is an amber-colored sweet dessert wine with a powerful citrus fragrance and herbal undertones.

The Islands
Sicily

Sicilia

If Italy is one of the most dramatic, sensual places in Europe, Sicily is its distilled and intensified essence—pure passion set in wild beauty. If you're coming from other parts of Italy, Sicily may feel similar…but it's not the same. The beauty is more rugged, the food is more flavorful, and the highs and lows are more extreme. Coming to this island requires not only patience and a sense of adventure, but also a willingness to be open to its seductions.

Sicily floats just off the toe of Italy's boot, like a soccer ball about to be kicked. At nearly 10,000 square miles, the island (which is Italy's biggest region) can be driven end to end in three hours—a journey that traverses a variety of landscapes, climates, and cultures.

Sicily's location at the center of the Mediterranean made it a strategic base for successive waves of invaders. Carthaginians from North Africa used the west side of the island as a trading base, even as the Greeks settled the east side—creating a cultural divide that persists today. It's

Foods and Drinks to Sample in Sicily

Arancina (or arancino)
Gooey, deep-fried ball of rice, often containing meat sauce, saffron, and other fillings.

Agrumi
Outstanding citrus fruits (including blood oranges, lemons, and tangerines) flavor many Sicilian dishes.

Pasta alla Norma
A sauce of eggplant, tomato sauce, basil, and *ricotta salata* cheese.

Caponata
Sweet-and-sour stew of eggplant and other vegetables, served as a side or a starter.

Cannoli
Deep-fried pastry tubes filled with sweet *ricotta*.

Granita
Sweet, slushy ice of fruit or coffee, incredibly refreshing on a hot day.

Marsala
One of the world's most famous fortified dessert wines.

Arancine

---

striking to think that 2,500 years ago, the second and third biggest cities in the Greek world—Syracuse (today's Siracusa) and Agrigento—were in Sicily. Later came wave after wave of further invaders: the Romans, barbarians, and Byzantines; the Arabs, who modernized the island, brought prosperity, and turned Palermo into a flourishing city; the Normans from France; the Swabians from Germany; the Angevins (again from France); the Spanish...all of this by the time Garibaldi was putting his country together, adding Sicily to the Italian mix in 1860.

Through those many centuries of foreign domination, Sicily often drew inward, building a magnificently complex culture. Sicilian life is full of color and spectacle, as evidenced in the religious observances at Easter and in the famous puppet shows of Palermo. It's also full of tragedy, of families separated by immigration, by war, by feuds, by people who leave in search of work.

Sicily is a historically poor land that knew great poverty and had a humble cuisine. And yet, it's also one of the foremost kitchens in Italy, bursting with flavor, color, fragrance, and high drama. Four factors (at least) contribute to this proud heritage: First, as with other impoverished areas (especially in the South), poverty loomed large. Much of Sicilian cooking is *cucina povera* ("food of the poor"), in which shrewd chefs use humble ingredients creatively.

Arabs arrived in Sicily in 827, and their rule gradually spread across the island, lasting until 1091. The Arabs brought irrigation and other farming techniques, increasing

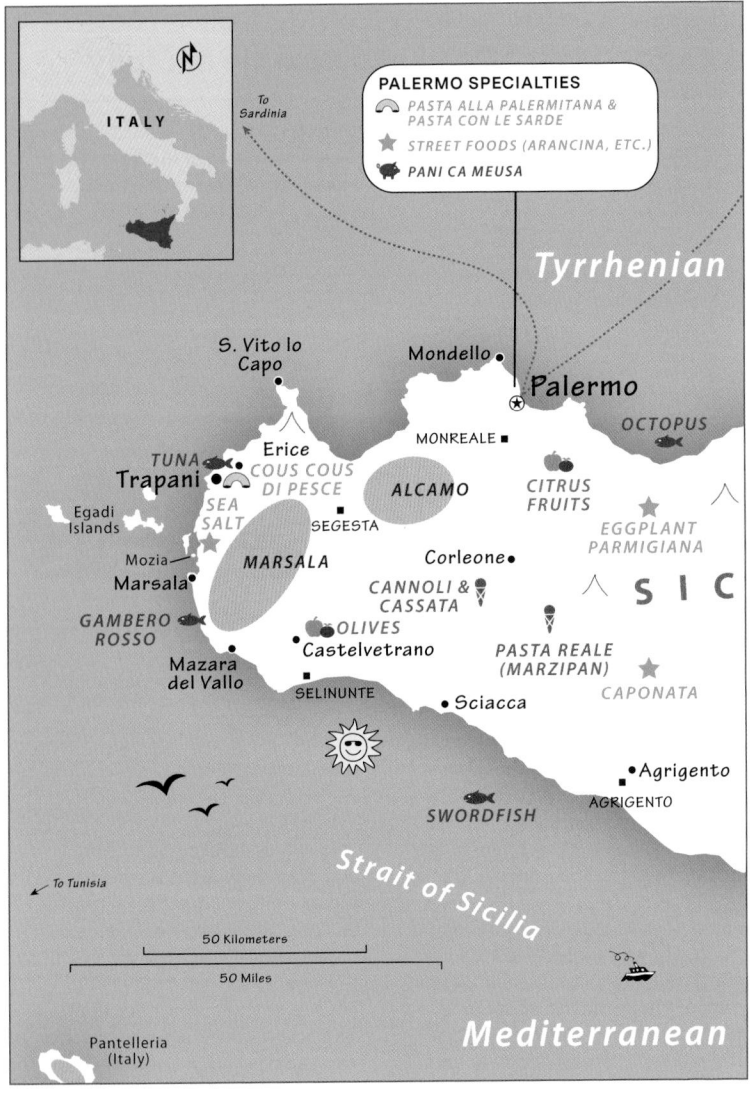

PALERMO SPECIALTIES
PASTA ALLA PALERMITANA &
PASTA CON LE SARDE
★ STREET FOODS (ARANCINA, ETC.)
🐷 PANI CA MEUSA

Tyrrhenian

S. Vito lo Capo

Mondello •

● **Palermo**

MONREALE ■

Trapani

Erice

TUNA

COUS COUS DI PESCE

ALCAMO

OCTOPUS

CITRUS FRUITS

EGGPLANT PARMIGIANA

Egadi Islands

SEA SALT

SEGESTA •

MARSALA

Corleone •

S I C

Mozia •

Marsala ●

GAMBERO ROSSO

Castelvetrano

CANNOLI & CASSATA

OLIVES

PASTA REALE (MARZIPAN)

CAPONATA

Mazara del Vallo ●

SELINUNTE

• Sciacca

SWORDFISH

• Agrigento

AGRIGENTO ■

Strait of Sicilia

← To Tunisia

50 Kilometers

50 Miles

Pantelleria (Italy)

Mediterranean

yields, and introduced many foods that have become Sicilian staples: citrus fruits, spices like cinnamon and ginger, almonds, pistachios, raisins and currants, candied citrus peel, an affinity for sweet-and-sour combinations *(agrodolce),* fried foods, couscous, and, perhaps most of all,

sugarcane—which explains why, even today, Sicilian desserts are the sweetest and most extravagant in all of Italy.

Another major factor were the cloistered nuns (and some monks) who cooked pastries to sell to support their orders. They were among

the first to preserve and candy citrus and other fruits, and they were the guardians of the tradition of making gelato. At various points in Sicilian history, nuns left the convent and were hired by wealthy families as pastry chefs. As the nuns' work grew more appreciated by a wider segment of the population, sweets-making became an honored profession on the island.

Finally, during the period of the Bourbon occupation (late 18th century), the noble families of Sicily wanted professional French chefs in their homes. At this point, chefs called *monzù* (or *monsù*—a corruption of *"monsieur"*) entered Sicilian kitchens—bringing with them butter—and developed a refined culinary tradition quite distinct from the peasant food that is usually associated with southern Italy.

The success of all four of these groups—poor cooks, Arabs, pastry-chef nuns, and the *monzù*—owed a great deal to the fact that Sicily is blessed with amazing raw materials. The seas here are generous, and luscious vegetables grow throughout the island. The citrus fruits (called *agrumi*) that grow near Palermo show up in every part of the meal. Exotic combinations of nuts, fruit, fish, herbs, and bread produce dishes of unselfconscious sophistication. Powerful wines add assertive flavors to many recipes. You might think that all of these intensely flavored ingredients would compete with each other, yet they partner and work together brilliantly.

Sicily's bounty of food is celebrated in its many vibrant street markets (best in Palermo, Catania, and Siracusa). As you stroll the narrow lanes of a market, your senses are assaulted by sights, smells, and sounds. Vendors here still maintain the tradition of calling out to passersby in a singsong way, like an auctioneer.

Only in recent years has Sicily been discovered by mainstream tourism. But that industry is still new and unrefined compared to the sleek machinery of Tuscany, Venice, and Rome. That's actually an asset, because Sicily retains its personality and charm, and its surviving rough edges add to its appeal. In most of Sicily, you'll encounter people going about their lives as they normally do. The food you eat will be their food. And if, at times, the Sicilians don't quite know what to make of you, it's only because you're as new to them as they are to you.

🗺️ CITIES, TOWNS, AND PLACES

Palermo (pop. 680,000)—Sicily's misunderstood, underrated capital—is a city of great beauty and considerable squalor that reflects the legacies of Siculi, Greek, Roman, Arab, Norman, Spanish, and Italian civilizations. It has splendid churches, squares, monuments, and architecture. The markets are vibrant, delicious food can be had at all prices, and the cultural and political tradition is strong. Yet parts of the city are only now being restored following the destruction of World War II. Unemployment is high, and many people are disenchanted and disaffected. And, while the *palermitani* have made great strides in reclaiming their city from governmental corruption and organized crime, the Mafia still makes its presence felt from time to time. Still, the city possesses a certain pride and elegance (if shabby at times); like Sicily itself, it's a place that gets under your skin.

Catania is Sicily's second city (with 315,000 people) and Palermo's cross-island rival, on the east coast. While Catania is spiffing up and its thriving markets rival the vibrancy of Palermo's, it lacks its rival's sophistication.

Catania sits on the lower slopes of **Mount Etna,** giving it access to excellent produce and wine that grows in that volcanic soil. Europe's most active volcano presides over her island like Mount Fuji over Japan. Mount Etna dominates the skyline

Above: Palermo; **Below:** Street performer in Catania

Top: Salt flats near Trapani; **Bottom:** Valley of the Temples at Agrigento

some of the world's best pistachios come from the town of **Bronte.**

There are some fine seaside resorts in this northeastern part of Sicily, most notably **Taormina** (pop. 11,000)—an elegant, clifftop town just below Etna. While the setting is undeniably stunning, and the old Greek theater hovering just above the main drag is striking, Taormina is swamped with tourists. For a beach break between Catania and Palermo, **Cefalù** (pop. 14,000)—Rick's favorite town on the island—is a fishing village with a striking Norman fortified cathedral, a picturesque harbor, a burly fortress topping the rock overhead, skinny pastel houses, and good seafood restaurants.

Trapani (pop. 70,000) is the main city of Sicily's west coast, facing Tunisia (geographically, culturally, and culinarily). This mellow, fun-to-explore town is the best place to try Sicilian couscous. Just down the coast from Trapani are salt flats where sea salt has been harvested since the eighth century BC (now well-explained by museums). And farther south down the coast is **Marsala** (pop. 83,000), which produces one of the world's most famous dessert wines.

On the less-discovered south coast of Sicily—far from the urban centers of Palermo and Catania—you'll find ancient ruins, including the stunning Valley of the Temples at **Agrigento** and, deep in the interior, the amazing mosaics at **Vila Romana del Casale.**

In the rolling hills of the southeast, **Ragusa** (pop. 76,000) is one of Sicily's undiscovered gems, built along a steep promontory and surrounded by a verdant gorge; it's also known for its cheese production. Ragusa is a handy home base for exploring other fine towns—most notably **Noto** (pop. 24,000), blessed with gorgeous Sicilian Baroque

of the east coast of Sicily, soaring to 11,000 feet. Gondolas and 4x4 buses take visitors to the summit, and on many days, you'll actually see steam and smoke.

But for food lovers, the big draw of Mount Etna is its soil, which nourishes remarkable ingredients. Wineries surround Etna to the east and north, but it's best along Etna's north flank, along the 12-mile stretch of rural road between the towns of **Linguaglossa** and **Randazzo.** This area boasts beautiful scenery, charming wineries, and world-class wines. You can stop in at various places for a tasting, a tour, and a look at the old, abandoned (or repurposed) wine cellar/presses called *palmenti.* Nearby,

architecture and some of Italy's best gelato, and **Modica** (pop. 54,000), famous for its chocolate.

And in the southeast corner of Sicily is the lovely town of **Siracusa** (a.k.a. Syracuse, pop. 125,000). We've saved the best for last, as this is Fred's favorite Sicilian city (and, truth be told, one of Rick's, too). The modern mainland city of Siracusa huddles around its expansive bay, as if protecting the little island of Ortigia like a jewel. Ortigia—which dates back to ancient times—features meandering lanes of eroding palaces and ruins side-by-side with hipster wine bars and sumptuous piazzas.

Ragusa

🍽 FOODS OF SICILY

The Sicilian diet relies on Italian staples such as pastas, olives, savory breads, and tomatoes—but it gives them a local twist. Sicilian cuisine has been influenced by the island's unique location, geology (with volcanic soil), and many occupiers. Thanks to centuries of North African and Middle Eastern influences, Sicilian cuisine includes distinctive ingredients such as couscous, almonds, ginger, cinnamon, and lots of citrus; you might also detect Greek and Spanish touches. Choosing between fish couscous and *pasta bolognese* on the same menu, you know you're at a crossroads of cultures.

STREET FOOD AND SNACKS

Sicily has little tradition for *antipasti*. Instead, it has among the most appealing street food scenes in Europe. Towns big and small have street markets where vendors serve up steaming munchies from rickety carts; the very best selection is in Palermo and Catania. Prices are affordable (most items cost just a euro or two). Don't be intimidated—just point to what you want and dig in. Most dishes are finished with a spritz of fresh lemon juice. Below are the main street foods you'll find in Sicily, some of which have now been appropriated and adapted by restaurants as *antipasti* or other courses.

Arancina (or **arancino**)	A breaded, deep-fried rice ball filled with *ragù* (meat sauce) and other ingredients. The specifics vary throughout Sicily. In Palermo and the west, where the rice balls originated in the 10th century, they're called **arancina** (feminine, plural *arancine*). The classic ones are round, flavored with saffron, and contain no tomatoes. In Catania and the east, they're called **arancino** (masculine, plural *arancini*). Typical ones are pointy and usually contain tomatoes, but rarely have saffron. The pointed shape resembles the profile of Mount Etna, and the molten *ragù* inside echoes the volcano's hot lava.

In either city, you'll find variations in shapes and fillings. The classic choices are **al burro** (ham and Béchamel sauce; in Catania, these are called **arancino al prosciutto**) and **al ragù** (with tomato, meat, and peas). And there are other, modern variations. The shape often indicates what's inside: *al burro* is spherical; eggplant is oval, with a darker crust; and *alla palermitana*—with sardines, wild fennel, pine nuts, and *pecorino*—is also typically oval.

Cacio all'argentiera	Fried or roasted cheese with a dressing of oil, anchovies, and oregano.
Crocché	Potato croquettes, usually filled with mashed potato, parsley, and mint, then deep-fried. **Cazzilli** are a smaller version of *crocché*.
Falso magro (or **farsu magru**)	Meat roll filled with cheese, sausage, and boiled eggs.
Frittola (or **frittula**)	Leftover veal parts, such as cartilage and bone, fried up and assembled into a chewy, salty meat fluff.
Mangia e bevi	Literally "eat and drink," this is thin strips of pork wrapped around a stalk of green onion, then tossed on a grill. Often, other meats are also available to grill (including *stigghiole,* described later).
Panelle	Deep-fried chickpea fritters. *Panelle* and *cazzilli* are often served together, sometimes inside a sandwich.
Pani ca' meusa (also **pane con la milza** or **guasteddu**)	Boiled spleen, lung, and other veal organ meat, served on a sesame-seed roll. It can be dressed with *caciocavallo* cheese (in which case it's called **maritatu**), or without **(schiettu).**
Polpo bollito	Octopus (often a small one, about the size of your hand) that's been boiled in salty, inky water, then chopped up and spritzed with lemon.

Left: *Arancina;* **Right:** Street food

Left: *Parmigiana di melanzane;* **Right:** *Panelle*

Rascatura	A mix of leftover *panelle* and *cazzilli,* sometimes with onion and lemon, refried into little greasy pieces.
Sfincione	Sometimes called "Sicilian pizza," this is a fluffy crust simply topped with tomato (and sometimes anchovy and cheese), sold on carts by the greasy slice. It doesn't look appetizing in the cart's display case, but the vendor grills it on a hidden oven.
Stigghiole	Lamb intestines wrapped around green onions. They may not sound appetizing, but they smell and taste amazing. For something a bit tamer, look for *mangia e bevi* (described earlier).

PRIMI (PASTAS AND OTHER FIRST COURSES)

Anelletti al forno	Ring-shaped pasta, originating in Palermo, baked with tomatoes, meat, eggplant, and cheese.
Cous cous (or *cuscusu*) *di pesce*	This North African-influenced dish is common mainly on the west coast, near Trapani. The couscous is served with a side of fish broth, which you ladle on to taste. Fancier variations are topped with a more elaborate array of shellfish and other seafood **(cous cous ai frutti di mare).**
Macco di fave (or *maccu*)	A simple, stick-to-your-ribs soup made of dried and crushed fava beans and fennel; sometimes served over pasta.
Pasta alla bottarga	Dried tuna roe—very salty and very fishy.
Pasta alla Norma	A tomato sauce with eggplant, basil, and *ricotta salata* cheese. It's named for the opera *Norma* by Vincenzo Bellini, native son of Catania.

Left: *Cous cous di pesce;* **Right:** *Pasta alla Norma*

Pasta alla palermitana	This simple "Palermo-style" topping began as a hardship food: sardines (the only fish poor *palermitani* could afford), wild fennel and pine nuts (to disguise the flavor of low-quality fish), and breadcrumbs (a cheap alternative to grated cheese). In general, anything *alla palermitana* often has breadcrumbs.
Pasta or ***risotto con frutti di mare***	Many varieties of seafood are served with pasta or rice.
Pasta con le sarde	This Palermo specialty is topped with fresh sardines and some combination of wild fennel, chopped onions, tomato sauce, saffron, olive oil, black currants, raisins, pine nuts, and sea salt; often eaten with spaghetti or *bucatini.*
Pasta 'ncasciata	Baked pasta dish made with *salame,* hard-boiled eggs, mozzarella, eggplant, and other ingredients.
Pesto alla trapanese	This variation on pesto (from Trapani, on the west coast) is a paste of almonds, garlic, tomatoes, and cheese—but not predominantly basil, as in Liguria, so it's red rather than green. It's often eaten with *busiate,* long twists similar to fusilli.
Spaghetti ai ricci	Spaghetti topped with sea urchin, a top-end choice for those who enjoy a taste of the sea.
Spaghetti alla siracusana	With breadcrumbs and anchovies, from Siracusa.
Zuppa trapanese di aragosta	Lobster soup, a specialty of Marettimo, an island off the coast of Trapani.
Zuppa di pesce	Fish soup.

SECONDI (MAIN DISHES)

An old Sicilian proverb says: *Quannu 'u piscaturi pigghia pisci, magari passa Cristu 'un lu canusci* ("When a fisherman catches a fish, he wouldn't even notice if Christ passed by"). The waters that surround Sicily provide an amazing bounty of fish and seafood, and if a fisherman has a good day, he can feed his family and earn money. Local menus are full of sea life: *tonno* (tuna), *pesce spada* (swordfish), *polpo* (octopus), *calamari* (squid), *seppie* (cuttlefish, similar to squid), *gamberoni* (large shrimp), *ricci di mare* (sea urchins), *vongole* (clams), *cozze* (mussels), *masculini* (small, lean anchovies), *spigola* (sea bass), *spatola* (ribbon fish), and on and on. Seafood is often served with some combination of pine nuts, pistachios, raisins, and breadcrumbs.

Beef and veal are precious commodities in Sicily, and goats and lambs (always consumed at Easter) are prized. Chickens and rabbit also show up in many dishes.

Alici	Fresh anchovies.
Gambero rosso (di Mazara)	These sought-after red prawns, of remarkably high quality, are caught off Sicily's west coast.
Neonata (or ***nunnata***)	This term refers to one of the many types of delicate young (literally "newborn") fish.
Nero dei Nebrodi	This "black pork from Nebrodi" comes from small, free-range, black pigs raised in the Nebrodi Mountains of northeast Sicily. The pigs, introduced under Spanish rule, are the same breed that produces Spain's most expensive *ibérico* ham.
Parmigiana di melanzane	Eggplant parmesan—fried eggplant layered with tomato sauce and cheese—is a classic that, some Sicilians claim, originated on the island.
Pesce spada	Swordfish is popular, in various preparations. Often it's simply grilled with a bit of olive oil, parsley, lemon, and garlic; or it can be spritzed with lemon, coated in breadcrumbs, and grilled; or it's topped with a sauce called ***la ghiotta*** (made of tomatoes, eggplant, olives, capers, raisins, and pine nuts). Or you may see it prepared ***involtini***—strips of swordfish rolled up with raisins, pine nuts, capers, olives, and lemon, then sprinkled with breadcrumbs and baked or grilled.

Sicilian fish markets

Polpo	Octopus, often served as a salad with celery and olive oil, or simply boiled, chopped, and accompanied by a wedge of lemon.
Polpette	Meat rolls or meatballs made with mixed meat, fish, or even veggies. Real Sicilian meatballs combine beef, veal, and pork.
Polpettone	A traditional meatloaf; its core is filled with spinach, carrots, and cheese.
Sarde	Fresh sardines. These are often served as **sarde a beccafico** (or **beccaficu**). First they're boned and stuffed with various fillings (perhaps raisins, currants, pine nuts, cheese, breadcrumbs, herbs, or a vegetable). Then they're either folded, dipped in egg and flour, and fried (Catania-style, **alla catanese**); or rolled and baked with bay leaves (Palermo-style, **alla palermitana**).
Tonno	Tuna, which first appears in the late spring or early summer, is a delicacy. When fresh, a big slab of bright-red tuna might be grilled extremely rare, like a top-quality cut of steak. One of the most dramatic things to observe in Sicily, especially near Trapani, is *la mattanza:* Fishermen in small boats encircle a school of tuna and stab wildly to catch as many as they can. As the water turns red with blood, the fishermen pull in their catch. While this can be upsetting to watch, Sicilians take great pride in the fact that this traditional method is more sustainable than modern fishing methods that predominate in international waters outside of the Mediterranean Sea—which catch the tuna before they have the opportunity to lay eggs, threatening their numbers.

CONTORNI (SIDE DISHES)

Sicily is blessed with vegetables of amazing variety and quality. Eggplant reigns, particularly in the east, and tomatoes, onions, capers, garlic, olives (and olive oil), broccoli, peppers, and cauliflower are wonderful. Look for the unusual purple cauliflower, and the comically long, skinny zucchini. Oversized olives from Castelvetrano are the local answer to Greek Kalamata olives, and the capers from Salina are said to be some of the world's best. Sundried tomatoes *(pomodori secchi)* are still traditionally made by drying tomatoes on wooden planks on sunny days.

Caponata	Simple yet luxurious sweet-and-sour eggplant stew, served either hot or cold. It usually contains zucchini, olives, sultanas, pine nuts, vinegar, and sugar, and can be served as a side or as a starter.
Insalata pantesca	A salad made with tender potatoes, tomatoes, onion, and capers; sometimes mackerel is added.
Insalata siciliana (or *insalata di arance*)	A popular springtime salad made with juicy chunks of orange, chopped wild fennel, black olives, and raw onions. You'll never see this prepared the same way twice.

Left: Sicilian produce; **Right:** *Caciocavallo siciliano*

FORMAGGI (CHEESES)

Many of the classic cheeses of southern Italy are found in Sicily, too. Listed below are a few that are especially popular.

Caciocavallo siciliano (or *cosacavaddu*)	A large, long cheese with a rounded bottom made primarily of cow's milk. Like other Southern Italian "horse cheeses" (as the name means), it's named not for its source, but because the big bulbs would be tied together and hung out to dry, like saddlebags. Sicilians use this similarly to a Parmigiano-Reggiano: a dry, crumbly, salty grating cheese. It's sometimes fried or grilled and served with oil and pepper.
Canestrato (or *incanestrato*)	A sheep's-milk cheese that, when fresh, is sold under the name **tuma.** Most *tuma* is put in small wicker baskets and aged; the rind of the harder cheese shows the imprint of the basket. The cheese is used for eating and for grating. An aged *canestrato* with black peppercorns and saffron is called **piacentino** (or **piacentino ennese,** as it comes from the province of Enna).
Pecorino siciliano	The local version of the sheep's-milk cheese common throughout southern and central Italy.
Ragusano	A 100 percent cow's-milk cheese from Ragusa. It can be eaten young and smooth or aged and granular.
Ricotta	This is Sicily's cheese staple, made from sheep's milk. It's used liberally, including sweetened as a filling for *cannoli.* **Ricotta salata** is the firmer, saltier version, often used for grating—it's similar to feta.

Sicilian *agrumi* (citrus fruits), including blood orange (left)

FRUTTA (FRUIT)

Sicily is famous for its sweet desserts (see next section). But the island also has a remarkable variety of fruit and nuts. In addition to the items listed here, Sicilian figs and grapes are delicious, and there are some unusual items, too—such as *nespole* (loquats).

Citrus fruits (*agrumi*)	Deep-red blood oranges (called *tarocco*) are especially prevalent, but every month during the winter, a new kind of orange ripens. Also look for *limoni* (lemons), *cedri* (citrons), and *mandarini* (tangerines). Dishes scented with orange and lemon are common, and you'll see tempting juice kiosks offering fresh-squeezed O.J. or a thirst-quenching *seltz*—fresh-squeezed lemon juice, a pinch of salt, and fizzy water (no added sugar).
Fichi d'india (prickly pears)	These spiny, rather ugly little cactus fruits taste delicious but can be treacherous to handle for the uninitiated. Ideally let the vendor peel it for you safely.

DOLCI (SWEETS)

In most of Italy, desserts tend to be lightly sweetened...but Sicilian sweets are sugar bombs. (This difference stems from 200-plus years of Arab occupation.) Many Sicilian pastries are made with some combination of sugar, almonds, citrus, and *ricotta*. The best almonds are said to come from Avola, in the province of Siracusa; the best pistachios are from Bronte, on the slopes of Mount Etna. Every town has a *pasticceria* crafting local specialties, many with odd names (like the *minnuzze,* or breasts, of Sant'Agata—a round, spongy cake topped with a cherry). Sicilian sweets are eaten any time of day, not just after a meal.

Cannoli	In the most famous Sicilian sweet, a crispy fried pastry tube is filled with sweetened *ricotta,* then dusted with powdered sugar. The ends can be dipped in nuts, chocolate chips, or candied fruit, depending on the local style. The mark of a high-quality *cannolo* is one that's filled right when you order it—otherwise, the shell gets soggy and loses its crunch. While traditionally made for Carnival, these can be found everywhere, all year round.

Cassata (or ***cassata siciliana***)	Sicily's classic, colorful layer cake. It's made of a sponge cake called *pan di Spagna* filled with lightly sweetened *ricotta*. More elaborate versions can have a base of liquor-infused cake, topped with *ricotta* and chocolate chips, then crowned with a layer of neon green marzipan and a sugar glaze; other fillings and flavors can include vanilla, pistachios, cinnamon, and candied fruit.
Gelato	This is a Sicilian specialty. Look for flavors that are less common elsewhere in Italy, such as ***fichi d'india*** (prickly pears) and ***cassata,*** a gelato version of the cake.
Granita	Another Sicilian classic, this is sweet fruit juice, nut milk, or coffee that has been frozen, then partially melted to a slushy consistency. Traditional flavors are ***mandorla*** (almond), ***limone*** (lemon), and ***gelsi*** (mulberry), but you'll find many others. ***Granita di caffè*** is a very refreshing way to consume your coffee. If they offer it **con panna** (with whipped cream)…do it. (Just never put *panna* on lemon *granita*—that's a big Sicilian no-no.) In the hot summer months, many Sicilians opt for *granita* at breakfast time. They might get a strong espresso accompanied by a glass of *granita di mandorla* and a sweet, warm brioche—which they dip into the *granita,* like a scoop.
Maritozzi	Sweet buns, often filled with whipped cream and raisins.
Paste di mandorla	Almond cookie made with almond flour, sugar, and egg whites. This basic recipe comes in many variations, usually named for the shape: little pyramids (*tette delle monache,* "nuns' breasts") or clumps of dough dropped roughly in the pan (*brutti ma buoni,* "ugly but good").
Pasta reale	Almond paste—or marzipan—is called "royal paste" because talented chefs used it to create extraordinarily beautiful confections that were considered suitable for a king. At Easter, Sicilians like to eat a marzipan lamb.
Pignolata	Little balls of dough deep-fried and rolled in honey and pine nuts. The ***pignolata messinese,*** from Messina, is covered with chocolate or lemon glaze.

Left: *Cassata* and *cannoli;* **Right:** Brioche with *granita*

♇ WINES OF SICILY

Sicily, with a variety of grape-growing areas of differing characteristics, has more vineyards than any other region. Yet per capita, Sicilians consume less wine than other Italians. Many grapes go to make raisins, which are a key ingredient in Sicilian cooking; are big, juicy table grapes bound for markets in Italy and the rest of Europe; or are used to make dessert wines, which require higher concentrations of grapes and are consumed in smaller amounts than table wine.

Some of the grape varieties grown here are common on the mainland, but others, such as the red nerello grape, can be found only in Sicily. The king of Sicilian grapes is **nero d'Avola,** known for its dark skin and juice, its deep ruby color, its cherry notes, its medium body, and its tannins. Other red grapes include perricone, nerello mascese, and nerello cappuccio. White grapes, making up two-thirds of Sicily's harvest, include catarratto, grillo, grecanico, zibibbo, inzolia, and carricante.

Sicily's claim to fame comes in its outstanding dessert wines, though in recent years its other production has improved radically. While this was once considered the land of plentiful, cheap, and cheery table wine, you'll now find upscale wineries ranging from big producers to small family operations.

Western Wines More than half of the vineyards in Sicily are in the relatively small area around Trapani, on the west coast. The Alcamo zone, between Palermo and Trapani, has long been known for its white wines, but now they're producing some excellent reds as well. These wines are inexpensive and generally good, but western Sicily is best known for its Marsala wine, described later.

Eastern Wines On this side of the island, wines are grown from the south coast around Ragusa and Noto to the slopes of Mount Etna (see next). Nero d'Avola grapes are now grown all over the island, but they originated in the southeastern corner, near the town of Avola. This zone, with its lower elevation and hotter temperatures, produces the famous **Cerasuolo di Vittoria**—Sicily's only DOCG wine.

Mount Etna Wines After a long period of poor production—due to depopulation and strict new EU regulations—a new generation of vintners is leading a renaissance in Etna wines. Grapes thrive in Etna's nutrient-rich volcanic soil, and some vineyards are steeply angled, allowing the vines to catch the sun just so. Etna's north slope—at about 3,300 feet in elevation—means cooler temperatures than elsewhere on the island, causing grapes to ripen very slowly. The black soil retains the heat of the sun, keeping vines warm during particularly cold nights.

Etna wines, distinguished by their strong minerality, include white, rosé, red, and classic-method sparkling wines. Whites typically use the indigenous grape called carricante (meaning, roughly, "overloaded," for its heavy yield; also known as Etna bianco), which results in high-acidity, savory (not fruity) flavors. The dominant red wine grape is nerello mascalese, yielding a pinot noir-like bouquet that has earned comparisons to Burgundy wines. Nerello cappuccio is a fruity grape used for blending.

Fine Etna wines are expensive by Sicilian standards. Because the rejuvenated Etna winemaking scene is so new, experts are waiting to discover how well these wines will age.

Marsala This world-famous, fortified dessert wine earned the first DOC designation in Italy. Marsala, typically 15 to 20 percent alcohol, is made with native grape varieties (including grillo, inzolia, perricone, calabrese, catarratto, and damaschino).

Outside of Sicily, Marsala is thought of as the rich, sweet dessert wine sold by Florio. But there are many variations. Some are lean and dry, while others are rich and robust. Longer aging (in wood) creates more depth of flavor and increases the price. Marsala comes in three colors: *ambra* (amber), *rubino* (ruby), and *oro* (gold), each of which has its own flavor.

Fine is the cheapest grade of Marsala, typically sold as a cooking wine (sometimes labeled "IP," for Italia Particolare). *Superiore* is aged two years; it's sometimes labeled "SOM" (Superior Old Marsala), "LP" (London Particular), or "GD" (Garibaldi Dolce). *Superiore riserva* is aged four years, *vergine* or *soleras* is aged five years, and *stravecchio* or *vergine riserva* sits in the barrel for a decade. Florio is by far the largest producer, and there are many other small producers worth trying.

The wine is made exclusively in the Marsala area, south of Trapani on the west coast. In 1773, John Woodhouse, a cloth merchant from Liverpool, came to this area and tried a local wine known as *vino perpetuo* ("everlasting wine"). The wine had been aged for decades in wooden barrels in which a fraction of wine was evaporated, and new wine continuously added. Woodhouse grasped the wine's sales potential as a competitor for Portuguese Madeira, which was very popular in England. He shipped 8,000 gallons from Marsala to Liverpool; to keep it from spoiling, he added brandy to the oak casks. When the wine arrived, it had taken on a new flavor, which became instantly successful in England. Later, when Madeira wine became scarce due to the Napoleonic Wars, Woodhouse supplied his wine to the British Navy, which helped strengthen its hold on the British market.

Other Dessert Wines Moscato di Pantelleria and **Passito di Pantelleria** are rich, spicy dessert wines made on the intensely sunny, remote Sicilian island of Pantelleria, which is near Tunisia.

Averna This flavorful *digestivo*—one of Italy's favorites—is a product of Sicily, and best served with a twist of orange or lemon peel.

Sardinia

Sardegna

While Sicily is just a few miles from the Italian mainland (and culturally, more tied to its mainstream), Sardinia is an island in the middle of the Mediterranean—isolated from the rest of Italy and Europe. When Sardinians talk about the rest of Italy, they refer to it as *il continente* ("the continent"). This reality gives Sardinia a strong sense of identity: *I sardi* are reeds to the wind, standing exposed to the elements, tossed about but never broken.

Sardinia is an island of about 9,300 square miles—approximately the size of Vermont or New Hampshire. The closest point on the Italian Peninsula is more than 200 miles away, but the French island of Corsica sits just eight miles to the north. This is, by far, the remotest outpost of "Italy," and it feels only remotely Italian.

Unlike most Mediterranean islands, Sardinia was traditionally not oriented to the sea. Except for the ancient port cities of Cagliari

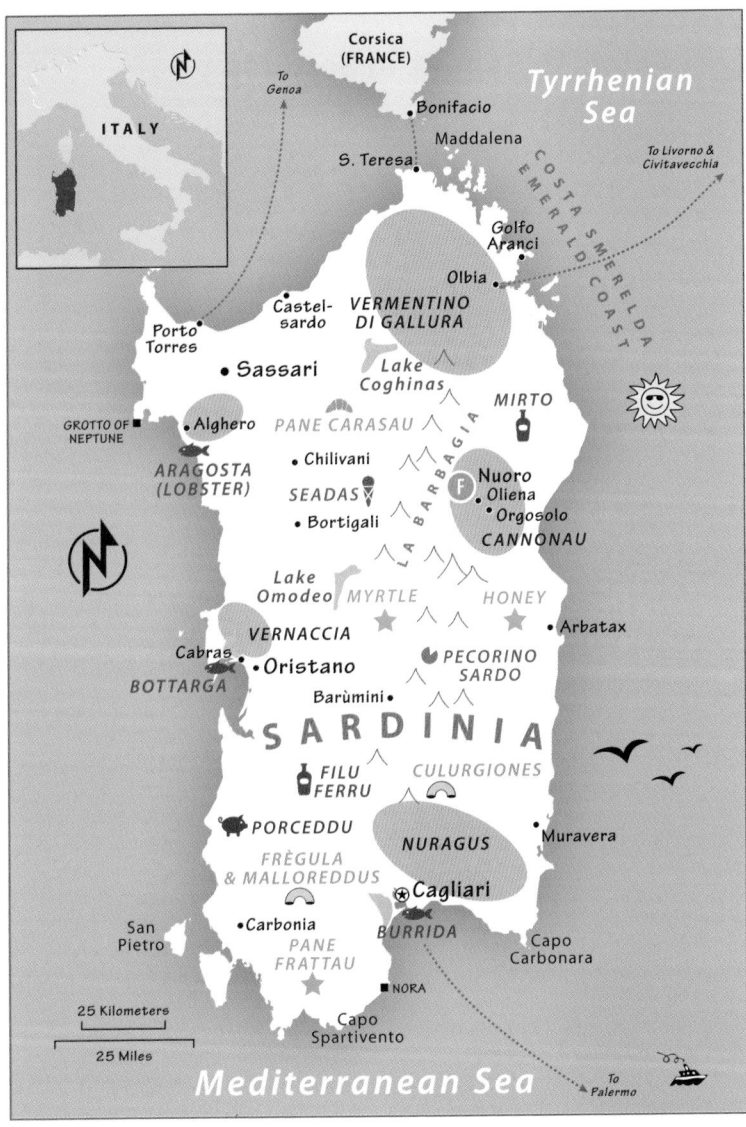

(the region's capital, on the south end) and Alghero (at the northwest corner), very little of the shore was inhabited until the mid-20th century. That's because the coastline was a marshy breeding ground for malaria, which was eradicated only in 1950.

Pirates were another threat that encouraged Sardinians to forge a life in the interior.

Foreigners—from the Phoenicians to the *piemontesi*—occasionally arrived on the coast, but had very little impact. Only the Catalans made

🍴 Foods to Sample in Sardinia

Pecorino
On this island of shepherds, sheep's cheese is at its best; it ranges from soft *ricotta* to hard, aged, and granular grating cheese.

Pane frattau
Simple, delicious dish of thin, crispy shepherd's bread *(pane carasau)* with tomato sauce, grated *pecorino,* and a fried egg.

Culurgiones
Puffy pasta pillows filled with potato purée.

Porceddu
Herb-flavored, slow-roasted suckling pig.

Seadas

Seadas
Deep-fried dessert ravioli filled with tangy, soft *pecorino* and topped with honey.

cultural inroads, arriving in Alghero in 1353 and bringing a new language and culinary influences to that city. People in Alghero speak an antiquated form of Catalan, which is studied today by philologists from the University of Barcelona. The rest of the island speaks Sardinian, a language that evolved directly from Latin. And, of course, almost everyone also speaks Italian.

The hills and mountains of the island's interior are strangely beautiful and very forbidding. A living had to be scratched out of the land, and the cuisine of Sardinia is a direct result of that struggle. Because people lived in tiny communities separated by natural boundaries, there was very little interaction between them—so dialects and recipes, while similar, had marked differences even in nearby areas.

One thing all of Sardinia had in common was that it was a pastoral society. Sheep provided milk, cheese,

wool, meat, and companionship for shepherds who would take their flock out for weeks at a time. The Sardinians baked breads (such as *pane carasau*) that could last a long time, which *il pastore* would supplement with cheese, wine, and whatever fruit or vegetables he might find during his travels. Many of the shepherds played pipes and other musical instruments. The most famous is the *launeddas,* a wind instrument whose origins date back to the 13th century BC.

While the men were away, women in the villages cooked, cleaned, made clothing and handicrafts that had practical applications, raised children, and prayed. Their handmade *(artigianato)* crafts are still made and used today. As they sat in circles and worked, the women also sang plaintive, haunting choral music—another artifact of Sardinian life that still survives.

Among Italians, Sardinians are

thought of as being quite intense and serious, and at times hot-tempered. Men, while courteous, are known to be withdrawn or abrupt in their dealings with strangers. Sardinian women, on the other hand, are famously strong and self-reliant, have a ready smile, and show great warmth and interest to someone new. This is likely because, traditionally, the wives of shepherds or fishermen spent a great deal of time alone, so they developed skills to support themselves emotionally and often financially. Many Sardinian women are shopkeepers, restaurateurs, bartenders, hotel managers, and so on.

In addition to its raw natural beauty, the Sardinian landscape comes with other fascinating elements—especially the *nuraghi,* cylindrical stone structures that date back at least to the early Bronze Age, 1800 BC. Some of these were sites for the veneration of pre-Christian deities; others provided shelter during bad weather.

Sheep still graze in the hills, occasionally taking refuge in the *nuraghi.* In fact, sheep outnumber people on the island about two to one. Throughout much of Italy, you'll find *pecorino* (sheep's cheese)—but here it's particularly outstanding. It comes in many forms, from soft

ricotta to very aged and granular cheese for grating. Most of the best cheese never leaves the island. Sardinia also has outstanding honey.

Since the mid-20th century, the Sardinians have finally made the sea a part of their lives. Fish and seafood have entered the cuisine even beyond those coastal outposts. Alghero is famous all over Italy for its lobster.

The part of Sardinia that has changed the most is the northeastern coast, from Castelsardo to Olbia. Because of its fine beaches, good conditions for scuba diving, and proximity to northern Italy, this area began to be developed in the 1960s and 1970s as a sprawling touristic resort—a sort of Cancún on the Med. Today the so-called Costa Smeralda (Emerald Coast) is very chic…and has very little to do with old Sardinia.

Somehow Sardinia, despite areas of great beauty and an absolutely gorgeous coastline, is not "romantic" in the way that so much of Italy is. But that's true to the story of Sardinia—the natural result of a legacy of insularity and a need to survive in harsh elements. If you'd made it through the last several centuries on an inhospitable (if beautiful) island in the middle of the Mediterranean, you'd be proud, too.

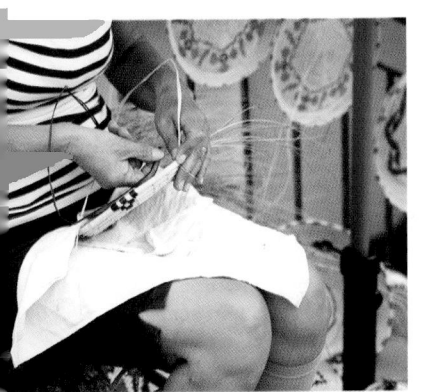

🗺 CITIES, TOWNS, AND PLACES

Cagliari is Sardinia's capital and biggest city, with 155,000 people. It sits near the southern tip of the island. Cagliari is a typical big-city port, with a good array of restaurants and ugly sprawl. Food lovers enjoy strolling the food shops along Via Baylle.

Above: Cagliari; **Below:** Alghero

Alghero, Sardinia's other historic coastal town, is in the northwest. This city of 44,000 was under the rule of Spain (particularly Catalunya) from the 14th century to the mid-18th century, and today's language and cuisine still reflect that influence. Locals use expressions like *más o menos* (Spanish for "more or less") and *bon di* (Catalan for "good day"), and some churches say Mass in *algherese,* the local dialect with heavily Catalan overtones. The town also has lovely beaches that attract day-trippers from the interior and vacationers from the Continent who can't afford the Costa Smeralda. The food here—especially the lobster and paella—is better than in the famous resorts, and the town also has great wine (especially the Aragosta, which goes well with lobster). The surrounding area has spectacular grottoes and rock outcroppings, formed by centuries of winds blowing across the sea from Provence.

Inland from Alghero is **Sassari,**

Left: Sardinian island beach; **Right:** Nuoro

Sardinia's second-biggest city (pop. 128,000). Its pink-and-ochre buildings, leafiness, student population, and grand, palm tree-lined main square (Piazza d'Italia) make it pleasant if you have time to spend in the stark central area of Sardinia.

At the island's northeast corner is the famous beach resort of the **Costa Smeralda** (Emerald Coast), accessed by the airport at Olbia. If you're visiting only for a beach vacation, spending time here could make sense. But you'll find far more satisfying cultural and culinary experiences elsewhere on Sardinia.

Specifically, don't miss the rugged, deeply traditional interior of Sardinia. **Nuoro** (pop. 37,000), Fred's favorite Sardinian town, isn't particularly beautiful. But it embodies so much of what's classically Sardinian: pastoral culture and cuisine, stone *nuraghi,* handicrafts, the rugged beauty of the mountains, and music—local choral groups periodically rehearse the haunting, ancient music of Sardinian shepherds.

The area surrounding Nuoro—called **La Barbagia,** roughly the

eastern half of the Sardinian interior—is a powerful display of nature that has conditioned the people who live there. If you have a car, journey deep into the nearby hills and valleys, and simply take in the winds, the clouds, the forests, the hills, and the rocks; villages worth a stop include Barùmini, Oliena, and Orgosolo.

Bortigali—halfway between Nuoro and the west coast—is a village of 1,300 people that's likeable precisely for its nondescriptness. It's built into a long curve in a hillock so that almost every house has a view of the valley below and the distant mountains. Townspeople like to gather in the tiny triangular piazza and in cafés along the main street. At the fringes of town you see dairy cows—a rarity on this sheep-crazy island; each evening at about 8 p.m., the main street fills with trucks carrying steel cans holding the results of the evening milking. This village—and, really, all of Sardinia—is a place where a 15-year-old shepherd and his flock always have the right of way on the narrow country roads.

🍴 FOODS OF SARDINIA

Outside the major cities and the Costa Smeralda, the selection on many menus is limited. While there are subtle local specialties, most are variations of the themes of bread, lamb, *pecorino* cheese, honey, certain vegetables, wine, and very sweet almond pastries (a legacy of the Moorish presence on the island centuries ago). Saffron *(zafferano)* shows up in several recipes, and herbs—rosemary, juniper, wild thyme—are abundant. Myrtle *(mirto)* is often used to flavor food (meat might be wrapped around a myrtle twig, or steaks and chops might be cooked over a fire made with myrtle wood). No matter what you eat, the food is fresh, flavorful, unpretentious, and served with pride.

ANTIPASTI (STARTERS)

Sardinia doesn't have much tradition for *antipasti*. But you will find something rather rare: **salumi di pecora,** created using many of the same types of curing methods normally applied to pork, but in this case applied to sheep.

PRIMI E PANI (PASTAS AND BREADS)

Culurgiones (or **culurgionis d'Ogliastra**)	Delicate pasta pillows filled with potato puree, *pecorino* cheese, and mint. They're often served with tomato sauce, or sometimes simply with butter and sage.
Frègula	Little toasted balls of semolina dough (like oversized couscous), often served with a seafood and saffron sauce, or with *bottarga* (dried fish roe, described later).
Impanadas	Baked meat-filled pasta; a specialty of Nuoro.
Malloreddus	Small gnocchi with saffron in the dough. They have a little notch along one side, allowing them to pick up a bit more sauce. The name means "little bulls" in an old dialect.

Left: *Pane frattau;* **Right:** *Malloreddus*

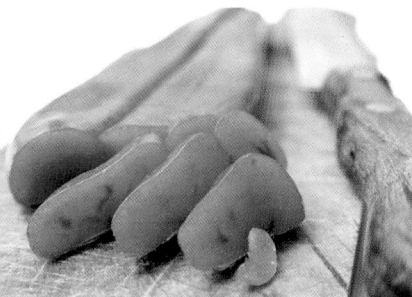

Left: *Bottarga;* **Right:** *Ricci di mare*

Pane carasau (or ***carta da musica***)	This crisp, almost wafer-like bread of the shepherds is a Sardinian classic.
Pane frattau	In this typical dish of the poor, *pane carasau* is soaked in hot water, layered, and topped with tomato sauce, grated *pecorino* cheese, and a fried egg.
Spaghetti all'algherese	With *arselli* (local clams—see below) and green olives, from the town of Alghero.
Zuppa gallurese (or ***suppa cuata***)	A lasagna-like casserole made with bread, meat, cheeses, and broth.

SECONDI (MAIN DISHES)

In lieu of a *contorno,* you may be served ***pinzimonio***—a palate-cleansing combination of chopped raw vegetables.

Aragosta	Lobster, a specialty of Alghero. Mediterranean lobsters are spiny and smaller—with much smaller claws—than the gigantic ones caught in New England. It's often served ***in insalata,*** lobster chunks tossed with lemon juice and olive oil; or ***all'algherese*** (or ***alla catalana***)—boiled and tossed with oil, lemon juice, tomatoes, and onions. When grilled, it's ***alla griglia.*** It can also be turned into a pasta sauce.
Arselle	A local type of clam with a delicate flavor, sometimes called "wedge clam" in English.
Bottarga (or ***butàriga***)	This specialty of Cabras—nicknamed "poor-man's caviar"—is made of the eggs of tuna or gray mullet. They're soaked in salt water, dried, and compressed so that they form a deep orange-colored block. *Bottarga* is used as a condiment with vegetables or blended with butter to flavor breads and pastas. You can also have shavings of *bottarga* topped with lemon juice.

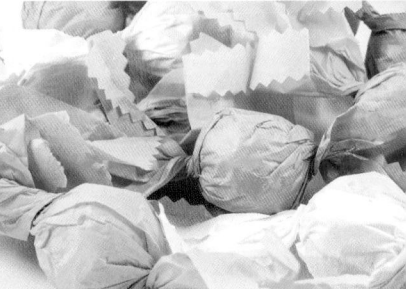

Left: *Pecorino sardo;* **Right:** *Sospiri*

Burrida	A small catfish (called *gattuccio di mare*), or sometimes an eel, is marinated in a sweet-and-sour sauce and then cooked with almonds and/or walnuts, often also with garlic, breadcrumbs, and nutmeg.
Cassola (or **sa cassola**)	Of Catalan origin, this is a stew with many types of fish and seafood (including octopus), tomatoes, onions, *peperoncino rosso,* and garlic.
Cefalo (or **muggine**)	Mullet.
Monzette	Snails, a specialty of the inland city of Sassari.
Pecora in cappotto	Slow-cooked mutton stew, a hardship food from the deep interior.
Porceddu	One of Sardinia's great specialties is spit-roasted suckling pig seasoned with herbs and cooked over a fire with myrtle leaves.
Ricci di mare	Sea urchin is popular in season (winter and early spring), often served with spaghetti.

FORMAGGI (CHEESES)

The sheep's cheese of Sardinia is among the best in Italy. While they're broadly called **pecorino,** each cheese is different. Sardinian *pecorino* can be very soft and creamy when young, but it becomes hard and granular when aged. Much of the *pecorino romano* grated over pasta in Rome actually comes from Sardinia. Other cheeses are made with the milk of a *vacca* or *mucca* (cow), or *capra* (goat).

Pecorino sardo	This excellent, tangy eating cheese is usually aged for two months, but no two are alike (so try as many as possible). Each one has the flavor of the herbs and grasses that the ewe consumed. Many of the best are made in Macomer and elsewhere in the province of Nuoro, although many towns throughout Sardinia boast great cheese.
Fiore sardo	A one-year-old *pecorino sardo* that's often shipped to Liguria for use in pesto.
Ricotta	Delicious soft cheese, which in Sardinia is almost always made of ewe's milk.

DOLCI (SWEETS)

Sardinia is famous for its pastries, which arrive at the end of almost every meal. Many are made with the famous local honey, which can be more bitter than sweet. This combines in interesting ways with other ingredients. The use of honeys, almonds, and other nuts is a legacy of the Arabic presence on the island centuries ago.

Aranciata nuorese (or *aranzata*)	Candied orange peel flavored with honey and tossed with almonds.
Ciccioneddas	Pastry filled with cherry jam, from Sassari province.
Dolci sardi	A bite-sized treat made with marzipan.
Miele	Sardinian honey comes in many flavors, which can be seasonal—based on when certain flowers and plants are in bloom. Honey made with nectar from the *corbezzolo* (strawberry tree), from October to December, tends to have a distinctly bitter taste. Other nectars, which produce more typically sweet honey, include *lavanda* (lavender) and mountain flowers in springtime, *cardo* (thistle) from the end of April through May, *agrumi* (citrus) in May, and eucalyptus in summer.
Pabassine (or *papassine*)	Pastry filled with raisins and almonds, originally eaten on All Saints' Day but now available year-round.
Sapa (or *saba*)	A syrup made with wine must from nuragus grapes. It can be used to flavor baked goods or other foods, or diluted with water and chilled to make a beverage.
Seadas (or *sebadas*)	A ravioli-shaped dessert filled with a tangy, soft sheep's-milk cheese; it's deep-fried and topped with either sweet or bitter honey.
Sospiri	Small, soft rolls filled either with *mirto,* chocolate, or almond paste.
Tilicas (or *tillicas*)	Crown-shaped pastries filled with marzipan.

♀ WINES OF SARDINIA

Traditionally, Sardinian wines were thought of as rough and heavy—like many poor regions of the South, the island produced *vini da taglio* (wines for cutting) that were used to blend with others in France or for making vermouth in Piedmont. But the *piemontesi* have had a strong positive influence on Sardinian winemaking, and the results are better than many visitors expect. Producers such as Sella & Mosca in Alghero have been in business for more than a century, and many newer, smaller producers have raised the quality of Sardinian wine even higher. There are 17 DOC wines in Sardinia, but the two names you should be sure to remember are Cannonau and Vermentino.

Cannonau A medium- to full-bodied red that goes well with roasted meats. It's made of 75 percent cannonau grapes and is blended with others, such as bovale di Spagna, bovale sardo, carignano, pascale di Cagliari, or Monica (and up to 5 percent vernaccia white grape). These other grapes are also made into wines of their own names, as well as blends.

Vermentino This grape, also found in Liguria and Tuscany, makes a delicious white wine to go with seafood. There are two varieties: Vermentino di Gallura (which is more prized) and Vermentino di Sardegna.

Nuragus The most cultivated white grape in Sardinia has a floral bouquet and produces a dry, slightly acidic wine.

Vernaccia di Oristano Vernaccia is a white-wine grape that shares its name with several others in Italy, but this one is not related to the others. It makes an intense, slightly liquor-like dessert wine.

Malvasia, Nasco, and **Moscato** Other grapes used for dessert wines.

Hard Drinks

Filu ferru (or **filu 'e ferru**) This high-powered liqueur (45 percent alcohol) was once contraband because it was made without governmental supervision or taxation. Its name—"iron string"—refers to the steel thread that would stick out of the ground when bottles were buried during periods of prohibition. Nowadays *filu ferru* has gone legit and is commonly served as a *digestivo*.

Limoncello The lemon-infused grappa popular in Campania (and other parts of mainland Italy) is also beloved in Sardinia.

Mirto This very popular after-dinner liqueur, which tastes of myrtle, may be red or white.

PART IV

The Details

100 Favorite Eateries in Italy

Every traveler has their personal favorites—those restaurants that have an ideal combination of good food, a warm welcome, a vibrant atmosphere, and that intangible quality that sticks in your memory long after you've gone home. This chapter collects the 50 favorite restaurants of each of your co-authors. Mind you, this isn't necessarily the 100 "best" restaurants in Italy—simply the ones that populate our happy trip memories, and that we hope may be a part of yours, too.

You may notice that your co-authors each bring a different perspective to dining out in Italy. That's why we've split them up the way we have—50 apiece, Rick's and Fred's.

Rick's choices favor the major destinations where most travelers spend their time. While a few options for high cuisine are mixed in, these are mainly unpretentious, crowd-pleasing favorites where he's enjoyed typical local meals, an engaging owner or waitstaff, and a memorable experience. (Rick's choices are all taken from his guide-books—which include many more suggestions than what's listed here.)

Fred—who has studied and lived in Italy—brings an in-depth mastery of the off-the-beaten-path areas of the country. Partly to complement Rick's listings, and partly to reflect his own preferences, Fred's favorites are a deep dive into parts of Italy that many travelers miss. More adventurous travelers will find these places worth the extra journey to experience a truly special, distinctive, local meal.

These listings include the street address and phone number (as you'd dial it from a mobile or international phone, always starting with Italy's country code: +39), and, where possible, the website. Take advantage of these details to check the current opening times and make a reservation.

In general, if a place is listed in this chapter, **reservations are highly recommended**—and sometimes required. (The only exceptions to this rule are some of the simpler takeout or market-grazing meals. In general, most places rated **$** don't require or accept reservations, though they can get very busy at peak times.) To avoid disappointment, always call ahead if you have your heart set on a particular place—especially one requiring a special journey. Remember, many restaurants in Italy close at least one day per week.

The dollar signs in front of each listing reflect the cost of a typical main course. Splurge items (steak, seafood) add to the price.

$$$$ Splurge—Most main courses over €20

$$$ Pricier—€15-20

$$ Moderate—€10-15

$ Budget—Under €10

Each group of favorites is listed by region, in the order the regions are described in this book—roughly from the North to the South. And there's also a list of our favorite gelato places, both Rick's and Fred's.

Buon appetito!

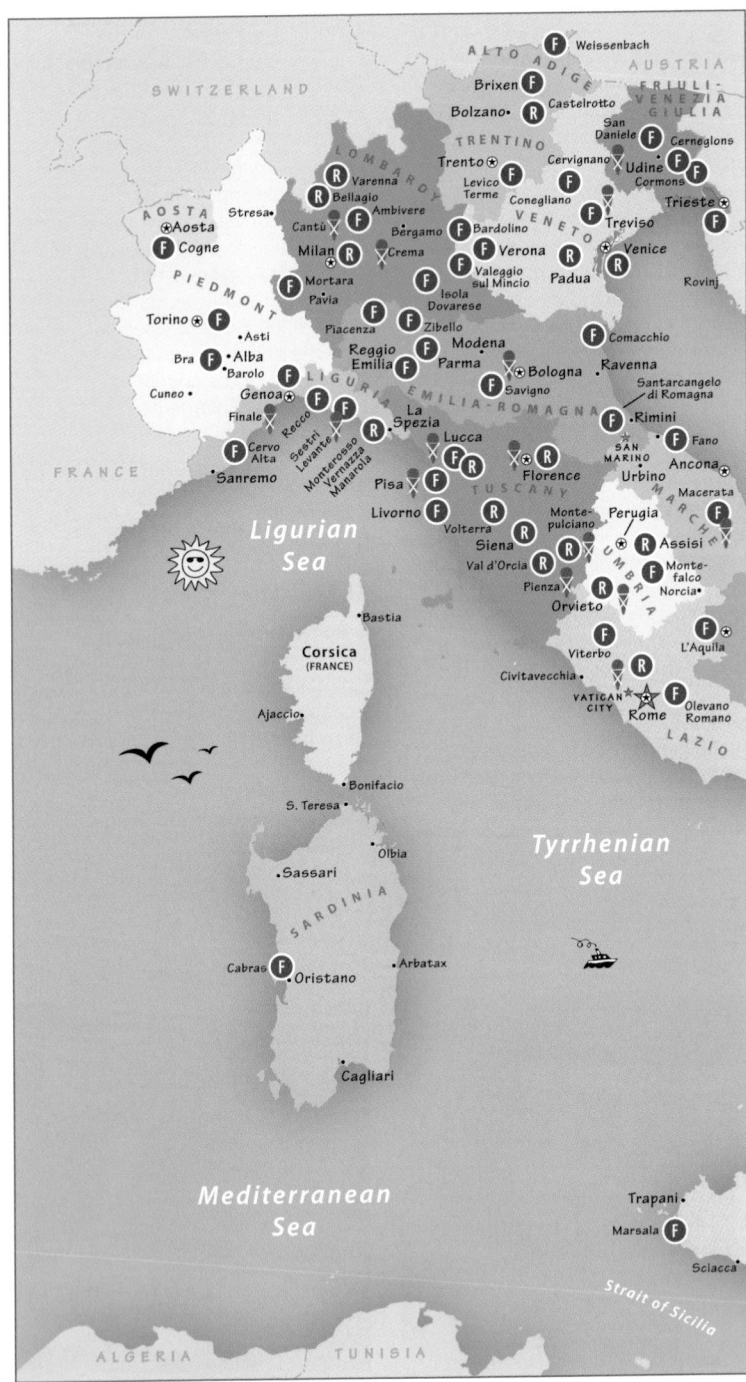

Weissenbach

Brixen

Bolzano · Castelrotto

ALTO ADIGE

AUSTRIA

FRIULI-
VENEZIA
GIULIA

SWITZERLAND

San
Daniele

Cerneglons

Cervignano · Udine
Cormons

Trento

TRENTINO

Coneglianno

Levico
Terme

Trieste

AOSTA

Varenna

Stresa

Bellagio

LOMBARDY

Ambivere

Treviso

VENETO

Aosta

Cantù

Bergamo · Bardolino

Venice

Cogne

Milan

Crema

Verona

PIEDMONT

Mortara

Pavia

Valeggio
sul Mincio

Padua

Rovinj

Isola
Dovarese

Torino

Asti

Piacenza

Zibello

Comacchio

Bra

Alba

Reggio
Emilia

Modena

Bologna

Ravenna

Barolo

Parma

Cuneo

Genoa

LIGURIA

EMILIA-ROMAGNA

Savigno

Santarcangelo
di Romagna

Finale

Recco

La
Spezia

Lucca

Rimini

Fano

Cervo
Alta

Sestri
Levante

Florence

SAN
MARINO

Ancona

Sanremo

Montarosso
Vernazza
Manarola

Pisa

Urbino

MARCHE

Livorno

Volterra

TUSCANY

Siena

Macerata

Montepulciano

Perugia

Assisi

Val d'Orcia

UMBRIA

Monte-
falco

Pienza

Norcia

Ligurian
Sea

Orvieto

Viterbo

L'Aquila

Bastia

Civitavecchia

VATICAN
CITY

Rome

LAZIO

Olevano
Romano

Corsica
(FRANCE)

FRANCE

Ajaccio

Bonifacio

S. Teresa

Tyrrhenian
Sea

Olbia

Sassari

SARDINIA

Cabras

Oristano

Arbatax

Mediterranean
Sea

Trapani

Marsala

Cagliari

Sciacca

Strait of Sicily

ALGERIA

TUNISIA

100 FAVORITE EATERIES IN ITALY

LEGEND

- **F** Fred's Favorite
- **R** Rick's Favorite
- Favorite *Gelaterie*
- ⊛ Regional Capitals
- ★ National Capitals
- • Other Cities

50 Kilometers

50 Miles

HUNGARY

ROMANIA

SLOVENIA

CROATIA

VOJVODINA

SERBIA

CROATIA

BOSNIA – HERZEGOVINA

MONTE- NEGRO

KOSOVO

Adriatic Sea

NORTH MACE- DONIA

ALBANIA

GREECE

Pescara

ABRUZZO

Sulmona

Termoli

Peschici

Larino

Vieste

Agnone

MOLISE

Campobasso

Foggia

PUGLIA

Bari

Martina Franca

CAMPANIA

Naples

Potenza

Matera

Alberobello

Ceglie Messapica

Brindisi

Lecce

Salerno

BASILICATA

Sorrento

Poscano

Amalfi

Paestum

Taranto

Maretea

Gulf of Taranto

CALABRIA

Ionian Sea

Crotone

Catanzaro

Tropea

Messina

Randazzo

Reggio Calabria

Palermo

Cefalù

Taormina

Castelbuono

SICILY

Enna

Catania

Agrigento

Siracusa

Ragusa

Noto

Modica

Mediterranean Sea

🔍 RICK'S 50 FAVORITES

Lombardy

MILAN

$$$ Trattoria Milanese, family-run and passionately Milanese, is on a back street. It has an enthusiastic clientele and a classic energy, with a curt and professional waitstaff. Expect an old-fashioned *milanese* ambience; eat early to avoid crowds (Via Santa Marta 11, behind the Pinacoteca Ambrosiana, +39 02 8645 1991).

$$$ Enoteca Boccondivino is a fun-loving place with no menu. You enjoy six courses for a fixed price, each paired with a different wine. A constant parade of food carts rolls through the happy dining room, keeping everyone entertained and happily fed. Fabrizio is the master of ceremonies, making sure English speakers understand what's being served: lots of quality meats and cheeses, pâté, pasta, and a token vegetable course—all "designed to maximize your cholesterol." You may share a bigger table; it's yours for the evening. The name is a play on words: It means both "divine mouthful" and "mouthful of wine" (Via Carducci 17, +39 02 866 040, www. boccondivino.com).

VARENNA (Lake Como)

$$$$ Ristorante la Vista feels like a private hotel restaurant (at Albergo Milano) but also welcomes nonguests. On a balmy evening, its terrace overlooking the town and the lake is hard to beat. Egidio (or Egi—pronounced "edgy") and his staff give traditional cuisine a creative twist, and his selection is great for food lovers with discerning tastes. While you can order à la carte, I'd go with the three-course *menù* (Via XX Settembre 35, +39 0341 830 298, www.varenna.net).

$$$ Ristorante il Caminetto is a homey, backwoods mountain trattoria in Gittana, a tiny town in the hills above Varenna. Getting there entails a curvy 10-minute drive (they'll pick you up for free at the ferry dock or the parking garage and bring you home after dinner). Moreno and Rossella take pride in their specialties, including grilled meats and *risotto* with porcini mushrooms and berries. They serve 22 diners a night…and that's it. Plan on the three-course, fixed-price *menù* and spending the evening—you won't regret it (Viale Progresso 4, +39 0341 815 127, mobile +39 347 331 2238, www.ilcaminettoonline. com). They also offer cooking classes during the day.

BELLAGIO (Lake Como)
$$$$ Alle Darsene di Loppia, the kind of place you'd expect jet-setters to dress up for, is a romantic gourmet restaurant serving Mediterranean cuisine. Consider their seared scallops and their tasting *menù.* It's a 15-minute walk south of town (through the exquisite Villa Melzi Gardens—worth paying admission to enter if dining here, as it lets you avoid the walk along the street). While seating indoors is OK, dining out on a historic little harbor under their *pergolato* is more memorable (on the far side of the Villa Melzi Gardens at Via Melzi D'Eril in Loppia, +39 031 952 069, www.ristorante darsenediloppia.com).

Trentino-Alto Adige

CASTELROTTO/KASTELRUTH (Bolzano Province)
$$$ Hotel zum Turm tries hard to up the culinary bar in this little town, focusing on locally sourced ingredients and serving good, meaty Alto Adige fare—including venison—and inventive vegetarian options. You can sit in the humdrum breakfast room, the cozy and very traditional *Stube,* or out on the oasis of a back terrace. The service is a bit Germanic (read: formal) but still welcoming (Viale Kofel 8, +39 0471 706 349, www.zumturm.com).

Veneto

VENICE
$ Rialto Market *Cicchetti* Crawl: The 100-yard-long stretch starting two blocks inland from the Rialto Market (along Sotoportego dei Do Mori and Calle de le Do Spade) is beloved among Venetian *cicchetti* enthusiasts for its delightful bar munchies, good wine by the glass, and fun stand-up conviviality. Before embarking, read the *cicchetti* information on page 183. Four places serve food all day, but the spread is best at around noon. At each one, look for the list of snacks and wine by the glass at the bar or on the wall. **Bar all'Arco,** a bustling one-room joint, is good for all-around *cicchetti* (San Polo 436). **Cantina Do Mori** serves a forest of little edibles on toothpicks and *francobolli* (a spicy selection of 20 tiny, mayo-soaked sandwiches nicknamed "stamps"). Go here to be abused in a fine atmosphere—the frowns are part of the shtick. It can be shoulder-to-shoulder crowded, and prices add up quickly (San Polo 430). **Osteria ai Storti** is more of a sit-down place (tables inside and on the street). It's run by Alessandro, who enjoys helping educate travelers (around the corner from Cantina Do Mori on Calle San Matio, San Polo 819). And **Cantina Do Spade** is run by Francesco, who clearly lists the *cicchetti* (mostly deep-fried) and wines of the day (30 yards down Calle de le Do Spade from Osteria ai Storti at San Polo 860, tel. +39 041 521 0583). When you're ready for dessert, try dipping a Burano biscuit in a glass of strawberry-flavored *fragolino* or another sweet dessert wine.

$$$$ Osteria alle Testiere is my top dining splurge in Venice. Hugely respected, Luca and his staff are dedicated to quality, serving up creative, artfully presented, market-fresh seafood (there's no meat on the menu), homemade pastas, and fine wine in what the chef calls a "Venetian Nouvelle" style. With only 22 seats, it's tight and homey, with a focus on food and service. They have daily specials, 10 wines by the glass, and one agenda: a great dining experience. This is a good spot to let loose and trust your host. They're open for lunch, and reservations are a must for their two dinner seatings (on Calle del Mondo Novo, just off Campo Santa Maria Formosa, Castello 5801, +39 041 522 7220, www.osterialletestiere.it).

$$$ Trattoria da Bepi, bright and alpine-paneled, feels like a classic, where Loris carries on his mother's passion for good, traditional Venetian cuisine. Ask for the seasonal specialties: The seafood *antipasti* plate and crab dishes are excellent. There's good seating inside and out. If you trust Loris, you'll walk away with a wonderful dining memory (half a block off Campo Santi Apostoli on Salizada Pistor,

Cannaregio 4550, +39 041 528 5031, www.dabepi.it).

$ Enoteca Cantine del Vino Già Schiavi, with a wonderfully characteristic *cicchetti*-bar ambience, is much loved for its inexpensive *cicchetti,* sandwiches (order from list on board), and wine. You're welcome to enjoy your wine and finger food at the bar (in the back room surrounded by wine bottles) or out on the sidewalk (specify *fuori* to sit outside and they'll provide plastic cups; please don't sit on the bridge). This is primarily a wine shop with great prices for bottles to go (100 yards from Accademia art museum on San Trovaso canal; facing the Accademia, take a right and then a forced left at the canal to the second bridge—it's at Dorsoduro 992, +39 041 523 0034, www.cantinaschiavi.com).

$$$$ Trattoria Antiche Carampane is a dressy, family-run place with an open kitchen and a local following. They have a passion for fish (and make a point: no pizza) and serve traditional Venetian dishes with a fresh twist that change with the season. It's small—just 30 seats, with six tables on the street (Rio Terà delle Carampane, San Polo 1911, +39 041 524 0165, www.antichecarampane. com, Francesco).

PADUA
$$ Osteria L'Anfora is a colorful if chaotic place serving classic dishes in an informal, fun-loving space. Don't be put off by the woody, ruffian decor, the squat toilet, and the fact that it's a popular hangout for a pre-meal drink. They take food seriously and serve it at good prices, and the fun energy and commotion add to the dining experience (Via dei Soncin 13, +39 049 656 629).

$ Padua's Market: Padua has one of Italy's most appealing markets, sprawling through Piazza delle Erbe and Piazza della Frutta each morning and all day Saturday. Exploring and grazing here is one of my favorite do-it-yourself meals in Veneto. As you wander, appreciate the local passion for good food: Residents can tell the month by the seasonal selections, and merchants share recipe tips with shoppers. Don't miss the indoor market zone on the ground floor of the Palazzo della Ragione. Wandering through this H-shaped arcade—where you'll find various butchers, *salumerie,* cheese shops, bakeries, and fishmongers at work—is a sensuous experience. Students gather in the squares after the markets have closed, spilling out of colorful bars and cafés, drinks in hand. Bars and food stalls offer plenty of refreshments and fun food; enjoy the Bar dei Osei sandwich stand, and the neighboring place selling squid.

Liguria

MONTEROSSO (Cinque Terre)

$$$$ Miky is packed with a well-dressed clientele who know their seafood. For elegantly presented, top-quality food that celebrates local ingredients and traditions,

it's worth the steep prices. It's a proud family operation—Miky (dad), Simonetta (mom), charming Sara (daughter, who greets guests), and the attentive waitstaff all work hard. Their "pizza pasta" is served in a bowl topped with a thin pizza crust dome to contain the flavor, then flambéed at your table. Many of the wines on their fine list are available by the glass if you ask. Their mixed dessert sampler plate, *dolce misto,* serves two and is a fitting capper (in the new town 100 yards from train station at Via Fegina 104, +39 0187 817 608, www.ristorantemiky.it).

$$ Ristorante Belvedere, big and sprawling, serves good-value meals indoors or outdoors on the harborfront. Their huge *anfora belvedere*—mixed seafood stew dumped dramatically at the table from a pottery amphora into your bowl—can easily be split among up to four diners. Their *misto mare* plate, a fishy treat, nearly makes an entire meal (2-person minimum). Mussel fans will enjoy the *tagliolini della casa.* The place is energetically run by Federico and Roberto (on the harbor in the old town at Piazza Garibaldi 38, +39 0187 817 033, www.ristorante-belvedere.it).

VERNAZZA (Cinque Terre)

$$$$ Ristorante Belforte serves a fine blend of traditional and creative cuisine, fishy *spaghetti alla Bruno, trofie al pesto* (hand-rolled noodles with pesto), and classic *antipasto misto di pesce*—an assortment of fish (2-person minimum). From the breakwater, a rope leads up to a web of tables embedded in four levels of the old castle. While their indoor seating is great, for the ultimate seaside perch, reserve a table on the *terrazza con vista* (view terrace) or request the "lovers' table" on its own little terrace. Most of Belforte's seating is outdoors—if the weather's bad, the interior can get crowded. Late in the evening, Andrea cranks up the fun (+39 0187 812 222, www.ristorantebelforte.it, Michela).

$ Il Pirata delle Cinque Terre,

located in the workaday zone at the parking lot at the top of town, is playful, efficient, comfortable, and serves tasty breakfast bruschetta, frittatas, and an array of fresh pastries, as well as lunches and dinners aimed squarely at American tourists' taste buds. The fun service of the dynamic duo Gianluca and Massimo (hardworking Sicilian twins, a.k.a. the Cannoli brothers) makes up for the lack of a view. They pride themselves on not serving bacon and eggs, since "this is Italy." While the atmosphere feels more like suburban Milan, this place exerts a strange and insistent charisma over its American clientele (Via Gavino 36, +39 0187 812 047).

MANAROLA (Cinque Terre)
$$$ Trattoria dal Billy, the best restaurant in town, is in the residential zone high above the touristy action. Many find it's worth the climb for Edoardo and chef Enrico's homemade black pasta with seafood and squid ink, green pasta with artichokes, and homemade desserts. Their antipasto misto di mare comes with a dazzling array of seafood treats—each one perfectly executed. Billy's outdoor terraces offer commanding views over Manarola, while across the street an elegant, glassy dining room is carved into the rock. Either setting is perfect for a romantic candlelight meal (Via Aldo Rollandi 122, +39 0187 920 628, www.trattoriabilly.com).

Tuscany

FLORENCE
$ Casa del Vino, Florence's oldest operating wine shop, has a crowded little bar offering an unforgettable stand-up lunch experience with a selection of wine by the glass from 25 different bottles (notice the prices chalked onto each bottle). Owner Gianni, whose family has owned the Casa for more than 70 years, is a class act. The sandwiches, crostini, and "Tuscany appetizer plate" of meat and cheese are perfect. During busy times, it's a mob scene—you'll munch and sip standing outside with workers on a quick lunch break. But if you come early or late, you can actually connect with Gianni (Via dell'Ariento 16 red, +39 055 215 609, www.casadelvino.it).

$ I Fratellini is a hole-in-the-wall, stand-up joint where the "little brothers" have served peasants more than 30 kinds of sandwiches and a fine selection of wine at great prices (see list on wall) since 1875. Join the local crowd to order, then sit on a nearby curb to eat, placing your glass on the wall rack before you leave. Be adventurous with the menu (order by number). Consider the sandwiches with finocchiona e caprino (a Tuscan salame and soft goat cheese), lardo di Colonnata (cured lard aged in Carrara marble), or cinghiale (spicy boar salame). It's worth ordering the most expensive wine they're selling by the glass (20 yards in front of Orsanmichele Church on Via dei Cimatori, +39 055 239 6096).

$$$ Antica Trattoria da Tito, a 10-minute hike from the Accademia along Via San Gallo, is great for a memorable meal with a local crowd and smart-aleck service. The boss, Bobo, theatrically serves quality traditional food and lots of wine. The food is good, and there's no pretense—it's a noisy playground of Tuscan cuisine. To gorge on a feast of *antipasti* (*salumi,* cheeses, a few veggies, and *bruschetta*), consider ordering *fermami* ("stop me")—for a set price, Bobo brings you food until you say, *"Fermami!"* Dinner is served in two seatings; the earlier one is a bit saner (Via San Gallo 112 red, +39 055 472 475, www.trattoriadatito.it).

$$ Trattoria Casalinga, an inexpensive standby, comes with bustling aproned waiters. Florentines (who enjoy the tripe and tongue) and tourists (who opt for *ribollita* soup and easier-to-swallow Tuscan favorites) both pack the place and leave full and happy (just off Piazza di Santo Spirito, near the church at Via de' Michelozzi 9 red, +39 055 218 624, www.trattorialacasalinga.it, Andrea and Paolo).

$ Trattoria Sabatino, across the river in untouristy Oltrarno, is a spacious, brightly lit mess hall. It's changed little since it opened in 1956. It's disturbingly cheap, with family character and a simple menu—a super place to watch locals munch, especially since you'll likely be sharing a table. Little English is spoken here, and that's a good thing (a 15-minute walk from Ponte Vecchio, just outside Porta San Frediano, Via Pisana 2 red, +39 055 225 955, www.trattoriasabatino.it).

LUCCA
$$$ Osteria dal Manzo is a classy restaurant run by classy Antonio, with an elegantly simple dining room and elegantly simple, seasonal cuisine. The menu is easy and enticing: five items for each of three courses—always two meat, two fish, and one vegetarian (Via Cesare Battisti 28, +39 0583 490 649, https://osteria-dal-manzo.business.site).

SIENA
$$ Osteria la Sosta di Violante, beyond the tourist zone, is a good value. You'll share this dreamy little spot with savvy locals. For 20 years, chefs Duccio and Enrico have offered gourmet food with no pretense—they make sure diners feel right at home. Order with a sense of adventure. They have great indoor and outdoor seating (walk down Via Banchi di Sotto to Via Pantaneto 115, +39 0577 43774, www.lasostadiviolante.it).

$$ Trattoria Papei is a sprawling place with festive outdoor seating under a big tent and a high-energy interior. It has a casual, rollicking family atmosphere and friendly servers dishing out generous portions of rib-stickin' Tuscan specialties and grilled meats (on the market square behind City Hall at Piazza del Mercato 6, +39 0577 280 894, https://anticatrattoriapapei.com, Amedeo and Eduardo).

$$$$ Osteria le Logge caters to a fancy crowd and offers pricey Tuscan favorites with a gourmet twist, made with seasonal local ingredients. Inside you'll enjoy a gorgeous living-room setting (books, wood, and wine bottles), and outside there's fine seating on a pedestrian street. I find dining inside on the ground floor most romantic (two blocks off Il Campo at Via del Porrione 33, +39 0577 48013, www. osterialelogge.it, Mirko).

$ Osteria il Grattacielo is a funky hole-in-the-wall with a tight and homey interior and three tables under a tunnel-like arch outside. It's perfect for a cheap, hearty, memorable yet no-frills meal. Luca, who's clearly found his niche in life, has no menu and just one solid house wine. You'll eat what he's cooking. Lunch is a mixed plate from the bar (be bold and point) or pasta (includes wine). Dinner is three courses—*antipasto* bar, pasta, and a *secondo*—for one fixed price; cap off your meal with a Vin Santo and cookies (Via dei Pontani 8, mobile +39 331 742 2835).

MONTEPULCIANO (Siena Province)
$$$ Osteria dell'Acquacheta,
beloved among locals for its beef steaks, is a carnivore's dream come true. Its long, narrow room is jammed with shared tables and tight, family-style seating, with an open fire in back and a big hunk of red beef lying on the counter like a corpse on a

gurney. Giulio and his wife, Chiara, run a fun-loving but tight ship—posing with slabs of red meat yet embracing decades of *trattoria* tradition (you'll get one glass to use alternately for wine and water). Steaks are sold by weight, and two diners typically share a 1.6-kilo steak (that's 3.5 pounds; the smallest they'll cook is 1.2 kilos). They also serve hearty pastas and salads and a fine house wine (Via del Teatro 22, +39 0578 717 086, www.acquacheta.eu).

ROCCIA D'ORCIA
(Val d'Orcia, Siena Province)
$$ La Cisterna nel Borgo is a rustic choice that's worth some effort to reach. Marta and Fede serve up simple yet beautifully prepared dishes that mingle big Tuscan flavors and exotic flourishes gathered from Marta's travels. The cavelike interior has character, but try to get an outdoor table, facing the namesake cistern on an enchanting, ivy-draped piazza where old ladies chat and stray dogs and cats beg for scraps (Borgo Mestro 37, +39 0577 887 280, www.cisternanelborgo.com). Dining here comes with a hike: Park at the lot below Rocca di Tentennano, huff up past the castle entrance, then keep going as the road crests the hill and twists downhill into the village.

CASTELMUZIO
(Val d'Orcia, Siena Province)
$$$ La Moscadella, just outside the village of Castelmuzio, a 10-minute drive from Pienza, is a gorgeous country hotel filling a historic monastery with guest rooms and an excellent restaurant. A limited number of tables are available to nonguests who book ahead. Chef Giancarlo's meals are top-notch: classic Tuscan recipes, occasionally with a modern spin, always delicious. You can dine either in the rustic-yet-elegant,

daughters Sara and Ilaria) invited you over for a dinner of classic Tuscan comfort food that's rarely seen on restaurant menus. They serve only two pastas and two *secondi* on any given day (listed on the chalkboard by the door), in addition to quality cheese and *salumi* plates. Committed to tradition, on Fridays they serve only fish. They also have fun, family-friendly outdoor seating on a traffic-free piazza (Piazza XX Settembre 4, +39 0588 86239, https://lacarabacciavolterra.it).

glassed-in veranda, or out on the pebbly terrace, both with views of Tuscan splendor. On occasion, owner Isabella combines dinner with a related activity—for example, a truffle hunt through the woods followed by a truffle dinner, or an olive oil tasting session combined with a meal of olive oil pairings (+39 0577 665 516, www.theisabellaexperience.com).

VOLTERRA (Pisa Province)
$$$$ Ristorante Enoteca del Duca, serving well-presented and creative Tuscan cuisine, offers the best elegant meal in town. You can dine under a medieval arch with walls lined with wine bottles, in a sedate, high-ceilinged dining room (with an Etruscan statuette at each table), in their little *enoteca* (wine cellar), or in their terraced garden in summer. Chef Genuino, daughter Claudia, and the friendly staff take good care of diners. The fine wine list includes Genuino's own highly regarded merlot and sangiovese. The spacious seating, dressy clientele, and calm atmosphere make this a good choice for a romantic splurge (near City Hall at Via di Castello 2, +39 0588 81510, www.enoteca-delduca-ristorante.it).

$$ La Carabaccia is unique: It feels like a local family (Patrizia and

Umbria

NEAR ASSISI (Perugia Province)
$$$$ Le Mandrie di San Paolo, in a 1,000-year-old farmhouse a 10-minute drive outside Assisi, makes many of its own ingredients and serves an exquisite dinner to guests and nonguests alike. This is a good example of a "zero-kilometer meal"—all the ingredients are sourced on the property (+39 075 806 40 70, www.agriturismomandriesanpaolo.it). It's about a 10-minute drive from Assisi, above the village of Viole (a.k.a. San Vitale). Just head southeast of Assisi following signs for *Viole;* when you enter town, turn left before you reach the arch and follow signs up the hill.

ORVIETO (Terni Province)
$$$ Trattoria la Palomba features excellent game and truffle specialties in a wood-paneled dining room. Giampiero, Enrica, and the Cinti family enthusiastically take care of their diners, offering a fine value, high quality, and classy conviviality. Truffles are shaved right at your table—try the *umbricelli al tartufo* (homemade pasta with truffles) or *spaghetti dell'Ascaro* (with truffles). Their *filetto alla cardinale* and mixed-cheese plates are popular. As Slow Food proponents, they use organic

Rick and Fred's Favorite *Gelaterie*

LOMBARDY

Milan: A classic from 1937, **Antica Gelateria Sartori** features old-school flavors with no gimmicks, plus the less traditional but delicious *pompelmo* (grapefruit). It's tricky to find, tucked at the far rear of the east side of the Stazione Centrale (closed in winter, Piazza Luigi di Savoia, near Via Pergolesi).

Crema (Cremona): **Bandirali,** as you might expect in a town called Crema, makes its gelato with exquisite local milk, eggs, and well-chosen flavorings. Be sure to try the *torrone*—nougat (Via Piacenza 93).

Cantù (Como): **Nonna Papera**'s offerings range from straightforward gelato made of local ingredients (such as superb raspberries) to unusual combinations—try the *ricotta,* honey, and walnuts (Via Borgognone 38).

FRIULI-VENEZIA GIULIA

Cervignano (Udine): **Gran Gelato** is an inviting shop with classics and unusual flavors (pomegranate, pine nut), delicious *cannoli*, and ice-cream cakes (Via Udine 47).

LIGURIA

Finale Ligure (Savona): **Bar Centrale** offers irresistible gelato in a beach town between Genoa and Sanremo (Via Torcelli 28).

Sestri Levante (Genoa): **100% Naturale,** as you might guess, features organic ingredients and gelato that's very flavor-forward—whether nuts, herbs, olive oil, divine fruits, or even some vegetables (Via XXV Aprile 126).

EMILIA-ROMAGNA

Bologna: Gelateria delle Moline is outstanding for its cream-based flavors such as hazelnut, pistachio, rum raisin, *stracciatella,* and eggy *crema* (Via delle Moline 13B).

TUSCANY

Florence: Edoardo features organic ingredients and tasty handmade cones (facing the southwest corner of the Duomo at Piazza del Duomo 45 red). **Perchè No!** ("Why not!") feels touristy but serves one of the widest range of flavors around, and the quality's top-notch (just off the busy main drag, Via de' Calzaiuoli, at Via dei Tavolini 19).

Pisa and **Lucca: De' Coltelli,** with locations both in Pisa (at Lungarno Antonio Pacinotti 23) and in Lucca (Via San Paolino 10), scoops up organic, artisanal, Sicilian-style gelato with unusual and vibrant flavors, and also has a fine selection of *granite.*

Pienza and **Montepulciano** (Siena): Nicola Sgarbi operates *gelaterie* in two of Tuscany's prettiest hill towns: **Buon Gusto** in Pienza (Via delle Case Nuove 26) and **Sgarbi Gelato Natura** in Montepuliciano (Corso 50). Nicola makes his gelato fresh every morning, using locally sourced ingredients from producers he knows personally, and he experiments with some creative flavors (such as carrot-ginger or creamy basil). The gelato is ready around midday...and when it's gone, it's gone.

UMBRIA

Orvieto: A great choice is **Pasqualetti,** with a handy location right next to Orvieto's stunning cathedral (likely closed in winter, Piazza del Duomo 14) and another nearby, steps off the main drag (Via del Duomo 10). They also have a branch in Bagnoregio, which you'll pass on your way to Civita (summer only, Corso G. Mazzini 30/32).

MARCHE

Civitanova Marche (Macerata): **Basium** features excellent ingredients, innovative flavor combinations, and a seriousness of approach that all result in excellent *gelati* (Viale Matteotti 14).

LAZIO

Rome: This city has many excellent options. Near the Pantheon, **Gelateria Artigianale Corona** feels like a time warp and is nothing fancy, but it has some of the finest homemade gelato in town (just south of Largo Argentina at Largo Arenula 27). Nearby is another classic, **Giolitti,** which has been in the same family since 1890. The *visciole* (local cherry) pairs nicely with *pompelmo rosa* (pink grapefruit), or try *gianduia* (chocolate-hazelnut paste) and pear (Via degli Uffici del Vicario 40).

For something less venerable, with a fresher approach, **Fatamorgana** features creative flavor combinations; portions are small but good-quality (in the Monti district at Piazza degli Zingari 5). **La Gourmandise,** in Trastevere, is quite formal but with very high standards. In addition to traditional *gelati,* they also have lactose-free versions plus goat's-milk gelato. Or you can just have perfect whipped cream (Via Felice Cavalotti 36B). And **Gracchi,** with multiple branches, is ideal for cooling your mouth while cooling your feet after long hours of touring Rome (Via dei Gracchi 272, Via di Ripetta 261, and Viale Regina Margherita 212).

CAMPANIA

Naples: Revered chocolate producer **Gay-Odin** also has great gelato based on variations in the key of chocolate. Don't miss the *foresta,* which pairs well with *ricotta*/pear (shops at Vico Vetriera 12, Via Benedetto Croce 61, Via Toledo 427, and Via Carducci 29).

Sorrento: Near the train station, **Gelateria David** has many repeat customers (they make 155 flavors, but have about 30 at any one time). In 1957, Augusto Davide opened a *gelateria* in Sorrento, and his grandson Mario proudly carries on the tradition today, still making the gelato on-site. Before choosing a flavor, sample *profumi di Sorrento* (an explosive sorbet of mixed fruits), "Sorrento moon" (white almond with lemon zest), or lemon crème (a block below the train station at Via Marziale 19; don't mistake this place for the similarly named Gelateria Davide, in the town center).

Amalfi: Andrea Pansa, known for its chocolate making, is also a destination for coffee, pastries, and delicious gelato and sorbet. Their chocolate gelato is terrific, but don't overlook things made with local lemons (Via Lorenzo d'Amalfi 9).

PUGLIA

Peschici (Foggia): **Pina Gel** prepares *gelati* with care and pride. Look for flavors made with local Gargano fruit such as wild blackberries, cherries, and oranges combined with ginger (Corso Umberto I).

SICILY

Palermo: Bar Lucchese, one long and characteristic block from the Vucciria Market, is a classic old café with a fine selection of gelato and *granita* (Piazza San Domenico 11).

Noto (Siracusa): This town is known for its top-quality gelato—and **Caffè Sicilia** is the gold standard bearer (Corso Vittorio Emanuele 125).

and locally sourced ingredients (off Piazza della Repubblica at Via Cipriano Manente 16, +39 0763 343 395).

Lazio

ROME

$$ Enoteca L'Angolo Divino is an inviting little wine bar run by Massimo Crippa, a sommelier who beautifully describes a fine array of wines along with the best accompanying *salumi,* cheeses, and pastas. With tiny tables, a tiny menu, great wines by the glass, intriguing walls of wine bottles, smart advice, more locals than tourists, and a smooth jazz vibe, this place can leave you with a lifelong memory (a block off Campo de' Fiori at Via dei Balestrari 12, +39 06 686 4413, www.angolodivino.it).

$ Testaccio Market abounds with colorful produce, fragrant meat and fish stalls, and stands dishing up tempting meals. At Mordi & Vai (#15), Sergio makes tasty sandwiches; try the *trippa* (tripe), *con allesso* (boiled beef dipped in broth), or *picchiapò* (stewed beef in a mildly spicy tomato sauce). Or survey the many nearby options, from pizza slices to pasta to creative pastries. In the center of the covered market are a lively café, public seating under a skylight, and a stretch of ancient Roman road littered with shards of broken amphorae (just south of central Rome near Piramide Metro stop).

$$ Enoteca Corsi, a wine shop that grew into a thriving restaurant, is a charming local scene with the family table in back, where the kids do their homework. The Paiella family serves straightforward, traditional cuisine to an appreciative crowd of office workers. The board lists daily specials (gnocchi on Thursday, fish on Friday, and so on). Friendly Manuela and her staff offer fine wine at a third of the price you'd pay in normal restaurants—buy from their shop and pay a corking fee (a block toward the Pantheon from the Gesù Church at Via del Gesù 87, +39 06 679 0821, www.enotecacorsi.com).

$ Filetti di Baccalà is a cheap and basic Roman classic, where nostalgic regulars cram in at wooden tables and savor fried cod finger-food fillets and slightly bitter *puntarelle* greens (slathered with anchovy sauce, available in spring and winter). Study what others are eating, and order from your grease-stained server by pointing at what you want. Sit in the fluorescently lit interior or try to grab a seat out on the little square, a quiet haven a block east of Campo de' Fiori. If you're not into greasy spoons, avoid this place (Largo dei Librari 88, +39 06 686 4018).

$$$$ Ristorante il Gabriello is inviting and small—modern under medieval arches—and provides a peaceful and local-feeling respite from all the top-end fashion shops in the area. Claudio serves with charisma, while his brother Gabriello cooks creative Roman cuisine using fresh, organic products from his wife's farm. Italians normally just tell their server, "Bring it on." Tourists are understandably more cautious, but you can be trusting here. "Claudio's Extravaganza" is created especially for my readers (not on the menu); specify whether you'd prefer fish, meat, or both. (Be warned: Romans think raw shellfish is the ultimate in fine dining. If you don't, make that clear.) While you're likely to dine surrounded by Rick Steves readers here (especially if eating before 9 p.m.), the atmosphere is fun and convivial

(3 blocks from Spanish Steps at Via Vittoria 51, +39 06 6994 0810, www. ilgabriello.com).

$$$ Hostaria Romana, near the Quirinale, is a busy bistro with a hustling and fun-loving gang of waiters. It's a good choice on your way to or from Trevi Fountain. The upstairs is a tight, tidy, glassed-in terrace, while the cellar has noisy walls graffitied by happy eaters. As its menu specializes in traditional Roman dishes, it's a good place to try *saltimbocca alla romana* or *bucatini all'amatriciana*. Their *antipasti della casa* plate, with a variety of vegetables and cheeses, makes a hearty start to your meal (midway between Piazza Barberini and Trevi Fountain at Via del Boccaccio 1, +39 06 474 5284, www.hostariaromana.it).

$$$$ Taverna Trilussa is your best bet for dining well in the Trastevere neighborhood. Brothers Massimo and Maurizio offer quality without pretense. With a proud hundred-year-old tradition, this place has the right mix of style and informality. The service is fun-loving (they're happy to let you split plates into smaller portions to enjoy a family-style meal), yet professional. The menu celebrates local classics and seasonal specials—as well as their award-winning *pasta all'amatriciana*—and comes with a big wine selection. The spacious dining hall is strewn with eclectic Roman souvenirs. Outdoors, Trilussa has an actual hedged-in terrace rather than just tables jumbled together on the sidewalk (Via del Politeama 23, +39 06 581 8918, www. tavernatrilussa.it).

$$ Pizzeria "Ai Marmi," also in Trastevere, is a noisy festival of pizza. Tight marble-slab tables (hence the nickname "The Morgue") fill the seating area in front of the oven and pizza-assembly line. It's a classic Roman scene whether you enjoy the chaos inside, sit at a sidewalk table, or take the famously good, thin, and crispy pizza home. They also serve fried cod, deep-fried rice balls *(suppli),* and bean dishes. Expect brusque service and a long line between 8 and 10 p.m. (Viale di Trastevere 53, +39 06 580 0919).

Campania

NAPLES
$ Real Neapolitan Pizza: Naples is the birthplace of pizza. You can drop in any neighborhood joint, and may just wind up eating the best pizza of your life. Or you can try one of the famous, venerable places (be prepared for long lines stretching out the door, and half-hour waits for a table; or arrive early or late). **Antica Pizzeria da Michele** is for pizza purists, serving just two varieties: *Margherita* (tomato, mozzarella, and basil) and *marinara* (tomato, oregano, and garlic, no cheese). Come early to sit and watch the pizza artists in action. If there's a mob, head inside to get a number (look for the vertical red *Antica Pizzeria* sign at the intersection of Via Pietro Colletta and Via Cesare

Sersale at #1; +39 081 553 9204). If it's just too crowded to wait, you can try their (less-exceptional) archrival, across the street and a few doors to the left, called **Pizzeria Trianon da Ciro.** It offers more choices, higher prices, air-conditioning, a cozier atmosphere, and a less chaotic upstairs (Via Pietro Colletta 42, +39 081 553 9426).

SORRENTO (Naples Province)
$$$$ Ristorante il Buco, once the cellar of an old monastery, is now a small, dressy restaurant—with spacious seating—that serves delightfully presented and creative modern Mediterranean dishes under a grand, rustic arch. Peppe holds a Michelin star, and he and his staff love to explain exactly what's on the plate— often sophisticated dishes with an emphasis on seafood, but a good vegetarian selection as well. They offer lots of fine wines by the glass (just off Piazza Sant'Antonino— facing the basilica, go under the grand arch on the left and immediately enter the restaurant at Il Rampa Marina Piccola 5; +39 081 878 2354, www.ilbucoristorante.it).

$$$$ L'Antica Trattoria enjoys a sedate, *romantico,* candlelit ambience, tucked away in its own little

world. The cuisine is traditional but with modern flair, and the inviting menu is fun to peruse (though pricey). Run by the same family since 1930, the restaurant has a trellised garden outside and intimate nooks inside. Aldo and sons will take care of you while Vincenzo—the Joe Cocker-esque resident mandolin player— entertains (good vegetarian options, Via Padre R. Giuliani 33, +39 081 807 1082, www.lanticatrattoria.it).

$$ Trattoria da Emilia, at the city-side end of the Marina Grande waterfront down below the town center, is good for straightforward, typical Sorrentine home cooking, including fresh fish, lots of fried seafood, and *gnocchi di mamma*—potato dumplings with meat sauce, basil, and mozzarella (Via Marina Grande 62, +39 081 807 2720, www.daemilia.it).

Sicily

PALERMO
$ Palermo Street Markets: Spend some time exploring—and eating at—Palermo's street markets. Each one is a combination of stalls for locals (clothes, housewares, bootleg CDs and DVDs, and so on), meat and fish, fresh produce, and street foods. Fearless eaters will head to the **Capo** or **Ballarò** markets and simply try a nibble from each cart, with choices ranging from sesame bread to veal penis. To make things easier, join a street food tour. Or, to sample a smorgasbord of classic Palermo street food in a graffiti-slathered square, make your way to Piazza Caracciolo in the heart of **Vucciria.** While this, too, was once a thriving market, most of its meat, fish, and produce vendors have moved elsewhere. But taking their place is an array of ramshackle food stands and cocktail bars. While it's open

for lunch and dinner, it's particularly lively after hours, when the square transforms into one of Palermo's trendiest nightlife spots. Take a spin around to consider your options: a classic cart selling *pani ca' meusa* (spleen sandwiches), an octopus man serving up *polpo bollito,* a fry stand selling *panelle* and *cazzilli,* and a sizzling grill with *stigghiola, mangia e bevi,* and other meaty choices. Once you've got your food, pull up a chair at a rickety plastic table near the fountain in the middle of the square. For more on the wonderful world of Sicilian street food, see page 335.

$$$ Casa del Brodo, a Palermo institution, is an old-school place for a reliably good meal. While it's just steps from the noisy Vucciria Market scene, it feels sedate and sophisticated, with photos of celebrity diners hanging on the walls. Their *antipasto* bar lets you pack a small plate with veggies for a set price, but you're there for the *brodo,* a clear broth with *tortellini* that's warmed bellies for generations (Via Vittorio Emanuele 175, +39 091 321 655, www.casadelbrodo.it).

RANDAZZO (Catania Province)
$$$ Ristorante Veneziano—on the north slope of Mount Etna, in the heart of that area's winegrowing zone—is a local favorite for a special-occasion splurge. While the restaurant is rooted in tradition, Chef Giuseppe prides himself on his modern preparation and technique. The space is casual and the menu features local specialties like Nebrodi pork and pasta with seasonal sauces, all served with Etna wines. The cuisine is high-end, the setting is unpretentious, and the remote location keeps prices reasonable (just east of Randazzo on SS-120, +39 095 799 1353, www.ristoranteveneziano.it).

🔍 FRED'S 50 FAVORITES

Piedmont

TORINO
$$ Trattoria Osto del Borgh Vej, a bastion of classic *piemontese* cooking, sits on an atmospheric piazza in central Torino, not far from the Duomo. Many of its specialties feature beef, veal, butter, and cheese, but you'll find a wide selection of vegetables as well as a discreet but well-prepared choice of fish and seafood from lakes, rivers, and the Ligurian Sea. Anything made with Castelmagno cheese (whether a *risotto,* gnocchi, or flan with *funghi porcini*) is a winner, as are the *agnolotti del plin*—dainty folded pasta with veal and cheese tossed in butter. The *brasato al Barolo* (slow-cooked beef in Barolo wine) is scrumptious. Desserts benefit from the *torinese* skill with chocolate and nuts, including a hazelnut flan with Moscato cream and *bonèt*—a pudding made of cocoa, coffee,

amaretti cookies, caramel, and rum (Via Torquato Tasso 7, +39 011 436 4843, www.losto.it).

BRA (Cuneo Province)
$$ Osteria del Boccondivino is an adherent to the Slow Food movement, whose offices are in Bra. It supports local food and wine producers who work sustainably, with respect for the environment as well as the preservation of ingredients threatened with extinction due to industrial agriculture. There's a lot of delicious food here, including the special *tajarin* pasta made with 40 egg yolks and tossed with butter and sage. Veal can be braised in Barolo wine or in an herb sauce. A house classic is rabbit cooked in white Arneis wine. The excellent list of wines by the glass allows easy pairings with each course (Via Mendicità 14, +39 017 242 5674, www.osteriadellarco.it).

Valle D'Aosta

COGNE
$$ Lou Ressignon is in the town of Cogne, which sits in the heart of the Gran Paradiso National Park. Here you'll find game, freshwater fish, and local Fontina featured on elegant cheese platters and in some pasta and main-course offerings. The Valle d'Aosta has the highest vineyards in Europe, and its sophisticated wines are prominent on the wine list. If you'd like to settle in to charming Cogne—which has many appealing restaurants—Lou Ressignon also rents a few rooms in its *locanda* (Rue des Mines 22, +39 016 574 034, www. louressignon.it).

Lombardy

AMBIVERE (Bergamo Province)

$$$ Trattoria Visconti, just seven miles from Bergamo and 28 miles from Milan, is your dream of a northern Italian country restaurant made real. Fiorella Visconti is the granddaughter of Ida Visconti, who opened her *trattoria* in 1932—drawing fruit, vegetables, herbs, eggs, and poultry from the garden out back, as well as rare varieties of corn for polenta. And so it remains today. You eat food picked an hour before, prepared with wisdom and respect for ingredients, and served with a smile of genuine hospitality. Don't miss *casoncelli della Nonna Ida,* the transcendent folded pasta with a jealously guarded recipe. *Lasagne ai tre ragù* is fresh sheets of pasta containing beef, chicken, and rabbit. *Tortelli di lago* are ravioli filled with four types of fish from nearby lakes. The *antipasti* are subtle and delicate, and the *secondi* are of exquisite local meats or lake fish with mountain mushrooms. These valleys produce some of Italy's best cheese—well worth savoring—including the unpronounceable *strachitunt*. The wine list is outstanding, too (Via Alcide De Gasperi 12, +39 035 908 153, www.trattoriavisconti.it).

ISOLA DOVARESE
(Cremona Province)

$$$ Caffè La Crepa occupies one corner of the town's surprisingly large and impressive piazza—much grander than you'd expect in a small agricultural town close to the Po River. Most dining tables are indoors, and the popular local bar in the front room sells local delicacies in jars and boxes (worth taking home). The province of Cremona is known for its beloved cows that provide superb meat, milk, butter, and cheeses. Those are honored at this restaurant, of course, but a unique specialty is the *storione* (fresh sturgeon from the Po) as well as eels and other river fish. Their folded pasta is divine: Local *marubini* in sumptuous broth are a must, as are the pumpkin *tortelli* and ravioli filled with herbs. For dessert, the home-made *gelati* are marvelous (Piazza Giacomo Matteotti 14, +39 0375 396 161, caffelacrepa.net).

MORTARA (Pavia Province)

$$ Trattoria Guallina showcases this town's distinct local cuisine: Because Mortara was historically Jewish, goose *(oca)* took the place of pork in foods such as *salumi.* Goose liver is prepared in different ways, and a real star of the menu are the ravioli filled with goose. Soups are delicious, and unusual local specialties include snails and fried frogs (Via Molino Faenza 19, +39 038 491 962, www.trattoriaguallina.it).

Trentino-Alto Adige

BRIXEN/BRESSANONE
(Bolzano Province)

$$$ Finsterwirt assiduously sources the best ingredients from local farms and respects seasonality not only of fruit and vegetables, but also meats—such as lamb in the spring and game in the fall. They have a superb list of local wines, especially whites. At the same location is the Vitis wine bar, with a small, carefully selected menu of more modern preparations (Vicolo Duomo 3, +39 0472 835 343, www.finsterwirt.com).

WEISSENBACH/RIO BIANCO
(Bolzano Province)

$$ Mösenhof offers specialties centered on one local product: *Graukäse* (gray cheese, described on page 175), which works well in soup,

which cooking techniques, especially from Asia, combine with foods found right here. Wines pair well with the delicious *torta di cipolle* (onion tart), beet-filled ravioli, *Gröstl di manzo* (veal and potatoes), and lovely desserts made with mountain berries (Via Garibaldi 9, +39 046 170 1670, www.boivin.it).

Veneto

TREVISO

$$$ Trattoria Toni del Spin does a good job with Treviso's two culinary specialties: red-leaf *radicchio* (called *trevigiano* here) and *tiramisù.* They also find many appealing ways to use grains. The barley-and-bean soup is good, and polenta appears as a companion to fish, meat, cheese, and mushrooms. *Polentina* (soft polenta) goes well with *schie* (fried gray shrimp from the Adriatic). For a taste of *cucina povera,* from when Veneto was impoverished, try the tasty *bigoli in salsa di acciuga e cipolla* (whole-wheat noodles with an anchovy-and-onion sauce). The outstanding wine list includes excellent Prosecco from nearby Conegliano (Via Inferiore 7, +39 393 986 3597, www.ristorantetonidelspin.com).

CONEGLIANO (Treviso Province)

$$ Trattoria Città di Venezia is a destination for those who love Venetian seafood dishes using crab, shrimp, mussels, clams, scallops, cuttlefish, squid, cod, sea bass, sole, and more. This Neptune's bounty appears in *antipasti,* pastas, *risotto,* with polenta, and as *secondi.* They also have meat options. Wines from Veneto and nearby Friuli-Venezia Giulia are perfectly suited to the cuisine; start with a glass of Prosecco, produced in or near Conegliano (Via XX Settembre 77, +39 043 823 186, www.trattoriacittadivenezia.it).

gnocchi, and as a spread. Also delicious here are braised lamb, locally caught trout, and a creamy local dessert called *Gibock'n,* which must be reserved ahead. The restaurant, open evenings only, is in a cozy hotel in the pretty valley called Ahrntal/ Valle Aurina (Kirchgasse 13, +39 047 467 1768, www.moesenhof.com).

LEVICO TERME (Trento Province)

$$$ Boivin showcases Trentino's longstanding vocation for producing outstanding wines. This cozy restaurant has been a site of winemaking since the 19th century. The dishes combine rigorous attention to local ingredients and traditions with what chef Riccardo Bosco calls *fantasia,* in

VERONA

$$ Trattoria al Bersagliere boasts a deep cellar of wines from throughout Italy and around the world. But stick to wines from Veneto, Trentino-Alto Adige, and Friuli-Venezia Giulia, which pair beautifully with all kinds of foods on this menu. Rather than do a traditional meal, make it an event to discover pairing wines (guided by Leo, the host) with foods such as *bigoli* with duck, spaghetti with rosemary, *maccheroncini* with sausage and beans, *stortina* (a small local *salame*) with soft polenta, fish from Lake Garda, veal *scaloppine* cooked in Soave wine, Monte Veronese cheese, *risotto* with Amarone wine, steamed or grilled vegetables, beautiful cooked fruit, and San Vigilini cookies (Via Dietro Pallone 1, +39 045 800 4824, www.trattoriaalbersagliere.it).

VALEGGIO SUL MINCIO
(Verona Province)

$$$ Ristorante alla Borsa is the best of the many restaurants in this small town that make exceptional *tortellini* and other filled pastas—which are just as good as anything you'll find over the border in Emilia-Romagna. They take special care in making their pasta, and you can taste the results. *Tortellini* come either in a fragrant beef/capon broth or tossed in butter and sage. *Tortelli* come with different fillings. And *tagliatelle* might be tossed with meat sauce or mushrooms or, most deliciously, in butter, Monte Veronese cheese, and fresh thyme. *Secondi* include meat options as well as local fish. Unlike many restaurants in this meat-focused part of Italy, Borsa has excellent options for vegetarians, who won't feel like second-class citizens here (Via Goito 2, +39 045 795 0093, www.ristoranteborsa.it).

CAVAION VERONESE
(Verona Province)

$$ Trattoria Villa is a lovely one-hour walk or half-hour bike ride from Bardolino on Lake Garda. Here you have the mediating weather effects of the lake wafting on hills where delicate wines and olive oil are produced. Lake fish appears in various forms and, in cold months, savory codfish is served with polenta. In the spring, local white and green asparagus shows up as *antipasti* and in pasta or *risotto*—not to be missed, especially with local white wines. Lamb is one of the better meats here, and tripe is a specialty of the house. Desserts are homemade and often based on the delicious local fruit— some of Italy's best (Strada Villa 32, +39 045 723 5426, www.trattoria-villa.it).

Friuli-Venezia Giulia

TRIESTE

$$$ Antica Trattoria Suban, an old stronghold of *triestine* cooking, is just outside the city center and has a small plot of land where they grow some of their own ingredients. Among these is fresh horseradish, which might be yanked out of the ground to directly grate on just-sliced *prosciutto in crosta,* ham baked in a rosemary-scented crust. That horseradish also goes into soups—the house specialty is *jota,* which has tender sauerkraut as its base. *Secondi* made with pork, venison, goose, lamb, or goulash all pair well with wines from the excellent list (Via Comici 2D, +39 0405 4368, www.suban.it).

CERNEGLONS (Udine Province)
$ Ai Cacciatori is a smiling *trattoria* that serves as this small town's gathering place. People come for delicious local wine and tasty food.

Be sure to try the *frico*—melted Montasio cheese that puffs up like a soufflé. Earthy polenta complements many things, including excellent pork products and stewed meats. Even the salads are prepared with care (Via Pradamano 28, +39 043 267 0132).

SAN DANIELE DEL FRIULI (Udine Province)

$$ **L'Osteria di Tancredi** offers a delicious reminder that, while the *prosciutto di Parma* in Emilia-Romagna is justifiably famous, the prosciutto from San Daniele in Friuli has many champions who insist that this one is more subtle. Come to your own conclusions: Start by having it on an *antipasti* platter, and then have more tossed in *tagliolini.* The remarkable filled pasta called *cjalsons* should not be missed if it's on the menu. Each restaurant guards its *cjalsons'* secret filling, but it might include chocolate, herbs, spices, rice, potato, and cheese. *Frico* (melted Montasio cheese fritter) is a wonderful match for fruity local red wines or a glass of Friulano (formerly known as Tocai). *Gubana,* a local cake, is an ideal dessert (Via Monte Sabotino 10, +39 043 294 1594, www.osteriadi tancredi.it).

CORMONS (Gorizia Province)

$$$ **La Subida,** just northeast of the town of Cormons and close to the border of Slovenia, is the sublime realization of the dreams of Joško and Loredana Sirk. This superb restaurant offers marvelous cooking, an amazing wine list, and careful though unfussy service. The food reflects the Sirks' research of the flavors of the area, including the influences of the Habsburg rule here as well as proximity to the local farms, the Adriatic Sea, prosciutto made by Gigi d'Osvaldo,

and traditional country cooking not found elsewhere. The *stinco* (shin of veal or pork) is excellent, but you can't go wrong with anything on the menu. You could splurge on wine, but there are many excellent choices at modest prices. There's also a more casual *osteria* and some rooms to rent if you want to base yourself in the area for a couple of days (Via Subida 52, +39 048 160 531 or +39 048 162 388, www.lasubida.it).

Liguria

GENOA

$$$ **Osteria Gigino** is devoted to meat—which almost feels exotic in this region of fish, vegetables, fruit, and herbs. If you come to Gigino, in the neighborhood known as Quarto dei Mille, you'll find outstanding beef from Tuscany, pork products from Emilia-Romagna, and starchy side dishes such as cannellini beans and roasted potatoes fragrant with olive oil and rosemary. The most Ligurian touch is the lovely meat-filled ravioli (Via Romana della Castagna 27/R, +39 010 377 2080, www.osteriagigino.com).

RECCO (Genoa Province)

$$$ **Manuelina**—in the humble but cuisine-focused town of Recco, between the Cinque Terre and Genoa—prepares many Ligurian

classics that are hard to find elsewhere: herb-filled ravioli called *pansoti* in walnut sauce, *trofie al pesto,* coin-shaped *corzetti* with wild mushroom sauce, excellent fish and seafood, and *cima alla genovese* (stuffed veal breast). The restaurant also has a simpler, adjacent **$ *focac-ceria*** where you can grab a cheap, fast, and delicious hunk of *focaccia col formaggio*—the cheesy focaccia this town is famous for (Via Roma 296, +39 018 574 128, www.manuelina ristorante.it).

SESTRI LEVANTE (Genoa Province)
$$$ Polpo Mario, in this pleasant and often overlooked beach town near the Cinque Terre, has its own boat that brings in fresh fish each day. This is the place to try *polpo* (octopus), either with potatoes *(con patate),* spicy *(alla diavola),* or as *ragù di polpo* tossed with spaghetti. Don't overlook the *acciughe al limone,* fresh anchovies cured in lemon, which might just change your mind about this humble fish (Via XXV Aprile 163, +39 018 548 0203, www. polpomario.com).

CERVO ALTA (Imperia Province)
$$$$ Ristorante San Giorgio breaks the old traveler's adage that restaurants with fabulous views can get away with so-so food. Here the cooking is so remarkable that you forget to notice the gorgeous Italian Riviera coastline below. Caterina Lanteri Cravet and her son Alessandro Barla run their restaurant with exquisite attention to detail. Caterina sources the finest local seafood, olive oil, herbs, vegetables, and fruit and exalts them in her cooking. She offers only what's the best that day, so the menu varies, but everything is memorable. If her hazelnut mousse is available, order it. Alessandro gently supports his mother while running the dining room and maintaining one of the best wine cellars around. They also run the adjacent **$$ San Giorgino,** which is more casual and wallet-friendly—but if you're contemplating a memorable splurge, the San Giorgio is worth it (Via A. Volta 19, +39 018 340 0175).

Emilia-Romagna

REGGIO EMILIA
$$$ Ristorante Canossa is a great excuse to visit this tragically under-appreciated city between Parma and Modena. The restaurant makes its own pasta throughout the day—you may well see that saintly work being done when you're there. The *quadrettini* in broth is a bowl of poetry, and the *tagliatelle, tortelli,* and *cappelletti* are transcendent. You can get samplings of three pastas if you ask for a *tris.* The go-to second course (unless you are a vegetarian) is the trolley of *bollito misto,* boiled meats (with some roasted meat and fowl, too) lovingly sliced and served with sauces—one of the best you'll find anywhere (Via Roma 37B, +39 052 245 4196, www.ristorantecanossa. com).

PARMA
$$$ Ristorante Cocchi serves fine examples of some of the pillars of *la cucina parmigiana:* prosciutto, *culatello,* and *salame* served

with *torta fritta* (crunchy, pillowy fry bread); *tortelli d'erbette* and *anelli pasta;* and veal stuffed with Parmigiano-Reggiano cheese and glorious vegetables. If they have *bollito misto* (described earlier), don't miss it. For dessert, get the *crostata* (fruit tart) of the day or crumbly *torta sbrisolona* with *zabaione.* Come with a serious appetite and be prepared for some seriously good eating (Viale Antonio Gramsci 16/A, +39 052 198 1990, www.ristorantecocchi.it).

ZIBELLO (Parma Province)
$$$ Trattoria La Buca is in a small town near the Po River, where generations of women have passed down their classic recipes and cooking secrets. Many of these dishes are based on the most famous local pork product, *culatello;* first taste it sliced thin, and then have it in pasta topped with Parmigiano-Reggiano. Then there's local meat and poultry—roasted or deliciously boiled—and vegetables whose flavor sings like a Giuseppe Verdi aria (the composer lived nearby, and this is the food he ate). Adventurous eaters will want to try local specialties, including eel with peas, tripe, snails, or calf's tongue with mushrooms (Via Ghizzi 6, +39 052 499 214, www. trattorialabuca.com).

PIACENZA
$$ Enoteca da Renato's meat-focused menu complements an appealing wine list focusing on reds from nearby (such as Gutturnio) and from throughout northern Italy. The platter of *salumi piacentini* is a succulent choice of exquisite local charcuterie. This town's famous small gnocchi (called *pisarei e fasò*) are made with beans, sausage, tomato, and cheese. Also delicious is a bracing bowl of *anolini* (meat-filled pasta) in a beef broth. Furthering the meat

theme, for those who want to go there, is horsemeat or delicious pan-fried guinea fowl. Non-carnivores can create a nice meal of cheeses and vegetables that show off the wines well (Via Roma 24, +39 052 332 5813).

SAVIGNO (Bologna Province)
$$$ Amerigo 1934, about an hour's drive from Bologna, is a calm oasis of the classic foods of the Apennine Mountains. The *tagliatelle al ragù* is impeccable, as are all the handmade pastas including *tortellini, tortelli,* and—for vegetarians—ravioli with *friggione* (tomatoes and onions topped with aged Parmigiano-Reggiano). Seasonality informs the menu; in autumn you might encounter a soup made with mushrooms, chestnuts, and truffles. A frequent *antipasto* item—*tigelle* flatbread served with Parmigiano-Reggiano gelato and traditional *modenese* balsamic vinegar—also makes a terrific dessert. The restaurant also has a *dispensa,* a store where you can purchase some of their products to enjoy at home (Via Guglielmo Marconi 14/16, +39 051 670-8326, www.amerigo1934.it).

SANTARCANGELO DI ROMAGNA (Rimini Province)
$$ La Sangiovesa has an unabashedly lusty feeling about it, as one would expect in the area that gave us Fellini. Romagna has excellent meat but also superb vegetables, so vegetarians can do very well here. Much of the food comes from their own farm. *Squacquerone* is a beguilingly creamy cheese that pairs well with fruit and vegetables and shows up in everything from *antipasti* to dessert. Homemade *tagliatelle* comes with either vegetable sauce or fragrant *ragù.* The *cappelletti* and *lasagne* are sensorial wonders,

grilled meats are excellent, and the *pollastro alla cacciatora* is perfectly cooked chicken and vegetables. The wine list suits every dish on the menu (Piazza Balacchi 14, +39 054 162 0710, www.sangiovesa.it).

COMACCHIO (Ferrara Province)
$$ Da Vasco e Giulia is in the town of Comacchio, at the delta of the Po River near the Adriatic. In a way, this area feels more like Veneto than Emilia-Romagna—not only for the fish, but also for the prominent use of rice and polenta. You can have fried fish and vegetables (based on what's available that day), or *risotto* flavored with fish, or a *brodetto* (stew) of eel and polenta. For Italians, Comacchio is synonymous with eel—and here, eel is perfectly grilled over wood. Grilled sea scallops, when available, are also delicious. Fresh fruit sorbets cleanse the palate nicely after a unique and savory meal (Via Muratori 21, +39 053 381 252, www.vascoegiulia.it).

Tuscany

LIVORNO
$$ La Barrocciaia is a youthful restaurant that captures the feisty working-class vibe of this port city. It's located near the fruit-and-vegetable market, which supplies ingredients for many of its dishes. If you just want a really good *panino,* this is the place to find it—but there's serious cooking going on, too, including pasta with crab or wild boar, delicious fried cod fillets, and braised cuttlefish, squid, and baby octopus. On Friday and Saturday nights and on Sunday, be sure to order ahead for *cacciucco,* Livorno's classic seafood stew that's worth the trip all by itself (Piazza Cavallotti 13, +39 058 688 2637, www.labarrocciaia.it).

LUCCA
$$ Il Mecenate prides itself on honest, genuine food to please carnivores and vegetarians alike. Lucca has excellent olive oil that appears in many dishes and soups, such as *garmugia* (a veritable bounty of spring vegetables). The leek pie is special, as are the meat-filled *tordelli* pasta and *testaroli,* an ancient bread-like pasta tossed with pesto. *Secondi* meats will raise your tab; instead, order a mixed plate of vegetable *contorni*. For dessert, the fig-and-walnut tart is delicious if available (Via del Fosso 94, +39 058 351 1861, www.ristorantemecenate.it).

PISA
$$ Osteria dei Cavalieri, on a back street between the Field of Miracles and the river, features good food from both land and sea—offering an escape from the tourist traps near the Leaning Tower. Ravioli, whether filled with fish or cheese, are delicious. Soups such as chickpea, bean, squash, or *farro* are hearty. Tuscan beef comes in many guises, and local seafood is prepared with vigor. Desserts are homey, if sometimes too sweet, but the cakes made with pear or hazelnuts are just right (Via San Frediano 16, +39 050 580 858, www.osteriacavalieri.pisa.it).

Umbria

MONTEFALCO (Perugia Province)
$$ Ristorante alla Via di Mezzo da Giorgione is located in the fortified hill town of Montefalco, which occupies a high position with grand views over Umbria. The surrounding hills are planted with the sagrantino red grape, used to make the famous red wine called Montefalco. Historically a communion wine, now it's complex and well matched to the hearty local cuisine. And this restaurant offers generous portions of good home cooking on a moderate fixed-price *menù* based on local olive oil and other products—and, of course, excellent wine (Via di Santa Chiara da Montefalco 52, +39 074 236 2074, www.ristorantealloviadimezzo.it).

Marche

FANO (Pesaro-Urbino Province)
$$$ Da Maria is in Fano, just south of the delightful city of Pesaro. Now run by the daughter of the founder, this restaurant offers Marche fish cookery with real finesse. The *brodetto* (seafood stew) is exemplary and complex. Boiled sole may sound unappealing, but here it's a model of delicacy. The *sugo di pesce* served with polenta or pasta is deeply satisfying. You'll notice the menus have no prices, since everything is market price (cash only, Via IV Novembre 86, +39 072 180 8962).

MACERATA
$$ Trattoria da Rosa is a good place to try Macerata's local specialty, *vincisgrassi*—a deluxe *lasagne* that's worth the trip. But you can't go wrong with whatever you order. The frittata with black truffle is exquisite, duck breast is succulent, and goose with caramelized onions and apple puree is a rich indulgence. The *ossobuco* is one of the best south of Lombardy. If you like fried foods, the *frittura mista* contains fried vegetables, lovely fried cream, and *olive ascolane*—deep-fried olives stuffed with meat (Via Leopoldo Armaroli 17, +39 073 326 0124).

Lazio

OLEVANO ROMANO (Rome Province)
$$ Sora Maria e Arcangelo, about an hour and a half southeast of Rome, conserves family recipes dating back to 1910. The *cannelloni* filled with ground veal, onion, carrot, mushrooms, and marjoram—and baked with tomatoes, basil, olive oil, Parmigiano-Reggiano, and cow's-milk mozzarella—is worth the journey all by itself. The *secondi* of goose, squab, and especially Roman lamb are excellent (Via Roma 42, +39 069 564 043, www.soramariaearcan gelo.com).

VITERBO
$$ Al Vecchio Orologio captures the ancient foodways of this town and surrounding countryside, which have roots dating back to the Etruscans. The wisdom of ancient agriculture results in a cuisine based on elemental ingredients such as wheat, olive oil, and vegetables. Here you can try *tonnarelli* with sausage and onion, *pizzicotti all'amatriciana,* and *pappardelle* with a wild boar sauce. *Secondi* include rabbit, chicken thighs, lamb, and oxtail. They also do wonderful vegetable preparations—order two or three if you want a non-meat alternative. The seasonal *crostata* is a delicious dessert, especially when made with *visciole*—Roman cherries (Via Orologio Vecchio 25, +39 335 337 754, https:// alvecchioorologio.it).

Campania

SALERNO
$$ L'Unico has its own fishing boat, and the menu changes based on what the sea provides—check the blackboard to see what's available. Always good are dishes made with *alici* (local sardines that might be combined with *scamorza* cheese or turned into meatballs), *totani* (delicate squid with tomatoes or potatoes), or *seppioline* (cuttlefish). If the *fettuccine con fiori di zucca e frutti di mare* (sauced with squash blossoms and seafood) is on the menu, get it. Lemon-based desserts are reliably good (Largo San Giorgio 14, +39 089 296 2671, www.lunicoristorante.it).

Abruzzo

L'AQUILA
$$ Trattoria da Lincosta is one of the restaurants that are helping reanimate Abruzzo's capital, L'Aquila, which suffered a devastating earthquake in 2009. Chef-owner Romina Muzi uses traditional *salumi* and cheeses and works wonders with lamb, whether as a filling for ravioli or chops on the grill. *Spaghetti alla chitarra* is made with cherry tomatoes, *ricotta,* saffron, and zucchini. She also has a special feeling for vegetables and grains, whether it's in *farro* soup, in the combination of chicory and potatoes, or in *frecandò* (a lightly cooked vegetable medley). Most of the wines on the list are from Abruzzo. Chef Romina maintains an *orto urbano* (city garden) that provides a steady supply of vegetables, fruit, and herbs, and also has a patisserie with elegant cakes for sale (Via Antonelli 6, +39 086 220 4358, www.dalincosta.it).

Molise

AGNONE (Isernia Province)
$$ Locanda Mammì is where chef Stefania di Pasquo flexes her creative muscles in ways that fascinate rather than perplex. Pasta with leeks and local saffron works better than one would imagine. Simple chicken and peppers with fried potatoes offer so much more than what the ingredients might imply. Local cheeses blend beautifully with peas in one recipe and squash in another. Even the thick, crusty, aromatic local bread is special (Contrada Castelnuovo 86, +39 086 577 379, www.locandamammi.it).

Puglia

BARI
$$ Perbacco is a friendly *trattoria* serving delicious food inspired by the sea, whose breezes waft through now and then. Good land-based dishes include polenta with mushrooms and melted Gorgonzola, or pork with onions and almonds. Otherwise, it's mostly pasta, fish, and vegetables. *Orecchiette* with a creamy fava-bean sauce with cheese and bits of pork is *pugliese* soul food, as is baked cuttlefish stuffed with eggplant, breadcrumbs, and yellow tomatoes. Desserts are simple and charming, though they tend to be a bit sweet; fresh fruit is a good alternative (Via Abbrescia 99, +39 080 558 8563).

CEGLIE MESSAPICA
(Brindisi Province)

$$ Ristorante Cibus is a family restaurant dating back many decades—and when it comes to cooking, they see no need to reinvent the wheel. Instead, they have relationships with farmers who provide superb raw materials that are transformed into delicious dishes, some quite consoling and a few a bit challenging. The red-chickpea-and-cod soup animates the soul. The selection of beautiful cheeses can be a course by itself or can flavor other dishes, such as pasta and tomatoes. Olives also appear, reaching a zenith when cooked with rabbit and tomatoes. Fava-bean puree, flan with fresh mint, and pork strips with capers, red onion, and rosemary cooked in vinegar are all transcendent dishes. If you're more adventurous, try donkey, horse, or *maretto* (grilled lamb offal, which is quite delicious). Charming desserts include peach *granita* and gelato made of either figs or walnuts (Via Chianche di Scarano 7, +39 083 138 8980, www.ristorantecibus.it).

Basilicata

MARATEA (Potenza Province)
$$ Il Giardino di Epicuro is in Massa, above the town of Maratea. Start with the *antipasti,* which include outstanding cow and sheep *ricotta* cheeses, delicious mozzarella, the spicy local 'nduja sausage, and more. The fresh pasta is special—particularly the ravioli filled with sausage, *ricotta,* and parsley. But then you might want the ravioli filled with *ricotta* and sauced either with *ragù,* fish sauce, or truffle. The *secondi* are grilled meats served with delicious seasonal vegetables cooked as a sort of stew; fish is only available if you order at least a day ahead

(Località Massa, +39 097 387 0130, a.bacchiglione@tiscali.it).

Calabria

REGGIO CALABRIA
$$ Baylik is the destination of some of the best fish from local waters—especially superb swordfish *(pesce spada)*. Swordfish becomes an *antipasto* flan made with cauliflower, and also appears in a pasta sauce with zucchini blossoms, tomatoes, and a touch of cream. An unusual carbonara has a sauce with swordfish, egg, parsley, and black pepper. And swordfish steaks are perfectly grilled with salt, lemon, and oil (Vico Leone 1, +39 096 548 624, www.baylik.it).

Sicily

PALERMO
$$ Trattoria ai Cascinari's straightforward, home-style cooking has been popular for decades. The *antipasto cascinaro* is a good way to start, and the *spaghetti con brodo di pesce* (fish broth) is a paragon of simplicity. Pasta also comes with sardines, and an appealing *secondo* is the *calamari ripieni*—stuffed squid (Via D'Ossuna 43, +39 091 651 9804).

CASTELBUONO (Palermo Province)
$$$ Nangalarruni is at the foot of the Madonia Mountains, a

destination for savoring local foods including wild mushrooms, black truffles, and products made of *maialino nero*—the succulent local black pig. The *pollo ruspante alla cacciatora*—local chicken cooked with vegetables—is a thing of beauty (Via Confraternite 7, +39 092 167 1228, www.hostarianangalarruni.it).

CATANIA
$$ La Cucina dei Colori is a convivial, vibrantly vegetarian restaurant with all kinds of attractions. You can dine in, take away, attend a cooking class, and always focus on what the markets offer that day. The emphasis is on freshness and sustainability, which are hallmarks in much of Italy but receive loving attention here (Via San Michele 9, +39 095 717 6146, www.lacucinadeicolori.it).

MARSALA (Trapani Province)
$$ Antica Trattoria da Pino is the place to savor the best of local seafood, starting with couscous with fish or pasta with pistachios, garlic, shrimp, and *peperoncino rosso*. Then have the catch of the day. In the springtime, fresh tuna is sensational. Save room for *cappidduzzi,* sweet ravioli filled with sheep's-milk *ricotta* (Via San Lorenzo 27, +39 092 371 5652, www.trattoriadapino.it).

Sardinia

ALGHERO (Sassari Province)
$$ Lo Romanì offers a good cross-section of Sardinian food, from seafood to meat—especially pork and lamb. Interwoven are fragrances and flavors including honey, myrtle, mint, citrus, and the island's incomparable *pecorino* cheese. *Culurgiones* are ravioli filled with potato, *pecorino,* and mint. The *porceddu* is a delicious suckling pig. Fresh tuna with caramelized red onions is a great fish option. If you want to splurge, Alghero is famous for its lobster *(aragosta),* which is otherwise rarely found in Italian waters; it's turned into a sauce for pasta or, famously, is a *secondo* with onion and citrus. Two classic desserts are flan made with sheep's milk and *menjar-blanc all'algherese,* a creamy dessert made with cornstarch, lemon, and honey. For wine, try a white vermentino or a red cannonau (Via Principe Umberto 29, +39 079 973 8479, https://loromani.unomenu.it).

CABRAS (Oristano Province)
$$ Sa Bell'e Crabasa is in Cabras, on a lagoon in western Sardinia. The town is famous for *bottarga,* which now shows up on fancy menus from Milan to New York to Tokyo. These dried mullet roe become firm and are served here sliced as an *antipasto* with artichoke, as a pâté, or grated over pasta and grains. Don't overlook the beautiful lentil-and-fava-bean soup. The west coast of Sardinia has gorgeous beaches, wonderful fish, native lobsters, and a pasta called *culurgiones* that can be filled either with seafood or sublime local *pecorino.* Pan-cooked tuna with poppy and sesame seeds is outstanding (Piazza Principe di Piemonte 2, +39 328 654 9725, www.trattoriasabellecrabasa.com).

Italian Food Glossary

So many foods, so little time. The food lover traveling in Italy encounters an almost endless array of new words on menus and in stores. While it's impossible to list all of these, I've assembled this chapter to be an as-comprehensive-as-possible glossary of the terms and phrases you're most likely to encounter as you travel through Italy. I've included a few dialectical variations (mostly to highlight major specialties from certain regions); remember that the lists of specialties in each regional chapter will be far more comprehensive.

When a dish is focused on a particular region (or several), I've noted it in parentheses—turn to that chapter for more information. (This doesn't necessarily mean that the item is found *only* in that region, simply that it's the place that's most associated with it.) I've also noticed specialties that are widespread either throughout the North (broadly, this includes Piedmont, Lombardy, Trentino-Alto Adige, Veneto, and Friuli-Venezia Giulia) or the South (typically Campania, Abruzzo, Molise, Puglia, Basilicata, Calabria, and sometimes also Sicily). And some items are specific to (or most closely associated with) a single city, such as Rome, Venice, or Milan.

When decoding menus, you'll often see these little words, which can be used in conjunction with the ones listed later:

alla, alle, della, delle → in the style of

con/senza → with/without

di → of, from

e → and

l'etto → price per 100 grams

in → in

-ine, -ette, -elle → small

-one → big

oppure → or

s.q. (secondo quantità) → price according to quantity

su → served over

If you see a phrase on a menu that begins with ***alla*** or ***della,*** the next word might not appear on this list. That's because these phrases mean "in the style of," and what follows is often a flowery, artsy, or obscure description. (Even if you knew the exact meaning, it might not make things much clearer.)

And remember: the best "menu decoders" of all are the Italian people, who have a passion for explaining their local specialties to visitors. When in doubt…ask.

A

Abbacchio Spring lamb. (Lazio, Abruzzo, Sardinia)

Abboccato Sweet or semisweet (wine).

Acciughe Anchovies, usually salted for preservation. Fresh anchovies are ***alici.***

Acero Maple.

Aceto Vinegar.

Aceto balsamico Balsamic vinegar, a specialty of Emilia-Romagna (especially Modena and Reggio Emilia).

Aceto di vino Wine vinegar.

Acqua Water, usually ***acqua minerale*** (mineral water)—either bubbly (***con gas*** or ***gassata***) or still (***naturale*** or ***non gassata***); tap water is ***acqua del rubinetto.***

Acquacotta Thin vegetable soup, literally "cooked water." (Tuscany)

Acquavite Firewater distilled from fruit ("water of life").

Affettato Sliced; **affettati** is a general word for cold cuts (salumi), and **affettato misto** is a mixed platter of salumi.

Affogato al caffè Ice cream with coffee.

Affumicato Smoked.

Aglio Garlic; **aglio fresco** or **germogli di aglio** is a garlic shoot, and **agliata** is garlic sauce.

Aglio e olio Spaghetti tossed with olive oil and garlic—a classic "hardship dish" that's still popular.

Agnello Lamb.

Agnolotti Folded, filled pasta similar to ravioli. (Piedmont)

Agretti Grass-like spring vegetable. (Umbria)

Agriturismo A working farm that receives government subsidies to also offer services to travelers, including accommodations and food.

Agrodolce Sweet and sour; usually vegetables cooked in vinegar and sugar. (Sicily)

Agrumi Citrus fruit.

Albicocca (plural **albicocche**) Apricot.

Albume Egg white.

Alcool Alcohol; something **alcolico** contains alcohol.

Al dente Toothsome—slightly undercooked and still a bit firm, the proper way for dry pasta to be cooked.

Alfabeto Letter-shaped pasta (for kids).

Alfredo A pasta preparation with lots of sweet butter and Parmigiano-Reggiano cheese; better known in Italy as **maestose al burro.** (Rome)

Alici Fresh anchovies. (Liguria, Sicily)

Alimentari Grocery store.

Alloro (or **lauro**) Laurel.

Amabile Semisweet wine ("amiable").

Amarena (plural **amarene**) Sour cherry.

Amaretti Bitter macaroons made with almond. (Piedmont, Lombardy)

Amaretto Sweet, almond-flavored liqueur.

Amaro Bitter; also a category of after-dinner drinks thought to aid digestion (see page 99).

Amatriciana, all' Pasta sauce of tomatoes, pork cheek, pecorino romano cheese, and chili peppers, usually

served with bucatini. (Lazio)

Americano American. Usually this refers to a **caffè americano,** espresso diluted with hot water, approximating American-style drip coffee (which is rare in Italy); or a cocktail of vermouth with bitters, brandy, and lemon peel.

Anacardo Cashew.

Analcolico Alcohol-free.

Ananas Pineapple.

Anatra Duck (**petto di anatra** is duck breast).

Anatra in porchetta Duck stuffed with prosciutto, duck liver, rosemary, fennel seed, and garlic. (Umbria and Tuscany)

Aneto Dill.

Anguilla Freshwater eel; **in umido** is stewed in tomato sauce.

Anguria Watermelon (in the North; in central and southern Italy, it's **cocomero,** while Sicilians call it **mellone**).

Anice Anise; **anice stellato** is star anise.

Animelle Sweetbreads.

Anitra Duck.

Annata Vintage (wine).

Anolini A type of filled pasta, usually stuffed with beef. (Emilia-Romagna)

Antipasto (plural **antipasti**) Appetizer. **Antipasto (ai frutti) di mare** is an assortment of fish and shellfish, while **antipasto misto** is an assortment of meats and veggies. See the *Antipasti* chapter.

Aperitivo Aperitif or pre-dinner cocktail, often served with snacks.

Apfelstrudel Apple strudel. (Alto Adige)

Apribottiglia Bottle opener.

Arachidi Peanuts.

Aragosta Crayfish or small lobster; the best is from Sardinia.

Arancia (plural **arance**) Orange.

Arancia rossa Blood orange. (Sicily)

Aranciata Orangeade or orange soda.

Aranciata nuorese Candied orange peel and almonds. (Sardinia)

Arancina (plural **arancine;** sometimes masculine: **arancino/ arancini**) Deep-fried rice balls stuffed with meat, cheese, or vegetables, sometimes served **al sugo** (in tomato sauce). (Sicily and the South)

Aringa (or **aringhe**) Herring.

Arista A roasted loin of top-quality meat (usually pork or veal).

Arrabbiata, all' Spicy pasta sauce made of olive oil, tomatoes, and chili peppers. (Rome)

Arrosto Roast or roasted; **arrosto misto** is an assortment of mixed roasted meats. (Tuscany and Umbria)

Arsella (plural **arselle**) A type of clam.

Asiago Hard cow's-milk cheese; it can come either **mezzano** (young, firm, and creamy) or **stravecchio** (aged, pungent, and granular). (Veneto)

Asino Donkey.

Asparagi Asparagus.

Assaggio (plural **assaggi**) A taste.

Assortiti Assorted.

Astice Large lobster.

Averna An *amaro* (herbal *digestivo*) from Sicily.

B _____

Babà (al rum) Mushroom-shaped, rum-soaked cake.

Baccalà Dried salt cod, an old staple that must be rehydrated, and the salt removed, before cooking. *Baccalà* can be deep-fried **(dorato)**, cooked with tomato and herbs **(alla livornese)**, prepared with milk and onions and served with polenta **(alla vicentina)**, or a variety of other ways. **Baccalà mantecato** is a spread made of cod whipped with olive oil.

Bacelli Fava beans. (Tuscany)

Bacio (plural **baci**) Chocolate-hazelnut candy ("kisses") from Perugia, in Umbria; can also describe a chocolate-hazelnut gelato flavor, or, in a bakery, a variety of small sandwich cookies (a.k.a. **baci di dama,** "lady's kisses").

Bagna cauda Hot-oil dip, seasoned with garlic and anchovies, for raw vegetables. (Piedmont)

Bagnet Sauce to accompany meats, eggs, or fish. (Piedmont)

Balanzoni Large, green filled pastas, with spinach in the dough and typically stuffed with more spinach and other ingredients. (Emilia-Romagna)

Bar Not a dark room for hard drinking, but rather an Italian social institution where you can have coffee, juice, a glass of wine, a stiff drink, a sandwich, or a sweet.

Barbabietola Beet.

Barbina Very skinny spaghetti often coiled into nest-like "beards."

Basilico Basil, best in Liguria.

Bavette Flank steak; this can also refer to a skinny *tagliatelle.*

Beccaccia Woodcock.

Bellini Cocktail of Prosecco and fresh peach juice. (Venice)

Bel Paese Mild cow's-milk cheese. (Lombardy)

Ben cotto/molto ben cotto Well-done/very well-done (meat).

Besciamella (sometimes called **balsamella**) Béchamel sauce. (Emilia-Romagna)

Bevanda (plural **bevande**) Beverage.

Bianco White, as in wine; also, something cooked **in bianco** is essentially "plain," without added fats or flavorings, such as a poached fish or simple boiled pasta.

Bibita (plural **bibite**) Beverage (typically soft drinks).

Bicchiere Drinking glass (including a wine glass).

Bietola Chard.

Bignè or **bignole (alla crema)** (Cream) puff.

Bigoli Long, thin whole-wheat pasta, often served **in salsa**— with anchovy sauce. (Veneto)

Biologico Organic.

Birra Beer; **birra artigianale** is craft beer, and **birra alla spina** is on draft.

Bis Split course— typically two pastas on one plate.

Biscotto (plural **biscotti**) Cookie; for **biscotti di Prato,** see *"cantucci."*

Bistecca Steak, usually one served on the bone—most famously **bistecca alla fiorentina,** a cut of Chianina beef rubbed with olive oil and grilled rare. (Tuscany)

Bitto Cow's-milk cheese; the young version melts luxuriously. (Lombardy)

Bocconcini Chunks or bits; this can refer to small balls of mozzarella, or to bite-size stew meat such as veal (especially in Lombardy).

Bollente Boiling hot.

Bollito Boiled.

Bollito misto An elaborate main course of boiled meats and sauces, popular in the wintertime throughout the North. Each region has its own special sauces.

Bolognese, alla "Bologna-style," usually referring to a rich meat sauce served with *tagliatelle;* this can also be any dish from Bologna (for example, **cotoletta alla bolognese,** veal cutlet topped with prosciutto and Parmigiano-Reggiano).

Bombolone (or **bomba**) Filled doughnut.

Bonèt Chocolate custard, sometimes with other flavors. (Piedmont)

Borlotti Red and white beans used in soups and pasta sauces. (The North)

Borragine Borage, greens popular for filling *pansoti.* (Liguria)

Boscaiola, alla Pasta sauce with mushrooms, herbs, and often sausage or ham.

Bosco, di Wild ("of the forest").

Bottarga (also **bottariga** or **butàriga**) Dried roe. (Liguria, Sicily, Sardinia)

Bottega A shop.

Bottiglia Bottle.

Brace, alla Charcoal-grilled.

Braciola Shoulder chop, usually of pork, veal, or lamb.

Branzino Sea bass.

Brasato Braised; can also mean beef braised in red wine.

Bresaola Dried, air-cured beef. (Lombardy)

Brioche Breakfast roll.

Broccoletti Turnip tops—a bitter, leafy green vegetable.

Broccolo romanesco A cross between broccoli and cauliflower.

Brodetto (or **brodeto**) Fish soup or stew.

Brodo Broth, typically of poultry; **in brodo** is a popular preparation for filled pastas in Emilia-Romagna.

Bruciatini Cured pork, similar to *pancetta*.

Bruciato Burned.

Bruschetta Toasted bread topped with olive oil, garlic, and some-times tomatoes or other toppings. (Tuscany, Umbria, Lazio, Marche)

Brutti e buoni (or **brutti ma buoni**) Deli-cious dry cookies, often with hazelnuts, that are "ugly but good." (Sicily)

Bucatini Long, spa-ghetti-like pasta with a hollow center (also known as **perciatelli**).

Buccellato Wreath-shaped anise-and-rai-sin bread. (Tuscany)

Budino Pudding.

Buridda A fish stew with tomatoes and other vegetables (Liguria); or, in Sardinia, a catfish marinated in sweet-and-sour and cooked with nuts (spelled **burrida**).

Burrata Cheese with a mozzarella-like shell containing a rich, oozing, creamy center called *stracciatella*. (Puglia and the South)

Burrino (plural **burrini**) Small cow's-milk cheese, usually filled with butter. (The South)

Burro Butter, typically unsalted.

Burro d'arachidi Pea-nut butter.

Burro e salvia Butter and sage, a common pasta preparation.

Busara A pasta sauce of seafood (often shrimp), garlic, and tomato.

Busecca Tripe stew. (Lombardy)

Busiate Small pasta twists, similar to *fusilli*.

Bussoli Easter cookies.

Bustina di tè Tea bag.

C

Cacciagione Game.

Cacciatora, alla "Hunter-style," usually with chicken, rabbit, or lamb prepared with olive oil, red wine, rosemary, garlic, and sometimes tomatoes or mushrooms. (Tuscany, Piedmont)

Cacciucco A fish soup from Livorno, usually made with red mullet, shellfish, and tomatoes. (Tuscany)

Cacia (or **cacio**) A generic term for cheese, especially in the South; **caciotta** is a small, soft cheese (often sheep's milk, but can be cow's milk).

Caciocavallo A mild-to-sharp, pear-shaped cheese; while called "horse cheese," it's named not for the source of its milk (which is usually from a cow), but for how the cheese hangs like sad-dlebags as it matures. (The South)

Cacio e pepe *Pecorino romano* cheese and pepper, a popular pasta preparation in the South (especially Rome).

Caco (plural **cachi**) Persimmon; also known as **diospero.**

Caffè Coffee. Ordering **un caffè** will get you a small cup of espresso; for a complete list of coffee drinks, see page 92.

Caffeina Caffeine.

Calamari Squid. **Calamari ripieni** are stuffed, usually with breadcrumbs, capers, garlic, and anchovies;

calamaretti are baby squid. And **calamarata** is squid-shaped pasta, often served with spicy tomato sauce and—you guessed it—squid.

Caldo Hot.

Calzone A pizza that has been folded; there are variations throughout the South—in Puglia, they're smaller, deep-fried, and called **panzerotti.**

Cameriere Server.

Camomila Chamomile tea.

Camoscio Chamois, popular in stews, sauces, and dried. (Valle d'Aosta, Trentino-Alto Adige, and the Alps)

Campanelle "Bell"-shaped pasta.

Canederli (or **Knödel**) Big, hearty bread dumplings that can be made with cheese, herbs, ham, spinach, or other fillings. (Trentino-Alto Adige and the Alps)

Canestrato A sheep's-milk cheese from Sicily.

Cannella Cinnamon.

Cannellini White beans. (Tuscany)

Cannelloni Big, stuffed pasta tube.

Cannolo (plural **cannoli**) Deep-fried pastry tube filled with sweet *ricotta* cheese. (Sicily)

Cannoncini Baked pastry tubes filled with cream.

Cantina Wine cellar; or, in a winery, the place where wine is produced.

Cantucci (or **biscotti di Prato**) Popular almond cookies, traditionally served as a dessert with a glass of Vin Santo. (Tuscany)

Capellini Long, very thin spaghetti-type pasta; this may be called **capelli d'angelo,** "angel's hair."

Capesante Scallops.

Capitone Saltwater eel. (The South)

Capocollo (or **coppa**) Spicy, tender *salame*. (The South)

Caponata Sweet-and-sour stew of eggplant, zucchini, olives, and pine nuts, served hot or cold, as a side or a starter. (Sicily)

Cappellacci "Hat"-shaped filled pasta, often filled with squash; the similar **cappelletti** are smaller. (Emilia-Romagna)

Cappelletti A brand of *amaro* (herbal *digestivo*) from Trentino; can also refer to small *cappellacci* (see above).

Cappero (plural **capperi**) Caper.

Cappone Capon (a small neutered rooster), often used to make broth. (Emilia-Romagna)

Cappon magro An elaborate cold dish of poached fish and cooked vegetables. (Liguria)

Cappuccino Espresso with steamed milk.

Capra Goat.

Capretto Kid (baby goat)—usually served roasted **(arrosto),** especially at Eastertime.

Capricciosa Chef's choice; often refers to a pizza with a variety of toppings.

Caprino Goat cheese.

Capriolo Venison.

Carabaccia Tuscan onion soup.

Caraffa Carafe.

Caramelle Candy; can also refer to filled pasta shaped like the twisted wrapper of a piece of candy.

Carbonada Braised beef. (Valle d'Aosta)

Carbonara, alla Pasta preparation with raw eggs, *pancetta, pecorino romano* cheese, and pepper.

Carbonella Charcoal.

Carciofo (plural **carciofi**) Artichoke; **alla giudìa** ("Jewish-style") is deep-fried, and **alla romana** ("Roman-style") is stuffed with garlic, mint, and parsley.

Carciofo romanesco Giant artichoke.

Cardamomo Cardamom.

Cardo Cardoon, an artichoke-like vegetable with a celery-like stalk. (Piedmont, Lazio, Molise)

Carne Meat, usually beef. **Carne di cervo** is venison, and **carne equina** is horse meat. **Carne bianca** is white meat (poultry), and **carne rossa** is red meat (beef and game). **Carne in umido** is meat stew, **carne macinata** is ground meat, **carne cruda** is raw veal or beef (a Piedmont specialty), and **carne salada** (or **carne sala**) is salted, raw beef, eaten in the Alps.

Carota Carrot.

Carpaccio Raw, air-cured beef often served as an *antipasto* with chopped greens, olive oil, lemon juice, and slivers of Parmigiano-Reggiano.

Carpione, in Pickled, usually with vinegar, lemon juice, wine, and herbs.

Carrè affumicato Pork shank that's smoked, then boiled. (Trentino-Alto Adige)

Carrè di Rack of.

Carrettiera, alla Spicy sauce with garlic, olive oil, and little tomatoes, named for the "cart-riders" who traditionally ate it.

Carta di musica Literally "sheet music," this is another name for the thin, crispy, unleavened shepherd's bread called *pane carasau*. (Sardinia)

Cartoccio, al Cooked in foil wrap or parchment (especially fish).

Casa, della Of the house.

Casalinga "Housewife," usually designating home-style dishes.

Casalinghi Housewares, or a store where they are sold.

Casarecce Short pasta with an S-shaped cross-section.

Casareccio "Home-style," especially relating to bread.

Casciotta Semisoft cheese made of a mix of sheep's and cow's milk. (Marche)

Casoncelli Folded pasta filled with meat, potatoes, and cheese, served in broth or melted butter. (Lombardy)

Cassa Cashier.

Cassata A rich Sicilian dessert made with sponge cake, *ricotta* cheese, candied fruit, almond paste, and other ingredients; it can also be a gelato with the same flavor.

Cassoeula Hearty Milanese stew of pork, cabbage, and vegetables. (Lombardy)

Cassola A Catalan-influenced stew made with fish, octopus, tomatoes, and onions. (Sardinia)

Castagna (plural **castagne**) Chestnut.

Castagnaccio Cake-like pudding (or pudding-like cake) made with chestnut flour and rosemary. (Tuscany)

Castagnole Little balls of fried dough, rolled in sugar, popular at Carnival time.

Castellane Pasta shaped like a castle tower.

Castrato Typically mutton, but can be any neutered male animal (horse, bull, or ram).

Cavallo (or **carne equina**) Horse meat, especially popular in Veneto.

Cavatappi Corkscrew (or corkscrew-shaped pasta).

Cavatelli (or **cavateddi**) Pasta shaped like small shells.

Caviale Caviar; domestic caviar is usually from Po River sturgeon.

Cavoletti di Bruxelles Brussels sprouts.

Cavolfiore Cauliflower.

Cavolo Cabbage; can also be used as an expression of surprise or disbelief. **Cavolo riccio** is kale, and **cavolo nero** is a type of Tuscan kale.

Cazzotto Small, folded sandwich. (The South)

Ceci Chickpeas; **farina di ceci** is chickpea flour, and **cecina** is a savory chickpea crêpe.

Cedro (plural **cedri**) Citron, a big, bumpy, pulpy lemon whose peel is candied or used to make marmalade. (The South)

Cefalo Mullet (fish).

Cellentani Corkscrew-shaped pasta.

Cena Dinner.

Centerba An *amaro* (herbal *digestivo*) from Abruzzo.

Cereali Cereal or grain; **cereali misti** is multigrain.

Cernia Grouper.

Cervello Brains, usually calf's brains; often served in Rome with fried artichokes.

Cervo Deer or venison.

Cetriolino Pickle.

Cetriolo Cucumber.

Chef consiglia, (lo) "The chef recommends."

Chiacchiere Literally "chatter," this refers to strips of dough topped with honey that are popular during Carnival.

Chianina Top-quality Tuscan beef.

Chiantigiana Chianti-style. (Tuscany)

Chicche Small potato dumplings; sometimes describes sweets.

Chinotto A bitter soft drink; in Liguria, a *chinotto* is an orange with myrtle leaves that is used to make jams or candied.

Chiocciole Hollow "seashell"-shaped pasta.

Chiodi di garofano Cloves (spice).

Chiodini Literally, "little nails"—a small mushroom, often pickled and sold in jars.

Chitarra, alla Fresh pasta that are cut on a device that looks like a guitar. (Abruzzo)

Chiuso Closed; most Italian restaurants close one day each week.

Ciabatta A loaf of crusty white bread.

Ciambella (or **ciambelline;** plural **ciambelle**) Ring-shaped, sugar-sprinkled cake or cookie, sometimes made with wine.

Ciambellone Pound cake.

Ciauscolo (or **ciavuscolo**) Pâté-like, spreadable *salame* spiced with pepper and garlic. (Marche)

Cibo Food.

Cicchetti Small appetizers. (Venice)

Ciccioli (or **ciccioli frolli**) Compressed dried pork belly; crispy pork belly.

Cicoria Chicory, served raw or cooked.

Ciliegia Cherry.

Cima ripiena Veal stuffed with vegetables, cheese, and other fillings. (Liguria)

Cime di rapa Broccoli rabe or rapini, often used to top pasta in Puglia.

Cinese Chinese.

Cinghiale Wild boar. Try it—it's delicious. Like pork but better. (Tuscany, Umbria)

Cioccolata Chocolate; *cioccolatini* are individual chocolate candies.

Ciociara, alla Typically a pasta sauce made with tomatoes, mozzarella, *pecorino romano* cheese, olive oil, and oregano; can also mean a pasta sauce to which cream has been added. (Lazio)

Cipolla (plural *cipolle*) Onion.

Cipollotti Mini-onions marinated in oil.

Ciuffi Tufts (i.e., clumps of herbs).

Ciuppin Fish soup. (Liguria)

Cjarsons (also *cjalsons* or *cialzons*) Delicious mountain dumplings with more than 40 ingredients. (Friuli-Venezia Giulia)

Classico Wine from a defined, select area.

Cocco (or *noce di cocco*) Coconut.

Cocomero Watermelon. (The South)

Coda Tail. *Coda di bue* is oxtail, and *coda alla vaccinara* is an oxtail stew popular in Rome.

Coda di rospo Monkfish tail. (Veneto)

Colazione Breakfast, also called *prima colazione.*

Collo Neck.

Colomba Dove. This is actually a dove-shaped Easter cake popular throughout Italy.

Colonnata, di Best-quality *lardo* (seasoned lard), from the Carrara marble quarries. (Tuscany)

Coltello Knife; *al coltello* means hand-sliced to order.

Con With.

Conchiglie Hollow "seashell"-shaped pasta.

Condito Seasoned.

Confetti Sugar-coated almonds, color-coded to honor various celebrations. (Abruzzo)

Congelato Frozen.

Coniglio Rabbit.

Cono Ice-cream cone.

Conserva Preserves.

Consigliamo "We recommend."

Contadina "Peasant-style"; rustic.

Conto The bill or check.

Contorno (plural *contorni*) A side dish that comes with the *secondo,* usually a vegetable (including potatoes, beans, or cooked greens).

Coperto Cover charge, added to the bill at some restaurants (see page 25).

Coppa This can refer to a small bowl or cup (for serving gelato), or to peppery, air-cured pork shoulder (see *capocollo*).

Coppa di testa Headcheese (organs in aspic).

Coppetta Small cup (for gelato).

Coriandolo Cilantro, coriander.

Cornetto (plural *cornetti*) Croissant, pastry.

Corposo Full-bodied (wine).

Corzetti Figure-8 or disc-shaped pasta. (Liguria)

Coscia Thigh, usually referring to a piece of poultry.

Cosciotto di agnello Leg of lamb.

Costata Rib-eye steak.

Costata di manzo Entrecôte of beef.

Cotechino Spicy sausage. (Emilia-Romagna)

Cotoletta (or *costoletta*) A cutlet, usually of veal (but *cotoletta* or *costoletta di agnello* is lamb chops). *Cotoletta alla milanese* is a veal cutlet dipped in egg and breadcrumbs and then fried in butter, similar to Wiener schnitzel (Milan); *cotoletta alla valdostana* is a breaded veal cutlet stuffed with Fontina cheese and a slice of prosciutto (Valle d'Aosta).

Cotto Cooked, as in **prosciutto cotto** (boiled ham) or **frutta cotta** (fruit that's baked or poached). **Cotto al forno** is oven-baked, and **cotto sul momento** is "cooked on request" (à la minute).

Cozza (plural **cozze**) Mussel.

Cozze ripiene Mussels stuffed with herbs, cheese, pork, and breadcrumbs (called **muscoli ripieni** in Liguria).

Crauti Sauerkraut; **crauti rossi** is red-cabbage sauerkraut. (Trentino-Alto Adige)

Crema Broadly meaning "cream," this is used in different ways: A dish that is **alla crema** is in a cream sauce; in gelato, *crema* is a custard cream flavor; and in soups, it means "cream of," as in spinach, broccoli, mushrooms, or asparagus. However, cream used for whipping is called **panna.**

Crema fritta A fried custard dessert. (Veneto)

Crème caramel Custard with caramelized topping.

Cremolata Mix of slushy ice and gelato.

Cren (or **Kren**) Horseradish.

Crescenza Mild, soft cheese.

Crescione Watercress.

Crespelle Crêpes; see also **scrippelle.** (Abruzzo)

Croccante Crisp; crispy.

Croccantino "Crunchy" gelato flavor with toasted peanut bits.

Crocchetta (plural **crocchette**) Croquette—a small ball of potato puree mixed with herbs and deep-fried.

Crosta Crust (bread); rind (cheese).

Crostacei Shellfish.

Crostata Fruit or jam tart; **crostatine** are smaller, individual-sized tarts.

Crostino (plural **crostini**) Small toast with topping.

Crudo Raw; **prosciutto crudo**—or simply *crudo* for short—is what English speakers call prosciutto.

Cucchiaio Spoon; **cucchiaino** is a teaspoon.

Cucina Kitchen; cuisine; cookery.

Culatello The most delicate part of a *prosciutto crudo.* (Emilia-Romagna)

Culurgiones Puffy pasta pillows filled with potato puree. (Sardinia)

Cumino Cumin.

Cuoco Cook, chef.

Cuscus (or **cuscusu**) Couscous. (Sicily)

Cutturiedd' (or **spezzatino di agnello**) Slow-cooked lamb flavored with herbs, onions, and potatoes. (Basilicata)

Cynar Cocktail of bitters flavored with artichoke.

D _____

Da portar via To go.

Datteri di mare Sea dates, delicious brown-shelled crustaceans. (Liguria, Trieste)

Datterini Sweet cherry tomatoes.

Dattero Date.

Decaffeinato Decaffeinated.

Deglassato Deglazed.

Degustazione A tasting, as in wine.

Delicato Mild (cheese).

Delizia al limone Cake with lemon-flavored whipped cream. (Campania)

Dello chef Chef's choice.

Diavola, alla "Devil-style," typically meaning quite spicy.

Diavolillo (or **diavolicchio**) A fiery sauce or powder made with spicy peppers. (The South)

Digestivo Digestif (after-dinner drink).

Diospero Persimmon; also known as **caco.**

Disossato Boneless.

Distillato Distillate, any clear eau-de-vie, usually derived from fruit.

Distilleria Distillery.

Ditali (or **ditalini**) "Thimble"-shaped pasta.

DOC Meaning Denominazione di Origine Controllata, this is a legal designation for wines that adhere to strict controls on the type, quantity, and location of the grapes grown.

DOCG This is a notch up from DOC wines (the extra G is "Garan-tita"—guaranteeing wine of an unmistak-ably high quality). DOCG wines are priced at a premium.

Dolce Sweet. The plural, **dolci,** is used generically to refer to desserts. See the *Dolci* chapter.

Dolci dal carrello "Desserts from the cart"—you may see this on a menu at a restaurant that has a little dessert cart circulating after the meal.

Dolcificante Artificial sweetener.

DOP Meaning Denominazione di Origine Protetta ("protected designation of origin"), this indicates foods that are produced in a specified, controlled geographical area.

Dorato Batter-dipped and deep-fried or sautéed (literally "gilded").

Dozzina Dozen.

Dragoncello Tarragon.

Drogheria Dry-goods store.

E _____

Effervescente Carbonated, sparkling.

Eliche "Propeller"-shaped pasta.

Emmental Swiss cheese.

Enoteca (plural **enoteche**) Store or bar featuring a variety of local wines, often serving well-paired snacks or even light meals.

Entrecôte Sirloin steak.

Erba (plural **erbe**) Herb.

Erba cipollina Chive.

Erbazzone Flatbread filled with Swiss chard or other greens. (Emilia-Romagna)

Erbette Swiss chard; **tortelli d'erbette** is pasta filled with *ricotta* cheese and Swiss chard. (Emilia-Romagna)

Erboristeria Store selling herb-based products, such as soaps, liqueurs, teas, and medicinal elixirs.

Etto (plural **etti**) This common unit of measurement is 100 grams, or about a quarter-pound.

Extravergine Extra virgin (top-quality olive oil).

F _____

Facile da bere Easy to drink (wine).

Fagiano Pheasant.

Fagioli all'uccelletto "Bird-style" beans with tomato and sage.

Fagiolino (plural **fagiolini**) String bean; can also refer to a green bean-shaped pasta.

Fagiolo (plural **fagioli**) Bean, often white bean.

Fagottino Puff pastry turnover.

Falsomagro (or **farsumagru**) Meat roll filled with cheese, sausage, and boiled eggs. (Sicily)

Faraona Guinea fowl.

Farcito Stuffed.

Farfalle "Butterfly"- or bowtie-shaped pasta.

Farina Flour.

Farinata Chickpea crêpe. (Liguria)

Farro Spelt, a grain found throughout Italy but especially in Umbria.

Fatto in casa Homemade.

Fave Fava beans.

Fave al guanciale Fava beans simmered with cured pork cheek and onion.

Fedelini Thin, long pasta noodle.

Fegatelli Pork liver wrapped in caul fat, flavored with herbs, and cooked in lard. (Tuscany)

Fegatini Chicken livers.

Fegato Liver, usually calf's liver; **fegato alla veneziana** is prepared with onions and white wine. (Veneto)

Fernet A dark, bitter after-dinner drink.

Ferratelle Anise cakes stamped with patterns. (Abruzzo, Molise)

Fetta Slice.

Fettucce Wider fettuccine noodle (see below).

Fettuccelle Skinnier fettuccine noodle (see below).

Fettuccine Strips of egg pasta, especially popular in Rome; **fettuccine al burro** (a.k.a. **fettuccine Alfredo**) is made with sweet butter and heaps of freshly grated Parmi-giana-Reggiano. (Lazio)

Fettunta Literally "oily slice," a basic and rustic *bruschetta* with olive oil. (Tuscany)

Fico (plural **fichi**) Fig.

Fico d'india Prickly pear. (Sicily)

Fiera Fair; festival; open-air market.

Fileja Short macaroni, often served in a spicy pork sauce. (Calabria)

Filetto Tenderloin, fillet.

Filetto di baccalà Salt cod fried in batter.

Filone Loaf of bread.

Filu ferru (or **filo di ferro**) High-octane liqueur. (Sardinia)

Finanziera, alla "Financier-style" sauce from Torino, made with chicken livers, mush-rooms, onions, and white wine. (Piedmont)

Finferli Small, delicious wild mushrooms found in the Alps.

Finocchio Fennel.

Finocchiona (or **finocchiella**) *Salame* containing fennel seed. (Tuscany, Umbria)

Fior di latte A cow's-milk cheese similar to mozzarella, but milder; also the name for a "plain" gelato flavor.

Fiorentina "Flor-ence-style"; when referring to steak, **bistecca alla fiorentina** is a top-quality cut of Chianina beef grilled very rare.

Fiori di zucca (or **fiori di zucchini**) Zucchini blossoms—typically stuffed with mozzarella or *ricotta* and ancho-vies, batter-dipped, and gently deep-fried.

Focaccia Pillowy, salty flatbread, often served with toppings; **focaccina** is a smaller, single-serving version. A **focacceria** is a shop that sells it. (Liguria)

Focolare An open hearth—a traditional place where family and friends gather in the home.

Foglia (or **verdura a foglia**) Leafy vegetable.

Foglia di vite Grape leaf.

Fonduta Italy's answer to fondue, with Fontina cheese. (The Alps)

Fontina Nutty, melty mountain cheese similar to Gruyère. (Valle d'Aosta)

Forchetta Fork.

Formaggio (plural **formaggi**) Cheese. **Formaggio di capra** (or **formaggio caprino**) is goat cheese, **formaggio di fossa** is cheese aged underground, and **formaggio spalmabile** is cream cheese. But *attenzione,* eh? **Formaggio di testa** is headcheese (organs in aspic).

Forno Oven, typically where bread is baked; **al forno** means "baked."

Fragola (plural **fragole**) Strawberry. Little wild strawberries (**fragoline**) are delectable; occasionally you will find giant strawberries **(fragoloni).**

Frangelico Hazelnut liqueur.

Frantoio A press to make olive oil.

Frappè Milkshake.

Frasca An informal restaurant similar to an *osteria,* often outdoors and near a vineyard. (Friuli-Venezia Giulia)

Frattaglie Giblets.

Freddo Cold.

Frègula Sardinia's answer to couscous.

Fresco This can mean cool, fresh, or young (in reference to cheese).

Friarielli The tips of **broccoletti;** in Naples, often sautéed and served with sausage. (Campania)

Fricassea Fricassee.

Frico Delicious fritter made of Montasio cheese; this can be thin and crunchy, or thick, with a runny center. (Friuli-Venezia Giulia)

Friggitoria A fry shop.

Frigo (or **Frigorifero**) Refrigerator.

Frisella Hard, dry, bagel-like roll that can be rehydrated before eating. (Puglia)

Frittata (plural **frittate**) Similar to an omelet, but the eggs are cooked in olive oil instead of butter, and vegetables and cheese are mixed in.

Frittella Fritter.

Fritto (also **fritta, fritti,** or **fritte**) Fried, usually deep-fried. A **fritto misto** (or sometimes **frittura**) is a combination of fried foods. When ordered in coastal areas, this usually contains fish and seafood (squid, octopus, perhaps a few shrimp) and might be called **frittura di mare, frittura di pesce,** or—in Naples—**frittura di paranza.**

Fritto misto all'italiana A smorgasbord of deep-fried foods: organ meats, lamb, and batter-dipped vegetables such as zucchini, eggplants, and artichokes. (Piedmont)

Frittole Small doughnuts eaten during Carnival.

Frizzante Sparkling.

Frullato A whipped or blended drink made with milk and fruit or chocolate—roughly equivalent to a milkshake.

Frumento Wheat.

Frutta Fruit.

Frutta cotta Cooked or stewed fruit.

Frutta secca Generic word for nuts and dried fruit.

Fruttato Fruity (young wine or olive oil).

Frutti di bosco Literally, "forest fruits," this refers to wild strawberries, raspberries, blueberries, blackberries, and currants. In a restaurant, these may be served in a bowl with lemon juice and sugar and called **sottobosco** ("under the forest").

Frutti di mare Shellfish.

Funghi Mushrooms; most famous are *funghi porcini,* which have large caps that can be grilled and eaten like steaks.

Funghi trifolati Sliced mushrooms cooked with garlic.

Fusilli Corkscrew-shaped pasta; *fusilli bucati* (or *busiate*) is long, tightly coiled, hollow pasta.

Fuso Melted, as in cheese or chocolate.

G _____

Galletti Pasta shaped like a rooster's comb; or chanterelle mushrooms.

Galletto Cockerel (rooster).

Gallina Hen.

Gamberi Prawns; *gamberetti* are small prawns, and *gamberoni* are jumbo prawns. *Gambero rosso* is the prized "red prawn" caught off Sicily's west coast (and also the name of a prestigious Italian food magazine). *Gamberi di fiume* are crayfish.

Garganelli Flat egg pasta rolled into a tube.

Garibaldi A cocktail (combining Campari bitters and orange juice) named for one of the creators of the modern Italian nation—described in the first pages of this book.

Gassata Carbonated.

Gastronomia High-end foods store selling cold cuts, cheeses, olives, and prepared dishes.

Gattafin Deep-fried pastry filled with greens.

Gelateria Ice-cream parlor.

Gelatina Jelly.

Gelato (plural *gelati*) Ice cream. For more on this delicious topic, see page 88.

Gelso Mulberry.

Gemelli Pasta shaped like a double helix ("twins").

Genovese, alla "Genoa-style," which usually means with pesto sauce; in the Naples area, it's a sauce of onions, carrots, and celery.

Germano (or *germano reale*) Mallard.

Ghiacciato Chilled.

Ghiaccio Ice.

Ghiotta, alla This term describes a sauce served with grilled meat or fish. In Umbria, it's made of the meat's natural juices with prosciutto, olive oil, wine, garlic, and other flavorings. In Calabria, Sicily, and the South, it's tomatoes, onions, garlic, olives, anchovies, and often other ingredients.

Gianduia (or *gianduja*) Chocolate with hazelnut paste. (Piedmont)

Ginepro Juniper.

Giorno, (del) (Of the) Day.

Giovane Young (wine).

Girasole Sunflower; also a ravioli shape.

Glassato Glazed.

Glutine Gluten.

Gnocchi Pillowy dumplings made with flour and, sometimes, riced potatoes; *gnocchetti* are tiny, thimble-sized gnocchi.

Gnocchi alla romana (or *gnocchi di semola*) Disks of semolina baked with butter and cheese. (Lazio)

Gomiti "Elbow" macaroni.

Gorgonzola Pungent, creamy, blue-veined cheese that comes in milder *(dolce)* and sharper *(piccante)* forms. (Lombardy, Piedmont)

Gramigna Coiled noodle with a tiny hole in the middle, often served with sausage sauce *(alla salsiccia).* (Emilia-Romagna)

Grana (or *grana padano*) Hard grating

cheese used on pastas, often as a less expensive alternative to Parmigiano-Reggiano. *Padano* means "from the Po Valley."

Granchio Crab.

Grande Large.

Granita (plural **granite**) Sweet, slushy ice treat flavored with coffee, lemon, fruit, almond, or other flavors. (Sicily)

Grano Wheat or grain.

Grano saraceno Buckwheat. (Lombardy)

Granoturco Corn.

Granseola A large crab found in the Adriatic Sea.

Grappa A powerful spirit distilled from grape skins and pits; for more, see page 100.

Grasso Cooking fat.

Gratin, (al) Topped with browned cheese.

Gratinate When referring to vegetables, this means baked with oil, spices, and breadcrumbs, but no cheese.

Grattachecca Slushy ice with sweet syrup. (Lazio)

Grattugia A grater, usually for cheese or nutmeg.

Grattugiato Grated.

Gremolada (or **gremolata**) A mixture of garlic, rosemary, and

lemon used to flavor *ossobuco.* (Lombardy)

Gricia, alla Pasta preparation with *pancetta,* black pepper, and *pecorino romano* cheese.

Griglia, alla Grilled.

Grigliata mista Mixed grill of meats; *verdure grigliata* is mixed grilled vegetables.

Grissini Breadsticks.

Groviera Gruyère cheese.

Guanciale Pork cheek.

Guarnizione Garnish.

Gubana Delicious, bready cake filled with raisins and nuts. (Friuli-Venezia Giulia)

Gulasch (or **Goulasch**) Spicy meat stew. (The Alps and Friuli-Venezia Giulia)

Guscio Shell, peel, or rind.

Gusto Flavor, taste.

Gustoso Flavorful; heavy (wine).

H

Hag Decaffeinated coffee.

Hugo Cocktail of Prosecco, elderberry syrup, and soda. (The North)

I

IGT A wine designation indicating high

quality and specific to a region, but often using non-traditional grapes and methods (such as the Super Tuscans).

Impanato Breaded.

Impepata (di cozze) Mussel soup (with mussels in the shell).

Importato Imported.

Incluso Included.

Indivia Endive—a pungent, curly salad green.

Insaccati Dried, hard *salame.*

Insalata Salad. It's usually considered a side dish with the *secondo,* rather than a first course or a meal in itself. Common choices include **Insalata verde** (a simple green salad) or **Insalata mista** (mixed salad, typically containing mixed greens and tomatoes). Other types are listed below.

Insalata caprese A "Capri salad" of fresh mozzarella cheese, tomatoes, and basil, plus a few drops of olive oil. (Campania)

Insalata di mare A mix of cold seafood, dressed with oil and lemon.

Insalata di riso "Rice salad" with vegetables, and occasionally meat, that's served cold and popular in the summer. (Piedmont, Lombardy)

Insalata russa Vegetable salad with mayonnaise.

Insalatone A main-course salad (literally "big salad").

Integrale Whole grain.

Involtini Rolled meat or fish fillets stuffed with vegetables or other fillings. **Involtini al sugo** are veal cutlets rolled with prosciutto and cheese in tomato sauce. (The South)

Inzimino Marinated in tomatoes and greens.

Inzuppato Soaked.

J _____

Jota A thick soup of beans, cabbage or sauerkraut, onions, sage, garlic, and sometimes pork. (Friuli-Venezia Giulia)

K _____

Kaiserschmarrn Eggy crêpe with raisins, jam, and powdered sugar. (Trentino-Alto Adige and the Alps)

Kasher Kosher.

L _____

Lagane (or **lacane**) Broad flat noodles, usually tossed with tomato sauce or with lentils and beans; smaller ones are **laganelle.** (The South)

Lampasciuoli (*or* **lampasciuni**) Small, bitter onions (actually hyacinth bulbs). (The South)

Lampone (plural **lamponi**) Raspberry.

Lampredotto Cow's stomach.

Lardellato Larded.

Lardo Salt-cured lard, sometimes scented with rosemary or other herbs; the best is **lardo di Colonnata.** (Tuscany)

Lasagne Sheets of pasta that are layered in baking dishes with various sauces and other ingredients.

Latte Milk. **Latte fresco** is fresh milk; **latte intero** is whole milk; **latte magro** is skim milk. Note that if you want what Americans call a "latte," you should order a **caffè latte.** (*Latte* by itself will get you just a glass of hot milk.)

Latte di mandorla Sweetened almond-milk drink that's very refreshing when served cold on a hot day. (The South)

Latteria A dairy or store that sells milk, cream, butter, and cheese; in Friuli, also a type of cow's-milk cheese.

Latterini Little poached fish served with lemon juice and olive oil.

Latticini "Milk products," usually referring to fresh cheeses. (The South)

Lattuga Lettuce; **lattuga romana** is romaine lettuce.

Lauro (or **alloro**) Bay leaf.

Leggermente Mild; mildly.

Leggero Light (not heavy).

Legumi Legumes.

Lenticchie Lentils, especially popular on New Year's Eve. Because they look like little coins, it's said that eating them will bring money in the coming year.

Lepre Hare.

Lepre in salmì Jugged hare. (The North)

Lesso Boiled.

Letto, su On a bed of.

Licurdia Simple soup with sweet red onions and other vegetables. (Calabria)

Lievito Yeast.

Limonata Lemonade or lemon soda.

Limoncello Lemon liqueur. (Campania)

Limoncino Ligurian version of *limoncello*.

Limone (plural **limoni**) Lemon.

Lingua Tongue.

Linguine Long, flat spaghetti; a skinny version might be called **linguettine.**

Liquirizia Licorice.

Locale Local.

Locanda Traditional word referring to casual eatery like an *osteria.*

Lombata (or **lombo**) Sirloin. **Lombatina** is a veal chop, and **lombata di maiale** is a grilled pork chop.

Lonza A freshly cured *salame,* popular in the fall and winter.

Lonzino Delectable air-cured pork loin.

Lucanica (or **luganega**) Spicy sausage. (Basilicata, Lombardy, Trentino)

Luccio Pike.

Lumache Snails.

M _____

Maccheroni A general term for dried, tubular pastas.

Maccheroni alla chitarra Fresh pasta that resembles squared spaghetti, made on a device that looks like the strings of a guitar *(chitarra).* (Abruzzo)

Macchiato Literally "stained," usually used in reference to coffee: **Caffè macchiato** is a small cup of espresso "stained" with a dash of foamed milk, while **latte macchiato** is a tall glass with milk and foam, "stained" with a splash of espresso.

Macco (di fave) Stick-to-your-ribs soup made of dried and crushed fava beans and fennel; sometimes served over pasta. (Sicily)

Macedonia Fresh fruit salad, a popular dessert.

Macinato Minced.

Mafalde (or **mafaldine**) Wide, flat, rectangular noodles ruffled on both sides.

Maggiorana Marjoram.

Maiale Pork.

Maiale sotto sale Salt pork.

Maionese Mayonnaise.

Mais Corn.

Malaga Rum raisin (gelato flavor).

Malloreddus Tiny, saffron-scented gnocchi. (Sardinia)

Maltagliati "Roughly cut" pasta.

Mandarino Tangerine. (Sicily)

Mandorla (plural **mandorle**) Almond; **pasta di mandorle** is almond paste, popular in desserts. (Sicily, Puglia)

Manicotti Big, stuffed pasta tube.

Manzo Beef.

Marasche Black morello cherries.

Margarina Margarine.

Margherita Classic pizza topping: simply tomatoes, mozzarella, and basil.

Marinara General term for tomato sauce. A **pizza marinara** is topped simply with tomatoes, garlic, and oregano, but no cheese. Confusingly, on pasta, **alla marinara** (which refers to "seafaring") can sometimes indicate a tomato and seafood sauce.

Marinato Marinated.

Maritozzi Sweet buns, often filled with whipped cream; in Sicily, they usually add raisins, too. (Lazio, Sicily)

Marmellata Jam or marmalade.

Marocchino This coffee drink (literally "Moroccan") is layers of espresso, cocoa powder, and foamed milk, with a dusting of cocoa powder; **mocaccino** is larger and uses hot chocolate instead of cocoa.

Marroni Chestnuts.

Marrons glacés Candied chestnuts. (Piedmont, Liguria)

Marsala, al With a sauce of sweet Marsala wine.

Marziani Pasta spirals resembling "Martian" antennae.

Marzolino A fresh, delicate sheep's-milk cheese, customarily made in March (marzo).

Mascarpone Rich, sweet, buttery dessert cheese. (Lombardy, Emilia-Romagna)

Mattarello Rolling pin.

Maturo Mature (wine).

Mazzancolle Giant prawns.

Mela (plural **mele**) Apple.

Mela cotogna Quince.

Melanzana (plural **melazane**) Eggplant.

Melanzane alla parmigiana Breaded, fried slices of eggplant, baked with fresh tomato sauce, mozzarella, and Parmigiano-Reggiano. (Sicily and the South)

Melograno Pomegranate.

Melone Melon, usually cantaloupe; in Sicily, **mellone** is a watermelon.

Melone d'inverno Honeydew melon.

Menta Mint.

Menù In Italian, menù can refer to the printed menu (also called **la lista**). Or it might refer to a fixed-price, multicourse meal, which might include the **menù del giorno** (of the day), **menù fisso** (fixed), or **menù turistico** (designed for tourists). A fancy, elaborate menù might be called a **menù degustazione** (tasting).

Merasca Sour cherry.

Mercato Market.

Merenda Snack.

Meridionale Southern Italian.

Meringa Meringue.

Merletti An amaro (herbal digestivo) from Marche, with cinnamon and anise.

Merluzzo Cod.

Mesciüà Soup made with white beans and chickpeas. (Liguria)

Mezzafegato Raw sausage made with pig's liver, pepper, sugar, raisins, pine nuts, and orange peel.

Mezzani Hollow, tubular pasta.

Mezzano Young, firm, creamy cheese (often Asiago).

Mezzelune Stuffed pasta shaped like "half-moons." (Trentino-Alto Adige)

Mezzo (or **mezza**) Half, as in mezzo-litro (half-liter) or mezza-bottiglia (half-bottle).

Midollo Marrow.

Miele Honey.

Millefoglie Layers of sweet, buttery pastry ("a thousand leaves").

Milza Spleen.

Minestra Soup; in some parts of the North, this term can also be used interchangeably with primo (first course).

Minestrone A rich soup with vegetables, beans, and either rice, pasta, or barley.

Mirtilli Mountain berries; **mirtilli rossi** look like cranberries, and **mirtilli neri** resemble blueberries, but the flavors are different. (Trentino-Alto Adige and the Alps)

Mirto Myrtle, a popular flavor in Sardinian cooking; also refers to an after-dinner liqueur made with myrtle. (Sardinia)

Missoltino (or **Missultitt**) Salted, air-dried, shad-like lake fish, often served with pasta or polenta. (Lake Como, Lombardy)

Misticanza Mixed green salad. (Lazio)

Misto Mixed; assorted.

Mocetta Dried veal, chamois, or other meat. (Valle d'Aosta)

Moka Distinctly Italian coffee pot (described on page 95).

Moleche Soft-shell crabs; ***moleche fritte*** are fried soft-shell crabs. (Veneto)

Mollicata (or ***con la mollica***) Simple pasta sauce, typically with tomato, onion, red wine, crumbs *(molliche)* from yesterday's bread, and sometimes anchovy. (The South)

Mollusco Shellfish.

Montasio Flavorful cow's-milk cheese. (Friuli-Venezia Giulia)

Monte Bianco "Mont Blanc"—a sweet, rich pastry made with cream, meringue, and chestnut paste. (Valle d'Aosta)

Montenegro Italy's most popular *amaro* (herbal *digestivo*), from Emilia-Romagna.

Montone Mutton.

Mora (plural ***more***) Blackberry.

Morbido Soft (cheese); smooth (wine).

Mortadella The original "baloney,"

a giant wheel made with pork, spices, pieces of fat, and sometimes pistachios. (Emilia-Romagna)

Moscardino (bianco) Baby octopus.

Mostaccioli "Moustache"-like cookies.

Mostarda Mixed fruit pickled with mustard seed, served with boiled meats or fine cold cuts; ***mostarda veneta*** is more like a spicy puree of fruits. (Lombardy, Veneto, Emilia-Romagna)

Mosto (del vino) The fresh juice of wine grapes, sometimes consumed as a drink in its own right, and also used (in Tuscany and Basilicata) as a flavoring in cooking and baking.

Mozzarella Soft, mild, melty, milky cheese; the very best is ***mozzarella di bufala,*** handmade from the milk of water buffalo. (Campania)

Mozzarella in carrozza Deep-fried mozzarella between two pieces of bread ("in a cart") that has been dipped in egg, sometimes with a bit of anchovy.

Muggine Mullet (fish).

Mursiellu Slow-cooked stew of organ meats, red wine, tomatoes, *peperoncino,* and herbs. (Calabria)

Muscoli In most of Italy, this means "muscles" (and *cozze* is mussels); but in Liguria, this means "mussels."

N

Napoletana "Naples-style"; when referring to pizza, this usually means mozzarella, anchovies, and tomato sauce.

Nasello Hake (whitefish).

Naturale Still (bottled water).

'Ncasciata Baked pasta dish made with *salame,* hard-boiled eggs, mozzarella, and eggplant. (Sicily)

'Ncapriata (or ***fave e cicoria***) Puree of fava beans and cooked chicory flavored with olive oil. (Puglia)

'Nduja Spicy, spreadable pork sausage, bright-red with *peperoncino rosso*. (Calabria and the South)

Negroni A potent cocktail of equal parts Campari, vermouth, and gin.

Nero, al Cooked with cuttlefish ink, with a black color.

Nero di seppia Cuttlefish ink.

Nervetti Chilled, boiled calf's foot. (Lombardy)

Nespola Medlar (a small, apple-like fruit).

Nettarina Nectarine.

Nocciola Hazelnut.

Noccioline Usually means peanuts ("little nuts").

Noce (plural **noci**) Walnut.

Noce di cocco Coconut.

Noce moscata Nutmeg.

Nocino Walnut liqueur.

Nodino Knuckle.

Nonna, della "Grandma-style," a generic term that suggests something made with loving care.

Norcina, alla (or **alla nursina**) In the style of Norcia—a town famous for its butchers; usually this means spicy sausage and, sometimes, truffle. (Umbria)

Norma, alla A tomato sauce with eggplant and *ricotta salata* cheese. (Sicily)

O

Oca Goose.

Offella (plural **offelle**) Soft round or oval cakes. (The North)

Oggi Today.

Olio Oil.

Olio di semi Seed oil.

Olio d'oliva Olive oil (see page 67).

Oliva (plural **olive**) Olive. **Olive nere** are black olives, and **olive verdi** are green olives. **Olive all'ascolane** is a stuffed-olive dish from Marche, and **olive con peperoni** are stuffed with red hot peppers.

Olivette Thin rolls of meat, usually veal, that are stuffed or spread with different flavors. (Marche)

Orata Gilthead, a delicious bream.

Orecchiette (or **recchietelle**). Ear-shaped pasta. (The South)

Origano Oregano.

Ortolano, dell' "Greengrocer-style," with vegetables.

Orzo Barley. This can refer to tiny barley-shaped pasta. Or it can be **caffè d'orzo,** a decaffeinated coffee alternative made with roasted barley. And **Orzata** is a nonalcoholic beverage made with barley.

Ossa dei morti "Bones of the dead" cookies. (Tuscany)

Ossobuco Braised marrow-bone veal steaks, cooked in butter, wine, and *gremolada* (garlic, rosemary, and lemon). (Milan)

Osteria (plural **osterie**) A tavern or humble restaurant where wine is served as the main attraction, paired with tasty food.

Ostrica (plural **ostriche**) Oyster.

Otto "8"-shaped pastry.

Ovotarica Dried roe, similar to *bottarga*. (Calabria)

P

Paccheri Short, very wide pasta tubes.

Padella Frying pan or skillet; **in padella** means "pan-fried."

Pajata (or **pagliata**) Slow-cooked lamb's intestines in tomato, often served with rigatoni. (Rome)

Pallina Scoop (ice cream).

Palombo Dogfish.

Pancetta Salt-cured pork belly meat; **pancetta arrotolata** is rolled into a tight, sausage-like bundle and sliced.

Pan di spagna Sponge cake.

Pandoro A yeasty cake often eaten at Christmastime. (Veneto)

Pane Bread. Some common types are **pane alle olive** (olive bread), **pane aromatico** (herb or vegetable bread), **pane bianco** (white bread), **pane casereccio**

(home-style bread), **pane di segale** (rye bread), **pane integrale** (whole-grain bread), and **pane scuro** (brown bread).

Pane carasau Thin, crispy, unleavened, Sardinian shepherd's bread; **pane frattau** is a simple dish that combines this with tomato sauce, grated *pecorino,* and a fried egg. (Sardinia)

Pane toscano Tuscan bread, made without salt.

Panettone Milanese Christmas yeast cake made with saffron, raisins, candied fruit, and eggs. (Lombardy)

Panforte A dense cake made of nuts, spices, and candied fruit. (Tuscany)

Panificio Bakery.

Panino (plural **panini**) Roll or sandwich. **Panini farciti** are premade sandwiches.

Paninoteca Sandwich shop.

Paniscia A rice dish made with sausage and vegetables. (Piedmont)

Panissa In Piedmont, this is the same thing as *paniscia* (see above). In Liguria, *panissa* refers to a chickpea tart, which is also called **paniccia.**

Panna Cream; **con panna** typically means topped with whipped cream *(panna montata).* With pastas and other savory dishes, **alla panna** is in cream sauce.

Panna cotta "Cooked cream"—a rich dessert often served with pureed berries.

Pansoti (or **pansotti**) Pasta filled with greens and herbs and served with walnut sauce. (Liguria)

Panzanella Bread salad with tomatoes. (Tuscany)

Panzerotto Savory, deep-fried turnover. (Puglia)

Papaia Papaya.

Papera (or **papero**) Duckling.

Pappa col pomodoro (or **pappa al pomodoro**) Soup of fresh tomatoes, stale bread, and olive oil. (Tuscany)

Pappardelle Broad, flat noodles often served with meat sauces. (Tuscany)

Parampampoli A brew of coffee, grappa, wine, and caramelized sugar served flambé at Christmas markets. (Trentino-Alto Adige)

Parmigiana With tomato, cheese, and breadcrumbs.

Parmigiano-Reggiano Italy's finest cheese—hard, nutty, and decadent, ideal for eating straight or for grating over pasta. (Emilia-Romagna)

Passata A puree that is either blended or passed through a sieve; **passata di pomodoro** is the base for tomato sauce, while a *passata* of vegetables is usually a soup.

Passatelli Fresh noodles for soup made with breadcrumbs, lemon, egg, and nutmeg. (Emilia-Romagna, Marche)

Passeggiata A stroll that's taken in the late afternoon or early evening by almost every Italian—an excuse to get some exercise, to socialize, and to enjoy an *aperitivo,* snack, or gelato before dinnertime.

Passito Sweet dessert wine.

Pasta (noodles) General term for the vast variety of noodles for which Italy is famous (for starters, see page 70). These come in a few broad categories: **Pastasciutta** (or **pasta secca**) is dry pasta, made of wheat flour and water in an almost infinite variety of shapes (including spaghetti, *maccheroni,* penne, and rigatoni). These can be stored on a shelf until needed. **Pasta fresca** is fresh-made pasta, including *tagliatelle,* fettuccine, *pappardelle,* and various types of filled pastas **(pasta ripiena). Pasta lunga,** also called strand pasta, are noodles long enough to twist around a fork (like spaghetti); **pasta corta** ("short pasta") are smaller, designed to be scooped or speared with a fork. And finally, **pasta al forno** is a baked pasta dish, such as *lasagne,* cannelloni, *timballi,* manicotti, and baked ziti.

Pasta (pastry) Confusingly, *pasta* can also refer to pastry and sweet rolls. **Pasta sfoglia** is puff pastry, and **pasta reale** is marzipan. (Sicily and the South)

Pasta e fagioli A soup of pasta and beans.

Pasticceria Pastry shop.

Pasticcino This is another word for pastry; **pasticcio di carne** refers to a hash.

Pasticciotto Small custard pie. (Puglia)

Pastiera napoletana A lemony Neapolitan *ricotta* cake served at Easter. (Campania)

Pastina Tiny pasta served in broth.

Patata (plural **patate**) Potato. **Patatine fritte** are french fries, **patate arrosto** are roasted potatoes, and **patate sabbiose** are deep-fried potato chunks.

Patatine Potato chips.

Patè di fegato Chicken liver paste.

Pearà A marrow-based sauce served with *bollito misto.* (Veneto, Emilia-Romagna)

Pecora Sheep.

Pecorino Sheep's-milk cheese; **fresco** is fresh and soft, while **stagionato** is aged. Aged, hard *pecorino* is often called **pecorino romano;** similar to but sharper than Parmigiano-Reggiano, it's often grated over pastas in Rome and throughout the South.

Pellizzoni Thicker spaghetti.

Penne Short, versatile "quill"-shaped pasta. **Pennette** is smaller, and **pennoni** is larger.

Pepe Pepper; **pepe nero** is black pepper. **Pepato** means "peppered."

Peperonata Side dish of cooked sweet peppers, sometimes with tomatoes.

Peperoncino Small, intense hot pepper, usually red **(rosso);** essential to the cuisines of Calabria, Basilicata, Puglia, Molise, and Abruzzo. (The South)

Peperoni Sweet peppers, which come in **verde** (green), **rosso** (red), and **giallo** (yellow). Italians don't recognize the American word pepperoni; for a spicy *salame,* they might instead say **salame piccante.**

Peperoni imbottiti Sweet peppers filled with capers, olives, anchovies, breadcrumbs, basil, garlic, and parsley. (Campania)

Peposo Highly peppered beef stew with red wine. (Tuscany)

Pera (plural **pere**) Pear.

Perciatelli Hollow, tubular pasta noodles (also called **bucatini**).

Pernice Partridge.

Pesante Heavy (rich, hard to digest).

Pesca (plural **pesche**) Peach (this also means "fishing").

Pescatora, alla "Fisherman's style," suggesting a combination of seafood and fish.

Pesce (plural **pesci**) Fish; **pesce gatto** is catfish, and **pesce**

spada is swordfish. (Sicily, Calabria)

Pescheria Fishmonger (also called *pescivendolo*).

Pesto Sauce made of fresh basil, garlic, pine nuts, olive oil, and *pecorino* or Parmigiano-Reggiano cheese. (Liguria)

Petto Breast, as in *pollo* (chicken), *oca* (goose), *anatra* (duck), or *tacchino* (turkey).

Pettole Fried dough balls popular at Christmas. (The South)

Peverada (or *salsa peverada*) Poultry sauce made with anchovy fillets, chicken livers, and pickles. (Veneto)

Pezzente A sausage made with leftover bits of pork and highly seasoned with pepper.

Pezzo Piece.

Piacentino ennese Hard, spicy sheep cheese with saffron and pepper. (Sicily)

Piacere, a "To order" (as you like).

Piadina A soft flatbread, often stuffed with fillings to make a wrap sandwich. (Emilia-Romagna)

Piatto Plate.

Piccante Sharp or spicy.

Piccata A meat—typically thin veal cutlets—cooked in butter and lemon.

Piccione (or *piccioncino*) Squab.

Piccolo Small.

Pici Hand-rolled thick pasta strands. (Tuscany)

Pieno Full.

Pignolo Macaroon. (Sicily)

Pinolata A pine-nut cake or cookie. (Tuscany, Liguria)

Pinoli Pine nuts.

Pinzimonio Raw vegetables dipped in olive oil. (Puglia, Sardinia)

Piselli Peas.

Pistacchio Pistachio.

Pizza You know what this is; for a list of toppings, see page 35. The style of pizza varies somewhat as you travel through Italy—for more on original Neapolitan pizza, see page 270. *Pizza rustica* (also called *pizza al taglio* or *pizza al trancio*) is a thick hunk of pizza sold by weight, cut out of a large, rectangular pan.

Pizzaiola, alla A way of preparing meat in the style of a pizzamaker (as the name means): with fresh tomatoes, oregano, garlic, and olive oil.

Pizzella Small, thin-crusted pizzas; sometimes the crust is cooked alone and dipped in honey or sugar to make a dessert. *Pizelle* can also refer to thin wafer cookies with a slight anise flavor.

Pizzicotti Round pasta. (Calabria)

Pizzoccheri Short, thick buckwheat pasta served with melty *bitto* cheese. (Lombardy)

Platessa Plaice (whitefish).

Poche calorie Low-calorie.

Pociacche Wider, flatter *orrechiette* pasta. (Puglia)

Polenta Cornmeal that is served as a mush or hardened and cut into blocks. This staple of impoverished times—which sustained Italians for generations—remains a key starch in much of the country, especially in the North. For more, see page 76.

Pollame Poultry.

Pollastrella Game hen.

Pollo Chicken.

Polmone Lung.

Polpa Pulp. (This also implies ground meat, such as *polpa di oca*— ground goose meat.)

Polpetta (plural **polpette**) Meatball, usually quite small. (Puglia, Campania, Sicily)

Polpettone Meat loaf.

Polpo (or **polipo**) Octopus; **polpetti** (or **polipetti**) are baby octopus.

Pomodoro (plural **pomodori**) Tomato. **Pomodorini** are cherry tomatoes, and **pomodori secchi** are sun-dried tomatoes.

Pomodoro gratinato Tomato grilled and dusted with breadcrumbs.

Pompelmo Grapefruit.

Porchetta Roast suckling pig, often sold in sandwiches from carts or roadside stands. In Sardinia, where this is a specialty, they call it **porceddu. Porchettato** refers to any meat that is stuffed and cooked in the style of roast pork.

Porcini See **Funghi.**

Porro (plural **porri**) Leek.

Prezzemolo Parsley.

Prezzo Price. **Prezzo al peso** means "priced by the weight," and **prezzo di mercato** is "market price."

Primo (or **primo piatto;** plural **primi**) The first course of a meal, typically pasta, soup, a *risotto,* or polenta. See the *Primi* chapter.

Profiterole Cream-filled pastry with warm chocolate sauce.

Prosecco Sparkling white wine. (Veneto, Friuli-Venezia Giulia)

Prosciutto Ham. This comes in two broad categories: **Prosciutto cotto** (often simply called **cotto**) is boiled. **Prosciutto crudo** is technically "raw" but air-cured—what Americans call "prosciutto." The two best are **prosciutto di Parma** (Emilia-Romagna) and **prosciutto di San Daniele** (Friuli-Venezia Giulia).

Prosciutto e melone/fichi Air-cured ham wrapped around melon/fresh figs.

Provola A semisoft cheese that can be made with buffalo or cow's milk, often lightly smoked. (Central and southern Italy)

Provolone This pear-shaped, cow's-milk cheese can be mild or sharp and is usually firm and aged. (The South)

Prugna (plural **prugne**) Plum.

Prugna secca (plural **prugne secche**) Prune.

Puledro Foal.

Puntarelle Dark-green Roman version of chicory. (Lazio)

Punt e Mes Sweet red vermouth and red wine.

Purè di patate (or **purè**) Mashed potatoes.

Puro Pure.

Puttanesca, alla "Prostitute-style" pasta sauce: tomato with anchovies and/or tuna, black olives, capers, and garlic.

Q _____

Quaglia Quail.

Quattro formaggi "Four cheeses"—a pasta sauce that varies by chef, but often contains Fontina, Parmigiano-Reggiano, Emmenthal, and Groviera (Gruyère).

Quattro stagioni With four separate toppings (pizza).

Quinto quarto Offal, literally "fifth quarter"—the parts of the animal that remain after it's been drawn, quartered, and the best cuts sold off.

R _____

Rabarbaro Bitter-tasting rhubarb liqueur.

Radiatori Radiator-shaped pasta.

Radicchio Bitter, red-leaf lettuce, originally from Treviso.

Radice Root.

Rafano Horseradish (also called **cren**).

Ragù In most places (especially Tuscany and Emilia-Romagna), this refers to a rich meat sauce for pasta, which may or may not contain tomatoes. In the South, *ragù* is a simpler sauce where scant meat is used as the base, but tomatoes and other vegetables are more prominent.

Ragusano Semi-hard cow cheese. (Sicily)

Ramazzoti An *amaro* (herbal *digestivo*) from Milan.

Rana (plural **rane**) Frog. **Cosce di rane** are frog's legs.

Rana pescatrice Monkfish.

Rapa Turnip.

Rascatelli Snail-shaped pasta, like *cavatelli*. (The South)

Raschiatelli Long, thick-cut pasta. (The South)

Ravanada A horserad-ish-apple sauce used for *bollito misto*. (The Alps)

Ravanello (plural **rava-nelli**) Radish.

Ravioli Filled pasta typ-ically containing *ricotta* cheese or chopped meat. **Raviolini** are tiny, and **ravioloni** are very large.

Ribes (plural **ribesi**) Currant.

Ribollita A thick, twice-cooked ("reboiled") soup made of old bread, vegetables, beans, and olive oil. (Tuscany)

Ricciarelli Small almond cookies topped with confectioners' sugar. (Tuscany)

Riccio di mare Sea urchin ("sea hedgehog").

Ricevuta Receipt (usually used for fiscal purposes); see also **scontrino.**

Ricoperto Coated.

Ricotta Soft, creamy cheese (made by cooking curds a second time—the name means "recooked") that's used a variety of ways, often in desserts. In Lazio, it's called **ricotta romana.**

Ricotta salata A salted, firmer *ricotta,* not unlike feta.

Rigatoni Large tubular pasta with grooves. **Rigatoncini** are a skinnier variation, and **mezzi rigatoni** are shorter.

Ripassate Sautéed with garlic and olive oil (usually a green vegetable).

Ripieno (plural **ripieni**) "Filling" or "filled"—either what you put in a pasta (such as ravioli or *tortellini*) or stuffed vegetables.

Riscaldare Reheat; when ordering foods such as pizza or pre-pared meals, request **riscaldata** (reheated).

Riso Rice, a staple in the North (**riso integrale** is brown rice). Popular dishes include **risi e bisi,** rice and peas (Veneto); and **ris e verz,** rice-and-cabbage soup (Lom-bardy). For more on rice dishes, see page 75.

Risotto Creamy, slow-cooked rice dish usually served as a *primo,* particularly in the North; it comes in a dizzying array of variations, but the most famous is **alla mila-nese** (with saffron and Parmigiano-Reggiano).

Ristorante Restau-rant—typically a rather formal establishment with servers, high-end ingredients, wine lists, and so on.

Robiola Rich, creamy mountain cheese. (Piedmont, Lombardy)

Rocciata Apple strudel with raisins.

Rognone (plural **rognoni**) Kidney.

Rombo Turbot (flounder-like fish).

Rosa Rose.

Rosato Rosé (wine).

Rosetta A round roll with an airy center, often used for sandwiches.

Rosmarino Rosemary; in Puglia, **rosmarina** is a pasta shaped like a large grain of rice.

Rosolato Browned.

Rospo (or **rana pescatrice**) Monkfish.

Rosso Red.

Rosticceria Takeout shop selling roasted chicken and hot side dishes.

Rotelle "Wagon wheel"-shaped pasta.

Rotini Short, spiral-shaped pasta.

Rubinetto, acqua del Tap water.

Rucola (sometimes called **rughetta**) Arugula.

Russa, insalata "Russian-style" vegetable salad with mayonnaise.

S _____

Sagnarelli Thick, flat, short noodles with wavy edges.

Salama da sugo Delicate, crumbly cooked sausage from Ferrara. (Emilia-Romagna)

Salame (plural **salami**) What in English is called salami: chopped meat (pork, goose, game) combined with fat and spices and stuffed in membrane, then cured with salt. This comes in many regional variations. **Salame di Sant' Olcese** is Genoa salami; **salame piccante** is spicy salami (similar to American pepperoni).

Sale Salt. **Salato** means salty.

Salmone Salmon. **Salmone affumicato** is smoked salmon; **salmone in bellavista** is braised salmon, usually elegantly presented.

Salsa Sauce. Very common is **salsa di pomodoro,** tomato and garlic sauce. **Salsa bruna** ("brown sauce") is gravy.

Salsiccia (plural **salsicce**) Sausage.

Saltato (or **saltata**) Sautéed.

Saltimbocca (alla romana) Literally, "jump in the mouth"—a Roman specialty made with thin-sliced veal, fresh sage, and prosciutto. (Lazio)

Salumeria (or **salsamentaria**) Store that sells cold cuts.

Salumi Cold cuts, which come in a

bewildering array of varieties and often show up as an *antipasto*. For much more, see page 60.

Salvia Sage.

Sambuca Syrupy, anise-flavored liqueur from Lazio. Adding water makes it cloudy (like ouzo), and it's sometimes served with coffee beans (**con la mosca,** "with flies"). It can also be called **anisetta.**

Sangue, al Cooked rare—literally "bloody." **Molto al sangue** means very rare.

Sanguinaccio Blood sausage; can also refer to a specialty in the South made with pig's blood, chocolate, sugar, vanilla, cinnamon, and candied citrus peel.

Sanguinelle Blood orange, with bright-red flesh. (Sicily)

San Pietro John Dory (fish).

Saor, in A sweet-and-sour marinade for fish made with vinegar, onions, raisins, and pine nuts; this is a common preparation for *sarde* (see below). (Veneto)

Saporito Tasty.

Sarde Sardines, often eaten fresh. You'll see them prepared other ways, too. In Veneto, **Sarde in saor** has a sweet-and-sour marinade (see earlier). In Sicily, **pasta con le sarde** is topped with sardines, wild fennel, tomato sauce, and saffron. Also in Sicily, **sarde a beccafico** is deboned sardines that are rolled around fillings and then fried.

Sartù di riso An elaborate rice tart made with mozzarella, sausage, peas, mushrooms, chicken livers, and more. (Campania)

Sbrisolona (or **sbriciolona**) A crumbly, buttery cake (Lombardy); can also refer to a less-aged "crumbly" fennel *salame*.

Scabecio Small fried fish, pickled in vinegar and spices. (Liguria)

Scaldato Heated.

Scalogno Shallot.

Scaloppine Thin boneless slices of meat, usually veal.

Scamerita (di maiale) Pork shoulder.

Scamorza Firmer version of mozzarella, sometimes smoked. (The South)

Scampi Large shrimp or prawns.

Scarola Escarole.

Schiacciata Thin, crispy, "squashed"

bread sprinkled with sea salt and olive oil.

Schiuma Milky foam on espresso.

Sciacchetrà Sweet dessert wine. (Cinque Terre)

Scialatelli Like linguine, but squared instead of rounded.

Sciatt Buckwheat fritters filled with *bitto* cheese. (Lombardy)

Sciroppo Syrup.

Scoglio, allo Pasta sauce with mussels, clams, and tomatoes.

Sconto Discount.

Scontrino Receipt you are given after paying. In a bar, you take this to the counter to get the item you ordered.

Scottaditto Thin strips of baby lamb that are quickly cooked in a frying pan (literally "scorched fingers").

Scottato Blanched.

Scremato Skimmed.

Scrippelle (or **scripelle**, also **crespelle**) Crêpes, either served with sauce, baked with cheese and sauce, or as **scrippelle 'mbusse**—in a rich chicken broth. (Abruzzo)

Seadas (or **sebadas**) Cheese-filled, deep-fried ravioli served with honey. (Sardinia)

Secco Dry (wine).

Secondo (or **secondo piatto;** plural **secondi**) The main course of a meal, typically meat, poultry, or seafood. See the *Secondi* chapter.

Sedano Celery.

Segale Rye.

Selvaggina Game.

Selvatico Wild-grown.

Seme Seed.

Semel A big, puffy roll used for sandwiches in Florence.

Semifreddo Frozen mousse-like dessert.

Semola Semolina.

Senape Mustard.

Senza Without.

Seppia Cuttlefish; **nero di seppia** is cuttlefish ink, a common seaside preparation for pasta or *risotto*.

Sfoglia Sheet of fresh pasta or pastry dough.

Sfogliatella (plural **sfogliatelle**) Crispy pastry filled with *ricotta* cheese and candied fruit. (Campania)

Sformato (or **sformatino**) Casserole, baked.

Sfusato Juicy lemon. (Amalfi Coast)

Sfuso "Loose," usually referring to house wine in a carafe that has already been decanted.

Sgombro Scad (like mackerel).

Sgroppino After-dinner drink of vodka and lemon gelato.

Sgusciato Peeled (shellfish).

Shakerato Espresso, ice, and sugar shaken up until frothy.

Siciliana, alla "Sicilian-style"; on a pizza, it's usually capers, olives, and often anchovies.

Sogliola Sole (fish).

Sopa cauda A soup made of layers of bread and squab. (Veneto)

Soppressata In the South, this is a spicy *salame.* In Tuscany, it means headcheese (organs in aspic).

Sorbetto Sorbet or sherbet.

Sorrentina, alla "Sorrento-style," with mozzarella, tomato sauce, basil, and occasionally eggplant. (Campania)

Sott'aceti Vegetables preserved in vinegar, often served with cold cuts.

Sottobosco See **"Frutti di bosco."**

Sott'olio Preserved in olive oil (usually refers to vegetables).

Sovracoscia Thigh (poultry).

Spaghetti Long, thin strands of pasta, native to Naples. **Spaghettini** is skinny spaghetti, and **spaghettoni** is thicker.

Spagnolo "Spanish-style" (spicy) *salame.*

Spalla Shoulder (of beef, pork, or lamb).

Spalla cotta Boiled pork shoulder, served cold and thinly sliced.

Specialità Specialty.

Speck Smoked cured bacon. (Trentino-Alto Adige)

Sperlano Smelt.

Speziato Spiced (flavorful).

Spezie Spices.

Spezzatino Stew, usually chunks of veal cooked with peas, onions, and wine.

Spiedino (plural **spiedini**) Shish kebab; **spiedini alla griglia** is grilled on a skewer.

Spigola Sea bass.

Spigoloso Sharp (wine).

Spina, alla On tap (beer).

Spinaci Spinach.

Spremuta Fresh-squeezed juice, typically orange **(d'arancia),** lemon **(di limone),** or grapefruit **(di pompelmo).**

Spritz In this favorite *aperitivo* cocktail, white wine and soda or Prosecco is mixed with the orange bitters Campari or sweeter Aperol.

Spuntino A little snack.

Squacquerone Young, very soft cheese often served in a bowl. (Emilia-Romagna)

Stagionato Aged, sharp, and hard (cheese).

Stagione, di Seasonal.

Stinco Roast joint of meat; the most popular are pork **(maiale)** and veal **(vitello).**

Stoccafisso Stockfish—dried cod imported from Norway.

Storione Sturgeon.

Straccetti Sautéed slices of meat with arugula and tomatoes or mushrooms.

Stracchino Creamy, spreadable cheese from "exhausted" cows (as the name means). (Lombardy)

Stracciatella This can refer to three things: chocolate-chip gelato flavor, a Roman egg-drop meat broth topped with Parmigiano-Reggiano cheese (called **stracciatella alla romana**), or the gooey center of *burrata* cheese.

Stracotto Slow-simmered (literally "overcooked"), usually with a lot of wine—typically referring to beef.

Strangolapreti "Priest stranglers"—an evocative name for a twisted pasta (also what gnocchi are called in Trentino).

Strapazzate Scrambled.

Strascinati Pasta resembling larger *orecchiette*. (Puglia, Basilicata)

Stravecchio Well-aged (cheese); can also refer to an aged, mellower variation on grappa.

Strega An *amaro* (herbal *digestivo*) from Campania.

Strichetti Bow-tie pasta, similar to *farfalle*.

Stringozzi (or **strangozzi**) Pasta shaped like and named for the long leather straps used to strangle medieval tax collectors. (Umbria)

Strozzapreti Pasta shaped like a "priest-choker."

Strudel Typically made with apples. (Trentino-Alto Adige and the Alps)

Struffoli Tiny fried balls of dough with honey. (Campania)

Strutto Pork fat.

Struzzo Ostrich.

Stufato (di agnello) (Lamb) stew.

Stuzzicadente Toothpick.

Su letto On a bed of.

Succo Juice, typically of fruit or vegetables.

Succoso Juicy.

Sughetto Gravy; sauce.

Sugo This can mean "juice" (as in the juices of meat), or tomato sauce that is used on pasta.

Sultana Sweet, golden raisin.

Supplì Deep-fried balls of rice, mozzarella, chopped meat, tomato sauce, and other ingredients (Rome); this is similar to the **arancine** of the South, but they're smaller and the fillings are all mixed up instead of stuffed.

Suprema (di pollo) (Chicken) breast, often with cream sauce.

Surgelato Deep frozen. Restaurants are obliged to indicate on the menu if they are using frozen fish or seafood.

Susina Plum.

T _____

Tacchino Turkey.

Tagliata Thin slices of grilled tenderloin, typically topped with arugula.

Tagliatelle Wide, flat noodles; **taglierini** are thinner (see below).

Tagliere Wooden platter with meats and cheeses.

Taglierini (or **tajarin**) Very thin noodles made with egg yolk. (Piedmont)

Taglio, al By the slice.

Taleggio A rich, creamy cheese. (Lombardy)

Tannico Tannic (wine).

Tapparelle Extra-large *orecchiette* pasta. (Basilicata)

Taralli Small bread rounds with a hole in the middle. (Puglia)

Tarocco Blood orange. (Sicily)

Tartine (or **tartine farcite**) Little tarts filled with truffle, meat, fish, vegetables, or cheese and served with an *aperitivo*.

Tartufata With truffles.

Tartufo (plural **tartufi**) Truffle (described on page 84); can also describe a ball of ice cream with chopped cherries and nuts that has been dipped in melted chocolate (Calabria).

Tavola calda Literally "hot table"—a shop selling prepared foods to eat standing up, at a table, or to go.

Tazza Cup. A **tazzina** is a small coffee cup.

Tè (or **thè**) Tea, which can come in various forms: **Tè nero** is black tea, and **tè verde** is green tea. **Tè freddo** is iced tea. There's also **tè agli agrumi** (citrus), **tè al limone** (lemon), **tè alla frutta** (fruit), and **tè alla menta** (mint).

Tegame alla vernazzana Anchovies with potatoes, tomatoes, white wine, oil, and herbs. (Liguria)

Temperatura ambiente Room temperature.

Terroso Earthy.

Testa Head.

Testa in cassetta (or **coppa di testa/ formaggio di testa**) Headcheese (organs in aspic).

Testicolo Testicle.

Tiella (or **tiedd**) A baking dish in which potatoes and other vegetables are combined and baked. (Puglia)

Tiepido Lukewarm.

Timballo Casserole-like baked dish including pasta, potatoes, or rice.

Timo Thyme.

Tintoretto Prosecco and pomegranate juice, named for the painter. (Venice)

Tiramisù Literally, "pick-me-up," this dessert is made of espresso-soaked ladyfingers, mascarpone, cocoa powder, and often sweet Marsala wine. (Veneto and the North)

Tisana Herbal tea.

Tiziano Prosecco and grape juice, named for the painter. (Venice)

Toç Milky, polentafortified soup. (FriuliVenezia Giulia)

Toma Generic name for "cheese." (Piedmont, Valle d'Aosta)

Tomini Little goat cheeses marinated in olive oil, pepper, and other flavors. (Piedmont)

Tonno Tuna.

Torchietti "Torch"-shaped pasta.

Toro Bull; a young bull (bullock) might be called **torello.**

Torrefazione Roasted.

Torrone Nougat. (Lombardy, Abruzzo)

Torta Cake or pie. **Torta di mele** is apple cake, **torta di ricotta** is *ricotta* cake with chocolate chips, and **torta della nonna** ("Grandma's cake") is a custard tart with pine nuts. In Liguria, **torta pasqualina** is an elaborate Easter dessert with 33 layers.

Torta de ceci Savory chickpea crêpe.

Torta salata "Savory pie," often similar to a quiche.

Tortelli (or **tordelli**) Small C-shaped pasta that may be filled with potatoes, cheese, vegetables, herbs, or squash. The smaller **tortellini** are little meat-filled, belly-button-shaped pasta; and **tortelloni** is a bigger version, typically filled with cheese. (Emilia-Romagna, Lombardy)

Tortiglioni Narrow rigatoni pasta.

Tortino A baked tart or quiche usually containing vegetables and cheese.

Totani Similar to squid.

Tovagliolo Napkin.

Tozzetti Small, hard nut cookies. (Tuscany)

Tramezzini Small, crustless sandwiches, often served as a light meal in bars.

Trancio Slice.

Trattoria (plural **trattorie**) A simple, family-run eatery that's more casual and affordable than a *ristorante*.

Trenette Flat strands of pasta, like linguine, usually served with pesto. (Liguria)

Triglia (plural **triglie**) Red mullet.

Tripoline Long, flat, thick noodle ruffled on one side.

Trippa Tripe. **Trippa alla fiorentina,** in Tuscany, is tripe and vegetables sautéed in a tomato sauce, sometimes baked with Parmigiano-Reggiano cheese. In Rome, **trippa alla romana** is braised with onions, carrots, and mint.

Tris Three foods (typically pastas) on one plate.

Tritato (or **trito**) Chopped.

Trofie (or **trofiette**) Short, skinny, dense pasta twists ideally suited for pesto. (Liguria)

Trota Trout.

Tuorlo Egg yolk.

U

Umbricelli Thick, chewy, rolled pasta. (Umbria)

Umido, in Poached or steamed.

Uova di pesce Fish roe.

Uova di riccio di mare Sea urchin roe.

Uovo (plural **uova**) Egg. These can be prepared **fritte** (fried), **strapazzate** (scrambled), or **in camicia** (poached). **Alla coque** means boiled, either soft **(molle)** or hard **(sodo)**.

Uva Grapes.

Uvetta Raisins.

V

Valtellina, bresaola della The best-quality air-cured beef, from the high mountain valleys of Lombardy.

Vaniglia Vanilla.

Vapore, al Steamed.

Vegano Vegan.

Vegetariano Vegetarian.

Veloce Fast.

Vendemmia Harvest (wine).

Ventriglio Gizzard.

Verace Authentic; fresh.

Verde Green.

Verdura Greens, as in vegetables; **verdura cotta** are cooked greens.

Vermicelli Long noodles shaped like "little worms," slightly thicker than spaghetti; **vermicelloni** are thicker.

Verza Cabbage.

Viennese, alla Pizza with tomato, mozzarella, and German-style sausage.

Vigneto Vineyard.

Vincisgrassi A very rich and elaborate *lasagne.* (Marche)

Vino Wine. Affordable **vino da tavola** (table wine) or **vino della casa** (house wine) is abundant, often served as **vino sfuso** ("loose," already decanted and available by the glass or carafe). Or you can spring for a bottle of higher-quality wine. For all the details, see the Italian Wine chapter.

Vin Santo "Holy wine" made from dried grapes, making it sweet and high in alcohol. (Tuscany and elsewhere)

Virtù A classic, elaborate soup with 49 ingredients. (Abruzzo)

Visciole Dark cherries. (Lazio)

Vitello (or **vitella**) Veal.

Vitello di mare Porbeagle shark ("sea veal"), similar to swordfish.

Vitello tonnato Chilled, thin-sliced veal served with a tuna-caper sauce. (Piedmont and the North)

Vongole Clams.

W_____

Weinsuppe A white-wine soup. (Trentino-Alte Adige)

Wurstel A generic word for Germanic-type sausages.

Z _____

Zabaione (or **zabaglione**) Dessert made with Marsala (or some other dessert wine), plus sugar and egg yolks, which may be served hot or cold; it's also a common gelato flavor, resembling eggnog.

Zafferano Saffron.

Zampone Stuffed pig's leg, boiled and sliced. (Emilia-Romagna)

Zelten A typical Christmas cake with candied fruit. (The Alps)

Zenzero Ginger.

Zeppola (plural **zeppole**) Deep-fried batter ball, like a doughnut hole.

Ziti Firm, elongated "groom" pasta.

Zucca An orange squash akin to pumpkin.

Zucchero Sugar. **Zuccherato** means sweetened, and **non zuccherato** means sugar-free. **Zucchero di canna** is brown sugar.

Zucchina Zucchini.

Zuppa Soup, which comes in many forms. **Zuppa di verdure** is vegetable soup, and **zuppa di pesce** is fish soup (sometimes also with shellfish). Regional specialties are noted below.

Zuppa alla volterrana Stew of white beans, veggies, bread, and olive oil.

Zuppa inglese Trifle.

Zuppa lombarda Tuscan bean soup.

Zuppa pavese A soup with chicken broth, a raw egg on toast, and Parmigiano-Reggiano. (Lombardy)

Buon appetito!

Appendix

This chapter is a travelers' toolkit for experiencing Italy, including conversions you'll encounter in Italy (from the currency to weights and temperatures), plus pointers on the Italian language.

TRAVEL SMART

This book is focused on Italian food. For the other aspects of your trip—planning an itinerary, budgeting your time and money, finding accommodations, using public transportation, sightseeing smartly, avoiding theft and scams, and much more—you'll find extensive, free information at Ricksteves.com.

For more in-depth travel advice, pick up a **Rick Steves guidebook**—which this book is designed to complement. My core *Rick Steves Italy* guidebook offers comprehensive coverage of Italy's top destinations, including self-guided town walks and museum tours, extensive listings of hotels and restaurants, and advice for how to plan your limited time. My full-color *Best of Italy* book is a condensed, beautifully illustrated version of the same content. I also have city and regional guidebooks covering Rome, Florence & Tuscany, Venice, and Sicily. My Pocket guides (on Rome, Venice, Florence, and the Cinque Terre) offer advice on those destinations in a compact package.

For sightseeing, be sure to download the free **Rick Steves Audio Europe app,** which includes entirely free walking tours of many of Italy's greatest museums, neighborhoods, and towns.

And you'll also find hours of free **video** clips (from my public television show, *Rick Steves' Europe*) and **audio** clips (from my public radio show, *Travel with Rick Steves*) at Ricksteves.com.

And we offer fully guided **tours** designed to personally lead you to Italy's top experiences—both culinary and otherwise.

CONVERSIONS

Currency

Italy uses the **euro** currency (€). One euro is broken down into 100 cents, like a dollar. While the currency rate fluctuates, generally €1 is equivalent to about $1.20—so to convert Italian prices to American ones, add 20 percent. Before your trip, check the latest exchange rate online. ATMs are widely available throughout Italy.

Phoning

To dial an Italian phone number from any mobile phone, begin with Italy's country code: +39. (To make the + sign, you may need to hold down the 0 button.) Then simply dial the rest of the number, which in Italy begins with a 0. If dialing from a fixed Italian line—such as your hotel room phone—skip the +39 and simply dial the number that begins with 0.

For much more detail on phoning in Europe—including tips for roaming with your mobile phone while abroad—see www.ricksteves.com/phoning.

Numbers and Stumblers

- Italians write a few of their numbers differently than we do. 1 = 1, 4 = 4, 7 = 7.

- In Italy, dates appear as day/month/year, so Christmas 2024 is 25/12/24.

- Commas are decimal points and decimals commas. A dollar and a half is $1,50, one thousand is 1.000, and there are 5.280 feet in a mile.

- When counting with fingers, start with your thumb. If you hold up your first finger to request one item, you'll probably get two.

- What Americans call the second floor of a building is the first floor *(primo piano)* in Italy.

- On escalators and moving sidewalks, Italians keep the left "lane" open for passing. Keep to the right.

Metric Conversions

A **kilogram** equals 1,000 grams (about 2.2 pounds). One hundred **grams** (a common unit at markets) is about a quarter-pound. One **liter** is about a quart, or almost four to a gallon.

A **kilometer** is six-tenths of a mile. To convert kilometers to miles, cut the kilometers in half and add back 10 percent of the original (120 km: 60 + 12 = 72 miles). One **meter** is 39 inches—just over a yard.

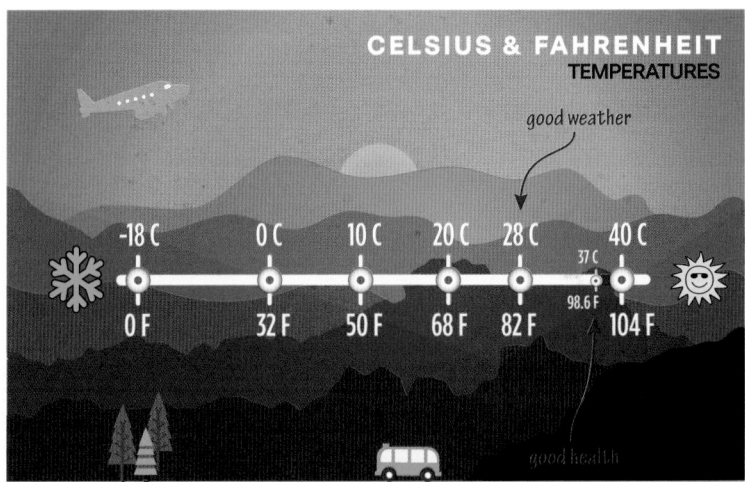

Europe takes its temperature using the Celsius scale, while Americans opt for Fahrenheit. Water freezes at 0° C and boils at 100° C.

For a rough conversion from Celsius to Fahrenheit, **double the number and add 30.**

For **weather,** remember that 28° C is 82° F—perfect. For **health,** 37° C is just right.

When doing **laundry,** 30° C is cold, 40° C is warm (usually the default), 60° C is hot, and 95° C is nearly boiling.

Your **air-conditioner** should be set at about 20° C.

PRONOUNCING ITALIAN WORDS

Italian words can be tricky for novices to pronounce. But the language is highly logical, and once you learn a few simple rules, you can say anything.

Italian is a phonetic language, so **every letter is pronounced.** This means that, for example, an E at the end of a word—which might be silent in English—must be pronounced in Italian. For instance, *possibile* is pronounced poh-SEE-bee-lay, *toilette* is twah-LEH-tay, and the five towns on the Italian Riviera are called the Cinque Terre, pronounced CHEENG-kway TEH-ray.

Most letters in Italian are pronounced as they are in English. Here are a few exceptions:

C followed by **A, O,** or **U** sounds like K, as in cat (*caffè,* kah-FAY).	However, **C** followed by **E** or **I** sounds like CH in chance (*dolce,* DOHL-chay; or *ciao,* "chow").

CH is always a hard C, as in cat, no matter what letter comes next (*chiuso,* kee-OO-zoh).

G followed by **A, O,** or **U** is a hard G sound (*prego,* PREH-goh).	However, **G** followed by **E** or **I** is a J sound (*gelato,* jeh-LAH-toh; or *buongiorno,* bwohn-JOR-noh).

GH is always a hard G, no matter what letter comes next (*spaghetti,* spah-GEH-tee).

GLI sounds roughly like LY—for example, *famiglia* (fah-MEEL-yah) or *biglietto* (beel-YEH-toh). You don't hear the G at all.

GN sounds like NY, as in *lasagne* (lah-ZAHN-yeh). Again—no G sound.

H only appears in letter combinations (such as CH or GH), or occasionally in loanwords from other languages (such as the cocktail called Hugo). If you ever see H on its own, it's silent.

I sounds like EE in seed (as in *si,* "see").

R can be rolled for emphasis, as in *brrravo!*

S usually sounds like an S. But when it's followed by **any vowel,** it has a Z sound (*scusi,* SKOO-zee; or *inglese,* een-GLAY-zay; or *cosa,* KOH-zah)

SC followed by **A, O,** or **U** sounds like SK in skip (as in *scusi,* SKOO-zee).	However, **SC** followed by **E** or **I** sounds like SH in shape (as in *Capisce?,* kah-PEE-shay; or *uscita,* OO-shee-tah).

Z usually sounds like TS in hits (*grazie,* GRAHT-see-ay; *stazione,* stat-see-OH-nay; or *servizio,* sehr-VEET-see-oh). **ZZ** sounds more like the DZ sound in kids (*mozzarella,* MOHD-zah-reh-lah).

Accent marks—such as à, è, or ò—suggest subtle changes in how a vowel is pronounced. For a beginner, these probably aren't worth worrying about.

Making Plurals

You'll notice that Italian forms plurals differently than in English. Italian nouns are grammatically either **masculine** (usually ending in *-o,* like *panino* or *gelato*) or **feminine** (usually ending in *-a,* like *pizza* or *trattoria*). Some nouns (both masculine and feminine) end in *-e,* like *ristorante.*

To pluralize a **masculine noun,** you change the O to an I:	One ***panino,*** two ***panini*** One ***gelato,*** two ***gelati***
If it ends in -IO, simply delete the O:	One ***formaggio,*** two ***formaggi***
To pluralize a **feminine noun,** you change the A to an E:	One ***pizza,*** two ***pizze*** One ***trattoria,*** two ***trattorie***
To pluralize a **noun ending in -E,** you change the E to an I:	One ***ristorante,*** two ***ristoranti*** One ***dolce,*** two ***dolci***

There is one exception: Since a C followed by an E or an I has a CH sound, you may have to change it to a **CH** to keep the K sound. For example, the plural of ***enoteca*** (eh-noh-TEH-kah) becomes ***enoteche*** (eh-noh-TEH-kay).

Also note that when you pluralize a noun, you also pluralize the accompanying adjective. For example, one ***primo piatto,*** two ***primi piatti.***

These are just a few basic rules to get you started. The next two pages feature "Survival Phrases" to help you navigate Italy. *Buona fortuna!* (Good luck!)

Italian Survival Phrases

Hello. (informal)	Ciao.	chow
Good day.	Buongiorno.	bwohn-**jor**-noh
Do you speak English?	Parla inglese?	**par**-lah een-**gleh**-zay
Yes. / No.	Sì. / No.	see / noh
I (don't) understand.	(Non) capisco.	(nohn) kah-**pees**-koh
Please.	Per favore.	pehr fah-**voh**-ray
Thank you.	Grazie.	**graht**-see-ay
You're welcome.	Prego.	**preh**-go
I'm sorry.	Mi dispiace.	mee dee-spee-**ah**-chay
Excuse me.	Mi scusi.	mee **skoo**-zee
No problem.	Non c'è problema.	nohn cheh proh-**bleh**-mah
Goodbye.	Arrivederci.	ah-ree-veh-**dehr**-chee
one / two / three	uno / due / tre	**oo**-noh / **doo**-ay / tray
four / five / six	quattro / cinque / sei	**kwah**-troh / **cheeng**-kway / **seh**-ee
seven / eight	sette / otto	**seh**-tay / **oh**-toh
nine / ten	nove / dieci	**noh**-vay / dee-**ay**-chee
How much is it?	Quanto costa?	**kwahn**-toh **koh**-stah
Write it?	Me lo scrive?	may loh **skree**-vay
Is it free?	È gratis?	eh **grah**-tees
Is it included?	È incluso?	eh een-**kloo**-zoh
Where can I buy / find...?	Dove posso comprare / trovare...?	**doh**-vay **poh**-soh kohm-**prah**-ray / troh-**vah**-ray
I'd like / We'd like...	Vorrei / Vorremmo...	voh-**reh**-ee / voh-**reh**-moh
...a room.	...una camera.	**oo**-nah **kah**-meh-rah
...a ticket to _____.	...un biglietto per _____.	oon beel-**yeh**-toh pehr _____
Is it possible?	È possibile?	eh poh-**see**-bee-lay
Where is...?	Dov'è...?	**doh**-veh
...the train station	...la stazione	lah staht-see-**oh**-nay
...tourist information	...informazioni turisti	een-for-maht-see-**oh**-nee too-**ree**-stee
...the bathroom	...il bagno	eel **bahn**-yoh
men / women	uomini, signori / donne, signore	**woh**-mee-nee, seen-**yoh**-ree / **doh**-nay, seen-**yoh**-ray
left / right / straight	sinistra / destra / sempre dritto	see-**nee**-strah / **deh**-strah / **sehm**-pray **dree**-toh
What time does this open / close?	A che ora apre / chiude?	ah kay **oh**-rah **ah**-pray / kee-**oo**-day
At what time?	A che ora?	ah kay **oh**-rah
Just a moment.	Un momento.	oon moh-**mehn**-toh
now / soon / later	adesso / presto / tardi	ah-**deh**-soh / **preh**-stoh / **tar**-dee
today / tomorrow	oggi / domani	**oh**-jee / doh-**mah**-nee

In an Italian Restaurant

I'd like / We'd like...	Vorrei / Vorremmo... voh-**reh**-ee / voh-**reh**-moh
...to reserve a table for one / two.	...prenotare un tavolo per uno / due. preh-noh-**tah**-ray oon **tah**-voh-loh pehr **oo**-noh / **doo**-ay
...the menu (in English).	...il menù (in inglese). eel meh-**noo** (een een-**gleh**-zay)
Is this seat free?	È libero questo posto? eh **lee**-beh-roh **kweh**-stoh **poh**-stoh
service (not) included	servizio (non) compreso sehr-**veet**-see-oh (nohn) kohm-**pray**-zoh
cover charge	(pane e) coperto (**pah**-nay ay) koh-**pehr**-toh
to go	da portar via dah **por**-tar **vee**-ah
with / without	con / senza kohn / **sehnt**-sah
and / or	e / o ay / oh
breakfast / lunch / dinner	(prima) colazione / pranzo / cena (**pree**-mah) koh-laht-zee-**oh**-nay / **prahn**-zoh / **chay**-nah
fixed-price meal (of the day)	menù (del giorno) meh-**noo** (dehl **jor**-noh)
specialty of the house	specialità della casa speh-chah-lee-**tah deh**-lah **kah**-zah
appetizer	antipasto ahn-tee-**pah**-stoh
first course	primo (piatto) **pree**-moh (pee-**ah**-toh)
main course	secondo (piatto) seh-**kohn**-doh (pee-**ah**-toh)
side dishes	contorni kohn-**tor**-nee
cold cuts / bread / cheese	salumi / pane / formaggio sah-**loo**-mee / **pah**-nay / for-**mah**-joh
sandwich	panino pah-**nee**-noh
soup / salad	zuppa / insalata **tsoo**-pah / een-sah-**lah**-tah
meat / chicken	carne / pollo **kar**-nay / **poh**-loh
fish / seafood	pesce / frutti di mare **peh**-shay / **froo**-tee dee **mah**-ray
fruit / vegetables	frutta / verdure **froo**-tah / vehr-**doo**-ray
dessert	dolce **dohl**-chay
tap water	acqua del rubinetto **ah**-kwah dehl roo-bee-**neh**-toh
mineral water	acqua minerale **ah**-kwah mee-neh-**rah**-lay
still / sparkling	naturale / frizzante nah-too-**rah**-lay / freet-**zahn**-tay
(orange) juice	succo (d'arancia) **soo**-koh (dah-**rahn**-chah)
coffee / tea / milk	caffè / tè / latte kah-**feh** / teh / **lah**-tay
wine / beer	vino / birra **vee**-noh / **bee**-rah
red / white	rosso / bianco **roh**-soh / bee-**ahn**-koh
glass / bottle	bicchiere / bottiglia bee-kee-**eh**-ray / boh-**teel**-yah
Cheers!	Salute! / Cin cin! sah-**loo**-tay / cheen cheen
The bill, please.	Il conto, per favore. eel **kohn**-toh pehr fah-**voh**-ray
Do you accept credit cards?	Accettate carte di credito? ah-cheh-**tah**-tay **kar**-tay dee **kreh**-dee-toh
Delicious!	Delizioso! day-leet-see-**oh**-zoh

For more user-friendly Italian phrases, check out *Rick Steves Italian Phrase Book* or *Rick Steves French, Italian, & German Phrase Book*.

Index

MAP INDEX

PHOTO CREDITS

Explore Italy

At ricksteves.com you can browse through thousands of articles, videos, photos, and radio interviews, plus find a wealth of money-saving travel tips for planning your dream trip to Italy. And with our mobile-friendly website, you can easily access all this great travel information anywhere you go.

TV Shows

Preview the places you'll visit by watching entire half-hour episodes of *Rick Steves' Europe* (choose from 21 shows covering Italy from top to bottom) on-demand, for free.

ricksteves.com

travel dreams into affordable reality

Radio Interviews

Enjoy ready access to Rick's vast library of radio interviews covering travel tips and cultural insights that relate specifically to your Italy travel plans.

Travel Forums

Learn, ask, share! Our online community of savvy travelers is a great resource for first-time travelers to Italy, as well as seasoned pros.

Travel News

Subscribe to our free Travel News e-newsletter, and get monthly updates from Rick on what's happening in Europe.

Classroom Europe®

Check out our free resource for educators with 500+ short video clips from the *Rick Steves' Europe* TV show.

Audio Europe™

Rick's Free Travel App

Get your FREE Rick Steves Audio Europe™ app to enjoy…

- Dozens of self-guided museum and walking tours for Rome, Florence, Venice, Assisi, Siena, Milan, and Naples.
- Hundreds of tracks filled with cultural insights and sightseeing tips from Rick's radio interviews
- For Apple and Android

With Rick whispering in your ear, Italy gets even better.

Find out more at ricksteves.com

Pack Light and Right

Gear up for your next adventure at ricksteves.com

Light Luggage

Pack light and right with Rick Steves' affordable, custom-designed rolling carry-on bags, backpacks, day packs, and shoulder bags.

Accessories

From packing cubes to moneybelts and beyond, Rick has personally selected the travel goodies that will help your trip go smoother.

Shop at ricksteves.com

Experience maximum Italy

Rick Steves Italy Tours

A Rick Steves tour takes you to Italy's most interesting places with great guides and small groups. We follow Rick's favorite itineraries, ride in comfy buses, stay in family-run hotels, and bring you intimately close to the Italy you've traveled so far to see. Most importantly, we take away the logistical headaches so you can focus on the fun—and food.

great tours, too!

Join the fun

Each year we take thousands of free-spirited travelers—nearly half of them repeat customers—along with us on nine delightful Italy itineraries, from Venice, Florence, and Rome to sun-soaked Tuscan hill towns and charming seaside villages.

Is a Rick Steves tour the right fit for your travel dreams? Find out at ricksteves.com, where you can also check seat availability and sign up.

Europe is best experienced with happy travel partners. We hope you can join us.

See our Italy itineraries at ricksteves.com

A Guide for Every Trip

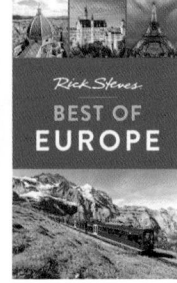

BEST OF GUIDES

Full color easy-to-scan format, focusing on Europe's most popular destinations and sights

Best of England
Best of Europe
Best of France
Best of Germany
Best of Ireland
Best of Italy
Best of Scotland
Best of Spain

COMPREHENSIVE GUIDES

City, country, and regional guides with detailed coverage for a multi-week trip exploring the most iconic sights and venturing off the beaten track

Amsterdam & the Netherlands
Barcelona
Belgium: Bruges, Brussels,
 Antwerp & Ghent
Berlin
Budapest
Croatia & Slovenia
Eastern Europe
England
Florence & Tuscany
France
Germany
Great Britain
Greece: Athens & the Peloponnese
Iceland
Ireland
Istanbul
Italy
London
Paris
Portugal
Prague & the Czech Republic
Provence & the French Riviera
Rome
Scandinavia
Scotland
Sicily
Spain
Switzerland
Venice
Vienna, Salzburg & Tirol

HE BEST OF ROME

me, Italy's capital, is studded with
ent ruins and floodlit-fountain
res. From the Vatican to the Col-
um, with crazy traffic in between,
e is wonderful, huge, and exhaust-
he crowds, the heat, and the

weighty history of the Eternal City where
Caesars walked can make tourists wilt.
Recharge by taking siestas, gelato breaks,
and after-dark walks, strolling from one
atmospheric square to another in the
refreshing evening air.

*d Pantheon—which
t dome until the
2,000 years old
y over 1,500).*

*f Athens in
s embodies the
e Renaissance.*

*adiators fought
other, entertaining*

Rome ristorante.

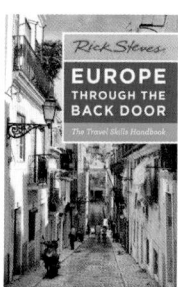

POCKET GUIDES

*Compact, full color city guides with
the essentials for shorter trips*

Amsterdam	Munich & Salzburg
Athens	Paris
Barcelona	Prague
Florence	Rome
Italy's Cinque Terre	Venice
London	Vienna

SNAPSHOT GUIDES

Focused single-destination coverage

Basque Country: Spain & France
Copenhagen & the Best of Denmark
Dublin
Dubrovnik
Edinburgh
Hill Towns of Central Italy
Krakow, Warsaw & Gdansk
Lisbon
Loire Valley
Madrid & Toledo
Milan & the Italian Lakes District
Naples & the Amalfi Coast
Nice & the French Riviera
Normandy
Northern Ireland
Norway
Reykjavík
Rothenburg & the Rhine
Sevilla, Granada & Southern Spain
St. Petersburg, Helsinki & Tallinn
Stockholm

CRUISE PORTS GUIDES

Reference for cruise ports of call

Mediterranean Cruise Ports
Scandinavian & Northern European
Cruise Ports

Complete your library with...

TRAVEL SKILLS & CULTURE

Europe 101
Europe Through the Back Door
European Christmas
European Easter
European Festivals
Europe's Top 100 Masterpieces
For the Love of Europe
Postcards from Europe
Travel as a Political Act

PHRASE BOOKS & DICTIONARIES

French
French, Italian & German
German
Italian
Portuguese
Spanish

PLANNING MAPS

Britain, Ireland & London
Europe
France & Paris
Germany, Austria & Switzerland
Iceland
Ireland
Italy
Spain & Portugal

ACKNOWLEDGMENTS

Rick and Fred wish to thank **Cameron Hewitt,** Rick's close collaborator since 2000. Cameron merged Fred's original text with our Rick Steves guidebook content, filled in gaps with original writing, and updated it all for contemporary sensibilities. Cameron ensured this book balanced the voices and insights of both Rick and Fred, and designed it for smart use by our travelers by injecting it with his own love of Italy and its food.

Dave Hoerlein, in addition to designing this book's gorgeous maps, also applied his many decades of Italian travel expertise by contributing savvy insights to important topics throughout the book.

Virginia Agostinelli gave this book a careful read from an Italian point of view. **Gene Openshaw,** the co-author of many Rick Steves guidebooks, contributed much material over the decades that made its way into this book. And **Sarah Murdoch** and **Alfio di Mauro** offered deep insight into Sicilian cuisine and culture.

Jennifer Madison Davis, Managing Editor at Rick Steves' Europe, applied her customary wisdom and commitment to excellence to running this project as smoothly as we could imagine. And **Sandra Hundacker** was instrumental in the design of the book, and in selecting hundreds of beautiful images from the Rick Steves' Europe photo archives that were perfectly suited to the text.

We thank our friends at **Avalon Travel Publishing** for their trust in Rick Steves' Europe's vision of how to best equip travelers with information for better travels. For decades, Avalon has ensured our books are beautifully produced and smartly distributed.

Fred thanks his mother, **Bernice,** who recognized my passion for Italy and took me there as a teenager. And my father, **Edward,** who brought Italian music, art, and Italian-American food to me as a toddler. *Grazie* to **David Black** (and his entire staff), **Susan Raihofer, Carole Lalli, Jennifer Josephy, Kyle Cathie, Abner Stein, Arabella Stein, Rachel Clements, Ben Fowler, Ruth Reichl, Corby Kummer, Carol Field, Donald Sloan,** and **Luciano Pavarotti,** all key figures in my trajectory as a writer about Italy's extraordinary food and wine culture. I am—and my contribution to this book is—a result of a life lived *italianamente*.

And most of all, we both thank our **thousands of Italian friends, colleagues, and acquaintances,** who—over five decades—have patiently and lovingly imparted their knowledge over a plate or a glass or *un caffè. Grazie infinite!*

Avalon Travel
Hachette Book Group
1700 Fourth Street
Berkeley, CA 94710

Printed in Malaysia for Imago
1st Edition. First printing January 2023.

ISBN 978-1-64171-511-9

For the latest on Rick's talks, guide-books, tours, public television series, and public radio show, contact Rick Steves' Europe, 130 Fourth Avenue North, Edmonds, WA 98020, +1 425 771 8303, www.ricksteves.com, rick@ricksteves.com.

RICK STEVES' EUROPE
Project Manager: Cameron Hewitt

Managing Editor: Jennifer Madison Davis

Assistant Managing Editor: Cathy Lu

Project Editor: Glenn Eriksen

Editors: Suzanne Kotz, Rosie Leutzinger, Jessica Shaw, Carrie Shepherd

Editorial & Production Assistant: Megan Simms

Graphic Content Director: Sandra Hundacker

Maps & Graphics: David C. Hoerlein, Lauren Mills, Mary Rostad

Digital Asset Coordinator: Orin Dubrow

AVALON TRAVEL
Senior Editor and Series Manager: Madhu Prasher

Associate Managing Editor: Jamie Andrade

Copy Editor: Maggie Ryan

Proofreader: Elizabeth Jang

Indexer: Stephen Callahan

Production & Typesetting: Rue Flaherty, Jane Musser

Interior Design: Toni Tajima

Maps & Graphics: Kat Bennett

Let's Keep on Travelin'

Your trip doesn't need to end.

Follow Rick on social media!